A History of Scottish Philosophy

A History of Scottish Philosophy

Alexander Broadie

EDINBURGH UNIVERSITY PRESS

First published in hardback in 2009 by
Edinburgh University Press Ltd
22 George Square, Edinburgh

This paperback edition published 2010

Typeset in 11/13pt Adobe Sabon
by Servis Filmsetting Ltd, Stockport, Cheshire, and
printed and bound in Great Britain by
CPI Antony Rowe, Chippenham and Eastbourne

A CIP record for this book is available from the British Library

ISBN 978 0 7486 1628 2 (paperback)

Contents

Acknowledgements

In writing this book I have benefited greatly from conversations with friends and I wish especially to thank Knud Haakonssen, James Harris, Laurent Jaffro, Michel Malherbe, Christian Maurer, M. A. Stewart and Paul Wood for their help. Patricia S. Martin read a complete draft, checked many things that I had rashly claimed to know and discovered for me many things that I needed to know. I am grateful to her for all she has done.

A.B.
Glasgow
15 January 2008

CHAPTER 1

Introduction

As a philosophy student at Edinburgh University in the 1960s I received a splendid education. We covered a great deal of ground and dealt with some major areas in serious depth; the programme was impressive and so was the delivery. However, with my student days behind me I found myself drawn increasingly to two fields, medieval philosophy and Scottish philosophy, on which my teachers had been almost totally silent. I had been taught David Hume's philosophy by George E. Davie and Páll Árdal, but there were no lectures on Hume's distinguished contemporaries who occupied philosophy chairs in Scotland, such as Francis Hutcheson, Adam Smith, Thomas Reid, Dugald Stewart and Adam Ferguson. As regards medieval philosophy there was nothing at all; the nineteen centuries between Aristotle and René Descartes were represented by silence.

The two areas on which I came to focus overlap in medieval Scottish philosophy, whose most spectacular representative is John Duns Scotus (c.1266–1308) from the village of Duns in the Scottish Borders. He was allotted not even a one-minute walk-on part during those four undergraduate years of intensive philosophical education. Scotus constructed a vast and intricate system that played a key role in shaping the philosophical and theological thinking of the High Middle Ages, both within the Franciscan Order to which he belonged and much more widely in the church. His thinking has had adherents in later centuries, as witness the remarkable statement, 'The school of Scotus is more numerous than all the other schools taken together', made in 1664 by Johannes Caramuel y Lobkowitz, who was well placed to make such a judgment.[1] Scotus's philosophy is still a major centre of attention, with perhaps particular regard paid to his writings on moral philosophy, on the nature of the human mind and on logic.

Scotus's compatriot Hume, whose family hailed from the Scottish Borders estate of Ninewells close to Duns, could in some ways hardly be more different. Two of these ways are especially important for this book. First, Scotus was a dedicated man of the church, but Hume did not believe in God or in attending church services. Secondly, Hume thought that the proper method of philosophy was that employed by the empirical sciences; he therefore despised scholastic metaphysics, thinking it contained nothing but sophistry and illusion, and would have had it committed to the flames.[2] Scotus, on the contrary, was the greatest of scholastic metaphysicians, and his works would assuredly not have survived if Hume had been in charge of the conflagration. But Scotus and Hume are alike in this, at least, that, as is characteristic of philosophical geniuses, they both made a major contribution to the shape that philosophical discourse would still be taking centuries after they wrote.

I have begun this opening chapter with reference to these two great Scottish philosophers because I want to make it clear at the start that Scottish philosophy is represented by thinkers of the very highest calibre. In any general account of the history of philosophy, even if very short, Scotus and Hume will feature, for they are among the universal figures of philosophy. But there are other Scottish philosophers; I have already mentioned Francis Hutcheson (1694–1746), Adam Smith (1723–90), and Thomas Reid (1710–96), each of whom is now (though was not in the 1960s) the subject of a major philosophical industry. There are many others, however, who had important things to say and whose work has not, I believe, received adequate recognition. In these pages I seek to make out a case for some of them. In the course of this book I hope to demonstrate that Scotland has a rich philosophical tradition, created by many people, and testifying to a deep interest in abstract speculation that has characterised Scottish culture for centuries.

The phrase 'Scottish philosophy' suggests that one part of the great western philosophical project has a nationality, that it is a citizen of Scotland or at least of Scottish culture. But what is it for something to be a piece of Scottish philosophy? Is it sufficient that it is written by a Scot? Or does there have to be something identifiably Scottish about the philosophy itself such that it can be identified as Scottish even if the identity of the author is unknown? The concept of Scottish philosophy might be contested on the grounds that philosophy is essentially a universal enquiry, asking questions that anyone from anywhere might ask and offering answers that might also be offered by anyone anywhere. There surely cannot be anything Scottish about the question whether our powers of sense perception deliver up truths about the world, nor anything Scottish about the answer. That is surely incontestable.

But it cannot be the end of the story. Philosophers have written histories of German philosophy, of early German philosophy, of German philosophy from Kant to Hegel, of twentieth-century German philosophy. There are likewise histories of French philosophy, histories of twentieth-century French philosophy, and histories of American philosophy. There are books on the history of philosophy covering American pragmatism, British empiricism and German idealism, and so on. Since these national-sounding concepts seem not to be thought problematic, there is no obvious reason why the concept of a Scottish philosophy should be ruled out of court just on the grounds that philosophy cannot be *Scottish*. Why can there be no Scottish philosophy when there can be German philosophy, French philosophy, American philosophy?

It has to be added that there have been many works explicitly on Scottish philosophy, including works by major figures in the Scottish philosophical tradition. I am thinking here of books such as *Scottish Philosophy: The Old and the New* by James Frederick Ferrier (1856), *The Scottish Philosophy, Biographical, Expository, Critical, from Hutcheson to Hamilton* by James McCosh (1875), *The Scottish Philosophy: A Comparison of the Scottish and German Answers to Hume* by Andrew Seth Pringle-Pattison (1885), the anonymous *Scottish Metaphysics Reconstructed in Accordance with the Principles of Physical Science* (1887), and *Scottish Philosophy in its National Development* by Henry Laurie (1902). Nor are we dealing here with a parochial Scottish conceit. In 1819–20 Victor Cousin, professor of philosophy at the Sorbonne, delivered a course of lectures which in 1829 he published under the title *Philosophie écossaise*. He had inherited his academic chair from his former teacher Pierre-Paul Royer-Collard, who himself had delivered lectures at the Sorbonne on what he termed the Scottish philosophy. Near the end of the nineteenth century Émile Boutroux published 'De l'influence de la philosophie écossaise sur la philosophie française' (1897), and the practice of identifying a Scottish philosophy continues to the present day with *Philosophie française et philosophie écossaise 1750–1850* edited by E. Arosio and M. Malherbe (2007). We can, if we wish, ask what Scottish philosophy is, but it is too late to question whether it exists.

Closely related to the concept of Scottish philosophy is the concept of a Scottish school of philosophy. There is such a school. It dominated the Scottish philosophical scene from the mid-eighteenth century to the mid-nineteenth and beyond. Its ideas are among Scotland's most successful invisible exports. It was pervasive in France and North

America throughout the nineteenth century and it also had a large impact on philosophical thinking in Germany. The school was generally known as the Scottish school of common sense philosophy. Its leading figure was Thomas Reid, but many others also made important contributions to it. In his 200-page introduction to the first French edition of the complete works of Thomas Reid, Théodore Jouffroy attempts to sum up the main features of the Scottish school. According to his account the three principal features are these: (1) Just as natural scientists investigating the material world must use observation as a basis for determining the laws governing the behaviour of material things, so also philosophers must use observation, by an inwardly directed faculty, as a basis for determining the laws governing the operations of the mind. (2) Knowledge of the human mind and of its laws is necessary for the solution of most of the questions with which philosophy deals. (3) Philosophy has to be assimilated to the natural sciences. That is, philosophy, properly done, *is* a natural science. The various sciences have different objects of investigation but they should all use the same fundamental method.[3]

Other accounts of the fundamentals of the Scottish school take a rather different line, paying particular attention to the role played in our lives by so-called 'principles of common sense', fundamental beliefs that structure any characteristically human belief system. But Scottish philosophy is a good deal wider than the school of common sense philosophy. I am speaking here of a long tradition of philosophising traceable back at least to the thirteenth century, though perhaps earlier still, to Richard of St Victor (c.1123–73), whose Latin name was Ricardus de Sancto Victore Scotus, from Scotland (as the name indicates) though he was prior of the Abbey of St Victor in Paris and may have spent most of his life in Paris. Mention might also be made of Michael Scot (died c.1236), better known these days as a necromancer, but who should be remembered chiefly because he made a major contribution to the transmission of the works of Aristotle to the Christian west.[4] He was also a member of a team working in Cordova, Spain, that produced Latin translations of Arabic commentaries on Aristotle, particularly commentaries by Averroes that were to have a large impact on philosophical and theological thinking in the Christian west.

But as regards the Scottish philosophical tradition the first major thinker was Duns Scotus. At the age of twelve, by which time he had almost certainly mastered Latin, he was taken south and there is no evidence that he ever returned. Across Europe he was known, however, by his nationality; he was Scotus, the Scot. His work evidently had an especial appeal for Scots. His political philosophy almost certainly had an impact on two of the great documents of early Scotland, the Declaration of the Clergy (1310) and the Declaration of Arbroath (1320), and his philosophical successors of the Pre-Reformation period, perhaps especially John Mair, were philosophically very close to him. John Mair indeed, while professor at the University of Paris, led a three-man team that produced an edition of one of Scotus's main works, the *Reportata Parisiensia*, and it may reasonably be supposed that while Mair taught at Glasgow (he was principal of the university from 1518 to 1523) and at St Andrews, where he was provost of St Salvator's from 1534 to 1550, his interest in Scotus's philosophy was on display to his students. Mair's persistent reference to Scotus as *conterraneus*, my fellow-countryman, my compatriot, indicates his sense of closeness to the earlier man.

Mair's interest in Scotus must also have been passed on to his many Scottish pupils at the University of Paris, where he taught for many years. Several of those pupils, such as William Manderston, George Lokert and Robert Galbraith, rose to senior academic positions and were important figures in Scotland as well as in Paris. They lived in each other's intellectual pockets as members of the circle of John Mair, producing a widespread and deep philosophy, taking forward the process by which philosophy became deep-rooted in Scottish culture and enabling the Scottish universities to teach philosophy at as high a level as was available in Europe.

After that generation, and with the arrival in Scotland of the Reformation and renaissance humanism, philosophy in Scotland, as elsewhere in Europe, went through a process of renewal. The philosophical drive was still there and became manifest in that wondrous event, the Scottish Enlightenment, an awesome act of the human spirit that burst upon western culture in the eighteenth century. The brilliant philosophy contributed by Scots of that period to the great western philosophical project did not come from nowhere, appearing in Scotland as if by miracle, but on the contrary was a continuation of a long tradition of Scottish philosophising, work done by men (almost all were men) who knew each other and for whom philosophising was a social act, something done in face-to-face conversation or by letter or in print. They responded to each other partly because they were close by and partly because they were so interested in each other's thinking. I speak here of many who were very good and some who were geniuses.

It is therefore appropriate to speak of Scottish philosophy, parallel to the way in which writers speak of German or French or American philosophy. Scottish philosophy is a unitary thing, but not in the sense of a school of philosophy with its set of doctrines to which all in the school subscribed; instead the unity derives from the circumstances of the philosophical activity, of people standing in the relation of friend to friend, of colleague to colleague, of teacher to pupil; they were influenced by the national church (and in many cases were officiants in it), lived under the same legal system, were brought up within the same educational system. In short they were at home with each other, working through their philosophy with each other, borrowing good ideas from each other, and being each other's fiercest (while yet friendly) critic when that was called for.

Two particularly significant sets of choices faced me. One concerned how far I should go in discussing the international network of influences within which Scottish philosophers were prominently situated. There is a large and important story to be told within that field but, aside from a number of especially significant elements, I have told very little of it, preferring to focus on the Scottish philosophy itself. Secondly, there have been many Scottish philosophers and this book names very few of them. My aim, however, has been not to write an encyclopedia covering every Scottish philosopher of whom I know anything but instead to give the reader an idea of what has gone on in Scottish philosophy. I have indicated something of its range and depth without also aiming for comprehensiveness. Some readers may regret that their favourite philosopher has been left out of the reckoning. I reply sadly that I have missed out some of my own favourites. In a work of this kind hard choices are inevitable.

Notes

1. Caramuel y Lobkowitz (1606–82), a Spanish Cistercian who was also bishop of Prague, was a close observer of the philosophical and theological schools of his day.
2. See Hume, *Enquiry Concerning Human Understanding*, XII.III, final para.
3. Reid, *Œuvres complètes*, ed. Jouffroy, vol. 1, pp. cc–ccviii.
4. Lynn Thorndyke, *Michael Scot* (London: Nelson, 1965). For the part Michael Scot played in the transmission of Aristotle see Kretzmann, Kenny and Pinborg (eds), *Cambridge History of Later Medieval Philosophy*, pp. 48–52, 58–9.

CHAPTER 2

John Duns Scotus

Section 1: Life and works

The Franciscan friar John Duns Scotus (c.1266–1308) was born in the village of Duns in Berwickshire in the Scottish Borders. The Scottish philosopher/theologian John Mair (c.1467–1550) reports that:

> When [Scotus] was no more than a boy, but had been already grounded in grammar, he was taken by two Scottish Minorite [i.e. Franciscan] friars to Oxford, for at that time there existed no university in Scotland. By the favour of those friars he lived in the convent of the Minorites at Oxford, and he made his profession in the religion of the Blessed Francis.[1]

It is supposed that it was in the late 1270s that Scotus began his studies at Oxford, first in arts and then in theology. On 17 March 1291 he was ordained into the priesthood, a date that permits an educated guess regarding his year of birth, for since twenty-five was the minimum age for ordination, and since Scotus was evidently a person of immense and precocious talent, it is probable that he was born on or not long before 17 March 1266.

While at Oxford he lectured on the *Sentences* of Peter Lombard (c.1100–c.1160), a theologian whose set of four books of *Sentences* (*Sententiae* = opinions) remained central to the teaching of theology in the Catholic church for at least the following three centuries. By 1300 Scotus had begun revising his lectures, but the revision was far from complete when he was sent to Paris to lecture there on Lombard's *Sentences*. His Paris lectures began in autumn 1302, but in June of the following year he was exiled from France for siding with the pope in an argument with the French monarch, Philip the Fair, regarding Philip's wish to tax church property. Scotus probably spent his exile in Oxford, though it is possible that he spent some or even all of the period in Cambridge. In late 1304 he was back in Paris, where he continued to lecture on the *Sentences*, and in addition lectured on the Bible and led several theological debates or 'disputations'. He remained there for a further three years before going to Cologne. Why he left Paris is not entirely clear, but the reason is probably related to the hostility he kindled through his teaching on the immaculate conception of Mary, Mother of Jesus. Contrary to the generally accepted judgment that Mary was conceived with original sin, Scotus taught that by divine agency Mary could have been conceived without original sin, and that this was probably what happened. Some prominent theologians thought Scotus's position heretical; he was therefore living dangerously. There is evidence that his departure from Paris was precipitate. He died in Cologne in the following year, 1308, on 8 November, and was buried there in the Minoriten Kirche, the Franciscan church. His remains are still there.

Scotus may have left for Cologne in such a hurry that he took none or few of his papers with him, and this is a plausible explanation, along with his early death, for the fact that his chief works, and especially his three commentaries on the *Sentences* of Peter Lombard, are unfinished. The three commentaries are the *Lectura* (his early lectures on the *Sentences* at Oxford), then the *Ordinatio* (also known as the *Opus Oxoniense* = the Oxford work), which is an extended and revised version of the *Lectura*, and finally the *Reportatio Parisiensis* or *Reportata Parisiensia* (student reports of his lectures on the *Sentences* at Paris). Of these three commentaries the *Ordinatio* is his grand commentary on the *Sentences* and is his single greatest achievement. The critical edition has been appearing, volume by volume, since 1950, though a great part of the editorial work remains to be done. Scotus also wrote a major set of *Quaestiones quodlibetales* (his replies to questions put to him on a wide range of topics) and a set of *Quaestiones* (*Questions* [on the *Metaphysics* of Aristotle]). In addition his works include several commentaries on logical writings of Aristotle, and a *Treatise on the First Principle*.

SECTION 2: TALKING ABOUT GOD

God was the focal point of almost all of Scotus's thinking and it is with his concept of God that I shall begin. God is said to be good, just, merciful and wise; and in seeking to make sense of these ascriptions we have to acknowledge the fact that our concepts of goodness, justice, mercy and wisdom are formed by us creatures looking out upon the created order and observing and reflecting upon creatures, particularly human creatures. Our concepts are therefore creaturely through and through, and hence it may seem that to bring God under these concepts implies that he also is creaturely. But God the creator is in no sense a creature, and surely therefore cannot be brought under these concepts. But is this not to deny that he is good, just, and so on? If we say that he is good and just, but that his goodness and justice are wholly unlike the goodness and justice with which we are familiar from our human experience of human beings, an experience that is the basis of our formation of these concepts, then a question arises as to whether we can properly understand these terms as applied to God. Some have held that we should understand the terms negatively. That is, even if they seem positive, they must be understood only to be denying things of God. Thus, the affirmation of God's wisdom is nothing more than a denial that he is 'foolish' as the term is ordinarily understood; the affirmation that he is just is nothing more than a denial that he is 'unjust' as the term is ordinarily understood.

Thomas Aquinas (c.1225–74), greatest of Dominican theologians, argued that we can indeed bring God under our concepts of moral and intellectual perfections, but that our concepts are imperfect representations of these perfections as they exist in God. Hence, though the corresponding terms, such as 'good' and 'just', can indeed be truly predicated of God, they signify him imperfectly; or, to put the matter otherwise, God is good and just in an 'analogical' sense of these terms. What makes the sense analogical is that the corresponding concepts in our minds represent God imperfectly. This 'doctrine of analogy' encompasses even the concept of God's existence, for Aquinas believed that we humans cannot form an adequate concept of God's existence; that even if we do not fail entirely, the concept we do form of it is an imperfect representation of his existence.

Scotus writes against both the negative interpretation and the analogical interpretation of religious language, while accepting that the two interpretations are not wholly wrong. As regards negativity, he argues that if we deny something of God, say 'foolishness', this must be because we wish to affirm something else of him, say 'wisdom', and the affirmation that he is wise is incompatible with the affirmation that he is foolish. In short, we never negate as a first move, only as a move subsequent to an affirmation, for it is only in the light of something that we know positively about God that we consider ourselves in a position to deny anything of him.[2] To take Scotus's example, we cannot know that God is not a stone unless we know something positive about God that is incompatible with his being a stone. Perhaps, for example, we have the positive belief that he is a pure spirit, and therefore is incorporeal, and therefore is not a stone.

Furthermore, if we can only deny things of God and cannot say anything of what he is then we imply that there is nothing that he is, from which it would follow that he is nothing, from which it would follow that he does not exist. This looks like atheism. But Scotus thinks that it is not even atheism. He writes: 'I never know, as regards something, whether it exists, unless I have some concept of that thing whose existence I know.'[3] The real problem with the systematic employment of the negative interpretation of talk about God is that we end by denying the existence of a God of whom we have no concept. But if we really have no concept of him then the proposition that God does not exist, or that there is no God, does not even make sense to us. This is not atheism, for at least the atheist has a concept of God; what the atheist says is that nothing can truly be brought under the concept. For Scotus, therefore, this doctrine of negativity reduces to incoherence.

Scotus is more kindly disposed to the doctrine of analogy. Aquinas held that the terms for intellectual and moral perfections are predicated primarily of God and secondarily and derivatively of creatures, and that accordingly God is the measure or standard by which we should measure his creatures in respect of these perfections. Thus the being of God is the measure by which we should measure the being of creatures, and just as our being falls short of his and therefore imperfectly represents his, so also our wisdom and justice fall short of his and imperfectly represent the divine wisdom and justice. Hence, though God has being, wisdom and justice in an analogical sense of the terms, the terms are more properly predicated of God than of us, for it is creatures that imperfectly represent the creator, not the converse.

Scotus agrees with Aquinas that the perfections of God are different from our creaturely perfections; but, as against Aquinas, he holds that a term can be used in the same sense, that is 'univocally', of God and humans. One metaphor deployed in this context is that of the relation between a measure and that which is measured. Another is that of the relation of excedent (that which exceeds) to excess (that which is exceeded). Scotus does not deny the propriety of saying that in so far as God's wisdom is the measure of ours by a certain proportion, God has wisdom in an analogical sense. But Scotus also thinks that analogy presupposes univocity or sameness of meaning.

Scotus writes:

> Things are never related as the measured to the measure, or as the excess to the excedent, unless they have something in common . . . When it is said: 'This is more perfect than that', then if it be asked 'A more perfect what?', it is necessary to ascribe something common to both, so that in every comparison something determinable is common to each of the things compared. For if a human being is more perfect than a donkey, he is not more perfect *qua* human than a donkey is; he is more perfect *qua* animal.[4]

In the phrase 'human animal', 'animal' is the determinable and 'human' is the determinant which qualifies 'animal'. The idea behind this medieval terminology is that the term 'animal' signifies any and every animal, whereas 'human animal' signifies more determinately, for it signifies only those animals that are human.

Let us then say that God is more perfect, even infinitely more perfect, than humans. We are then asked: 'A more perfect what?' or 'More perfect *qua* what?' and we reply '*Qua* wise being'. In the light of the foregoing argument we must say that 'wise' must be predicated, with the same sense, of God and humans if the comparison in respect of wisdom is to be coherent. In short, comparison implies univocity. Scotus is not saying that God and humans are wise in much the same way. He is saying that if we cannot form a univocal concept of wisdom under which we can bring the wisdom of God and of humans, then we cannot form the concept of God's wisdom as infinitely greater than ours. To form that latter concept, we must be able to form a concept of something, one and the same thing, which is infinite in God's case and finite in ours.

The foregoing arguments hold with equal force in respect of the concept of being. As against the doctrine of the analogy of being, which is perhaps the central doctrine in Aquinas's religious philosophy, Scotus holds that it is possible to form a concept of being which is neutral as between the being of God and the being of creatures, and is contained in both. He writes:

> The intellect of a person in this life can be certain that God is a being though doubtful as to whether he is a finite or an infinite being, a created or an uncreated being. Hence, as regards God, the concept of being is other than this concept [i.e. of infinite or uncreated being] and that concept [i.e. of finite or created being]. And thus in itself the concept is neither of these and is included in each. Hence it is a univocal concept [of being].[5]

We can form a concept of finite being and one of infinite being. We can also form a concept of being without qualification. Having this latter concept we can then construct a more determinate concept by adding the qualification 'finite' or 'infinite' to it. But we should not lose sight of the fact that the two concepts, of finite being and infinite being, are formed by adding a qualification to one and the same concept, being, which is logically antecedent to the more determinate concepts. This neutral concept, that is, neutral as between finite and infinite, is equally predicable of both a finite being and an infinite one.

Scotus's doctrine of the univocity of being does not imply that there can be in the world a being which is neither finite nor infinite, neither created nor uncreated. For being is known, not directly, that is, by intuition, but only by an intellectual act of abstraction, in which, starting with a concept of determinate being, we form a concept of what remains if we think away the determinant, that which determines being. Being, considered as such or without qualification, does exist, but only in the sense that (1) we can form a concept of the being of things that have determinate being, and (2) by a process of abstraction we can reach the concept of being as such.

Suppose we deny Scotus's doctrine of univocity. What then? Two consequences may be noted. First, as against Aquinas, Scotus thinks that a doctrine of analogy that does not presuppose univocity is in fact a doctrine of pure equivocity. That is, the terms 'being', 'wise' and so on have a totally different sense when applied to God and to creatures and we are unable to give more than a merely negative characterisation of these concepts as applied to God. This position, as already noted, is unacceptable to Scotus since he holds that it can only be in the light of an affirmative belief about God that we can deny anything of him.

Secondly, the denial of the Scotistic doctrine of univocity strikes at the heart of the medieval project of natural theology, a project by which conclusions were to be drawn about God's being and attributes on the basis of a suitably slanted investigation of the created order. Thus, for example, there is an argument in natural theology which begins with the fact that some things in the world, such as human artefacts, bespeak the existence of intelligent creatures and, on the basis of this concept of 'signs of intelligence', points out that there are signs of intelligence in the natural world which bespeak an intelligent creator of nature. But this argument cannot work unless there is a concept of intelligence which applies in the same sense to both the creator of the natural world and the creator of creaturely artefacts.

This matters greatly to Scotus. If the doctrine of univocity is rejected it follows that:

> from the proper notion of anything found in creatures nothing at all can be inferred about God, for the notion of what is in each is wholly different. We would have no more reason to conclude that God is formally wise from the notion of wisdom derived from creatures than we would have reason to conclude that God is formally a stone.[6]

Natural theology is especially to be ruled out if there is no univocal concept of being, for in a valid argument that starts from the fact that there are finite and contingent things and infers that there must be an infinite and necessary cause of their being, the concept of being must have the same sense throughout. If the concept is different in different parts of the argument then the argument is invalid. It is plain therefore that for Scotus a good deal hangs on the doctrine of univocity.

It should be added that Scotus's doctrine of the univocity of being does not accord with Aristotle, who writes of ten categories of being, such as substance, relation and action,[7] the list of ten being complete in the sense that there is nothing whatever that is not in one or other of the categories. Aristotle holds that no concept transcends all ten categories in the sense of being univocally predicable in them all. Thus, although we can predicate 'good' of things in the various categories, 'good' is not predicated univocally of a substance, a relation and an action. But against this, Scotus takes himself to have demonstrated that there are indeed transcendental terms, that 'being' is such a term, and that the so-called proper attributes of being, namely, unity, truth and goodness, must likewise be transcendental if being is.[8]

SECTION 3: UNIVERSALS AND INDIVIDUALS

This cat, which I am now looking at, is an individual – it is a *this* – and it also has a universal feature or a 'common nature', call it 'cathood' or 'felinity', which is universal in the sense that everything that is a cat has felinity and everything that is not a cat does not have it. Let us therefore distinguish between the individuality and the universality of the creature; and let us also notice that the distinction between individuality and universality can be made in respect of perhaps everything, for everything is an individual in virtue of being a *this* and it is universal in virtue of being *of a given kind*. In this section I shall consider Scotus's immensely influential doctrines regarding individuals and universals.

Almost from the start of the western philosophical tradition philosophers have asked questions about universals, and especially about their location. Where are they? Are they in the mind? Are they in external objects of the relevant kind? Or somewhere else? Perhaps they are in the mind, existing as concepts or as principles of classification. For example, we have in our minds a concept of cathood which is universal in the sense that every cat, past, present or future, falls under that concept. On the other hand, we must ask what it is in every cat as a result of which cats falls under that concept rather than under some other concept, and surely the answer is that there is some shared quality, a common nature, that every cat has and that exists not in the mind but in the cats. But there is a problem here. How can the common nature of a cat be in each of the many cats that there are? If it is in any one cat then surely it cannot also be in any other, unless the common nature is somehow divided up, and part is in one cat and part in another. But then, it might be argued, something that has only part of the common nature of a cat is only partly a cat.

Philosophers who hold that universals are, at least primarily, in the real world and are mind-independent or partly mind-independent are 'realists' on the subject of universals. Those who hold that universals are only in the mind and are mind-dependent are 'nominalists' or perhaps 'conceptualists'. We are dealing here with a spectrum of views, and not just with two homogeneous schools. Within this spectrum Scotus can be located on the realist side, though only just. I shall discuss briefly certain aspects of Scotus's realism. The question of the relation between universals and individuals will be centre stage.

The great Franciscan philosopher/theologian William Ockham (c.1285–c.1349) held that universals exist only in the mind and that everything in the real world is individual. As regards the common natures of things he held that the so-called common nature that given individuals have is individual in each and every thing that has the nature. Thus we have a concept of cat which is universal in the sense that it can be truly predicated of each and every cat in virtue of the cat's nature. In an important sense, Ockham privileges individuals and problematises universals. He starts by accepting the existence of individuals and then asks: if what really exist are individuals then how is universality possible? To which his reply is: universality is a property not of individuals but of predicates, and a predicate is universal in the sense that it is truly predicable of many individuals.

In adopting this line, Ockham was writing against several philosophers, but especially against Scotus, who might fairly be said to have privileged universals and problematised individuals. For Scotus starts from the fact that there are universals, common natures, and then asks the question: how are individuals possible? Here, as almost everywhere in Scotus's writings, it is theology that provides the space within which his philosophy flourishes. He asks his question at the start of his investigation of the fact that there is a plurality of angels, each one an individual. This fact about angels is a problem because, as was generally held, (1) there are individual angels, (2) angels are wholly immaterial, and (3) it is the matter of an individual, the material of which it is composed, that individuates that individual.[9] Given (1) and (2) it follows that matter does not individuate individuals; given (1) and (3) it follows that angels are at least partly material beings; and given (2) and (3) it follows that there are no individual angels. It is as a prelude to resolving this dilemma that Scotus poses the question: what makes something an individual? Or, in Scotistic language: what is the principle by which a common nature contracts to an individual?

William Ockham's answer to Scotus's question is in effect that there is something wrong with the question, for a common nature cannot exist at all except as an individual. A common nature arrives individuated as, say, *this* bundle of felinity or *that* bundle – both bundles being individual cats, which 'share' a nature or have a 'common' nature only in the sense that we have a concept of what it is to be a cat and can bring these two bundles and indefinitely many other such bundles under this same concept. So, wonders Ockham, why not accept that the unity of the common nature is also the unity that the individual has – a unity that constitutes the individual's being a *this*?

Scotus, in the generation before Ockham, could not of course argue against Ockham's precise formulation; but Ockham's position – that in the real world there are nothing but individuals and that therefore in so far as there are common natures in the real world these must have the unity that individuals have – was familiar to Scotus and was rejected by him. He argued, against it, that if the nature of an X were of itself a *this*, then there could never be more than one thing of a given kind. Since the nature of a stone is itself a this, a singular thing, every stone would be *this* one. Any other stone would have identically the same nature as this one and therefore would be this one – it could not be another.

Scotus does not deny that common natures have a kind of unity, but he does deny that they have the kind that individuals have. It is in virtue of the nature that each cat has that it is possible to bring all cats under one and the same concept of felinity. Cats are, so to say, united under the concept because of some one thing that they all have. But the unity of an individual thing is of a different order. Put simply, an individual thing is unrepeatable – there cannot be any person other than Ockham who is Ockham, though of course there can be someone else who is *similar to* Ockham.[10] That there cannot be a multiplicity of Ockhams can also be expressed by saying that Ockham is indivisible – he cannot be divided into two Ockhams. In contrast, a common nature is repeatable and divisible, and is in fact repeated in, and divided amongst, everything that has that nature. In that sense the unity of a common nature, a unity which is repeatable and divisible, is less than, or weaker than, the unity of an individual, a unity which is neither repeatable nor divisible.

With the aid of his insight into the different degrees of unity possessed by an individual and by a common nature, Scotus goes in search of the principle that, as he says, 'contracts' the nature to an individual. His tactic is first to consider several principles that had recently been canvassed and then to present his own solution. Among the contemporaries or immediate predecessors to whom he turns is Henry of Ghent (d.1293), the philosopher at whom Scotus perhaps most frequently takes aim. Henry's principle of individuation, as reported by Scotus, is a conjunction of negations: an individual substance is individual through being (1) not divided (or repeated) in itself and (2) not identical with anything else. However, though Scotus accepts that an individual is neither divided in itself nor identical with anything else, he thinks that this pair of negatives cannot account for individuality, for an individual is not merely not divided, but is of such a nature as to be indivisible. The double negation does not explain this; instead it prompts the question: What positive thing pertains to this individual such that the double negation is true of it? It is this positive thing that Scotus will identify.

Scotus considers briefly the suggestion (from an unnamed source) that it is the very existence of an individual that individuates the individual, but he rejects the suggestion on the grounds that existence is no less common than common natures. Several individuals of the same kind have the same kind of nature and the same kind of existence, and just as we must ask what makes a nature a *this* because the nature itself is not the explanation for its individualisation, so we must ask what makes existence *this* existence and not some other, for existence is not the explanation for its individualisation. In short, invoking existence as a principle of individuation merely prompts the question of how a given existence is itself individuated.

Scotus also considers matter as a possible principle of individuation, at least in respect of material substances. Why not say that two things which have a common nature differ in the matter which the common nature informs? A human being is composed of flesh and blood of which no other being, human or otherwise, is even partly composed. Human beings, therefore, though having a common nature, are individuated by the matter of which each is composed. This doctrine, commonly attributed both to Aristotle and to Aquinas, is, however, rejected by Scotus. Individuals have the greatest possible unity in that they are absolutely unrepeatable or indivisible, and yet matter, which is here supposed to explain this unity, is traditionally seen as a principle of potentiality in individuals; it has the form it has but could have some other form instead. Thus a lump of clay is in potency to any of an indefinitely large number of forms that the potter could impose on it. Since matter is a principle of multiplicity it seems impossible that it should perform the role of being a principle of the greatest possible unity.

What then is left? Scotus's investigation of plausible, but in the end unsatisfactory, solutions is a valuable exercise in that it produces clarification, even if of a negative sort, regarding the criteria being sought. Above all, he is looking for something that confers unrepeatability or indivisibility. What makes me an individual is something that ensures that I cannot be repeated, something through which, to put it plainly, there cannot be another me. Of course, I can be cloned and my clone is very similar to me, and indeed is indistinguishable in respect of genetic make-up, but my clone is no more another me than anyone else is. If two people have, as we say, the 'same' genetic make-up, then the genetic map of one of them is repeated, for it is also the genetic map of the other. But the map is a universal – it can be instantiated indefinitely many times. But that which is universal cannot confer individuality. What can?

Scotus describes something that he believes must exist if individuals are to exist; but he has never experienced this 'something' nor thinks it experienceable by us in this life, so his exposition proceeds in a sideways fashion. Tibbles is a cat and Fido is a dog. Both are animals, but Tibbles has something by which she is in the species cat and Fido something by which he is a dog. Let us say then that Tibbles and Fido are generically the same, that is, they belong to the same *genus*, animal; and that each is specifically different from the other, that is, they belong to different *species* of animal. The genus animal is differentiated into the species cat by a given *specific difference*, and it is differentiated into the species dog by a different specific difference. The genus animal is repeatable, for it is repeated in every species, such as cat, dog and so on, which falls under that genus, and the species cat is repeatable, for it is repeated in every instantiation of the species, that is, in every cat. Scotus hypothesises an *individual difference*, which he sometimes calls a 'thisness' (= *haecceitas*), which relates to a species in somewhat the way that a specific difference relates to a genus. The thisness confers on the common nature a unity that the common nature cannot have in itself, for in itself a common nature is divisible and is in fact divided among all its instantiations, whereas each instantiation has the unity of something that is absolutely indivisible.

Of course, an instantiation of the common nature cat is divisible in the sense that a limb can be separated from the body, but the cat's limb is not related to the cat as the instantiation of a common nature is related to the common nature. The instantiation is just that, an instance of the common nature cat – it is, in Scotus's terms, a contraction of the nature to the individual cat. But the limb is in no sense an instantiation of the individual cat. It is one part of the cat, but the cat itself is not one part of the common nature. It is therefore plain why Scotus wishes to distinguish between different sorts of unity, and to maintain that the unity of a common nature is weaker than the unity of the individual that instantiates it.

On this account, much as the genus contracts to a species by a specific difference, so a species contracts to an individual by an individual difference. The individual difference is a positive entity that contracts the species to an individual, a something that is so determinate that it cannot become more determinate. Animal becomes more determinate when it contracts to cat, and cat becomes more determinate when it contracts to Tibbles. But Tibbles cannot contract to anything; it cannot be a head of division in relation to subordinate heads of division, and therefore is neither repeatable nor divisible.

SECTION 4: WILL AND INTELLECT

Scotus treats the human mind as a principle of activity; it forms concepts, remembers, imagines, intuits, deliberates, wonders, wills, and so on. Each of these various sorts of activity is referred to a faculty or power of the mind. Thus, we have an intellect, a memory, an imagination, a will, and so on. The question how the various faculties are related to each other and to the mind is one that Scotus regards as central for an understanding of the mind and as hardly answerable without deployment of the concept of unity, to which concept we therefore now turn.

We have already noted that Scotus believes there to be different kinds of unity; for example, the unity of a genus, which is less or weaker than that of a species falling under the genus, and the unity of an individual, which is greater or stronger than that of the species it instantiates. A genus is divisible, so is a species, but an individual is not. An individual is therefore a very strong unity, though not so strong as to be entirely lacking in multiplicity, for it does after all include not only the common nature but also the individual difference which, though inseparable from the common nature, is conceptually distinct from it. The relation between mind and its faculties bears a striking resemblance to the relation between, on the one hand, an individual thing and, on the other, the common nature and the individual difference that compose the individual.

A pile of stones has a unity of sorts, but not a strong one, since the removal of a stone need have no perceptible effect on the heap as a whole or on any other stone in it. A tree has a stronger unity in the sense that excision of part of the tree has an effect on other parts and perhaps throughout, due to the fact that the tree forms a botanical system. However, excision of a branch does not destroy every part, or even any other part, of the tree; the tree can accommodate the loss of the branch and go on to flourish. But the mind is not quite like that. Malfunction of one faculty impacts on the others, and total loss of one faculty will have catastrophic effects on others and on the mind as a whole. One need only think of the effect that comprehensive loss of memory would have on the intellect. I shall here focus on the relation between intellect and will and the nature of the unity that they form. It is appropriate to begin by giving some indication of the nature of the intellect, as a route to a grasp of Scotus's concept of will.

Different faculties are directed to different things which are their proper objects. Memory is properly directed towards past events, as sense perception is properly directed to objects in the external world. What is it to which intellect is properly directed? Scotus says it is being, being as such or without qualification, and therefore not simply the being of this kind of thing or that kind. Thus, for example, given Scotus's doctrine of the univocity of being, it follows that the being of God, in so far as it is being, and irrespective of its being infinite and

uncreated, is a proper object of our intellect. To us therefore, in so far
as we have a grasp of being, being without qualification, God is not a
completely closed book.

Scotus makes a distinction between two sorts of act of intellect, a
distinction that was to reverberate through the logical and theological treatises of the fourteenth century. First, the intellect can conceive
of something while abstracting from the thing's existence or non-
existence, that is, without judging whether the thing conceived does
exist or does not. Pure acts of imagination (such as my imagining a
unicorn or a goat-stag) are of this kind. An act of this kind is termed
an 'abstractive cognition'. Secondly, the intellectual act by which we
conceive of a thing may, on the contrary, be of the thing precisely in
so far as it exists and is present to the mind. Such an act, which
permits the judgment that the thing exists, is termed an 'intuitive cognition'. Our intellectual grasp of our own mental acts may be of just
such a nature; my intellectual grasp of an act of recollection in which
I am now engaged permits the judgment that the act exists. In each
case, that is, of intuitive and of abstractive cognition, the intellect
forms a concept of something. The something which is conceived is
termed the 'object' of the intellectual act.

In so far as an intellectual act by its nature has an object, something to which the act is directed, it resembles an act of will. As we
do not conceive without conceiving something, so also when we will
we will something. To will without willing something is to will
nothing, and there is no difference between willing nothing and not
willing. The something which is the object of an act of will is an act
or a state of affairs produced by an act, and for us to will this object
we have to form a concept or idea of it. But it is the intellect that produces concepts. It forms or formulates a plan of action or an object
to be aimed at, and presents this to the will, which then either acts on
it or rejects it. Intellect proposes and will disposes, and will cannot
dispose unless a proposal of intellect is in place for will to deal with.
Dependence of will on intellect is therefore absolute.[11]

Scotus raises conversely the question of the dependence of intellect
on will. He does this in the context of a discussion on St Jerome's
dictum that there is sin in thought, word and deed. Jerome's dictum
is problematic for the following reason. Let us grant that a willed act
must be preceded by a concept of what it is we will. If therefore we
will to have a given thought we must first form a concept of that
thought, that is, we must think the thought before we will to think it.
But then the time to will to think the thought is already past – we have

had the thought antecedent to an act of will. This consideration impacts directly on Jerome's dictum because according to Catholic teaching every sinful act is willed or voluntary. Hence sinful thoughts are willed. But how can that be if they come unbidden and therefore unwilled into our head?

Scotus's solution to this problem is based on the acknowledgement that we can find thoughts in our heads that have simply come into being without an act of will. Whether we invoke the principle of association of ideas to explain their presence or invoke some other natural causal principle is not to the point, which is simply that if the explanation is not an act of will then the thought, no matter its content, cannot be a sinful act. But Scotus also acknowledges that once the thought is in our head then what happens to it next may well be subject to voluntary control.

Here the similarity to the case of visual perception is instructive. When we focus upon an object in our visual field then we see the object with greater clarity and distinctness than other objects which are also in the visual field but are closer to the periphery, and the closer they are to the periphery the less they are clear and distinct. The fact that something is closer to the periphery does not mean that it is not seen at all. It can therefore attract our attention. We may have a momentary awareness of some delightful or otherwise attention-grabbing quality, and in that moment we can focus on it or we can decide, for whatever reason, that it would be better not to do so.

Much the same thing happens where it is imagination and not visual perception that is at issue. Thoughts or ideas simply occur to us. We just find ourselves thinking them without having had any intention to think either those precise thoughts or any thoughts cognate with them. There they are, in our minds as if from nowhere. Some of the ideas are in intellectual focus – they are the ones on which we are concentrating – and others are peripheral within the field of intellectual vision. Of those towards the periphery one might attract our attention for whatever reason. We might have a sense that exploration of that idea may afford us pleasure. Or on the contrary, we might have a sense that closer inspection would be painful to us. In either case, according to Scotus, what happens next is subject to voluntary control. We can willingly either focus on or withdraw all attention from the peripheral idea. Scotus considers the example of a lecherous or lascivious idea on the periphery of our intellectual field. If voluntarily we focus on the lecherous thought so that we may delight in it then the thought is sinful. It is not sinful on its first appearance in the mind, for then it is not voluntary, but the deliberate preservation of the thought with a view to satisfying a lustful desire is another matter entirely. Such thinking is judged by the church to be a contravention of God's law and such an act is therefore a sin. From this it follows that our original problem regarding the possibility of sinning in thought is resolved. We cannot be culpable for a thought on its first occurrence (what Scotus terms a *cognitio prima*), but we are culpable for the retention of that thought when that retention is motivated by a wish to dwell delightedly on its content.

Scotus draws a practical conclusion from his analysis. It is that one way to avoid committing a sin in thought is to avert our intellectual gaze from an object to which it would be better for us not to attend. The underlying consideration here is that almost all our thinking is subject to voluntary control. A thought might come to us involuntarily, but thereafter whether we attend to that thought for a minute or for an hour, or whether we refuse to attend to it any further – these things are all subject to will. The conclusion is that while in an obvious sense will is dependent on intellect, there is also a sense in which our intellectual life, almost in its entirety, is dependent on will. Without will, the life of the intellect would be utterly chaotic; no kind of intelligent, systematic consideration of anything would be possible; ideas would come and go according to principles of association of ideas, and not according to rational considerations. This is not the way human beings think.

If will cannot function without intellect nor intellect without will, this fact contributes significantly to the concept of the human mind as a strong unity. Intellect and will are really inseparable in the sense that within any human mind the will could not survive destruction of the intellect, nor the intellect survive destruction of the will. None the less, intellect and will are not identical in all respects, for they are conceptually distinct, in the sense that an act of thinking is a different sort of act from an act of willing. The fact that intellect and will are really inseparable implies that in a sense, one deployed by Scotus, they are really identical. He holds further that they are really identical with mind. Put otherwise, it is really the mind that engages in these various sorts of act, 'mental' acts. In so far as the mind wills, it takes on the *form* of a willer, and in so far as it thinks, it takes on the *form* of a thinker. I use this mode of expression as a way to introduce crucial terminology. Scotus holds that intellect and will are *formalities* of mind and that the distinction between intellect and will is therefore a *formal* distinction only. It is not a real distinction since not even God can preserve one of these faculties in a human mind while annihilating the other. Nor is it a mere 'distinction of reason',[12] since it is grounded in something real, namely, the fact that acts of will and acts of thinking are not the same sorts of act.

It should be added that the concept of the formal distinction is also deployed by Scotus in his philosophy of religion, for he holds that there is a merely formal distinction between the attributes of God. The fact that God has many attributes seems incompatible with the absolute oneness of God, and Scotus's solution is that the many attributes are absolutely inseparable in God, and that therefore the distinction between them is not real; it is, however, more than merely a distinction of reason, for conceptually an act of wisdom is not the same as an act of justice or of mercy. The formal distinction also appears in Scotus's discussion of individuality, for he holds that within a given individual substance the individual difference which contracts a common nature to *this* is only formally distinct from the common nature. Really the two are the same in being inseparable even by God. The concept of the formal distinction is a unifying principle in Scotus's philosophy.

The thesis, that intellect and will are inseparable and therefore really identical, prompts a question as to whether the will is free. Its inseparability from intellect surely implies that it must will in accordance with the directives of intellect and therefore cannot be free. How, if the two faculties are inseparable, can will stand at the distance from intellect that is required if it is to be able to reject intellect's directives?

To pursue this question further it is necessary to note that Scotus speaks of two kinds of will, a free will and a natural will, and he holds that the latter is not free. There are things that we desire by our biological nature, things such as warmth, rest, nourishment and, above all, survival. This natural desire is a kind of will. When hungry we naturally desire food – we will to eat; when threatened with death we naturally desire to survive – we will to stay alive. Scotus believes that such willing is willing only in a qualified sense precisely because it is not free; it is instead a purely natural inclination to obey a biological imperative.

The free will is free in a double sense, one negative and the other positive. As regards the negative side, free will is free from nature for, whatever nature demands through us or of us, we can will not to satisfy that natural demand. Though starving, we do not eat food that is to hand because to take it would be theft. Though desperate to live, a person chooses to do what he knows will lead to his death because he is not prepared to betray his friends or his values. As regards the positive side of freedom, we are always open to opposites in the sense that whatever act we perform, we could in those very same circumstances have performed some other act instead. Even if intellect proposes a line of action as the best in the circumstances, we can reject that proposal and do something else instead, or (if this is different from doing something else) do nothing at all. We might be crazy to reject the eminently reasonable proposal of intellect, but that does not imply that we will not reject it, for freedom includes the freedom to do crazy things. This concept of freedom prevents Scotus from being an intellectual determinist. Even though we almost always act as reason dictates, we are always free not to; and right up to the moment of the act being performed, and right through the period of the performance, the possibility of its not being performed has a kind of reality.

We are reasonable beings, which is to say that normally we do as our intellect dictates. That we always listen to its dictates and usually obey is the least we would expect given the metaphysical fact, as Scotus believes it to be, that intellect and will are really the same, both being identical with the mind. Given this relation it is not to be expected that will could behave as if intellect did not exist. However, intellect and will are distinct forms of mind, that is, they are formally distinct; and this metaphysical fact about their relation constitutes a distance of will from intellect that permits the possibility of not acting as intellect dictates.

Earlier I noted the concept of the biological imperative, an imperative which is a natural inclination of the will towards things that constitute or contribute to our good. To cover this concept Scotus uses, courtesy of St Anselm of Canterbury, the Latin phrase *affectio commodi* – affection for the beneficial or the advantageous. It is a good affection in so far as it is an affection for the good, but at the same time it is for the good for the sake of the agent, not for the sake of the good. This latter concept, an affection for the good for its own sake, which Scotus signifies by the phrase *affectio iustitiae*, affection for justice, is a principle of freedom in us in so far as it enables us to liberate ourselves from the insistent demands that we, as natural creatures, each make for ourselves. Among these natural demands is our natural inclination to our own happiness. But, as we have seen, Scotus does not believe that we necessarily act to secure our happiness. Our affection for justice can stand up to the natural demand and it can win, as it does when, though hungry, we refuse to eat available food because to take it would be to steal and therefore to act unjustly. It is in such acts informed by the affection for justice that, for Scotus, our free will is most manifest.

As regards the contents of justice, the broad picture can be gleaned from the Ten Commandments. Here a question arises as to whether we could work out the commandments by reason or whether it is only by revelation that we could know them. Scotus's answer starts from the fact that Moses came down from Mount Sinai with two tablets of the law, the first three commandments on one tablet and the remaining seven (concerning honour of parents, murder, adultery, theft, false witness, and covetousness of one's neighbour's house and of his wife) on the other. As regards the first two commandments, that we should have no other gods and that we should not take God's name in vain, Scotus is clear that these follow from our very concept of God, and that therefore God could not exempt anyone from them, and could not have given us commandments incompatible with those two. In that sense they are necessary. In a more low-key way he also thinks that this is true of the commandment to keep the Sabbath day holy. But none of the commandments on the second tablet is necessary, even though they are all highly consonant with the commandments of the first tablet.

Section 5: Scotus's political theory and the Declaration of Arbroath

We have already observed that for Scotus we are independent beings in the double sense that we are both free *from* nature and free *to* choose one or another of the several mutually opposed possibilities that are always open to us. We can do otherwise than we do, and this is because we are independent of nature. Our principle of change lies within us, with our own judgments and choices. Features of this doctrine are duly modulated by Scotus into a concept of political independence. The concept is constructed in the context of the theological question whether a thief can be truly penitent if he has not made restitution.[13] This might seem an odd context but it is not really so, for restitution of property to its rightful owner naturally raises a question about the origin of property rights, and that question is a central one in political theory. As Scotus puts the question: 'What is the source of distinct ownership such that this may be called "mine" and that

"yours"? For this is the basis of all injustice through misappropriation of another's property and consequently of all justice in restoring
it.'[14] It is natural to think that Scotus has in mind such things as an
ordinary thief might steal, but I wish to hold in the background the
thought that Scotus might also have in mind a non-ordinary thief,
such as a king, who has stolen another country, and who also (as with
the ordinary thief) cannot be a true penitent unless he restores to its
rightful owners the property he has stolen.

The source of property rights, argues Scotus, cannot lie in the 'state
of innocence', the state of nature prior to the Fall, for there was then
no mine or thine; instead everything was held in common. Scotus
invokes in support of this claim a proposition in the *Decretals* of
Gratian: 'By the law of nature all things are common to all.'[15] They
are common to all because, as Scotus puts the point, such an arrangement will contribute to a peaceful and decent life and will provide
needed sustenance.[16] In the state of innocence a person would not
seek by violence to take from another what another needed for life or
comfort. It is therefore only after the Fall that property rights come
into existence.

According to Catholic theology the loss of innocence involved a
radical change in human psychology, in the direction of covetousness
and a willingness to use violence against one's neighbour. A covetous
and violent person would take more than he needs of the things held
in common and would be willing to use violence to withhold them
from another who has a genuine need of what the covetous person
has needlessly appropriated. In the face of this new psychological
reality it becomes necessary to divide up what had previously been
held in common. The division could not be by natural law, since that
law, as already stated, sanctioned the common ownership of things,
and hence positive law was required for the task. A legislator is therefore required, and Scotus argues that the legislator must possess two
qualities: prudence and authority.[17] Prudence is needed for the
obvious reason that the legislator must form a correct judgment as to
the principles of division that would result in a decent and peaceful
life for the citizens, and such judgment involves the exercise of practical right reason, that is, prudence. Furthermore authority is
required, because prudence by itself is not enough. The mere fact that
the legislator is prudent does not imply that others will attend to him.
A legislative authority's word must be sufficient to bind others also,
and for that he must be recognised as having just command over
others.

But from where does this just command come? It is in his answer to this question that Scotus moves into territory that is also occupied by the Declaration of the Clergy (1310) and the Declaration of Arbroath (1320). According to Scotus authority takes two forms. The first, parental, is entirely according to nature, not according to any human convention or voluntary arrangement. Hence even in the state of innocence the parent has a right to command and the child has a duty to obey; and after the Fall it remains a part of the natural order. It is simply a natural feature of parenthood. This is to be contrasted with the other kind of authority, the political. There are several differences. First, political authority is not exercised solely over members of the authority's own family, and indeed it is possible that no member of the authority's family is subject to his political command. Secondly, political authority can reside with either a single person or with what Scotus terms a community (*communitas*), a group to which he assigns no upper size. Thirdly, in contrast to parental authority, whose justice is a natural endowment, political authority, as Scotus states the matter: 'can be just by common consent and election on the part of the community'.[18] While it is not by 'common consent and election' that parents justly command their children, the just rulership of a political authority, by contrast, derives from the choice of those who will be ruled by that authority. Scotus continues:

> Thus, if some outsiders [*extranei*: that is, people who are not all in the one family] banded together to build a city or live in one, seeing that they could not be well governed without some form of authority, they could have amicably agreed to commit their community to one person or to a group [*communitas*], and if to one person, to him alone and to a successor who would be chosen as he was, or to him and his posterity. And both of these forms of political authority are just, because one person can justly submit himself to another or to a community in those things which are not against the law of God and as regards which he can be guided better by the person or persons to whom he has submitted or subjected himself than he could by himself.[19]

There are several elements in this doctrine that we should take with us into the question concerning the major political scheme in the minds of Scottish political leaders in the two decades after Scotus devised and taught his doctrine. The first element is that of a social contract. The people are to choose their ruler by agreeing among themselves as to who the ruler should be. Secondly, and consequently, the people also choose the principle of transference of authority. It is not that the people choose the first ruler, and that thereafter the question of who is to rule is out of their hands; on Scotus's scheme, it is never out of their hands. It could be agreed by the people that the transference of authority could be by birth, say, the principle of primogeniture, or at the end of one ruler's rulership the people could agree among themselves as to who should be the next ruler. Thirdly, the ruler is put in place because there is a job to be done, one that requires exercise of practical right reason, that is, prudence. As Scotus says, the ruler must be able to guide the people better than the people individually can guide themselves. I should add, as a fourth element, the fact that the people can choose as a ruler either a single person or a 'community'. This should be mentioned if we have it in mind to support the claim that there is a close relation between Scotus's political theory and the politics of Scotland. For in the decades from 1286 the phrase 'community of the realm', referring to the political elite in Scotland, had become a term in rather frequent use in Scottish documents, and the phrase gives particular significance to Scotus's use of the term 'community' in his description of one kind of just rulership. But whether the political authority be a single person or a 'community', the outcome is that a nation governed in the way described by Scotus is independent in the sense that, as with individual independence, the principle of change lies within and is not external. The people come together and decide among themselves and for themselves who is to govern them and what the principle of change of ruler should be. Scotus, in political theory, as in so much else, was his own man. None of his contemporaries and predecessors produced a theory quite like his. Some did argue for a form of social contract theory, though in that feudalistic age very few did, but nevertheless Scotus's form of the theory was unique.

I turn finally, and briefly, to the question of how Scotus's doctrine stands in relation to the politics of Scotland in the first two decades of the fourteenth century, and in particular to the Declaration of the Clergy and the Declaration of Arbroath. The date of the Declaration of the Clergy is disputed, though the document itself bears the date 24 February 1310.[20] In the Declaration the clergy of Scotland declared themselves in favour of King Robert Bruce. The Declaration begins by affirming that John Balliol was made king of Scotland by the king of England. This is the nub of the clergy's criticism of Balliol's status, for they argue that the English king does not have the authority to determine who will be king of Scotland; only the Scots themselves have that authority. I quote at length:

The people, therefore, and commons of the foresaid Kingdom of Scotland . . . agreed upon the said Lord Robert, the King who now is, in whom the rights of his father and grandfather to the foresaid kingdom, in the judgment of the people, still exist and flourish entire; and with the concurrence and consent of the said people he was chosen to be King, that he might reform the deformities of the kingdom, correct what required correction, and direct what needed direction; and having been by their authority set over the kingdom, he was solemnly made King of Scots.[21]

The Declaration then refers to the cardinal virtues by which Robert Bruce is fitted to rule and be worthy of the name of king, a point to be borne in mind in view of Scotus's emphasis on the ruler's possession of the cardinal virtue of prudence. The Declaration continues: 'and if any one on the contrary claim right to the foresaid kingdom in virtue of letters in time past, sealed and containing the consent of the people and the commons, know ye that all this took place in fact by force and violence which could not at the time be resisted'.[22]

It is clear that the political doctrine in this document is Scotus's so far as it focuses repeatedly on the doctrine that legitimate rulership depends on the consent of the people; the *'people agreed'* upon Lord Robert; it was *'with the concurrence and consent of the said people'* that Robert was King; it was *'by their authority'* that he was set over the people. If anyone has documents to the contrary , including documents containing *'the consent of the people'*, then the people were not then, that is, at the time of giving their consent, acting freely or voluntarily; their consent was extracted by force and was therefore not real consent. In the light of the fact that the political theory underlying the Declaration is thoroughly Scotistic, it is of particular interest that the document was presented in the General Council of Scotland in the Church of the Friars Minor, the Franciscan Church, in Dundee. Scotus's own order provided the venue for the occasion.

The Declaration of Arbroath, ten years later, repeats the message of the Declaration of the Clergy that a king does not rule except by the consent of those who are ruled, for it states that Robert was made prince and king 'by the dutiful consent and assent of every one of us'.[23] It then adds a new element to the Scotistic story that we have extracted from the Declaration of the Clergy. I quote in full:

Unto him [sc. King Robert Bruce], as the man through whom salvation has been wrought in our people, we are bound both of right and by his service rendered, and are resolved in whatever fortune to cleave, for the preservation of our liberty. Were he to abandon the enterprise

begun, choosing to subject us or our kingdom to the king of the
English or to the English people, we would strive to thrust him out
forthwith as our enemy and the subverter of right, his own and ours,
and take for our king another who would suffice for our defence.[24]

Nothing could more clearly encapsulate Scotus's doctrine that the
ruler justly rules his people solely by their choice and consent. From
this doctrine it follows immediately that the ruler's authority can be
transferred solely by an act of the people and not at all by an act of the
ruler. Of course, the people, unwilling to lose their political power,
which is, above all, the power to decide who will rule, are bound to
replace the errant ruler by one who will work for and not against them.

The independence of the people resides, more than in anything
else, in their freedom to determine who will rule; and having determined this the people's will is not followed by a period of passivity –
their will is not switched off. They remain watchful, judging the
quality of the task performed by the person they have elected, and
ready to withdraw their consent to his rule if he fails them. In this
collective act of self-determination lies their independence. It is formally the same as with the individual person, whose actions are
determined from within, and whose act of will is not followed by passivity – the will is not switched off. The person remains watchful,
judging whether the line of action decided upon remains appropriate
in all its aspects, or whether it requires modification or abandonment
in light of developments.[25]

I have argued that Scotus's theory of freedom is articulated in the
two great Declarations that were issued within a few years of his
death. There remains a question of historical causation, which I am
not competent to answer, of whether this identity of doctrine in the
theological work of Scotus and in the Declarations was a coincidence
or not. But I do note that Scotus was much the most prominent
Scottish philosopher/theologian of his time and that his doctrine was
therefore one that the senior Scottish clergy were likely to know.

My conclusion is that while Wallace was fighting for Scottish independence, Scotus was developing precisely the intellectual framework
that the Scots within a few years would deploy in the chief documents
that defined that independence. I also believe it possible that the documents in question were compiled with Scotus in mind. There
remains an intriguing thought, that I have not pursued, that Scotus
was actively engaged in the development of Scottish thinking on the
matter of Scottish independence, through discussions that he might

have had with Scots whom he met at the great centres where he worked.[26] If such discussions did indeed take place then my suggestion, made some years ago,[27] that the relation of Scotus to the Wars of Independence was one of theory to practice, is false. Scotus may, after all, have been on the side of practice as well as theory, by working to the same end as the Scottish military leaders, even though by utterly different means.[28]

Notes

1. Mair, *History*, p. 206.
2. 'negatio non cognoscitur nisi per affirmationem . . . Patet etiam quod nullas negationes cognoscimus de Deo nisi per affirmationes, per quas removemus alia incompossibilia ab illis affirmationibus.' 'A negation is not known except via an affirmation . . . It is also obvious that we know no negations about God except by means of affirmations. It is on the basis of those affirmations that we deny other things that are incompatible with them.' Duns Scotus, *Philosophical Writings*, p. 15.
3. 'Numquam enim cognosco de aliquo si est, nisi habeam aliquem conceptum illius extremi de quo cognosco esse.' *Philosophical Writings*, p. 16.
4. 'quia numquam aliqua comparantur ut mensurata ad mensuram, vel excessa ad excedens, nisi in aliquo uno conveniant . . . Quando enim dicitur "hoc est perfectius illo", si quaeratur "quid perfectius?", ibi oportet assignare aliquid commune utrique, ita quod omnis comparativi determinabile est commune utrique extremo comparationis; non enim homo est perfectior homo quam asinus, sed perfectius animal.' Duns Scotus, *Opera Omnia*, ed. Balić, vol. 4, p. 191 (my trans.).
5. 'Sed intellectus viatoris potest esse certus de Deo quod sit ens dubitando de ente finito vel infinito, creato vel increato; ergo conceptus entis de Deo est alius a conceptu isto et illo, et ita neuter ex se, et in utroque illorum includitur; igitur univocus.' *Philosophical Writings*, p. 20.
6. 'quod ex nulla ratione propria eorum prout sunt in creaturis, possunt concludi de Deo, quia omnino alia et alia ratio illorum est et istorum; immo non magis concludetur quod Deus est sapiens formaliter, ex ratione sapientiae quam apprehendimus ex creaturis, quam quod Deus est formaliter lapis.' *Philosophical Writings*, p. 25.
7. See *Aristotle's Categories and De interpretatione*, tr. with notes by J. L. Ackrill (Oxford: Clarendon Press, 1963).
8. These are not the only transcendentals. Scotus also recognised 'disjunctive transcendentals', such as 'infinite or finite', 'necessary or possible', 'actual or possible', where the first term is predicable of God and the second of creatures, and also where the fact that there is something of which the first is predicable follows from the fact that there is something of which the second is predicable.

9. For example, a sculptor can make ten bronze statues from the same mould. The statues are identical – they have the same identical form (this being universal) – and they are different individuals because each one is composed of a different piece of bronze.

10. There can of course be many people who are *called* 'Ockham', but that means only that they all have the same name, not that they are all the same person.

11. 'volitio est effectus posterior intellectione naturaliter, et intellectio phantasmate vel phantasiatione, et propter illum ordinem necessarium, non potest causari volitio a voluntate, nisi prius causetur ab intellectu intellectio.' 'Willing is an effect that is naturally after an act of intellect, and the act of intellect is naturally after an image or an act of imagination, and on account of this necessary ordering relation an act of will cannot be caused by the will unless antecedently an act of intellect has been caused by the intellect.' Duns Scotus, *Opus Oxoniense*, II d.25 q.unica, n. 19, in *Opera Omnia*, ed. Wadding, vol. 13, p. 212b (my trans.).

12. The distinction between a definition and what is defined is a distinction of reason only. For example, and assuming the correctness of Aristotle's definition of 'man' as 'rational animal', there is no basis in reality for the distinction between man and rational animal; the difference exists solely at the conceptual level.

13. *John Duns Scotus's Political and Economic Philosophy*, ed. Wolter, pp. 24–85.

14. Ibid. p. 29.

15. *Corpus Iuris Canonici*, ed. A. Friedberg (Leipzig: Bernhard Tauchnitz, 1979), vol. 1, col. 742.

16. *John Duns Scotus's Political and Economic Philosophy*, p. 29.

17. Ibid. p. 35.

18. Ibid. p. 33.

19. Ibid. pp. 33–5.

20. In fact it gives the date 24 February 1309, which is 1310 by modern reckoning.

21. Dickinson, Donaldson and Milne (eds), *Source Book of Scottish History*, vol. 1, p. 124.

22. Ibid. p. 126.

23. Ibid. p. 133. The 'us' are the numerous barons who sealed the Declaration. No clergy sealed the document, though it was probably written by Bernard de Linton, abbot of Arbroath, who was also the chancellor of King Robert, an interesting circumstance given that the document spells out the circumstances under which the signatories would oust the king.

24. Ibid. p. 133.

25. For discussion of this aspect of will see A. Broadie, 'Duns Scotus on sinful thought', *Scottish Journal of Theology*, 49 (1996): 291–310, reprinted in *Classical and Medieval Literature Criticism*, 59 (2003).

26. Arguments in support of this position are developed in considerable detail by Fr. Bill Russell, who has generously given me access to his as-yet-unpublished writings on this topic.
27. Broadie, *Why Scottish Philosophy Matters*, p. 34.
28. I first raised the question of the relation between John Duns Scotus and William Wallace in a BBC Scotland Radio programme 'The brilliant dunce' in 1993 on the occasion of Scotus's beatification. More recently I have benefited from conversations on the topic with Fr. Bill Russell.

CHAPTER 3

The Fifteenth Century

SECTION 1: THE CONTEXT

Scotland's first three universities were founded in the fifteenth century, and prior to the earliest of them, St Andrews, almost all young Scots in search of a university education had gone to the continent. Oxford and Cambridge were not in the main an attractive option, chiefly because of the political relations between Scotland and England, at best uncertain and at worst fraught. The French universities, especially Paris, received Scottish students in the largest numbers, but other countries, such as Germany, Austria, Poland, Spain and Italy, also welcomed them. However, with the founding of St Andrews University in 1411, Scots could receive a university education in their own country, and very quickly they were being educated in Scotland at as high a level as was available anywhere in Europe. Glasgow University was founded by Pope Nicholas V in 1451 and King's College, Aberdeen, followed in 1495. Almost all the teachers in those earliest years were Scots, educated on the continent, most commonly at the University of Paris, and indeed St Andrews was explicitly modelled on Paris. Glasgow, in accordance with its foundation bull, adopted the statutes of the university of Bologna, but Glasgow's practices were increasingly modelled on Paris, where most of the university's regents had been educated. And likewise King's College, Aberdeen, whose first principal was the Dundee-born and Paris-educated Hector Boece, was heavily influenced by Paris.

Nevertheless in fifteenth-century Scotland some philosophy was written by men who were not university teachers. There are philosophical ideas in *The Kingis Quair*, a long poem ascribed to King James I,[1] and philosophical ideas are close-woven in the poetry of the makars, such as Robert Henryson and William Dunbar. For example, Henryson's 'The preaching of the swallow'[2] is a rich mine of scholastic philosophical allusions. However, much of the extant philosophy of fifteenth-century Scots is in substantial treatises by university teachers, of whom the first of distinction is Lawrence of Lindores (1372–1437), master of arts (1393) and bachelor of theology (1403) at the University of Paris, where he also taught in the Faculty of Arts. He was among the first teachers at St Andrews, where he lectured both in arts subjects and in theology, besides twice occupying the post of rector. Aside from his academic life, but closely related to it since he was a professional theologian, Lindores was also Scotland's first inquisitor-general. In that capacity he was directly responsible for the burning of two men, one the English Wycliffist James Resby and the other the Hussite Pavel Kravar, whom Lindores judged guilty of heresy. Since St Andrews was founded expressly as a bulwark against heresy and 'errors', Lindores no doubt saw himself, *qua* inquisitor-general, as a faithful servant of the university's values.

Lindores wrote commentaries on several of Aristotle's treatises, including *Super Physicam* (On the *Physics*), *De anima* (On the mind) and *De interpretatione* (On interpretation). All these commentaries demonstrate Lindores to have been in the nominalist camp, as is indicated, for example, by the fact that he offers an account of the mind that does not involve positing the real existence of mind. Instead he started from things of which we are immediately aware, namely mental acts – acts of conceiving, imagining, reasoning, remembering, willing, and so on – and sought to give an account of the existence of mind in terms of a set of dispositions to perform such acts. On this account there is no such thing as mind other than our disposition to perform acts of the kind just listed. Notoriously Lindores sought to ban the teaching of a contrary, realist philosophy at St Andrews,[3] but in so far as he had any success in this it was not one that long survived his death.[4]

Section 2: John Ireland and *The Meroure of Wyssdome*

John Ireland (c.1440–95), possibly a native of St Andrews, was certainly a student there, though he left in 1459 without a degree. He immediately enrolled in the University of Paris, from which he gained his MA in 1460. Thereafter he rose through the ranks in Paris, teaching arts subjects and then also theology, and twice holding the post of rector. In 1474, as a reversal of the earlier experience at St Andrews, Louis XI of France prohibited the teaching of nominalist texts at Paris, and a deputation which included Ireland went to the king to argue the case for the retention of the nominalist texts in the syllabus – to no avail.[5] The ban was lifted in 1481. In the latter years of the seventies and the first two or three of the eighties Ireland wrote a great deal, mainly in the field of theology, and much of it now lost, though of his massive commentary on the *Sentences* of Peter Lombard books three and four survive.[6] By late 1483 Ireland was back permanently in Scotland. Amongst his several positions were those of confessor to James III and to James IV, and it was to the latter that Ireland dedicated his *Meroure of Wyssdome* (= *Mirror of Wisdom*). This very large book, written in Scots, is in the 'advice to princes' genre. It contains a number of philosophical ideas relating in particular to politics and religion, and I shall here give a brief indication of its philosophical contents.

Though an advice to a prince, the *Meroure* is a theological text with a good sprinkling of philosophy. This, for Ireland, is how it must be since, as regards the broad sweeping principles of good governance, only theology, bolstered by philosophical consideration, can provide a sound intellectual basis. We are given a hint of Ireland's perspective within a few lines of the start of the *Meroure*:

> for god that is omnipotent, though he be of infinite power to govern the world, the heaven, the earth, the angels, the men and all creature and though his power may not err in regimen and governance, nevertheless to give kings, lords, and princes example how they should rule and govern their people committed to them, his high majesty governs not by strength or force, but with his power ruled by wisdom, clemency, virtue, and benevolence.[7]

The position, therefore, developed across seven books of the *Meroure*, is that princes should adopt, as far as is humanly possibly, divine rule of the world as the model for their rule of their principality.

SECTION 3: FREEDOM AND GOOD GOVERNANCE

Central to the philosophical considerations underlying Ireland's advice on good governance is the fact that we human beings have free will, a fact that is bound to interest the moral theologian John Ireland in view of the church's teaching that an act cannot be sinful unless it is freely willed. The teaching is motivated partly by the consideration that sins are punishable and that we surely would not be punished by a just God for an act that we were not free not to perform. Yet this prompts a question, duly posed by Ireland, as to whether God could have so made us that though free we were by nature not free to sin,[8] a question that Ireland anwers in the negative, perhaps surprisingly since his answer seems to imply a rejection of the doctrine of divine omnipotence. For apparently there is one thing that God cannot do – create a being with free will whose nature prevents it sinning. Ireland is not explicit as to why he takes this line but it may be surmised that he thinks the alternative incoherent. Faced with a divine commandment, our freedom is really no freedom at all if we are not free to say no. This is not to imply that God cannot prevent us from sinning but if he does then the principle of prevention is directly from God, not from the nature that he has given to us. If our very nature prevents us sinning then our freedom is not true freedom.

Our freedom comes therefore at an awesome cost, of opening up the possibility of disobedience to God, something not available to other created things such as beasts and plants, below us in the chain of creation, who lack free will and are therefore wholly incapable of disobeying God. On the other hand the fact that we can sin implies that our obedience to God's law is meritorious and worthy of reward. Since the reward in question is eternal salvation there is a sense in which meritorious behaviour has cosmic significance, and Ireland stresses both this aspect of it ('of that comes great perfection in the world') and also the contrary condition, the cosmic significance of sin: 'in that [a man] displeases God he works his own lack and confusion and causes great discord and confusion in the world among all creatures.'[9]

The awesome cost of freedom is not, from Ireland's perspective, too high a price to pay. True, it means that we are free to sin and thereby to act against God and also to render the created world more imperfect. But it also means that we are able to bring added lustre to the created world by the performance of meritorious acts. On balance the gain must outweigh the loss, otherwise God's creation of creatures with free will is inexplicable. It should be added that the formulation of the question at issue needs to be watched. The question is not whether it is better that we human beings be free but peccable or be unfree but impeccable. It is whether we be peccable or we humans not exist at all. For our free will is an aspect or feature of our nature – one of the elements that conjointly make us human beings. Hence beings that lack the capacity for free acts are not human beings however much like us, biologically and mentally, they may otherwise seem. Indeed given the inseparability of intellect and will, had God created us without free will he would also have created us without a recognisably human intellect. These mental or spiritual characteristics no less define our humanity than do our biological characteristics, and a medieval Catholic theologian would therefore regard himself as having an argument from authority to deploy: since God prefers human beings peccable to the universe containing no human beings, it is in fact better that we should sin and thereby morally deform the universe than that we not sin because we don't exist.

At first sight Ireland seems to be working from a moral intuition that he regards as able to serve as a proof of the existence of God. Writing of the acts, good and bad, that we perform, he affirms:

> And thus since they must be rewarded or punished it is necessary that there be but one above the man to reward and punish his works and operation after, as they require by true justice. For and were there no thing above the man to reward him for his good deeds and punish him for his sins, wicked deeds, and trespasses, God has made the man in vain . . . without this all the world would be broken in the perfection of it.[10]

Ireland has in mind here the moral analogue of a physical vacuum. Aristotle argues that there cannot be a vacuum in the corporeal world, and Ireland adds that likewise there cannot be what he terms a 'voidness regarding justice'. Such a voidness or vacuum would exist if virtue were not rewarded or sin were neither punished nor forgiven. It is as if a sinful act creates a space into which a punishment or the forgiveness of the sinner must move, and the world would be saddled with a vacuum, an impossibility, if the sinner were neither punished nor forgiven. Hence we find Ireland stating:

> Therefore necessary is [it] that there be a lord of great power above the man that may remit and forgive him the sin and fault that he has made and committed or else punish it after his pleasure. And that lord is God of high power and majesty. And the sin that the man commits and also the merit that he does concludes and argues that there is a high lord that is God.

Hence Ireland formulates the argument: 'Homo potest peccare ergo deus est. Et homo potest mereri ergo deus est'[11] (= A human being can sin, therefore there is a God. And a human being can be meritorious, therefore there is a God).

Seemingly therefore Ireland starts from a deep sense that the world cannot be an ultimately unjust place (just as it cannot be a place that sustains a physical vacuum) and draws the conclusion that there must therefore be an agent who ensures that the world is indeed not ultimately unjust – not that it is a place in which injustice cannot occur but that it is one in which just acts and unjust ones, if they occur, are appropriately recompensed. Since only a God could dispense due recompense there must be a God.

Ireland moves to a discussion of several implications of the fact that God bestows due recompense on his creatures, the first being that:

> he that reward or punish the works of man have perfect and infallible knowledge of all men's works and operation, thought, word and deed. And he must know and see perfectly all the good deeds of the whole nature of man and also all the evil works that men wreak, have wrought and shall wreak.[12]

To which he adds that knowing that the acts have occurred is insufficient, for the acts have to be judged 'by true wisdom and justice'. However, even this is not sufficient, for the judgment has to be acted on:

> power is required to put the judgment and sentence in execution, and since the merits and demerits, the good and evil operation of human nature, of men and women, are almost infinite, and to part of them should be given more reward and part less, for part more punishment, for other less, necessary [it] is that this lord and judge have infinite power to reward and punish all their things, thought, word and deed.[13]

This does not, of course, imply that our world is a just place in the sense of containing not only free acts but also the corresponding rewards and punishments, for recompense is not necessarily bestowed in this world. Heaven and hell are also part of Ireland's narrative, as for example in his assertion: 'His noble justice shines in hell in the punishment of the damned person, as his high and noble mercy in heaven.'[14] In a sense this is a surprising sentiment since hell is portrayed as the worst of all possible places, yet it is structured by divine justice, and therefore by something of infinite value. How can the worst possible place have a structuring principle of infinite value? Can the worst possible place have anything of positive value in it? For Ireland the answer to the latter question is an unequivocal yes. He was heir to the doctrine that 'good' is a transcendental term, that is, that 'good' is true of whatever exists. To be is to be good. Behind this doctrine are at least two large theological considerations, first, that if something were absolutely valueless then God would have no reason to create it; and secondly, that existence is pre-eminently divine in that God not merely has existence (as do all created things) but is identical with his existence. As the medieval thinkers formulated this position,

God's essence is his existence. From this it follows that the existence
of every created thing is an imperfect representation of God's. This is
no less true of hell than of anything else. Merely as existing it imperfectly represents God's existence. Additionally it was created as the
place where God deals justly with certain kinds of sinner, and therefore serves a morally good purpose, one answering to the moral imperative, which we all recognise, that sins should be punished just as
meritorious acts should be rewarded.

Let us now move on from the doctrine that divine governance of
the created world is conducted on the basis of the fact that the ruler
of the universe is a God of justice with perfect knowledge of his subjects and infinite power. It is this foregoing feature of divine governance that powers the moral theologian, John Ireland, towards his
conclusion that earthly princes should, as far as possible, govern as
God does. Medieval theologians had a good deal to say about the *imitatio dei* – imitation of God – structuring our lives as far as possible
with the ideals and principles that God has revealed either to his
prophets or directly to us by the 'law written on our heart'. The
medieval 'advice for princes' literature develops a corner of the practical doctrine of *imitatio dei* by drawing parallels between God *qua*
governor of the universe and the earthly prince *qua* governor of his
earthly domain. In particular, God has promulgated for us a set of
laws that perfectly articulate his perfect concept of justice, and an
earthly prince therefore should likewise legislate in accordance with
justice. God has perfect knowledge of his subjects and therefore the
earthly prince should judge his subjects on the basis of the fullest and
soundest knowledge that he can gain regarding his subjects. Of course
the prince is always at risk of bestowing recompense unfairly, but
Ireland insists that the prince does not sin in his princely rule if he does
everything in his power to make his governance of his domain as
similar as he can to divine governance of the universe.

SECTION 4: FREEDOM AND FOREKNOWLEDGE

In the large picture just outlined there are the makings of a theological problem that Ireland prefers not to duck even though he is writing
for the king of Scotland and not for other theologians. It concerns a
tension between two propositions that Ireland accepts, one concerning freedom and the other concerning knowledge. The first proposition is that we are free, in the Scotist sense that we are open to
contrary possibilities such that even in the moment of initiating one of

the possibilities the alternative is open to us as a real possibility. Our future free acts are therefore contingent in the sense of being non-necessary. Whatever act we do perform, we could have done something else instead. Within Ireland's conceptual framework, contingency is dependent upon freedom; if there is no free will in the world then nothing that happens in the world is contingent.

Yet Ireland has furnished grounds for arguing that no creature is free and if there is any contingency in the world it cannot therefore be due to the nature of any creature. Earlier we noted Ireland affirming of God: 'And he must know and see perfectly all the good deeds of the whole nature of man and also all the evil works that men wreak, have wrought and shall wreak.' To which he adds the second of the two propositions I alluded to: 'great thing [it] is to know at once all men and thing that ever was or is or ever shall be, all their works, their words, their thought'.[15] He is not saying that whenever a man performed a deed God then knew about it, that now that a man performs a deed God now knows about it, and that when he will perform one God will know about it. The claim is much stronger: 'it is necessary that God that is the judge, the rewarder and punisher of all good and evil, see and know at once all the works and deeds of word, heart, mind, intention, thought and cogitation of all men that ever is or was or ever shall be. For in God grows no knowledge of the new.'[16]

Ireland's argument depends on that last sentence. Our learning is sequential; we learn first one thing then another. And in particular as events unfold before us we learn about them; our learning of them is temporally sequential, much as the events are. That is to be expected. Our knowledge of what happens in the world is almost entirely dependent upon those events happening. Once they happen we can know about them, either through our perception of them (which is simultaneous with the event), or by another's testimony (which may be accessed after the event), or by memory (which can only be accessed after the event). God's knowledge is otherwise, for he knows all at once our past, present and future acts. Yet if, antecedent to the performance of our free acts, God knew those acts, then in what sense are they free? How can we really be open to contraries if God 'always knew' which of the contraries we would will into existence? If he 'always' knew and we then choose a different contrary from the one that God knew we would choose, then he was wrong and is therefore not omniscient. There seems no escape from this. If to be able to do otherwise is the heart of our freedom and if to do otherwise falsifies

God's knowledge then we cannot do otherwise and hence are not free. But if we are not free then at a stroke practically the whole of moral theology is undermined, for without freedom there is neither merit nor sin. Plainly Ireland has to reject this line of argument.

Lurking in this argument is the corrosive thought: 'God knows all what should come eternally before ever he made the world, he knows who should be saved, who condemned. And since it shall come as God knows, it profits not to do good more than evil.' To which Ireland responds that 'this is true heresy'.[17] As regards the future acts of human beings we cannot know what they are until they have been performed and hence our knowledge has to await the performance. God's knowledge, however, cannot be constrained in this way. He is not a temporal being, for he who created the spatio-temporal framework cannot himself be limited by that framework. It is for this reason that religious writers speak about God knowing things 'from all eternity'. But if God is non-temporal does this not imply that nothing is present to him either? Ireland replies that on the contrary everything is present to God, that what is present to us is also present to him and that what is past or future in relation to us is also present to him. On this account the whole history of the universe is simultaneously present to God's gaze.

On this matter Ireland paraphrases an influential narrative by Boethius, a great thinker of the late-Roman Empire: 'God stands in the high tower of eternity and sees the people, men and women, pass by diverse ways of delight and pleasure wherein they put their beatitude and felicity.'[18] The metaphor is readily intelligible. From a high place we gaze down upon many people round about, and we see them simultaneously. We are invited to consider things spread out in time, some earlier and some later, as somewhat like things spread out in space, and just as we can simultaneously see things in different places, some in front of others, so God simultaneously sees events that are not simultaneous with each other.

The metaphor seems helpful, at least as regards the problem of free will. We naturally think about certain acts, for example, acts that we plan to perform, as lying in the future in relation to us and wonder how they can be free if God now knows them. But on the Boethian interpretation, though the acts are future in relation to us they are not future in relation to God. Nothing is future in relation to him just as nothing is past in relation to him either, for all is present to his gaze. This permits a familiar medieval move that Ireland duly makes:

> And when I see a thing, as a man sit or stand, I am certain that he sits or stands. But my sight neither puts nor causes necessity in him. Likewise the spiritual eye and sight of God, though he sees this evil person fall in sin and persevere therein, and finally condemned therefore, yet the knowledge of God is not the cause whereof he falls and perseveres in sin.[19]

Hence God's eternal knowledge of our acts does not make it impossible for us to act freely.

Boethius's metaphor of a person looking down from a high tower became a common one in medieval literature, even if occasionally adapted in a small way, as when Aquinas speaks of God's gaze on the created world as like that of someone from high up on a hill who simultaneously sees the wayfarers walking along the path below, though, because of the curvature of the slope, the wayfarers cannot see those coming behind.[20] However, it may be argued that, taken too literally, the metaphor of the divine gaze is incoherent. If I see two people at different places on a path I see them simultaneously and they are walking simultaneously. That is, the seeing and the two lots of walking all happen at the same time. And logically that is how it must be. If my seeing is simultaneous with A's steps and it is simultaneous with B's steps then A's steps and B's must be simultaneous with each other. But if we unpack this metaphor by deploying this same logic in relation to God's gaze we face a problem. For if God's gaze takes in simultaneously the birth of Boethius and the birth of John Ireland then the two births must have been simultaneous with each other, and yet they were in fact about a millennium apart. For this reason the metaphor seems unhelpful as an aid to clarifying the concept of God's timelessly present knowledge of future human acts.

But it should be said that even if we accept Boethius's metaphorical account of the divine gaze we are hardly nearer to showing how human free acts are compatible with divine knowledge. God's knowledge of the world is not merely theoretical. He knows what is happening in the world not because he watches it and learns from what he is seeing, but because he is its creator. We cannot suppose God surprised at what he found when he looked at the world he created, and the reason for this is that he had a concept of the world antecedent to willing it into existence. But if the history of the world is the unfolding of a divine plan, then what we do must have been planned (as must everything else that occurs in the created order), in which case our acts cannot be free. If they are otherwise than God planned them to be then we have thwarted God's intention for us, which is impossible for he is omnipotent.

However, these considerations do not affect Ireland's idea of the role of the earthly prince, which is to set before himself the ideal of *imitatio dei*, especially with respect to God's justice, knowledge and power, by establishing just laws and by ensuring both that those who have infringed the law are punished and that their punishment is no more severe than justice requires.

SECTION 5: THE ACCESSION OF RULERS

Given that Ireland cites Duns Scotus more frequently than any other medieval thinker, and that Scotus is the only medieval thinker who is cited in all the extant writings of Ireland, it is of interest to consider how Ireland's discussion on the principles of accession to the throne compares with that by Scotus.[21] We noted that Scotus considers the principles of election and of heredity, and that though he allows for the possibility of heredity as a principle of succession, he insists that the ruler's authority to rule depends on the people's consent, so that the people always have the last word. Ireland asks whether succession by natural inheritance or by election is best for the people, and in his reply he deploys Aristotle's *Politics*. On Ireland's not unreasonable interpretation of the *Politics*, Aristotle argues that the principle of natural inheritance is unsatisfactory since the ruler's heir may be incompetent, that is, lacking in the virtues of rulership. As Aristotle notes, some might say that if a ruler is virtuous he will not let his child inherit the crown unless the child also is virtuous. But this point, as Aristotle also notes, ignores the fact that parental love might lead a ruler to allow his natural heir to inherit the crown whether he is virtuous or not. Hence, so far as Aristotle resolves the question at issue, it is on the side of election by the people as the principle of succession.

Ireland's discussion of the merits of election operates within this Aristotelian framework and attends particularly, as did Scotus, to the need to have a ruler who is prudent. Thus Ireland argues as follows:

> he that the people choose anew is more obliged to the people that choose him to that honour and he knows that, and that he has great honour through them and therefore he would put more pain, labour and diligence for the people and realm than he that does not hold the realm of the people except through his progenitors. Also it appears that he that is newly chosen would put more diligence to govern the people virtuously and cause his children to be good that, for their virtue and love of him, one of them would be chosen to be king after him.[22]

Nevertheless Ireland argues that once a king is in place then heredity is a better principle of succession than election, partly on the grounds that one takes best care of one's own property (the realm being the property of the king in the case of a hereditary monarchy), partly also on the grounds that a hereditary monarch will feel freer to punish high nobles if he knows that his son will inherit his power, and will therefore be better able to take care of himself if the nobles dare to try to take revenge on the son for the punishments inflicted on them by the father. As to the principle by which the first king comes to power Ireland argues that that should be by election – after which heredity should be the sole principle. All in all it is not clear that the arguments Ireland musters in support of a hereditary monarchy are stronger than those in support of an elected monarchy. Perhaps there is an element of prudence behind his decision in favour of the hereditary principle, for a book written for James III and dedicated to his son James IV would not have been the most opportune place to argue in favour of an election of a monarch by a people who would choose on the basis of the candidate's practical wisdom. But in any case the space devoted to the case for election, the strength of the arguments mustered in support of that position, and the fact that the arguments on the other side seem at best no stronger, indicate that Ireland has at least considerable sympathy for the principle of election and therefore for the position developed by Scotus, even if he does not at the last declare himself for that principle.

Notes

1. James I, *The Kingis Quair of James Stewart*, ed. Matthew P. McDiarmid (London: Heinemann, 1973).
2. In Robert Henryson, *The Poems*, ed. Denton Fox (Oxford: Oxford University Press, 1987), pp. 64–75. The poem's structure, forty-nine verses, each seven lines long, is a gift to numerologists, especially in view of the poem's preoccupation with the passage of time.
3. A. I. Dunlop (ed.), *Acta Facultatis Artium Universitatis Sanctiandree, 1413–1588*, 2 vols, Scottish History Society, 3rd ser., nos. 54–5 (Edinburgh: Oliver & Boyd, 1964). Entry for 16 February 1418.
4. Ibid. Entry for 14 November 1438.
5. The decree, probably instigated by the king's confessor, who no doubt thought, as many did, that nominalism had heterodox theological implications, banned among other authors William Ockham and Gregory of Rimini. Duns Scotus's thinking, however, was acceptable to the king.

6. The sole copy is in Aberdeen University Library, MS 264. A working edition of this ms is a major desideratum for the study of Pre-Reformation Scottish theology.

7. Ireland, *Meroure of Wyssdome*, vol. 1, p. 5. The *Meroure* is in Middle Scots. Hereinafter my quotations from it are transliterated into modern English.

8. *Meroure*, vol. 2, p. 115.

9. Ibid. vol. 2, p. 117.

10. Ibid. vol. 2, p. 119.

11. Ibid. vol. 2, p. 121.

12. Ibid. vol. 2, p. 121.

13. Ibid. vol. 2, p. 122.

14. Ibid. vol. 2, p. 150.

15. Ibid. vol. 2, p. 121.

16. Ibid. vol. 2, p. 121.

17. Ibid. vol. 2, p. 140.

18. Ibid. vol. 2, p. 143. See Boethius, *Consolation of Philosophy*, IV, vi.

19. *Meroure*, vol. 2, p. 143.

20. Aquinas, *Summa Theologiae*, 1.14.13 ad 3.

21. It has been demonstrated by Dr Sally Mapstone that the chapter in which Ireland's argument unfolds, *Meroure*, vol. 3, pp. 144–54, is based substantially on passages in the *Defensor Pacis* (1.16) by Marsilius of Padua. See Mapstone, 'The advice to princes tradition in Scottish literature, 1450–1500', unpublished DPhil thesis, Oxford University, 1986. Nevertheless Marsilius supports the principle of election. It might be added that on this topic Ireland acknowledges his debt to Marsilius; see *Meroure*, vol. 3, p. 142. All Ireland's aguments, for and against election and heredity, are helpfully summarised by Craig McDonald in *Meroure*, vol. 3, pp. xl–xlii.

22. *Meroure*, vol. 3, p. 146.

CHAPTER 4

The Circle of John Mair

SECTION 1: JOHN MAIR AND HIS CIRCLE

The late-fifteenth and early-sixteenth centuries were a period of transition for the European universities, as humanistic values encroached increasingly on late-medieval modes of thinking. Scottish philosophers participated in the various stages of the transition, and in this chapter I shall focus on aspects of their work. In the next chapter attention will be directed to the new scene that was opening up as the 'modernisers' started to dominate. John Mair (whose name appears in his lifetime, whether in print or in his own hand, as Mair, Maior and Major) is the dominant figure in the earlier part of the story. He was the centre of a circle at the University of Paris, a circle that included prominent Scottish and Spanish thinkers. Among the Scots were George Lokert, William Manderston and Robert Galbraith, all of whom returned to Scotland to take up major posts and thus in one form or another continued at home the work they had conducted abroad. Three other Scots who were in the circle of John Mair in Paris were David Cranston (c.1480–1512), Gilbert Crab (c.1482–1522) and William Cranston (c.1513–62). Of these only one, William Cranston, returned to Scotland, and I shall be writing about him in the next chapter since he is part of the new beginning that came with the encroachment of renaissance humanism into Scotland. David Cranston did not return to Scotland; he died in his early- to mid-thirties some weeks after receiving his doctorate in theology at Paris. I shall say something about him in my discussion on Mair, for Mair published an illuminating dialogue between Cranston and Gavin Douglas, the poet and scholar. Gilbert Crab took his master's degree in Paris in 1503 and taught there for some years before taking up a position at Bordeaux, where he died, a member of the Carmelite order. In this chapter I shall focus on the work of Mair himself and of the three members of his circle, Lokert, Manderston and Galbraith, who returned to Scotland to continue their work.

Section 2: John Mair

Mair was born in the village of Gleghornie, south east of Edinburgh, in c.1467 and attended the grammar school at Haddington. It seems that his first university was Cambridge, where he spent a year c.1491 as a student of God's House,[1] called Christ's College from 1505, which focused on the teaching of Latin grammar – a field in which Mair demonstrates a strong interest throughout his writings.

He then transferred to Paris, to the College of St Barbe, receiving his master's degree in 1494 and incepting in the following year as regent in arts, at the same time beginning his studies in theology under the Flemish scholar Jan Standonck at the College of Montaigu, where Erasmus was one of his fellow students. Mair, with his colleague Noel Beda, took charge of the college in 1499 when Standonck, its principal, was banished from Paris. At about that time Mair also became attached to the College of Navarre, which boasted among its fifteenth-century members Pierre d'Ailly, bishop of Cambray, and Jean Gerson (who bore the honorific title 'Doctor Christianissimus'), both men distinguished for their work on behalf of the idea, accepted by Mair, that in certain circumstances a general council of the church can overrule the pope. In 1501 Mair became bachelor in theology.

In 1506, while still at the College of Navarre, Mair took his doctorate in theology, and began to teach theology at the College of Sorbonne, the pre-eminent college for theology in Paris, and one of the great centres in Europe in that field. The Faculty membership, which consisted solely of doctors of theology of Paris, was a highly conservative body, as witness the fact that as late as August 1523, and therefore at a time when the humanist movement was well established in the universities of western Europe, the Faculty passed judgment that translations of sacred texts from Greek into Latin, or from Latin into French, should be entirely suppressed and not tolerated. Throughout his life Mair remained a conservative on doctrinal matters, despite his periodic severe criticism of the behaviour of the church and of churchmen.

Mair was not wholly opposed to the encroachment of renaissance humanism. When the Italian scholar Girolamo Aleandro introduced the teaching of Greek to Paris against a background of official criticism, Mair was one of his pupils. Aleandro affirms: 'There are many Scottish scholars to be found in France who are earnest students in various of the sciences and some were my most faithful hearers, John Mair, the Scot, doctor of theology, and David Cranston, my illustrious friends.'[2]

Mair wrote on ethics, metaphysics, theology, biblical commentary, history and above all logic, on which he was one of the pre-eminent writers in Europe. His first book was *Exponibilia*, published in 1499. There are exponible terms and exponible propositions, and the detailed investigation of the logical properties of such terms and propositions constitutes a major achievement which took the medieval logicians far beyond Aristotle. Mair writes: 'An exponible proposition is a proposition which has an obscure sense by reason of a sign placed in it . . . What are the signs at issue? I think this depends more on usage than on art.'[3] Among the signs on which Mair focuses are 'every', 'only', 'except', 'in so far as', 'begins', 'ceases' and 'becomes', and he enquires also into the exposition of comparative and superlative forms of terms. The deployment of propositions such as 'Only an A is a B', 'No A except a B is a C', 'A in so far as it is a B is a C' calls for the formulation of rules of inference that are not to be found in any classical source, and Mair's treatise contributed to the development of logic in this field.

In addition to the contribution to logic proper, Mair's discussion of the logic of exponibles has immediate relevance to the physics of the period, for the interest in terms such as 'begins' and 'ceases' derives from issues to be found in Aristotle's *Physics*, and places the terms within a formal logical framework. For example, Mair affirms that 'begins' concerns what is and was not, and concerns also what is not but will be.[4] Hence, to say that X is beginning is to say that X exists now but did not exist immediately beforehand, or to say that it does not exist now but will exist immediately after now. This analysis seems to imply that if something begins to exist, then at one instant it does not exist and at the next instant it does. But whether this simple analysis is coherent depends on one's view of the nature of time in that it implies the possibility of adjacent instants, one instant and then the next one, which in turn implies that time is composed of a succession of discrete instants. But Mair believed time to be not discrete but continuous in the technical sense that there are no two instants so close together that there is no intervening instant. On this account, between any two instants there are infinitely many instants. Hence there is no such thing as a 'next instant', and hence whatever it is for something to begin, it cannot consist in the thing not existing at one instant and existing at the next, for there cannot be a next. A question is therefore to be raised, one which held Mair's attention, concerning the term 'immediately'. What is it for something to happen 'immediately' after something else if it does not mean that the second thing happens at the next instant? Mair composed a lengthy treatise on the concept of infinity, and that treatise is testimony to the fact that Mair's interest in the logical analysis of propositions concerning beginning, and also propositions concerning ceasing, takes him far beyond what we now think of as the merely logical to embrace also questions concerning the metaphysics of time. But Mair was heir to the doctrine that logic is 'the art of arts and the science of sciences', and he believed that it should be on or close to the surface of all scientific endeavours.

Many of the topics dealt with in the *Exponibilia* are of relevance to philosophical and logical issues of present-day concern. To take one example, Mair presents a logical analysis of so called 'reduplicative propositions', these being propositions in which the term 'in so far as' (*inquantum*) plays a crucial role. We are dealing therefore with propositions such as 'Every A in so far as it is B is C', Mair's example (a stock example of the period) being: 'Every man in so far as he is rational is risible [i.e., able to laugh]'. This proposition should be analysed, according to Mair, into a conjunction of four propositions: 'Every man is risible & Every man is rational & Every rational thing is risible & If something is rational it is risible.' The last of the four conjuncts is crucial. There must be a causal relation (in some sense of 'causal') between rationality and risibility for the reduplicative proposition to be true; it must be in virtue of the person's rationality that he is able to laugh (or more precisely, is able to see the funny side of things). Mair accepted this causal relation in the case of rationality and risibility – he was heir to the Aristotelian doctrine that only rational beings can see things as funny.[5]

Mair's *Exponibilia* was sufficiently popular to go into a second edition within two years, in 1501, when he also published his *Termini*, a treatise on terms. He offers a number of definitions of 'term', though his subsequent discussion of types of term is based on an acceptance of just one of the definitions, namely that a term is a sign, placeable in a proposition, representing some thing or things, or representing in some way. A sign X represents something in so far as there is something to which one can point and say truly: 'That is an X' (where the pointing can be by a directing of the mind, and not necessarily a pointing with the index finger). Mair adds that a sign can represent 'in some way', to accommodate the fact that some signs, such as 'every', 'no', 'only', 'and' and 'if' – that is to say, signs of particular interest to logicians – do signify but there is nothing to which one can point while saying truly: 'That is an every' (or 'That is a no', and so on). As Mair states the matter: '"In some way" is said because of syncategorematic terms.' A syncategorematic term is one which does not itself signify anything but which does affect the way that other terms signify in the context of a proposition. For example, in 'Every donkey is running', the 'every' does not signify anything but it affects the way 'donkey' signifies, for it ensures that in the context of that proposition 'donkey' signifies universally, so that it stands not for some donkey or other but for *every* donkey.

Having discussed the nature of terms, Mair proceeds to a discussion of so-called 'divisions of terms,' such as the division into spoken, written and mental terms, into categorematic terms (which signify something or things) and syncategorematic terms, and into complex and incomplex terms. Spoken and written terms are terms known by hearing and by sight respectively. A mental term, Mair affirms, is a concept of the mind or an act of understanding. A mental proposition is a proposition composed of mental terms; it is the act of intellect performed when we think something that would be appropriately expressed in a spoken or written proposition. Mental terms and propositions are parts of a mental language, and mental language was conceived by Mair to be essential to the work of a logician. For Mair held that mental language sets the limits of those features of spoken and written language that can be of interest to the logician. In particular, the rules of valid inference, as customarily formulated, were stated in terms of propositions which revealed in their grammatical form the form of the mental propositions of which the written ones in the logic textbooks were visible expressions. The language of the logic textbooks had therefore to approximate as closely as possible to mental language, the language of thought.

During this earlier part of his career in Paris Mair wrote numerous logic textbooks, and in 1506 published those writings in a single enormous volume.[6] He tells us in the preface that it was at the insistence of his favourite pupils that he decided, despite bouts of fever and an overwhelming workload, to prepare his lectures for publication. The pupils he names include the Scots David Cranston, George Lokert and Robert Galbraith.

However, theology was playing an increasingly important role in Mair's life, and it has to be recalled that in the year in which Mair's collected logic works were published he received his doctorate in theology. Four years later, and having delivered a full course of theology lectures, he published the first of a series of four volumes of theology, forming his commentary on the *Sentences* of Peter Lombard. Mair's theological search begins with the question: how can the wayfarer

(*viator*) acquire faith? 'Wayfarer' is a technical term in theology referring to us human beings on our pilgrim path. Mair considers several
definitions of the term without settling for any one of them, but he is
explicit that a wayfarer is a person on a journey whose destination is
either salvation or damnation. Since faith can save us, it is upon the
nature of faith that Mair focuses in the opening pages of his theological *magnum opus*. In its 'strict' sense, he tells us, it is 'assent without
hesitation to propositions whose truth one does not know except
through the testimony of others' (a definition for which Mair finds
support in St Augustine's 'What is faith if not belief in what one does
not see?'). In addition Mair presents as a 'proper' definition of 'faith':
'Assent without hesitation to propositions which are pertinent to salvation.' It is in this latter sense that Mair uses the term in his commentary, though he is sympathetic to the 'strict' definition which, in
his view, emphasises central features of the act of faith, including the
fact that faith concerns the things that 'are not seen.'

But Mair wishes to know how we come to believe in the existence
of things that are not visible to us. The evidence for their existence is
insufficient to compel the intellect to give its assent, and Mair argues
that the only possible explanation for the occurrence of faith is that
will plays a role. He finds a proof text for this in Romans 10:16, at a
point at which Paul the apostle is himself using Isaiah 53:1 as a proof
text. Mair quotes the verse: 'O Lord, who believes what we have
heard?' and he refers us to the *Glossa Ordinaria*, which asks why the
Jews do not believe and which replies that it is because they will not
to. Hence, concludes Mair, to will not to believe is incompatible with
the production of faith, and hence the faculty of will cooperates in the
production of acts of faith. 'And again,' continues Mair, 'since God
obliges us to believe, and does not oblige us to do what transcends
our powers, believing and not believing will both be free acts.' And
Mair also quotes the Vulgate Bible, Mark 16:16, 'He who does not
believe will be condemned', and comments: 'There is no precept
unless the will cooperates in its implementation.' Mair's argument
here is that since God would not condemn us for not performing an
act the performance of which is not under our voluntary control, and
since God would condemn us for not obeying his commands, obeying
God's commands, all of them, is subject to our will. Since, furthermore, God commands us to believe, belief also must be subject to will.
I have considered this matter at some length, partly because the question of the nature of faith and its relation to will is central to Mair's
philosophical and theological concerns, and partly because his style

of procedure in the passage just discussed is typical of the entire commentary. On every page of it, whether Mair is enquiring whether God is in any sense mutable, whether the Father generated the Son by necessity or by will, whether God could have made the world a better place than he made it, whether there is a real difference between God's creation of the world and his conservation of it, whether there is an evil which is so evil that it has absolutely no good in it, whether it was necessary for Christ to die – on every page there is clear evidence of the author's grasp of logical principles. Syllogisms abound, and there is a consistent display of logic of a high level of rigour and subtlety. When Mair moves from formal logic to philosophical theology he takes his logic with him.

Although most of Mair's writings on formal logic concern demonstrative logic, where relations between premisses and conclusion are necessary and not merely probable, a different sort of logical thinking is deployed at many points in the commentary on the *Sentences*, particularly where practical problems are at issue. For example, in the fourth book of the commentary on the *Sentences*,[7] Mair addresses the question whether it is permissible to accept payment for taking on a risk that another person runs. What is at issue here is mercantile insurance. Mair rules that if the contract is 'a contract based on location', then safe arrival of the goods means that the insurer should be paid and non-arrival means that he should not. This contract is permissible according to Mair. But what of a contract stipulating that if the cargo is lost at sea the insurer who receives payment must give the merchant whatever the value of the cargo was? Would such a contract be morally permissible? The question had significant practical implications in an age when usury was generally regarded as being against the law of God. Mair deals with this issue within a scholastic framework of dialectical reasoning, but he deploys analogical reasoning, features of common experience, and calculations of utility, in an attempt to solve this practical moral problem. The outcome is a discussion that has all the appearance of a piece of casuistical reasoning. In the light of this case, and others also that Mair deals with in the commentary on the *Sentences*, it is not surprising that he has been seen as a seminal figure in the development of casuistry.[8] Although leading humanists, such as Juan Luis Vives (1493–1540) in his *In pseudodialecticos*, were contemptuous of Mair's logic, he was nevertheless in important ways in the vanguard of applied logic, as well as contributing to late-scholastic discussions on matters concerning pure logic.

A last point might be made about the quasi-casuistical case just considered. Mair was writing on maritime insurance rather less than two decades after the discovery of America. Trade routes were being opened up, and questions of maritime insurance were being raised as a matter of real urgency. Mair was one of the first to grapple with these problems at a serious intellectual level. Likewise he was an originator in the field of international law, a field that burgeoned in the wake of the growth of international trade, and it is not surprising that Francisco Vitoria, the first great authority on international law, quotes extensively from his teacher John Mair, as indeed does Francisco Suarez in the course of his own legal writings. These considerations prompt the thought that though some have believed Mair to be one of the last of the major scholastic thinkers, his mind was open to new influences and new ideas, and he was willing to think creatively about the rapidly changing cultural environment. At least some of his thinking was in the vanguard.

Some of the above discussion, concerning areas where philosophy and theology meet, prompts a question concerning Mair's perception of the relation between the two disciplines, and he provides us with insight into this matter in one of his shorter works, the *Dialogus de materia theologo tractanda*, published in his commentary on the first book of the *Sentences* (1510). The two *dramatis personae* were friends of Mair's, of whom one was David Cranston, whose premature death in 1512 cut short the career of one of the rising stars of the philosophical scene, and the other was the young aristocrat Gavin Douglas (1476–1522), provost of the collegiate church of St Giles in Edinburgh, who would in due course be recognised as one of Scotland's greatest poets.

Douglas is portrayed (no doubt faithfully) as highly sceptical about the methods of the academic theologians, his scepticism being based upon the fact that the theologians are more dependent upon Aristotle's philosophical and natural scientific writings than upon the writings of the doctors of the church. In this context Douglas refers particularly to Aristotle's *Metaphysics* and to its 'commentator', that is to say, the medieval Persian philosopher-theologian Avicenna (980–1037). There may be a hint in this that the Christian theologians put themselves doubly in the wrong by depending on the writings of a pagan philosopher and also of his Muslim commentator. Cranston on the contrary regards theologians as being doubly in the right for, first, one way to get at the truth is to do philosophy, and if philosophy has discovered the truth about some matter, then it is important to be able to demonstrate that theology is not inconsistent with that truth; and secondly, there are many matters which can be accepted on faith but can also be discovered by philosophy without the aid of faith, and since faith can be an uncertain thing, it makes sense to use philosophy to bring people to truths that they might not otherwise come to accept. A theologian, affirms Cranston, should be prepared to give people arguments in support of the hope that they find in themselves.

Gavin Douglas, sounding like a typical humanist critic of scholastic theology, rejects this position on the grounds that the countless frivolous discussions one meets with, concerning such niceties as the intensity of forms and the possibility of there being points on a continuum, can be of no use to theology, and confuse and obscure the issues rather than otherwise. The humanists wished people to return to the source of their religion, the Bible, and to turn away from the obfuscatory work of the theologians. Douglas therefore quotes Paul's letter to Timothy: 'You stay within these things that you have learned and which have been entrusted to you, knowing by whom you have been taught, and because from infancy you have been familiar with the holy books they can educate towards salvation.' (II Tim. 3:14–15) Mair, whose education in dialectic taught him how to argue both sides of a case, is here using his skill to argue against himself. But his reply, via Cranston, is that we have to consider the case for philosophy on its merit. No doubt sometimes theological nonsense is taught in the name of philosophy, but if you give yourself time to consider the theological problems and to recognise that they are genuine problems that call for solution it becomes clear that philosophy is indeed one of the essential disciplines that must be called into play to solve the problems. He does not persuade Douglas, who quotes first the great humanist Aeneas Sylvius Piccolomini (who was Pius II from 1458 to1464), and then Lorenzo Valla in support of the claim: 'Whatever it is that they handed on in infinite books, I note that it could have been passed on in a very few precepts. So what else do you believe to have been the cause of such prolixity, if not the vain pride of those thinkers.'[9]

The Dialogue ends indecisively shortly after this thoroughly humanist criticism is voiced, though Mair's answer would assuredly be that if theological problems call for the exploration of newly perceived complexities, then it is necessary to go down that route, and if the humanists do not like the apparently endless multiplication of rules of logic that are plainly called for as a means to solving the problems, then this could only be because the humanists are failing to treat theology with the required seriousness.

Mair left Paris in 1518 to take up the principalship of Glasgow University. His duties were primarily administrative, but there was little pause in his writing. It was during this period that he wrote the book for which he is best known today, *Historia maioris Britanniae tam Angliae quam Scotiae* (*A History of Greater Britain as well England as Scotland*, 1521, which may be translated *A History of Mair's Britain*, though 'Greater Britain' can also be understood as contrasted with 'Lesser Britain,' i.e., Brittany). It is probable that it was written with the intention (among others) of promoting the idea of a union of the two countries; and the dedicatee, James V, son of James IV and (as son of Margaret Tudor) grandson of Henry VII, was an appropriate symbol of the closeness of the relations between the two countries.

Though the argument of the *History* points to the conclusion that a justly established union of the two kingdoms was desirable, the reason Mair gave for writing the book was that 'you may learn not only the thing that was done but also how it ought to have been done.' He adds that the first law of the historian is to tell the truth and that it is 'of more moment to understand aright, and clearly to lay down the truth on any matter, than to use elegant and highly coloured language.'[10] Armed with a keen sense of what is probable, what incredible, and what incoherent, Mair rejects Scotland's foundation myth, the claim that the Scots are descended from prince Gathelus of Greece (who gave his name to the Gaels) and Pharaoh's daughter Scota.

Mair says not only what was done but also what ought to have been done or ought not. For example, he criticises David I of Scotland for endowing religious foundations with great wealth, arguing that such endowments eventually damaged the church and then, in a discussion of the excommunication of the Scottish king Alexander II, he writes: 'If it [an excommunication] is unjust to the degree of being null, it is in no way to be dreaded . . . unjust excommunication is no more excommunication than a corpse is a man . . . Whence it comes that we reckon a vast number of excommunicated persons who are in a state of grace.'[11] Some theologians would regard this judgment as theologically, and perhaps also philosophically, problematic, for excommunication is an act in the public domain. If the priest has followed the correct church procedures in excommunicating someone, then the excommunicate has indeed been excommunicated and the fact that the excommunication was unjust does not affect its reality. Nevertheless, Mair is not courting controversy in suggesting that if the *fidelis* had been in a state of grace up to the moment of excommunication then the grace which had been bestowed on him would not be withdrawn in response to his being excommunicated if the excommunication was unjust.

Mair is silent on the issue of the structure that a Greater Britain should have. It is plain that he thought that a single monarch, justly established, is essential for the peace of the island, and that a powerful nobility is more likely to do harm than good, and as evidence for these judgments he turns repeatedly to the conflicts amongst the nobility of medieval Scotland. But what constitutes the 'just establishment' of a monarch? This question, as we noted in Chapter 2, was discussed in an innovative way by Duns Scotus, and I should like here to indicate briefly the closeness of Mair's position in relation to that earlier discussion, a closeness of which Mair must have been well aware given that he edited the text by Scotus in which the discussion of just establishment of a monarch is dealt with.

Mair accepts Scotus's doctrine that it is not up to the king and the king alone whether he remains on the throne. If the king demonstrates his unfitness to rule then, as Scotus holds, he can be deposed by others. Who are these others? Mair is as explicit as Scotus: 'A free people confers authority upon its first king, and his power is dependent upon the whole people.'[12] Mair's argument, like Scotus's, is in effect an argument from elimination, for there is no plausible candidate, apart from the people, for the role of bestower of authority: 'And it is impossible to deny that a king held from his people his right to rule, inasmuch as you can give him none other; but just so it was that the whole people united in their choice of Robert Bruce, as of one who had deserved well of the realm of Scotland.'[13] The implications of the act by the people go beyond the king to those who would otherwise be his natural heirs to the throne: 'A people may deprive their king and his posterity of all authority, when the king's worthlessness calls for such a course, just as at first it had the power to appoint him king.'[14] It might seem that the only matter on which Mair does not pronounce in harmony with Scotus concerns Scotus's doctrine that the people can choose as their ruler a community of persons, but neither does he explicitly reject the idea. He is simply silent on it. The overall picture concerning Mair's teaching on the just establishment of a ruler is therefore that he is very close indeed to Scotus's position and may in fact agree with the whole position, whose overarching consideration is that the king has a job to do, it is the people's right to decide who should do that job, and it is the people's right to retain him if he does it well and to depose him if he does it badly. The king's possession of his kingdom is conditional on the people's judgment. As Mair says: 'For a king has not the same unconditional possession of his kingdom that you have of your coat.'[15]

In June 1523 Mair left Glasgow for the University of St Andrews, but by 1526 he had returned to Paris. During this latter period in Paris students working in his field, who may therefore be assumed to have heard him lecture, include John Calvin, Ignatius Loyola, François Rabelais and George Buchanan. In 1529 he published his *In quatuor evangelia expositiones* (= *Exposition of the Four Gospels*), a work highly conservative in form and content, and paying little if any attention to the considerable strides made by the humanists in their critical investigations of the texts. Thereafter, Mair produced one more book, his commentary on Aristotle's *Nicomachean Ethics* (1530), a work on which he had lectured while at Glasgow. The commentary, which is based on the Latin translation made in 1457 by John Argyropoulos,[16] makes concessions to the encroaching humanism, as for example in the occasional use of Greek terms rather than the standard Latin translations, but the commentary as a whole is highly consonant with the attempts of the high and the late-Middle Ages to locate Aristotle within a Christian world view:

> In almost all Aristotle's opinions he agrees with the Catholic and true Christian faith in all its integrity. He constantly asserts the free will of man. He declares with gravity that suicide, to avoid the sad things of life, is the mark not of a truly brave but of a timid spirit. He separates honest pleasures which good men may seek after from the foul allurements the Turks propose for themselves. He places in the exercise of the heroic virtues the happiness which man may attain. And he pursues with admirable judgment the examination of the two kinds of life, each of them praiseworthy. I mean the active and the contemplative kinds, once represented for the Jews by the sisters Rachel and Leah, and now represented for us also by the sisters Martha and Magdalena. For he ascribes one kind of life to higher beings and the other kind to mortals. In short, in so great and manifold a work [i.e., the *Ethics*] if it be read as we explain it, you meet scarcely a single opinion unworthy of a Christian gentleman.[17]

Categories of medieval Christian theology are deployed throughout Mair's commentary and there is no attempt by him to question their propriety. Many of his contemporaries must have regarded the work as hopelessly out of date. It has, however, many revealing passages that make it worth reading today for the philosophical insights it has to offer.

The commentary is detailed. Thus, for example, Aristotle affirms (fol. 34v) that animals cannot choose, and Mair raises a doubt about this doctrine. In fol. 35v Mair argues:

> It seems that animals do choose. For a cow accepts this grass and rejects that grass. And, granted two things which have been posited, choice is acceptance of one of them rather than the other. Hence the Philosopher is wrong to say that animals do not choose . . ... Reply: properly speaking there is no choice in animals, for it is of the nature of choice freely to accept one thing while rejecting another – which animals cannot do. For if there is food round about a horse sick with hunger it takes the food which is most convenient for it, especially the food right in front of it. It goes for what it senses and it cannot do otherwise.

Mair sides with Aristotle, accepting that choices are made only by rational beings. But there is a separate question concerning whether rational beings must behave rationally. Let us say that, faced with a choice between two mutually incompatible goods of which one is greater than the other, it is rational to accept the greater and reject the lesser. Mair reports (fol. 36r) that some have held that if reason judges that of two mutually incompatible goods one is greater than the other, then the will cannot will the lesser good as against the greater. But Mair argues against this as follows: let us suppose that the lesser good is presented to the will before the greater good is presented to it and that the will wills the lesser good. If during this act of will the greater good is presented to the will this does not necessitate the will to will the greater good instead. It can continue with the lesser good even though it is in the presence of the greater. But more generally Mair holds that the will, being free, is free to choose something and also not to choose it. If the choice is between a greater good and a lesser, then if the will really is free to choose the greater good and free not to choose it, then it might not choose it, and in that case, Mair adds, it might actually choose the lesser good. Mair supports this argument by reference to the way people do in fact behave: 'Many people deliberately and by an act of free will reject the greater good and accept the lesser.'

However, Mair recognises that this position is not entirely plain sailing. For, he argues, let us agree that of two mutually incompatible goods between which a person has to choose, a greater good and a lesser, the lesser is, comparatively speaking, an evil. Now, no one chooses anything under the description of 'evil'. From which it seems to follow that faced with what appears to us to be a greater good and a lesser, we will always choose what appears to be the greater good. This argument, however, is rejected by Mair on the grounds of experience, for people do knowingly reject the greater good in favour of the lesser. Of course, Mair is considering here our choice of an evil only in so far as the evil is a lesser good and is not simply evil in itself. Whether we could choose something which we recognise to be simply evil is another matter, one which Mair postpones to a later occasion. But the point is clear; the fact that intellect presents an alternative as a greater good does not imply that the will will choose that good in preference to a lesser good which is also available. Intellect proposes but will disposes, and it can dispose in a direction contrary to that dictated by the intellect.

The foregoing discussion is important as regards the location of Mair in the schools of thought of the late-Middle Ages, because the doctrine Mair here espouses is especially associated with John Duns Scotus, who, as we have seen, holds that the will is free to reject the greater good in favour of the lesser, even though such a rejection is irrational. Scotus holds that what is essential to will is its openness to opposites, even where the opposites are judged by the agent not to be of equal value. It should be added that in many ways Mair shows his admiration for Scotus. For example, he led a three-man editorial team which prepared an edition of Scotus's Parisian commentary on the *Sentences*. Throughout his career Mair wrote about Scotus, referring to him, not as 'Scotus' or as '*doctor subtilis*' (his honorific title), but as *conterraneus* – my fellow-countryman. And indeed in his *History of Greater Britain* Mair stresses the proximity of Scotus's birthplace to his own. He writes: 'Near to [Richard Middleton] in date, only later, wrote John Duns, that subtle doctor, who was a Scottish Briton, for he was born at Duns, a village eight miles from England, and separated from my own home by seven or eight leagues only.'[18] To return to a point made earlier about Mair's political thought, it is noteworthy that even in such a detail as Scotus's nationality Mair's championing of unionism is on display, for he describes Scotus not as a Scot but as a Scottish Briton.

Mair returned to Scotland in or shortly before 1534. From 1534 he was provost of St Salvator's College and also dean of the faculty of theology. Among the friends with whom he was reunited on his return was William Manderston, who had been elected rector of the university in 1530. During this lengthy final period of his life Mair tutored John Knox, who probably matriculated in St Andrews in 1529. In a famous phrase Knox refers to Mair as a man 'whose word was then held as an oracle on matters of religion.'[19] Knox was a leading instigator of the new order, whereas his teacher Mair was to the end a schoolman of the Middle Ages. By the time Mair died, just ten years before the Reformation in Scotland, he must have known that the world to which he had dedicated his life was gone forever.

SECTION 3: GEORGE LOKERT

George Lokert (or Lockhart) (c.1485–1547), philosopher and logician, son of John Lokkart and Marion Multray (d. 1500), was a native of Ayr, on the south west coast of Scotland. He entered the University of Paris, along with his half-brother John, and studied arts under David Cranston at the College of Montaigu, one of the poorest and yet also one of the most prestigious colleges in the University of Paris, where the leading players were John Mair, Noel Beda and David Cranston. Lokert took his master's degree in 1505 and that same year became a regent in arts, while at the same time beginning the study of theology. In 1514, after teaching a course on the *Sentences* of Peter Lombard he became a bachelor of theology, and in that same year published *Scriptum in materia noticiarum* (*On the subject of notions*). The book ran to eight editions during his lifetime, impressive testimony to its popularity. We shall consider the book in some detail.

As a preface to my discussion of Lokert's *Scriptum in materia noticiarum* I should say that he was not the first Scot of his generation to write on the subject. The first was Jacobus Ledelh (= James Liddell) from Aberdeen, who in 1495 became the very first Scot who, while yet alive, had a book of his printed.[20] The book was *Tractatus conceptuum et signorum* (*Treatise on concepts and signs*). Liddell received his master's degree in Paris in 1483, began his teaching career there in 1484, and two years later he became official examiner to a large group of Scottish students there. His little treatise on notions presents in highly condensed form material that was in due course to be developed in detail by George Lokert, and it is therefore to the latter's treatise that I shall now turn.[21]

A notion is 'a quality which immediately represents something or in some way to a cognitive power'. In seeing something one forms a concept of the visual appearance of the thing, in hearing something one forms a concept of the sound, and so on for the various sensory modalities. In thinking about numbers and geometric shapes one forms concepts of numbers and geometric shapes. These concepts are termed 'notions' by Lokert. Their status, according to him, is that of mental acts; they are not the objects of mental acts, things to which the acts are directed, but are instead the acts themselves. In the same spirit, Mair affirms that 'notion' and 'act of understanding (or thinking) [actus intelligendi]' signify the same thing.[22] David Cranston offers a simple example: '[T]he seeing by which I see a wall is called a notion because through that seeing, the mind knows the wall.'[23] The mental acts that are notions are described by Lokert as 'representing' the objects at which the mental acts are directed. Let us say, then, that to have a notion of an external thing is not to be apprehending something in the mind through which apprehension we come indirectly to apprehend the external thing; it is instead to be engaged in the very act of mind by which the external thing is directly apprehended. The mental representative of the external object is the act of mind by which the external object is directly apprehended. 'Representationalism', as commonly understood today, is the doctrine according to which a mental image of something external is the mental representative of the external thing and it is through our apprehension of the mental representative that we apprehend the external thing. No member of Mair's circle subscribed to this latter doctrine of representationalism.

Notions are said to be either sensory, as when one has a concept of something one is seeing or hearing or touching and so on, or intellectual, if the object is available for inspection by the intellect but does not exist in the outer world, as for example the concept of a thought process. To have notions implies the power to have them, and Lokert states that he uses the term 'cognitive power' to cover two sorts of power, the sensory and the intellectual, the powers which enable us to have sensory and intellectual notions.

However, it is not necessary actually to be seeing something in order to have a visual notion of it, for we can form visual notions in the absence of the object, as when we remember what something looks like or we imagine something. The chief difference between a perceptual notion of an X that we have because we are perceiving an X and a notion of an X that we have when we are not perceiving one is this, that in the former case the notion is of such a nature that we give unhesitant assent to the proposition that there is an X, and in the latter case we are not in a position to do that because it might have been annihilated by a natural cause or by God while we are not looking. The former kind of notion is 'intuitive' and the latter 'abstractive'.

If we understand a proposition we are reading or hearing then we form a complex notion of the proposition and in so doing form notions, which are the parts out of which the complex is formed. Thus on hearing the proposition 'A donkey is running' we form a complex notion corresponding to it. This complex notion is the act of understanding the proposition. The theory of notions, such as Lokert develops, is therefore a theory of understanding, and therefore is also, in an important sense, part of a theory of meaning or sense, for to understand a proposition is to know what its sense is. In that respect Lokert's investigation of notions contributes to the field now designated 'philosophical logic' and articulates well with his more formal logic researches.

Logicians, as noted in our account of Mair, are particularly interested in the logical constants, terms such as 'every', 'some', 'no', 'and', 'or', 'if' and so on. Lokert believes that there are notions corresponding to such terms, and this doctrine is signalled by the clause 'or in some way' in his definition of 'notion'. There are, he says, notions which immediately represent *in some way* to a cognitive faculty. What he has in mind is the following: any propositional notion, that is, any notion whose linguistic expression is propositional in form, includes terms that signify something X to which one can point and say truly 'that is an X'. But the proposition must include more than that for otherwise it does not say anything, but is instead simply a string of nouns. The propositional notion that no dog is five-legged, the notion one entertains in the act of understanding the proposition, includes a notion of a dog and of being five-legged. But the 'no' does not signify anything – there is nothing one can point to and say truly 'That is a no'. But 'no' is plainly not without significance, since its presence in the proposition affects the sense of the proposition. Lokert holds that the fact that a notion does not signify something does not imply that it does not signify at all, for it might signify 'in some way'. 'No' affects the way 'dog' signifies in the context of the proposition, for in understanding the proposition we think about dogs universally and negatively – that is, thinking about *each and every* dog and thinking about each and every dog that there is something that it does *not* have. Likewise we are thinking predicatively about being five-legged, for we are thinking that five-leggedness is not truly predicated of any dog. Hence, although 'is' does not signify anything, it signifies in some way, that is, by affecting the way we think about the relation between dogs and five-leggedness.

Notions are of two sorts: categorematic and syncategorematic. The former are notions that signify something, and the latter are notions which signify in some way. Mair made this distinction in respect of terms. Lokert accepts the common view that thinking is a linguistic activity, with the language of thought, mental language (let us call it mentalese), being different in many respects from conventional languages, for its terms cannot be spelled. I think that there is a dog and a French person thinks exactly the same thought – the same mental act involving the same mental terms. What corresponds in English to the thought of a dog is 'dog' and in French is 'chien'. But the fact that these written terms are spelled differently does not in the least imply that the corresponding thought is different. Letters of the alphabet, or rather of the various alphabets, are for spoken languages, not for composing our thoughts.

There are other differences between mentalese and conventional languages. Mentalese is a truly natural language, for one thinks naturally, and it is antecedent to all conventional languages for before we can say anything we must think of something to say. What we say has categorematic and syncategorematic terms, and since what we say corresponds to what we think, there must be in mentalese notions corresponding to such terms. In short, mentalese has categorematic and syncategorematic notions. Lokert raises a question concerning the objects of such notions. The object of a categorematic notion is what the notion signifies. As regards syncategorematic notions Lokert holds that their objects are the terms covered by such notions in a mental proposition. For example, in 'Every man is an animal' the objects of 'every' are the remaining terms in the proposition. To this claim Lokert presents an interesting corollary, namely that any complex expression which contains categorematic and syncategorematic terms must have an order of construction, for the categorematic terms must be formed before the others (in some sense of 'before'). To return to 'Every man is an animal', Lokert holds that 'man' must be in place before 'every', since we cannot think universally unless there is something for us to think universally about. We cannot think universally about men (i.e., think about every man) unless we first (in the order of time or of nature) think about a man, and we cannot think unitively about a man and an animal, unless the notions of a man and an animal are in place; that is, the 'is' must be put in place after the two categorematic notions. There are in Lokert's comments in this area clear hints of doctrines associated with modern logic concerning the order of construction of a proposition.

There is another ordering relation on which Lokert insists in his discussion of notions, for he argues that there is a distinction between apprehensive propositional notions, which are the mental acts we perform in grasping the sense of a proposition, and judicative notions, which are the acts of assent in which we say 'yes' to the proposition whose significance we have grasped. It is plain that the assent must come second; that is, unless there is a proposition in place there is nothing for us to give our assent to. These points are presented by Lokert as prefatory to a lengthy discussion on the relation between assent and dissent, and on the relation between different sorts of assent.

It might be held that dissent from a proposition is the same thing as assent to the proposition's contradictory; so that to dissent from P is to assent to not-P. But Lokert rejects this. He affirms: 'If assent to a proposition were dissent from its contradictory it would follow that someone could naturally dissent without having an apprehensive proposition from which he would be dissenting. But that is false.'[24] Lokert's position is compelling. Suppose you dissent from P. It does not follow from that fact alone that you have formed the proposition not-P, which is the contradictory of P. But if you have not even formed the proposition you are not in a position to assent to it. From which it follows that dissent from a proposition is distinct from assent to the proposition's contradictory. Lokert is emphatic on this matter. It may be speculated that the reason that the distinction in question was emphasised relates to an interest that a theologian is bound to have in the distinction between confession of faith and abjuration of error.

Lokert discusses several sorts of assent, for example, evident assent, which is unhesitant assent to a true proposition, where the assent has causes necessitated by the cognitive power, as happens when the thinker has an overwhelming argument in support of the proposition to which he assents. There is also opinative assent, or 'opinion' for short, where the assent is hesitant, as happens where the argument the thinker has is quite strong but not irresistible. In addition there is the assent of faith, in which Lokert was greatly interested.

Lokert asks how an assent of faith is produced and argues that it has two conjoint causes.[25] One of the causes is a 'probable argument' (*motivum probabile*), that is, the assenter has evidence sufficient to support hesitant assent. The kinds of evidence that Lokert has in mind here are testimony and authority. The second of the two causes of the assent of faith is an act of will by which the agent wills to adhere firmly to a proposition and does not seek reasons for believing things to be otherwise. Will does not provide the conclusion to which assent is given; that is provided by the probable argument. Instead will affects the manner of one's assent, in that it removes the hesitation that characterises opinion, and renders the assent firm. For Lokert the assent of faith is a free rational act, free because the will cooperates in the production of the assent, and rational because the proposition to which the assent of faith is given is supported by sufficient evidence to justify at least an opinion that the proposition is true.

Can faith be blind? Lokert would have said no and indeed would probably have rejected the concept as contradictory or incoherent. He seems committed to the view that every person who has faith has at least a probable argument on which to base their faith and is therefore not giving assent blindly. But since the assent of faith requires input from the faculties of intellect and will, a distinction should be made regarding the two sources of output. No doubt the part of the output for which intellect is responsible is reasonable, namely the part which is an opinative conclusion of a probable argument. But what should be said about the part of the output for which will is responsible, namely the certainty? It is perhaps reasonable to hold that the religious claim is plausible or probable or likely. But is it reasonable to be certain of its truth in the absence of further evidence beyond the evidence that supports a merely hesitant assent?

This last question is important because it is on account of its certainty that an assent is specifically an assent of faith. Suppose we say that the act of will by which we become certain of the truth-claim is an unreasonable act. Does it follow that the assent of faith is itself unreasonable? Perhaps not, for an act does not need to be reasonable all the way through to count as a reasonable act, so long as some part of the act is dictated by reason and no part of the act is in conflict with reason. Nevertheless, the certainty of an assent of faith is not a peripheral element or feature, and this fact has to be represented in our solution to the problem. If the part of an assent of faith that makes it an assent of *faith* is not sanctioned by reason, surely this implies that the assent of faith is not reasonable, for the certainty goes beyond the evidence.

This oscillation between two mutually opposed positions threatens to be interminable because there seems to be no agreed basis for arbitration. Faced with an assent of faith one person says that the assent is unreasonable because the certainty of the *fidelis* is not sanctioned by reason, and another person says that the assent is reasonable because, even if the certainty is not sanctioned by reason, that to

which the *fidelis* assents is sanctioned by reason since there is a probable argument that supports it.

It is no doubt predictable that the secular priest George Lokert
would think the assent of faith reasonable, but he must have supposed
there to be a way to end the oscillation between the opposed positions. On this matter help is at hand from John Mair, with whose
teaching on this matter Lokert would have been familiar. The 'help'
is Mair's doctrine that an act of faith inheres primarily in the intellect:
'If intellect and will were mutually distinct (no matter whether such a
thing were possible) then the act would inhere in the intellect and not
in the will.'[26] What he has in mind appears to be this: if the assent of
faith could be located in one and only one faculty, then it must be
located in the intellect rather than the will. The will produces certainty but does not produce something for us to be certain about.
Therefore, in the absence of any act by the intellect, the will does not
produce any part of the assent of faith. On the other hand, the intellect does produce the conclusion of a probable argument – this being
part of the assent of faith – even if it does not also produce the certainty of the assent; and this seems a good reason to follow Mair in
ascribing primacy to the act of intellect in the production of an assent
of faith. Since in this important respect the act of intellect has primacy
in relation to the assent of faith, and since the act of intellect, which
is a partial cause of the assent of faith, is reasonable, it is appropriate, following Lokert, to describe the consequent assent of faith as
reasonable.

In 1516 Lokert published an important edition of medieval writings on physics,[27] and in the same year he prepared the alphabetic
table of contents of the fourth edition of Mair's commentary on the
Sentences of Peter Lombard. In 1519 he was elected prior of the
College of Sorbonne, the headquarters of the faculty of theology in
the University of Paris, and about this time he moved from Montaigu
to the College of La Marche, where he lectured on logic, publishing
in 1520 a commentary on the *Posterior Analytics* of Aristotle. In that
same year he was awarded a doctorate in theology.

Lokert returned to Scotland in 1521 to take up the provostship of
the Collegiate Church of Crichton, in the village of Crichton a few
miles south of Edinburgh, and at about the same time (December
1521) he was incorporated in the University of St Andrews, a move
that seems to have been made as preparation for his election in
February 1522 as rector of the university. During his three years as
rector he continued to publish logic works, bringing out in 1522 a

work, *Tractatus exponibilium* (*Treatise on exponibles*) on exponible terms and propositions, the subject of John Mair's first book. In all probability Lokert attended the lectures Mair delivered on the subject. An exponible proposition, Lokert writes, is 'a proposition in which there is an exponible sign'. Among these signs, he tells us, are 'only', 'except', 'in so far as', 'begins', 'ceases', 'differs from' and, as Lokert put it, 'any other term which obscures the sense of a proposition'. The psychological criterion of obscurity is not entirely satisfactory, since a proposition obscure to one person may not be so to another, and indeed some of the propositions Lokert classes as exponible do not seem to be the sort that would be obscure to any native speaker of the language. For example, the exclusive proposition 'Only animals are cats' is surely not obscure, and in any case does not seem to be more obscure than its very clear, non-exponible equivalent 'Every cat is an animal.' What underlies the reference to obscurity is the fact that exponibles were seen as more complex than the non-exponible proposition in terms of which the exponibles were expounded. The basic proposition is of the form 'A is B.' This can be universal, particular or singular, and it can be affirmed or denied. Next, such propositions can be connected by connectives such as 'and', 'or' and 'if'. Exponible propositions were expounded in terms of such propositions, as connected in these various ways. For example, Lokert expounds 'Only A is B' as 'A is B & Every non-A is non-B', and he expounds 'Every A except B is not C' as 'No A which is non-B is C & Every B is A & Every B is C.' Lokert's work in this field is detailed and painstaking and some of the material, particularly regarding 'begins', 'ceases' and 'immediately', is of abiding interest.

The year 1522 also saw the publication of Lokert's *Sillogismi*, a detailed investigation of syllogistic reasoning. In the *Sillogismi* he formulates the rules of inference for syllogisms containing propositions that have three categorematic terms. The theory of syllogistic reasoning presented by Aristotle in the *Prior Analytics* was wholly unable to cope with syllogisms such as the following: 'Some man's donkey is running and every donkey is a quadruped, therefore some man's quadruped is running', and 'Every donkey is a quadruped and something running is a man's donkey, therefore something running is a man's quadruped.' But Lokert provided the rules that enable the conclusion of these two syllogisms and many others to be drawn. His discussion ranges far beyond Aristotle's in the further respect that whereas all the propositions in Aristotelian syllogisms are strictly present-tensed, Lokert's are not. Work on these distinct forms of syllogistic reasoning was a casualty of the humanist revolution, and only during the twentieth century did the logic of non-present-tensed propositions again begin to receive sustained attention.

De oppositionibus, a highly technical treatise on the relations of contradiction, contrariety and sub-contrariety, was published in 1523. The work, notable for the detailed investigation of four types of quantifier that had recently been invented, appeared at about the same time as Lokert's *Termini*, on the nature and variety of terms. In this latter work Lokert discusses the nature of a term considered as a sign that can be placed in a proposition. He investigates the concept of signification, particularly the signification that was called 'supposition', this being the signification that a term has in the context of a proposition. The reason the propositional context of a term is important is that the signification of a term, what a term stands for, is affected by its propositional context. In 'A donkey is running', 'Donkey is a species' and '"Donkey" is bisyllabic' the term 'donkey' does not stand for the same thing. In the first proposition it signifies a thing of flesh and blood, in the second it signifies (as many held) a concept in the mind, and in the third it signifies the term itself in that proposition and signifies all other terms that have the same form as that occurrence of 'donkey'.

As well as terms which signify something there are also terms which signify nothing, but instead signify in some way. These are the syncategorematic terms mentioned earlier in this chapter. Lokert discusses the role that they play in propositions. An important part of the discussion concerns the detailed account of truth conditions of categorical propositions, propositions of the subject-predicate form. It quickly emerges that his account of the truth conditions of universal propositions is not the modern one. According to the teaching in the *Termini* 'Every A is B' implies that there is an A. For suppose that there are no As, that is, that As do not exist. In that case there is no A to be anything, and if no A is anything then no A is B – which is incompatible with 'Every A is B.' Hence if 'Every A is B' is true there must be As. This position contrasts with the modern account according to which the universal proposition states that for every x, if x is A then it is B, and this does not imply the existence of As, but states merely that if there are As they are Bs.

A final work of Lokert's should be mentioned, the *Questio subtillissima de futuro contingenti* (1524), a work of four folios on so-called 'future contingents', that is, propositions that concern contingent events and which have a future-tensed main verb, for example, propositions affirming that a person will perform a given act. Since the person, being a free agent, is free not to do whatever it is that he actually does, the act, when performed, is contingent. More generally, a proposition is contingent if it is neither necessary nor impossible or, as Lokert puts the point, things can be as is signified by the proposition and they can be otherwise than as is signified by it. The principal question with which the work deals is whether a future contingent proposition is determinately true or determinately false. The question, which was asked by Aristotle in his *De Interpretatione*, is motivated in part by the thought that whatever the truth value of a future contingent proposition turns out to be, there is nothing now that determines its truth or determines its falsity, and hence it seems that it cannot now be either true or false. Lokert also poses a subsidiary question: whether truth is found differently in future contingent propositions and in present- and past-tensed propositions. Lokert interprets Aristotle as holding that future contingent propositions do not have a determinate truth value, but on the way to this conclusion he finds it necessary to make many distinctions and deal with many apparent counter-examples. The work is in the field of logic despite the fact that an important reason for the medieval interest in future contingents was specifically theological, for it was thought that if God is omniscient then he now has knowledge of the truth value of future contingent propositions concerning human acts. Hence those propositions now have a determinate truth value. A question therefore arises as to whether human beings are really free, for we cannot in the future perform acts which are not the acts that God now knows we will perform. Although this little book of Lokert's includes no theology it is likely that its contents reflect material in Lokert's lectures on the *Sentences* of Peter Lombard. There is, however, no evidence that Lokert published the lectures as a whole.

In 1525 Lokert returned to Paris from St Andrews, resuming his fellowship of the College of Sorbonne and his membership of the faculty of theology, and becoming also provost of the Scots College in Paris, an institution founded in 1325 by the bishop of Moray. At about this time Lokert became involved in an attempt to have certain of Erasmus's works condemned as heretical. Lokert was one of the thirteen members of a commission established by Noel Beda to investigate an attack by Erasmus on Beda. Lokert's position was difficult. Erasmus had the support of the king, François I, and Lokert no doubt felt his vulnerability as a foreign national criticising a man whom the king was trying to attract to the newly founded Royal College in Paris.

In March 1534 he was appointed dean of Glasgow, a post he held till his death on 22 June 1547. He was a devout man on the conservative wing of the church, and he was also a logician of formidable power, who wrote with great lucidity on highly technical and complex issues. The Reformation and the encroachment of renaissance humanism must have been deeply distasteful to him. He dedicated himself to the maintenance of the old order, and died some thirteen years before the new order took a firm grip on his native country.

SECTION 4: WILLIAM MANDERSTON

William Manderston (c.1485–1552) was a leading figure in Scottish academic life in the decades preceding the Reformation in Scotland. In 1503 he matriculated at the University of Glasgow, graduating three years later. Next he transferred to Paris, where he worked under, and then as a colleague of, John Mair. He rose to become professor at the College of St Barbe and in December 1525 rector of the university. In 1530 he was elected rector of the University of St Andrews, and most of his days thereafter were spent in Scotland. In 1517 he published a massive three-part work (*Tripartitum*) on logic,[28] which was followed a year later by a two-part work on moral philosophy, *Bipartitum in morali philosophia*. In 1523 he published a brief treatise on future contingent propositions, *Tractatus de futuro contingenti*. It is with the second of these three works that I shall be concerned here.

Manderston's moral philosophy is broadly Aristotelian. Indeed many of the details of Aristotle's system surface intact in the *Bipartitum*, though the latter work also contains distinctions and arguments not found in Aristotle. This is true even of the specifically natural, or secular, teachings of the *Bipartitum*. But Manderston's philosophy is Christian, and therefore contains elements foreign to Aristotle, including ideas concerning grace and the willing assent to articles of faith. We shall have to attend to these ideas especially.

Two related features of the *Bipartitum* justify its classification as Aristotelian, namely the central role assigned to the virtues and the account of virtues as dispositions of the soul. But Manderston goes on to ask[29] in which faculty virtue, considered subjectively, should be placed, and replies that it should be placed in the will because virtue is a disposition not merely of the soul, but of the soul in its practical employment. Having a given virtue we are thereby disposed to will actions which embody the virtue. In this sense virtues are dispositions of the will, and that is the sense captured by Manderston's metaphor of the will as the place of virtue.

But the point should not be so interpreted as to rule out the obvious fact that virtues dispose us not only to perform actions but also to judge them, and indeed, as Manderston was aware, the judgment is prior to the action since actions are willed only in the light of judgments based on the agent's cognitions. Manderston, following Aristotelian traditions, speaks of three kinds of desire, natural, sensitive, and rational, the first of which is the inclination which everything has towards its own perfection, a tree's, for example, to grow and bear fruit. Such desire does not presuppose either a particular cognition or even the object's possession of a faculty of cognition. On the other hand sensitive desire, by which the agent, in virtue of its sensitive nature, tends to pursue what will help it and flee what will harm it, does presuppose cognition. In this respect rational desire resembles sensitive desire. The chief difference between the latter two kinds of desire is that sensitive desire determines the agent by natural necessity to act, whereas the action performed at the urging of rational desire is free.[30] Rational desire, by which an agent freely pursues or flees its object, is will, and will, on this interpretation, requires the cooperation of understanding if it is not to be merely abstract will. To use Manderston's metaphor, will is blind and its adviser is understanding, for it is by the understanding that the will is presented with its object as something worthy of pursuit or of flight.

The cognition supplied by the understanding is not merely of something present but also and always of something that lies in the future, the end of the willed action. Manderston, without invoking Aristotle, has him in mind when he distinguishes between two kinds of acts of will: intention (*intentio*) and choice (*electio*).[31] Intending is an act of willing of some end, by which act the will reaches out to (*fertur in*) an object for the sake of the object itself. Choosing is an act of willing some end, by which act the will reaches out to an object for the sake of something other than the object itself, as when a person aids a pauper from love of God. But whether the end of the willing is for itself or for something else, that end is classed as a final cause, and that classification presents a problem which Manderston believes he has to resolve. For if we call the end of willing a cause of the willing, we must at least note that in general the end does not exist at the time of the willing, and we must ask how what does not exist can cause an act of will (or indeed can cause anything whatever). Manderston's answer is that the causality of a final cause consists of the efficient causation of acts of the appetite or appetitive faculty. Strictly speaking, therefore, it is not the end (still non-existent) which moves the agent, but the willing of the end. It is in this context that Manderston invokes the principle: the end is the cause of the means to that end (*Finis est causa mediorum ad finem*).

To call the end a cause, whether final or efficient, is to imply that it has an effect. But of course for humans, unlike God, willing may not lead to what is willed. Here a distinction must be drawn, as much at home in canon law as in moral philosophy, between internal acts and external acts.[32] Manderston invokes the distinction because he is interested in two kinds of acts related to the will and wishes to specify the order of priority in respect of freedom. To take his example, I will to walk, and then I walk. There are two acts here, the willing and the walking. But they clearly stand in very different relations to the will, for though the walking is willed the willing is not, for I did not will to will, I willed to walk. To mark this distinction Manderston speaks of the act of choice (*actus elicitus*), which is the act of will commanding the agent to walk, and the commanded act (*actus imperatus*), which is the walking itself.[33] Of these two kinds of act it is the interior kind, the willing, that was classed as primarily free, and the exterior kind, commanded by the will, that was classed as free only secondarily.[34]

If therefore a question is to be raised concerning the limits on an agent's freedom, attention must be focused on the act of choice rather than on the commanded act. Manderston raises a variety of points on this topic. First, let us return to our starting point, the fact that virtues are dispositions of the will. The disposition is produced by an act of will, for it is by acting as we do that our virtues (and vices) are formed. But here it has to be noted that though the acts by which a disposition is formed are free, the formation of the disposition by the performance of those free acts is not itself free but is due to natural causation, and this is the case even where a person performs those free acts precisely for the sake of forming the disposition. However, though the disposition is naturally produced, the acts of will which are embodiments of the disposition, say the courageous acts performed by the man with a courageous disposition, are free.[35] Manderston does not hold that every act produced by a given disposition is of the same species as the act by which the disposition is produced. For a disposition can incline us both immediately and mediately. Immediately it inclines us to produce an act like the act which caused the formation of the disposition – as, for example, a courageous disposition, formed by courageous acts, disposes us immediately to act courageously. Mediately it disposes us to perform an act which removes an impediment to the performance of an act to which the disposition immediately disposes us, or in some other way it facilitates the act which is proper to that disposition.[36]

Regarding both of these kinds of commanded act, immediate and mediate, a question can be raised as to whether there could be a disposition so intense or a passion so vehement that the will is necessitated to conform to that disposition or passion. For the will to be necessitated, Manderston explains, is 'for someone to receive or produce in himself an act from which he cannot freely desist'. The disjunction 'receive or produce' is presumably used here to indicate a role for the agent which is less than that implied by 'produce' simply; where an agent performs an act from which he cannot freely desist, it would be as true to say that he receives or even 'undergoes' the act as to say that he produces it. For example, the damned cannot freely desist from enduring their punishment; they are eternally trapped against their will. And in the same way the blessed cannot freely desist from their enjoyment of the beatific vision.[37] These examples are chosen by Manderston because the damned and the blessed are enduring or enjoying their recompense in accordance with the irreversible ordination of God. It is the irredeemability of the damned that grounds the necessitation of their will. This situation contrasts with that of the wayfarer, the person in his pilgrimage through this life (*viator in hoc statu*), whose will is, in general, not necessitated since he remains free to do good or evil. It is not in doubt that God can give us a spiritual push (*impulsus spiritualis*) in the direction of the good. But such a push, though having persuasive force, does not necessitate the will. Manderston's picture of the wayfarer, therefore, is of a person whose future state is not yet determined. By an act of full contrition, or by a refusal to repent, he contributes to the determination of his future state. In stressing the agent's contribution to his salvation Manderston goes some way, however short, towards semi-Pelagianism. The point we have to attend to here is that Manderston likens our dispositions and passions to the spiritual push by which God puts pressure on our will. That pressure falls short of necessitation. By the same token our dispositions and passions, however strong or vehement, are at most persuasive and cannot by any means necessitate our will.

Thus Manderston rejects the notion of an ungovernable rage which pitches us into action contrary to will. It is not just that, however vehement the passion, we can always distance ourselves sufficiently to give the will a chance to command. The point is that that is what always happens. The passion might be so vehement as to be highly persuasive in its urgings; but there is always a question as to whether the will will in fact yield to those urgings, and, if it yields, the resulting action is no less willed than if the passion had been calm. Manderston mentions temptation in this context. If it is vehement the agent might yield to it, then say that he acted unwillingly, would rather not have yielded, but the temptation was too strong. However, to say that the act was performed unwillingly is to say, not that the act was not willed, but that it was regretted even while being performed. Since however urgent the temptation, the act was willed, the agent was not caught helpless in the trap of temptation as the damned are trapped in hell. In just the same way we are not trapped in our dispositions and passions. On the other hand, with all the power of their being, the damned can say 'no' to their punishment, but their dissent might as well not exist for all the difference it makes to what they seek to reject.

I shall now pursue further the question of the limits properly assigned to an agent's freedom, by considering whether belief, especially belief in articles of faith, is in the free power of the will. The problem arises for Manderston because he has to deal with an argument which purports to prove the theologically objectionable proposition that some meritorious acts are non-free. The argument is that every act of believing is a non-free act and some acts of believing are meritorious. It is the first of these premises that concerns us for the present. One argument in favour of the major premiss is that the claim that it is in the free power of the will to make the understanding assent to any proposition is contrary to experience.[38] When this argument is brought to bear on immediate theological concerns we seem forced to the conclusion, widely considered to be heterodox, that the will does not cooperate in the believing in articles of faith. The Oxford Dominican Robert Holkot (d. 1349) expounded this piece of heterodoxy at the start of his commentary on the *Sentences* of Peter Lombard. Holkot's thesis was that every act of believing is purely natural and is caused purely naturally by motives which necessitate the understanding. Thus I believe there to be a sheet of paper on the desk before me. My reason for holding the belief is that I am sitting at the desk and can see the sheet on it. There is apparently no role here for the will to play; having seen the sheet I am not at liberty to deny that it is there. I can *say* it is not there or even entertain a hyperbolic doubt about its presence, but that is beside the point. I am not going to look elsewhere for paper to write on because I have willed not to believe in the presentness to me of the sheet I see to be there as plainly as I could see anything anywhere. The strength of Holkot's position is plain.

But Manderston had two arguments against it. The first is that only what can be subordinated to, or brought under, the will can be commanded, but God commands us to believe. Hence believing can be subordinated to the will. This argument does not establish that all believing can be subordinate to the will, but only that believing commanded by God can be subordinate. However, even this more limited claim is, if true, quite sufficient to undermine Holkot's thesis. The second argument is that if the act of believing were purely natural and effected by causes which necessitate the understanding, then an act of errorful belief should not be called unmeritorious. This argument relies on the unstated premiss that an act which cannot be willed should not be judged unmeritorious. If we could not do otherwise we should not be blamed or punished for what we did. On this concept of merit, we earn merit by our free actions. This concept is not the only concept of merit, and in particular it contrasts with the concept of merit as an absolutely free acceptance, by God, of a person for eternal reward. This point is important in view of the fact that the theology of good works was one of the great battlegrounds of the Reformation. However, each side in this dispute might hold that an act of infidelity could be seen as proof of demerit, whether the act was itself subject to the will or not.

Of the two opinions given above, Holkot's and its contrary, Manderston judges the second as likelier, though at least as much on the basis of scriptural authority as on the basis of the two arguments just cited. However, Holkot was much too distinguished a protagonist simply to be dismissed. There was perhaps some truth in his position even if not the whole truth, and Manderston, an attractive person who was always inclined to be charitable in dealing with his opponents, was happy to make distinctions on Holkot's behalf. The main distinction, already noted in our discussion of Lokert, is that between evident and inevident assent. The evidence for some propositions is so great as to leave no room for doubt. I have only to understand the proposition that the whole is greater than each of its parts to assent to it. I have only to look at the desk in front of me to assent to the proposition that there is a sheet of paper before me. In each case my assent to the proposition is evident assent. But often evidence is not so great as to leave no room for doubt, and though we do assent to many propositions whose evidence leaves room for doubt, we might not, and in such cases assent is called 'inevident'. Two points are crucial here. The first is that evident assent is given without the will being immediately engaged – there is no room for the will to work – whereas will can cooperate in the formation of inevident assent.[39] The second is that certain propositions which might be evident in themselves are not evident to us but are offered to us on the authority of another person. We might be immediately acquainted with very little, if any, evidence for the truth of the propositions, but we decide to take the authority's word for it. Our will is immediately engaged in such a decision. An article of faith can be accepted on such a basis, in which case our assent to it is partly caused by a free act of the will. However, we can still allow that Halkot is correct in saying that believing is purely natural and is caused by purely natural motives which necessitate the understanding, so long as we suppose Holkot to be speaking about assent to evident propositions.

There is therefore no moral value in evident assent, but because inevident assent is subject to the will it can be assessed morally, in which case certain considerations have to be borne in mind which apply no less to all other kinds of freely willed acts. Perhaps the most important consideration is the object intended. Manderston's position is orthodox: 'The absolutely ultimate end of all good human acts should be God Himself, so that no act is morally good unless it is done ultimately for God's sake.'[40] Of course other things have to be taken into account in assessing the moral worth of an action. For example, the means adopted to secure the end must also be good. Here Manderston takes issue with Aquinas, who held that an act is good-and-bad if it is a morally bad means for the sake of a good end. Manderston gives the example of a theft committed to aid a pauper for the sake of God, an act which he describes as entirely false and erroneous.[41] He defends his judgment against the Thomist position by pointing out that more things are required for an act to be good than are required for it not to be good. We need not pursue here the detailed argumentation that must lie behind this briefly stated reason, but shall for the present note his position, and keep it in mind as we take up the crucial issue of his identification of God as the ultimate end of morally good acts. The issue provides a link with Manderston's teaching on grace to which I shall turn shortly.

If all morally good acts are performed for the sake of God, does that not imply that only those persons who accept the revealed God (in particular, those accepting the God of the Trinity) are morally good, and that therefore those who are guided only by the light of nature are not morally good?[42] Manderston replies 'no'. Philosophers guided solely by the light of nature and in no way vouchsafed a divine revelation have learned a great deal about God. They have discovered, Manderston affirms, that there is a highest being, who is supremely good and supremely perfect, ruler of all things, upon whom depend all goodness and perfection, and who gives being to all things. These facts about God, he adds, are sufficient to persuade us he should be loved for his own sake. We should therefore conclude that 'it is false that to be morally good an act must be done for the sake of the Father, or of the Son, or of the Holy Spirit'. It is sufficient if it be done for the sake of God as known to us by the light of nature.

But Manderston knew that he could not let the matter rest there, for his conclusion was in conflict with an important body of opinion in the church. The problem at issue concerned the role of grace in the moral life. Grace is described by Manderston along traditional lines as 'a quality infused by God as a sign of his love (*amicitia*) of a rational being, with which quality every good act performed in this life merits beatitude'.[43] This is the realist concept of grace, firmly established in Christian theology by Aquinas, distinguished by its Aristotelian overtones of a disposition existing in the soul, though whereas Aristotle spoke of dispositions produced in a person's soul by his own efforts, grace was seen by Aquinas as poured into the soul by a free act of the divine will. But as well as this dispositional concept of grace there is another concept, that of special grace, a kind of grace to which Scottish writers seem to have paid particular attention. Manderston had a good deal to say on it, as also did John Mair. Among other sources we find reference to it in the Bannatyne draft of Robert Henryson's *The Prais of Aige*.

> The stait of yowth I reput for na gude,
> for in that stait sic perrell now I se;
> but speciall grace, the regeing of his blude
> can nane ganestand quhill that he aigit be.[44]

Moreover John Ireland reports, tantalisingly, that he had written a book

> proving that the help and supplement of god, that is called *speciale auxilium* . . . is necessary to evade and eschew sin, and that we may not through our proper virtue do works of merit. And this is a high and great matter in theology, for the same singular and special help of god and grace is necessary to all merit and good works.[45]

The book, which is possibly called *De speciali auxilio*, is thought not to be extant, but even this brief passage from *The Meroure of Wyssdome* is helpful to our understanding of the concept.

Special grace is a certain help by which God, preceding our will, moves it to produce a good act.[46] Manderston also speaks of it as an internal push (*impulsus interior*) or a special motion (*specialis motio*) which moves the will. This kind of language suggests that special grace is not to be understood as grace in the Thomistic dispositional sense but is instead episodic. There is room for speculation on how determinative such grace is, but it should be noted that Manderston nowhere speaks about it as efficacious or irresistible, and this would accord with his general position that in this life the will cannot be necessitated or forced, even by God. Where we are truly determined the will is not operative. In this context we should recall that Henryson speaks of special grace as if it is a necessary rather than a sufficient condition. Without special grace youth cannot control its passions. The implication is that with such grace it can – but not that it will. Likewise we observed that Ireland speaks of special grace as necessary if we are to eschew sin, but he does not suggest that it is sufficient. We can, even with special grace, will to sin.

Ireland's position is in line with the views of Gregory of Rimini (c.1300–58) to which Manderston refers. Let us therefore attend to Manderston's reading of Gregory, who is addressing theologians. In book II of his commentary on the *Sentences* Gregory presents two theses that take us to the heart of the matter. First, without God's special help in addition to habitual grace one cannot have a sufficient cognition of what ought to be done. Secondly, even with a sufficient cognition of what ought to be done, we cannot in this life produce a morally good act without God's special help. Manderston notes that Gregory specifies as the cause of this weakness original sin, through which man is so immersed in and united to sensuality that without an interior impulse from God he could never rise above that sensuality and produce a good act.[47]

Manderston, respectful as he is of Gregory of Rimini, nevertheless describes Gregory's view as a *fantasia*. To it he opposes another 'common opinion' which, he points out, gives more weight to free will. According to this common opinion, which is also Manderston's, 'a person's free will is able to produce an act which is morally entirely good without God's special help, though it could not produce a meritorious act [that is, an act meritorious of eternal life] without the special help and grace of God.'

Now, it is true that certain authoritative texts affirm that the free will is unable to fulfil the commands of God and, reluctant to dismiss such texts out of hand, Manderston draws a distinction. For there are two kinds of act which constitute a fulfilment of his commands. First, an act might not only accord with a divine command, but also be accompanied by God's intention that the agent be rewarded with eternal life. Secondly, an act can accord with a command of God, where the act is not accompanied by such an intention. We can call an act morally good if it 'fulfils a command of God' in the first sense. And in that case any morally good acts must be done by special grace. And on this interpretation of 'fulfils the commands of God' the authoritative texts to which Manderston refers are correct. But the situation is quite otherwise as regards the second way of taking the phrase, for according to that an act can be morally good without God's special grace.

This is not to say that Manderston believes that a morally good act can be performed entirely without God's help, for he believed that our acts, whether morally good or not, are produced by the agent with the general cooperation (*generalis concursus*) of God, just as fire produces its effect with God's general cooperation. Manderston is not, for our purposes, sufficiently explicit on this matter, but it is possible that what he has in mind here is the notion of the divine ordering of the circumstances within which the agent wills, as opposed to God working directly on the will itself. But aside from this general concept of God's cooperation or help, and focusing solely on special grace, it is plain that Manderston is not, except on a very particular interpretation, prepared to say that whereas our will is sufficient to produce a morally bad act it is not sufficient to produce a morally good one. He places the full weight of responsibility on our free will (*liberum arbitrium*).

I wish to make one further point about special grace, that is, that we have now identified two distinct aspects to it. First, it is an impulse or push by God which puts pressure, resistible pressure, on our will, and secondly, it involves a divine intention to accept a willed act as meriting eternal reward. In so far as the emphasis is placed on this latter aspect of special grace – and there is reason to place the emphasis just there – the concept of special grace has a distinctly nominalist ring to it, for special grace would be understood as God's acceptance of an action as meriting a certain reward for the agent. Thus in so far as a person acts by special grace his nature is not changed. He is still fallen man, naturally concupiscent and absolutely unable to save himself by his own efforts however capable he might be of producing, from his own will, morally good acts. This concept of grace is far removed from the realist concept developed by Aquinas, according to which grace, as a disposition of the soul, cannot be acquired by the agent without his nature thereby being changed. The inpouring of grace makes the agent a new man, effects his rebirth.

SECTION 5: ROBERT GALBRAITH

Robert Galbraith (c.1483–1544) was a Scottish member of the circle of John Mair. In 1506 Mair mentioned Galbraith as one of the members of his circle who persuaded him to prepare his logic lectures for publication. Some five years later Galbraith published the only book he wrote that has come down to us, a four-part work, *Quadrupertitum* on propositional opposites, propositional conversions, hypotheticals and modal propositions, in which he claims to have resolved almost all problems of dialectic (i.e., logic). He wrote another book, the *Liber Caubraith*, which was probably on legal decisions, but it seems not to have survived.

Though his *Quadrupertitum* is one of the great logic works of the late-scholastic period, Galbraith was no less a lawyer than a logician. He occupied the post of professor of Roman law at the College of Coqueret in the University of Paris, and it was to law that he dedicated the rest of his life. Galbraith was evidently a poet also, for his name appeared in the list of poets in 'Testament of the Papyngo' by David Lindsay, and it is therefore of interest that Galbraith's intellectual circle included the poets Gavin Douglas and John Bellenden.

Galbraith was a senator of the College of Justice in Edinburgh and, in 1528, advocate to Margaret Tudor. He was also treasurer of the Chapel Royal in Stirling, in which role he was John Mair's successor. Galbraith was murdered on 27 January 1544 in Greyfriar's kirkyard in Edinburgh.[48]

The *Quadrupertitum* is wide ranging, covering most of the topics to be found in the logic textbooks of the late-medieval period. Here I shall consider just one topic in order to give a sense of the kind of complex and subtle discussion characteristic of this difficult, highly technical book. This brief section dedicated to Galbraith is difficult. It is hard to present an account of the *Quadrupertitum* which can be readily understood by those not immersed in medieval logic. But the circle of John Mair did make a major contribution to the flowering of logic in the early sixteenth century and it is therefore necessary in a book such as this to attempt to give some sense at least of the style of the logic writing.

The second of the four parts of the *Quadrupertitum* is on so-called 'conversion', a term that Galbraith defines as follows: 'It is a formal inference whose premiss and conclusion share each term explicitly or implicitly, formally or virtually, with the order of the terms transposed.'[49] The terms which are transposed are the terms which occur in the subject and predicate positions in the premiss. For example, the universal negative proposition 'No dog is a cat' (call it the 'converse') is the premiss which is convertible to 'No cat is a dog', which is the conclusion. This is a 'simple' conversion since both propositions in the inference have the same quantity and the same quality, that is, both are universal and both are negative.

What of particular negative propositions, those of the form 'Some A is not B'? Galbraith had a good deal to say about the convertibility of such propositions. 'Some animal is not a human' is not convertible into 'Some human is not an animal' since, as indicated in the definition, conversion is a form of valid inference, and the inference 'Some animal is not a human, therefore some human is not an animal' is invalid, for the premiss is true and the conclusion false. But Galbraith believed, with a qualification to be mentioned shortly, that the particular negative can be converted if it is permitted to employ 'infinitising negation'. Such a negation is one which negates not a proposition but a term. Thus from 'Some animal is not a human' we can infer 'Some non-human is not a non-animal.' It can also be argued, again with a qualification, that from 'Every A is B' we can validly infer 'Every non-B is non-A.' This kind of conversion is called 'contrapositive conversion'. Galbraith believes that fundamentally it is sound but that the foregoing account of the contrapositive convertibility of universal affirmatives and of particular negatives will not do as it stands. I shall expound here an aspect of his position on this matter[50] in order, as said earlier, to indicate the style of Galbraith's thinking about logic.

Galbraith holds, as do most logicians, that if an argument is valid then every argument of the same form is also valid. Let us therefore, with Galbraith, consider the argument: 'Every human is an animal, therefore every non-animal is a non-human.' If this is valid then so also is every argument of the same form. In that case, affirms Galbraith, the following must be valid: 'Every human is a being, therefore every non-being is a non-human.' The premiss is uncontroversially true, but what of the conclusion? Galbraith held that an affirmative proposition, such as one of the form 'Every A is B', is not true unless there is at least one A. For if there is no A, there is no A to be anything and hence there is no A to be a B. Consider therefore, 'Every non-being is a non-human.' Since no non-being exists, no non-being is anything and hence no non-being is a non-human. Hence 'Every non-being is a non-human' is false. Galbraith resolves this difficulty by laying down a requirement that the contradictory of the predicate of the converse (that is, the premiss) in a contrapositive conversion must stand for something. This requirement is to be represented by a second premiss in the conversion. Thus, instead of arguing: 'Every human is a being, therefore every non-being is a non-human', we should argue: 'Every human is a being & A non-being exists. Therefore every non-being is a non-human.' This latter inference contains a false conclusion, as has just been demonstrated. But since the newly added second premiss is also false, a falsehood is not being inferred from a truth. Of course, if the second premiss were true, like the first, while the conclusion was false, the inference would be invalid. But it is only the falsity of the second premiss that prevents the conclusion from being true. That is, as Galbraith makes clear, if both premisses were true, then so also would be the conclusion. Galbraith is therefore satisfied that the contrapositive conversion of a universal affirmative is a formally valid inference so long as the existence requirement is satisfied.

Reverse considerations are brought to bear by Galbraith in dealing with the contrapositive conversion of particular negative propositions, those of the form 'Some A is not B.' In this case Galbraith deploys the doctrine that if nothing of a given kind A exists, then a proposition which denies that an A has some particular quality is true. For example, no chimera exists. But it is necessary for something to *be* if it is to be *something*. Since there is no chimera, there is no chimera to be anything, and therefore there is no chimera to be a human, and therefore a chimera is not a human. Let us therefore consider with Galbraith the inference: 'A chimera is not a human, therefore a non-human is not a non-chimera.' The premiss is true, as has just been demonstrated. As regards the conclusion, both the subject and predicate terms signify something. The term 'non-human' signifies all the many things that you can point to while saying truly 'That is not a human', and 'non-chimera' signifies everything, for you can point to anything that exists and say truly 'That is not a chimera.' That is to say, since everything that exists is a non-chimera, every non-human is a non-chimera. But this last clause, the true proposition 'Every non-human is a non-chimera', contradicts the conclusion 'A non-human is not a non-chimera' in the inference we are here considering, namely, 'A chimera is not a human, therefore a non-human is not a non-chimera.' Hence though the premiss of the inference is true, the conclusion is false. How therefore are we to protect the claim that particular negative propositions are convertible? Galbraith's solution is to lay down an existence requirement to the effect that a particular negative proposition cannot be contrapositively converted unless there exists something which is signified by the subject of the converse. The full consequence that we have been investigating should therefore be: 'A chimera is not a human & A chimera exists, therefore a non-human is not a non-chimera.' Since the second premiss is false (indeed, impossible according to sixteenth-century logic textbooks), the inference does not go from truth to falsity.

The *Quadrupertitum* is hard work from start to finish. It never relaxes, but instead is full of close argumentation that is presented in a highly technical language about highly technical topics. Nevertheless, the book repays close attention. It is a superb presentation and discussion of the state of the art of logic in the early sixteenth century. It is a great pity that there is no modern edition, and that hardly a word of it has been translated into English.

Notes

1. Although it has been supposed that Mair was a student at St Andrews University, a passage in his commentary on the *Sentences* of Peter Lombard, bk 1, fol. 34 r (first published Paris, 1510) demonstrates that as late as 1510 he had not been in that city.
2. Augustin Renaudet, *Préréforme et humanisme à Paris pendant les premières guerres d'Italie (1494–1517)*, 2nd edn (Paris: Librairie d'Argences, 1953), p. 614n.
3. Mair, *Exponibilia*, sig. a 7v. All translations from Mair's works are my own.
4. Ibid. sig. e 5r.
5. After a lengthy absence the problem of the logical analysis of reduplicatives is again on the philosophical agenda. See Allan Bäck, *On Reduplication: Logical Theories of Qualification* (Leiden: E. J. Brill, 1996).
6. Mair, *Libri quos in artibus in collegio Montis Acuti Parisius regentando compilavit* (= *Books which he [Mair] compiled while regent in arts at the College of Montaigu, Paris*). Both the *Exponibilia* and the *Termini* were included in this volume.

7. Mair, *Quartus sententiarum*, d. 15, q. 31, case 15.
8. James Keenan, 'The casuistry of John Mair, nominalist professor of Paris', in James F. Keenan and Thomas A. Shannon (eds), *The Context of Casuistry* (Washington, DC: Georgetown University Press, 1995), pp. 85–102.
9. Lorenzo Valla, *Dialectices* (Paris, 1530), fol. 34 recto.
10. Mair, *History*, p. cxxxiii.
11. Ibid. pp. 172–3.
12. Ibid. p. 213.
13. Ibid. pp. 213–14.
14. Ibid. p. 214.
15. Ibid. p. 216.
16. Mair also displays familiarity with the 1416–17 translation made by Aretino (the name by which Leonardo Bruni was generally known).
17. Mair, *Ethica Aristotelis*, dedicatory epistle. It may seem that Mair is over-defensive regarding the Christianliness of the *Ethics*, but his position needed defence since there was a rather common view in the late-medieval universities that the moral philosophy of Aristotle (who was, after all, no Christian) was an inappropriate subject for the students, and in St Andrews at that time a course on biblical wisdom literature was available as an alternative.
18. Mair, *History*, p. 206.
19. John Knox, *History of the Reformation in Scotland*, ed. W. C. Dickinson, 2 vols (London: Nelson, 1949), vol. 1, p. 15.
20. W. Beattie, 'Two notes on fifteenth-century printing: I. Jacobus Ledelh', *Edinburgh Bibliographical Society Transactions*, 3 (1950): 75–7.
21. There is discussion of Lokert's treatise in A. Broadie, 'James Liddell on concepts and signs', in M. Lynch, A. A. Macdonald, and I. B. Cowan (eds), *The Renaissance in Scotland* (Leiden: E. J. Brill, 1994), pp. 82–94.
22. Mair, *Libri quos . . . compilavit*, fol. 2, recto.
23. Cranston, *Tractatus noticiarum*, sig. b, fol. 1 recto col. 1 (my translation).
24. Lokert, *Scriptum*, sig. e 6 recto. All translations from Lokert are my own.
25. Ibid. sig. f 5 recto.
26. 'si intellectus et voluntas per possibile vel impossibile distinguerentur inhaereret intellectui et non voluntati' (Mair, *Super tertium sententiarum*, 56vb).
27. G. Lokert, W. Manderston and G. Waim (eds), *Quaestiones et decisiones physicales insignium virorum* (Paris, 1516).
28. For discussion of this work see my *Circle of John Mair*, passim.
29. Manderston, *Bipartitum*, sig. d ii verso col. 1. All translations are my own.
30. Ibid. sig. a i verso col. 2.
31. Ibid. sig. c v recto col. 1.

32. Ibid. sig. f v verso col. 1.
33. Ibid. sig. v i verso col. 2.
34. Ibid. sig. b iii verso col. 1.
35. Ibid. sig. d i verso col. 1.
36. Ibid. sig. d ii recto col. 2.
37. Ibid. sig. d iii recto col. 1.
38. Ibid. sig. e viii recto col. 2.
39. Ibid. sig. f i verso col. 1.
40. Ibid. sig. c i verso col. 2.
41. Ibid. sig. c vii recto col. 2.
42. Ibid. sig. i vii verso col. 2 to viii recto col. 1.
43. Ibid. sig. b i verso col. 1.
44. Robert Henryson, *The Poems*, ed. Denton Fox (Oxford: Oxford University Press, 1987).
45. Ireland, *Meroure*, vol. 2, p. 131.
46. *Bipartitum*, sig. k i verso col. 1.
47. Ibid. sig. k i verso cols. 1–2.
48. The murderer, John Carkettill, was ordered to pay 2,000 merks in compensation, and the sum of 500 merks was to be laid aside for the foundation of a chaplain to pray for the soul of Galbraith at the altar to St Thomas in the Collegiate Church of St Giles in Edinburgh.
49. Galbraith, *Quadrupertitum*, fol. 48 recto. All translations from Galbraith are my own.
50. Ibid. fol. 57 verso.

CHAPTER 5

Humanism and After

In this chapter I shall consider the developments in philosophy in Scotland after the heyday of the circle of John Mair and pay particular attention to the contrasts between that earlier period and its aftermath. In considering the contrasts we should bear in mind that all members of Mair's circle had been logicians and that even those of their works that are neither logic textbooks nor commentaries on books of logic are suffused with the terms, logical categories and logical principles of distinction that are expounded in the logic textbooks. Deploying the extensive vocabulary of formal logic, they argued every point, analysing criticisms of their theses, and criticising the criticisms, and so on, until their defence of these theses was as strong as they could make it. Inevitably most of their works were long. However, that could not be a criticism in the eyes of those authors, for their purpose was to reach the truth however many pages it took. In this respect the members of Mair's circle inherited the scholastic way of philosophising. As well as having their own intrinsic interest, the main positions that were established were seen as contributing to an understanding and appreciation of the saving truths of Christianity. For a Christian, those truths were the most important thing, and if brevity had to be sacrificed in the interests of getting at the truth it was a small price to pay. The logic and philosophy developed by the medieval logicians were theologians' tools. That the logic and philosophy had to be as right as possible was indisputable, but the sheer length of the textbooks in due course came to be seen as a serious drawback. In short, change was on the way as Scotland started belatedly to be active in the cultural revolution that brought renaissance humanism to the fore. Comment on this cultural revolution is therefore necessary.

Humanists were committed to the study of the great works of classical antiquity, particularly those of Greece and Rome, but also the

Bible in the original Hebrew and Greek. Among the classical writers particularly revered were Cicero and Quintilian, authors of definitive accounts of the art of rhetoric, accounts that probe deeply the nature of humanity, for successful exercise of the art of the orator requires deep insight into the nature of the audience. Humanity was investigated as thoroughly by the rhetoricians, those who theorised about the art of the orator, as by anyone, including the philosophers. Nevertheless philosophers, from classical antiquity and ever since, have also seen as a primary philosophical task the study of humanity. Nobody went deeper than Plato and Aristotle in this task, though they were matched by Cicero and Quintilian.

During the Middle Ages Plato, Cicero and Quintilian were hardly, if at all, on the agenda of the philosophers. And Aristotle, who was at the top of the agenda, was there not *in propria persona* but, as we shall shortly note, in the *persona* of a Latin text that stood at a considerable distance from the one Aristotle wrote. All this changed with the humanist revolution, when philosophers read Plato, Aristotle and other classical philosophers in the original Greek and Latin. At the start of the sixteenth century there was little sign of Greek scholarship among Scottish philosophers – though in the last chapter we noted the presence of John Mair and David Cranston at Girolamo Aleandro's Greek lectures in Paris – but by the end of the century the situation was greatly altered, to the extent that the theologian/philosopher Robert Rollock, first principal of Edinburgh University, gave to his undergraduates logic lectures which consisted of little more than a dictation of Aristotle's works in the newly edited Greek texts. In consequence of their close study of Roman authors, especially the orators and rhetoricians, Scots acquired the characteristic humanist prejudice against scholastic Latin and began instead to use 'neo-Latin' (the name given to classical Latin as written by post-medieval writers). An understandable reason for this change in practice was aesthetic; the Scots were enchanted by the beauties of the classical Latin writers, not only the classical philosophers and orators but also the rhetoricians, poets and historians. They wished to emulate them and accordingly ceased to use the so-called 'Sorbonnic Latin' that was standard in the University of Paris during the days of Mair.

A second reason for the change in practice concerns the fact that over the centuries scholastic Latin became a 'scientific' Latin which was intended to help philosophers and logicians communicate their ideas with the greatest possible precision and the least possible risk of ambiguity. But the renaissance humanist thinkers were not interested in saying the kinds of things that the schoolmen had said. This is especially true as regards scholastic logic, the kind of logic whose last great flowering was the achievement of John Mair and his colleagues. The renaissance was a rebirth of the great cultural achievements of classical antiquity, a rebirth that created a space for a new beginning in the arts and sciences.

This interest had a parallel in the new-found interest in the Hebrew Bible and the Greek New Testament; there developed a perceived need to prepare critical editions of the Bible and to understand the divine word in the light of the newly edited texts. The Vulgate translation of the Bible was no closer to the Hebrew Old Testament and the Greek New Testament than the Latin Aristotle was to the Greek original, and of course people wished to get as close as possible to the original texts in order to get as close as possible to the mind of their author. Admiration for the classical texts and admiration for the language of the texts were connected. An obvious correlate of the admiration for the great texts of classical antiquity was that something was bound to seem amiss with any work written in a 'Latin' that Cicero would not have understood. How good could a logic be that could not be expressed except in a form of Latin that was so distorted as to be beyond the comprehension of Rome's greatest orator?

It has to be stressed that from the time of the reintroduction of Aristotle's writings into the Christian west, a process under way by the early thirteenth century, philosophers, logicians and theologians, in fact scholars in all disciplines, were reaching back to him as a *fons et origo*, a spring and source of insights that could help propel further the great intellectual enterprise of the Middle Ages, an enterprise that became in Aquinas's hands the Christianisation or baptism of Aristotle. The ubiquity of Aristotle in Christian Europe from the thirteenth century is therefore not at issue. But Aristotle arrived in western Europe in a far from pristine condition. Near the start of this book I referred to the role of Michael Scot in the reception of Aristotle in the Christian west. The Arabic translations of Aristotle that reached Michael Scot's team in Toledo were surrounded on every page by commentaries in Arabic by Muslim commentators. The Latinised versions of the Arabic versions of the Greek Aristotle duly arrived in the Christian west in the context of Latin translations of the commentaries of the Muslim philosophers, thus making it even more difficult than it otherwise would have been for the Christian thinkers to get close to the mind-set of Aristotle himself. The humanists, though sharing with the scholastics a wish to get close to Aristotle, realised that one could get closer to Aristotle if the approach was not mediated by first Muslim and then Christian translators. Aristotle had to be mastered, if at all, in the original Greek. It may have been just such an insight that took Mair and Cranston into Aleandro's class at the Sorbonne, in which case they would have been among Scotland's proto-humanists.

In post-Mair Scotland Aristotle's writings, that is to say, the original Greek texts, acquired almost the status of holy writ, and philosophers were mainly concerned both to expound his writings and to avoid regression into scholastic modes of interpretation. Though largely unoriginal, philosophical activity in Scotland continued in a lively fashion during the century after Mair; hence when the amazing philosophical flourish of the Scottish Enlightenment came into its own it did not come out of nothing, for the country had already had a centuries-old tradition of philosophising. Philosophy in post-Mair Scotland was biding its time. During that same period great advances were being made elsewhere in philosophy in Europe. There were, for example, Francis Bacon's *New Organon*, René Descartes's *Meditations* and Thomas Hobbes's *Leviathan*. But no Scottish philosopher was operating at or near that level. In this brief chapter, which covers a period of comparative quiet, I shall indicate some of the main players and the chief areas, usually areas of Aristotle's system, within which they operated.

Section 2: Abbreviated logic

An early Scottish example of the new way of doing things is provided by William Cranston (c.1513–62), a student at Paris, where he rose to be regent in arts and then university rector. From 1553 to about 1560 he was provost of Mair's former college, St Salvator's in the University of St Andrews. Cranston had been a friend of Mair's and was also on friendly terms with the great Latinist and historian of Scotland, George Buchanan, though unlike Buchanan Cranston remained a Catholic after the Reformation in Scotland. In 1540 he dedicated to Cardinal David Beaton of St Andrews his *Dialecticae compendium Guilielmo Cranston Scoto authore* (*A compendium of logic, by the Scot William Cranston*), a pamphlet seven folios in length which consists of a diagrammatic presentation of logic. It opens with a diagram representing the fact that a term is a subject or predicate of a proposition, and that a term can usefully be brought under one or other of the following headings: (1) univocal or equivocal, (2) material or personal, (3) absolute or connotative, (4) common or singular, and (5) name of a name, or name of a thing. All other divisions and definitions, Cranston adds, are omitted because they are of little use to philosophers. But he does not provide an analysis of the five headings despite their obscurity and complexity. As regards the other divisions and definitions that are omitted because they are of little use to philosophers, they include many items that had been of great interest to philosophers for centuries – philosophers who had dedicated countless pages to their elucidation.

An important aspect of William Cranston's clean break with his medieval predecessors is that he did not merely leap-frog his late-medieval predecessors and return to positions won in the earlier Middle Ages; he went straight back to the words of Aristotle, the original logic texts known as the *Organon*. There are only a few elements in Cranston's diagrammatic presentation of logic that are not taken directly from Aristotle. One element is the so-called 'hypothetical –syllogism', a form of argument in which a premiss consists of a molecular proposition, that is, a complex of propositions, such as 'If P then Q', 'P and Q' and 'P or Q', where P and Q stand for propositions. Thus we can construct valid argument forms such as 'If P then Q. P. Therefore Q'; 'If P then Q. It is not the case that Q. Therefore it is not the case that P'; and 'P or Q. It is not the case that P. Therefore Q.' Aristotle did not investigate logic forms such as these though they were studied by his successors in classical antiquity.

Five years after the first edition of this very brief logic book Cranston published a second edition, which is markedly different. One difference is that he abandoned exclusive reliance on diagrams. Plainly he thought that his diagrams were simply too terse for the undergraduate arts students for whom the book was written, and he augmented the text with numerous examples of definitions and divisions of terms and of varieties of argument-forms.

A further difference concerns the introduction into the second edition of the distinction between logicians and grammarians. They both deal with language but not with the same parts of language. The grammarian recognises four levels of complexity, namely letters, syllables, words and propositions, whereas the logician proceeds from terms to propositions and then to forms of argument. Thus the logician deals with nothing more complex than arguments and nothing simpler than terms, and hence he ignores letters and syllables. Cranston does not here formulate the distinction between logic and grammar, but he is evidently relying on the doctrine that logic concerns items of language only in so far as they have signification or sense, and hence the simplest thing in which the logician has an interest is a linguistic item that has signification but that lacks parts the signification of which contributes to the signification of the whole. Thus the term 'thousand' has parts, namely the syllables 'thou' and 'sand'; but though each syllable, if considered as a single word, has a sense, the syllables have no signification which contributes to the signification of the whole. That is, knowledge of the sense of 'thou' and 'sand' would not enable us to work out the sense of 'thousand'.

An additional distinction between the editions of 1540 and 1545 is that, while each provides an account of Aristotle's logic, the later edition names a number of writers, including Cicero, Porphyry and the Italian humanist Rudolph Agricola, who are not named in the earlier edition but who influenced Cranston. The latter two are quoted whereas in the first edition no one is quoted.

In the second edition Cranston displays sympathy for the humanist conception of logic as primarily a tool for the orator, and indeed he remarks that the only difference between the logician and the orator is that the orator is eloquent. The extreme brevity of his treatment of logic also indicates his accord with Melanchthon's criticism of late-scholastic logic as 'wagon-loads of trifles'. The many hundreds of rules of inference devised by previous generations of logicians, rules designed, in most cases, to help logicians cope with very fine differences of meaning between terms, could not be expected to help the orator to persuade anyone of anything. The rules were therefore useless and could profitably be ignored – 'profitably' because logic was a compulsory subject for arts students and they, and their parents who were paying the education bills, were increasingly coming to think that time spent on 'logic chopping' could perhaps be spent on things which would better fit the student for the new era. In Scotland William Cranston seems to have been the first to provide the kind of textbook required.

Shortly after William Cranston's *Compendium* came Patrick Tod's *Dialecticae methodus Patritio Todaeo Scoto authore* (*The method of logic, by the Scot Patrick Tod*), published in Paris in 1544. The *Dialecticae methodus* says hardly more than the first edition of Cranston's *Compendium*, though Tod eschews the diagrammatic mode of exposition. Tod's humanist sympathies are clearly expressed in his preface to the reader. In it he congratulates his era, in which liberal disciplines are handed down by the revived studies of languages, and very famous authors are brought from the shades to the school, and from darkness to light. The languages in question are of course Greek and classical Latin, and Tod's book is written in Ciceronian style with Greek words used wherever necessary. He does not claim originality for his book, since his approach was to bring together some of the more noteworthy things found in 'the prolix and excessively verbose commentaries of others'. Much of the book consists of the briefest of expositions of Aristotles's account of the categories, of the different kinds of proposition, of the various forms of valid argument, and of other forms of argument.

SECTION 3: SOME SCOTTISH ARISTOTELIANS

I turn now to a contemporary of Cranston and Tod, John Rutherford (d. 1577) from Jedburgh, a friend of George Buchanan, and a tutor of the Montaigne household.[1] He was also successor to William Cranston as provost of St Salvator's College, St Andrews. In 1557 Rutherford published in Edinburgh his *Commentariorum de arte disserendi libri quatuor* (*Four books of commentaries on the art of reasoning*) and in 1577 there appeared a second edition, this time with a preface containing an effusive reference to the anti-Stoic Scottish lawyer Edward Henryson. Apart from revealing a friendlier attitude to Plutarch the second edition differs little from the first. The book, written in neo-Latin and sprinkled with Greek, is a commentary on Aristotle's logic and reveals no knowledge of important advances gained by the late-scholastic thinkers.[2]

Occasionally Rutherford strikes out on his own,[3] but the significance of the book lies chiefly in its status as a particularly fine example of the humanists' attempt to return to the pure thought of Aristotle, to understand him without the disadvantages implicit in using medieval commentators as intermediaries. Even Rutherford's examples of arguments are unscholastic and instead exhibit the humanists' preference for examples that have a moral content. The opportunity to exhort students to civic virtue was not to be passed over, even in the context of an exposition of Aristotle's logic.

Nevertheless Rutherford criticises Aristotle's logic for being often more difficult than useful, and for being hard to remember;[4] and he refers several times to the importance of writing what the students can be expected to remember. He was as exercised by this consideration as were William Cranston and Patrick Tod.[5]

An interesting contemporary of Rutherford was the Aberdonian John Dempster (writing under the name 'Johannes Themistor'), whose book *Dialogus de argumentatione (Dialogue on reasoning)* appeared in Paris in 1554. The book has Platonic and Ciceronian overtones, the former in so far as it is in the form of a Platonic-style dialogue, and the latter because of the Ciceronian examples used to illustrate the logical points, but Dempster certainly owes more to Aristotle than to any other classical author. Though the book is on argumentation, it starts by acknowledging that argumentation cannot be the first act of the mind, for an argument is itself a composite collated by the mind, which in turn implies that something has already been grasped by the understanding and recorded by the memory. Dempster does not discuss these matters in detail, but launches quickly into an exposition of logic, a logic which is largely but not entirely Aristotelian. For example, Dempster discusses molecular propositions, that is, complexes within which propositions are linked by such words as 'and', 'or' and 'If . . . then . . .', in itself an un-Aristotelian topic.

He employs a wide concept of conditionality according to which both 'if' and 'since' are signs of conditionality, for from both 'Since P, Q' and 'If P, Q' we learn that P is in some sense a condition for Q. In fact the two concepts of 'if' and 'since' have a different logical character, because 'P' follows from 'Since P, Q' but not from 'If P, Q'. However, in bringing the two concepts under the one heading Dempster was deploying standard medieval teaching, though in the case of his account of 'or', or more precisely in his account of 'disjunctive propositions' (these being molecular propositions in which two propositions are linked by 'or'), his teaching is more distinctive. A disjunction, he tells us, is a molecular proposition only one of whose parts is asserted, and it is asserted in a confused, not a definite fashion. Thus, where 'or' is a sign of disjunction of the kind Dempster describes, if the molecular proposition 'P or Q' is true then P is true or Q is true, but not both. Additionally 'P or Q' does not give an indication as to which of P and Q is true – this is what Dempster means by saying that the part that is true is asserted in a confused fashion. This kind of disjunction, now called 'exclusive disjunction' (in contrast to 'inclusive disjunction', in which it is not ruled out that *both* P and Q are true), is presented by Peter of Spain in his *Summulae logicales*, one of the most influential logic textbooks of the Middle Ages. But Peter of Spain's account of disjunction was generally disregarded by subsequent generations, who favoured the inclusive variety. It is therefore of interest to observe the neglected concept reappearing in Dempster's work.

In his discussion of argumentation Dempster shows independence of mind on a matter that is of importance in the history of logic. This concerns the number of figures of the syllogism. The best-known syllogism, nicknamed 'Barbara' by medieval logicians, has the form 'Every A is B. Every C is A. Therefore every C is B.' The premisses have a shared term, the 'middle term', which occurs as the subject in the first, the 'major' premiss, and as the predicate in the second, the 'minor' premiss. The predicate of the conclusion (called the 'major term') also occurs in the major premiss, and the subject of the conclusion (also called the 'minor' term) also occurs in the minor premiss. An inference whose terms are arranged in the order just described is said to be a syllogism in the first figure. A syllogism in the second figure answers to the description just given except that the middle term is the predicate in each premiss. For example, 'No A is B. Every C is B. Therefore no C is A' is a second-figure syllogism. A syllogism in the third figure is like one in the first figure except that the middle term occurs as subject in each premiss. For example, 'Some A is B. Every A is C. Therefore some C is B' is a third-figure syllogism.

Aristotle discusses these three sorts of figure in detail but he does not investigate syllogisms in any other figure, nor does he give any hint that he thinks there are any other figures. Almost all medieval and renaissance logicians follow Aristotle faithfully on this matter, but in fact there is a fourth figure. It is like the first except that the middle term is the predicate in the major premiss and the subject in the minor premiss. Thus 'Every A is B. No B is C. Therefore no C is A' is in the fourth figure. Some commentators do mention this figure, but only to reject it as in some way or other unsatisfactory. For example, the Italian renaissance thinker Jacopo Zabarella complains that it is 'unnatural' to reason with the aid of a fourth-figure syllogism, and others say the fourth figure is redundant, for it is merely a version of the first figure, differing from it only in that the order of the premisses is reversed. But Dempster saw that there is a fourth figure and that it is not simply the first figure with the order of premisses reversed. He describes five kinds of valid syllogism in the fourth figure, including 'Every A is B. No B is C. Therefore no C is A'; and 'No A is B. Every B is C. Therefore some C is not A.' There are in fact six kinds of valid syllogism in the fourth figure. The one that Dempster omitted has the form 'Every A is B. No B is C. Therefore some C is not A.'

The theory of the syllogism was of interest largely because of its utility in demonstrating the validity of arguments. As we noted, Zabarella claimed that reasoning with the aid of fourth-figure syllogisms was somehow 'unnatural'; but this claim, even if true for some sense of 'unnatural', seems to imply that the point of syllogistic theory is to help one reason well by using syllogisms, when it may be held that that is simply not the point of the theory of syllogism. For it can be maintained instead that the point of the theory is this: that it is possible to demonstrate what forms of syllogism are valid, and that in consequence if we can rephrase an argument so that it has the form of a valid syllogism we have in effect demonstrated that the argument is valid. Hence the theory of the syllogism is a powerful tool. This point deflects Zabarella's criticism. It is further deflected by the following consideration: even if it were unnatural to think in the form of the fourth figure of the syllogism, it does not at all follow that it would be unnatural to have a thought that could be translated into a fourth-figure syllogism. If such a translation were possible and the syllogism were shown to be valid then the original thought would thereby also be shown to be a valid piece of reasoning. For these reasons I think that even had Dempster known of Zabarella's criticism of the fourth figure he would probably have been unmoved by it.

Another logician whose work should be noted is the Aberdonian William Davidson. Active in Paris at the time of the Reformation in Scotland, he remained a Catholic, unlike his brother John, who became the first Protestant principal of Glasgow University. In his *Gulielmi Davidson aberdonani Institutiones luculentae iuxta ac breves in totum Aristotelis organum logicum (Clear and brief institutions on the whole of Aristotle's logic, by the Aberdonian William Davidson)* (Paris, 1560), Davidson gives a clear exposition of the logical writings of the ancient masters, in particular Aristotle and Porphyry, though he displays the customary humanistic predilection for arguments in which the virtues are commended and the vices opposed. But the substantive logical points are in every case from Aristotle and Porphyry, whom Davidson had evidently read in Greek, if his liberal use of Greek terms and phrases is a sound witness.

Davidson is in the Rutherford mould and as such he is one of the quite large number of Scottish Aristotelian purists carefully expounding Aristotle's ideas. Mention may be made in this context of Robert Boyd of Trochrague, Walter Donaldson, Arthur Johnston, Gilbert Burnet, Andrew Aidie, and Scots associated particularly with Leiden such as John Murdison and Gilbert Jack.[6] In the field of logic this was the age of Aristotle-as-guru. Nevertheless there was also a Ciceronian climate of thought, for Cicero was frequently named as among the wisest of men, he served as a model for literary style, and logical examples used were of the moral and civic kind with which his own writings abound.

Section 4: Florentius Volusenus (Florence Wilson)

Space must be made here for an interesting man, Florentius Volusenus (whose name may be a Latinised form of 'Wilson'), who was at least as much his own man in ethics as Dempster was in logic. He was born near Elgin in Moray c.1504 and studied under Hector Boece at King's College, Aberdeen, before travelling first to England and then to France. He was familiar with the writings of Erasmus and of Melanchthon, who seems to have been an important influence on him. He was also familiar with the latest writings of the Italian humanists, and admired the Spanish humanist Juan Luis Vives. From the late 1540s he spent a good deal of time within a circle of humanists, many of them Italian, at Lyons. The last firm date we have for him is 1551, when he was made public orator for the feast of St Thomas at Lyons. He died at Vienne south of Lyons.

Amongst other writings he published commentaries on the Psalms, in which his Greek and Hebrew scholarship are much in evidence (he quotes the medieval rabbis Abraham ibn Ezra and David Kimchi).[7] He was also a poet. However, we are chiefly concerned here with two books by Volusenus.[8] The *Commentatio quaedam theologica (A theological commentary)* (Lyons, 1539) is a devotional work, largely in the style of a litany, emphasising our absolute dependence on God: 'O my mind, thou art indeed subject to God, thy salvation is indeed from him, he is assuredly thy Father who possessed, made and created thee' (p. 6); we who are mortal and made from gross visible matter do not clearly discern the invisible God, powerful king of the ages, 'wherefore to you, immortal invisible king, God alone, let all the honour be and all the glory' (p. 9). God's otherness is emphasised. For example, Volusenus reproduces Boethius's doctrine, which subsequently received its classic formulation in Thomas Aquinas's *Summa theologiae*, that there is neither past nor future in relation to God, but in a single eternal vision he sees all things which occur separately in the flux of time (pp. 13–14).

This God is sometimes spoken of by Volusenus in humanistic terms, such as 'the highest Jupiter' (p. 31) and 'ruler of immense

Olympus' (p. 8). But he is the Christian God, and in Volusenus's main work, *De animi tranquillitate dialogus* (*Dialogue on peace of mind*) (Lyons, 1543), knowledge of God is identified as the goal of man. The title is resonant of Boethius's *The Consolation of Philosophy*, in which we find Boethius's account of the nature of the divine perspective on his creatures, and one may indeed regard Volusenus's book as a sixteenth-century version of Boethius's masterpiece. The problem Volusenus addresses is that of how to secure a tranquil mind, one steadfastly at peace and devoid of a tumult of passions. The efficient cause of this happy state is the 'sedation' of the passions (p. 19). Here Volusenus takes issue with many Stoics, though elsewhere their influence on him is strong, for he attributes to them the doctrine that all passions are bad, a doctrine he thinks absurd. Tranquillity involves an absence not of passion but of a 'tumult of passions'. On this matter he judges 'our Aristotle' to have 'by far the more humane' position, for he prescribes moderation of the passions, not their privation (p. 47). In this context Volusenus invokes Plutarch's rhetorical question: the passions are part of our nature, and who except the impertinent would call nature the author of evil (p. 48)?

Volusenus, aware of the high level of abstraction of these thoughts, seeks to make the *De animi tranquillitate* a practical handbook by listing a number of classical precepts and discussing each in turn, for example: 'We should not judge to be proper to us, or to be ours, what are alien to us'; 'Shamefully and in vain do we seek rest in external things'; 'Vainglory disturbs the peace of human society and impels one to every sort of injury'; 'Since you are the servant, not the master of providence, obey willingly and cheerfully', this last precept leading to the injunction to despise death. Since death is the departure of the mind from the body, death is not an evil – a doctrine that Volusenus places in the context of a Christian piety which endures suffering unto death, and which thereby leads to *imitatio Christi*, the theological ideal of likeness to Christ. Not surprisingly, Volusenus shows little enthusiasm for physical pleasures and least of all for those of touch and taste, since these do not contribute to the likeness to Christ. Nevertheless we must not court suffering for its own sake. Suffering 'is not consistent with the happiness of life now or in the future. For it greatly impedes contemplation and the study of wisdom, in which happiness has been placed' (p. 212).

Volusenus is a theologian no less than a philosopher, and in certain areas, such as the one I have just expounded, the resultant synthesis has strong Thomist overtones. Nevertheless we must not forget that he was also a renaissance figure and in several respects transitional, as is indicated by his contact with a number of people whose religious orthodoxy was in question, for example the first dedicatee of the *De animi tranquillitate*, Francesco Micheli, who was put on trial for heresy and escaped to Geneva. The book evidently had a rather wide appeal, as witness its publication history: a paraphrase of it by Orazio Lombardelli was published in Siena in 1574; the original book was republished in Amsterdam in 1637 and then in The Hague in 1642; and it was published in Edinburgh in 1707 on the threshhold of the Scottish Enlightenment, and again in Edinburgh in 1751, in a version prepared by William Wishart, the Arminian principal of Edinburgh University, whose intention was to produce a user-friendly edition for the pupils at the city's High School. This is a rare example of a sixteenth-century Scottish book that was still making an impact at the height of the Scottish Enlightenment.

SECTION 5: SOME SEVENTEENTH-CENTURY TEXTS

Robert Balfour (d. c.1625) from Tarrie in Angus studied under John Rutherford before attending the Collège de Guyenne in Bordeaux. Through Rutherford he is connected with Nicolas de Grouchy (whom he quotes) and he shares with both men a deep respect for the *ipsissima verba* of Aristotle. His two main philosophical works, *Commentarius R. Balforei in organum logicum Aristotelis (Commentary on the Logic of Aristotle, by R. Balfour)* (1616) and *Commentarii in Aristotelis Ethica (Commentaries on the Ethics of Aristotle)* (1620), are both commentaries on Aristotle, written in an exuberant rhetorical style. Balfour, who was as much at home with Greek as with Latin, quotes in Greek a wide range of Hellenic and Hellenistic authors from Homer to Philo Judaeus and Plotinus, and his numerous references to Latin writers include many to important renaissance authors such as Rudolph Agricola, Lorenzo Valla and Peter Ramus (Pierre de la Ramée).

The splendour of logic, affirms Balfour, illuminates all parts of philosophy. When he considers the arts attentively there is just one art, logic, which by the light of its doctrines sheds light on all the other arts. It informs, that is, gives form, to the method of enquiry of the other disciplines, and it aids the making of sound connections and the exposing of 'monstrous and false connections'.[9] In certain areas Balfour goes beyond Aristotle's logic, as for example when he discusses, though unreliably, the fourth figure of the syllogism. Little of the important innovative work of the medieval logicians finds a place in Balfour's *Commentary*, and where there is discussion of his medieval predecessors it is a pale reflection of those earlier subtle, complex discussions. But Balfour was aiming to draw attention to Aristotle's text and he no doubt judged that inclusion of substantial sections of innovative medieval material would have the opposite effect.

The aim to keep Aristotle in focus also helps to shape Balfour's *Commentary* on Aristotle's *Nicomachean Ethics*. First Aristotle's ethics have to be placed in the context of his four kinds of cause. The four are: (1) the final cause, which is the end to which a thing is drawn by its nature, as the seed is drawn to the flowering plant that it will become by its nature. We have a tendency to see purpose in nature, for example, our tendency to see the purpose of a seed as being that of growing into a flourishing or well-functioning plant, and it is roughly this way of seeing nature that is at issue when the question of a thing's 'final cause' is raised; (2) the efficient cause, which precedes its effect and pushes it into a changed state or position, as when a falling raindrop bends the leaf it strikes; (3) the formal cause, which is the nature or essence of the thing, what it is that makes something a member of the species or class to which it belongs, as for example rationality is all or at least part of the formal cause of a human being, for a human being is essentially a rational animal (on Aristotle's account); (4) the material cause, the matter out of which a thing is formed, as marble is the material cause of a marble statue. Balfour begins by stating that for Aristotle the final cause of good acts is happiness – that is what they aim at by nature. The efficient cause is right reason, or the faculty of will governed by right reason. (It later becomes plain that Balfour holds that it is will governed by right reason rather than right reason itself which is the efficient cause.) The formal cause is virtue, which is a disposition to act according to a principle given by right reason; and the material cause of good acts is desire or passion. Balfour evidently approves of this account of the four causes of good acts. It is to be noted that like Volusenus he is no despiser of passion, he regards it as part of our nature and bad only if not moderated by reason. In its moderate state it takes its place along with reason in good acts.

Balfour's interest in the utility of intellectual disciplines, which emerges in his *Commentary* on Aristotle's logic, re-emerges in his *Commentary* on Aristotle's ethics. His defence of moral philosophy is vigorous: no part of philosophy is more fertile or more fruitful than ethics, which supplies us with the idea of living well (p. 11). Its teaching, placed in us by nature, assists and increases the seeds of virtues.

Many passages in Aristotle's *Nicomachean Ethics* which had attracted the close attention of previous generations of commentators go entirely unremarked by Balfour. Certain of these silences are surprising in view of the facts that some of the unremarked passages have an immediate and important bearing on law, and that in many places Balfour displays a lively interest in legal writings, ecclesiastical as well as civil. I shall mention one example. Balfour attends to Aristotle's discussion (*Nicomachean Ethics*, III.1) on excusing conditions. A person has a good excuse if he is compelled by force to do something which has a bad outcome, as when somebody, pushed by another, suffocates someone. He is no more thought blameworthy than a person is thought meritorious if, against his will, he does something that has a good outcome, as when someone accidentally falling from a height destroys a tyrant. But Balfour accepts that if a person does wrong in ignorance and is the author of his ignorance (as when he has failed to learn something that he should have taken the trouble to learn) then by law he should be punished. This is *ignorantia affectata* (affected ignorance) and it is not a good excuse. Balfour holds therefore that there are two kinds of ignorance, (1) that of which we are the author, and (2) that of which we are not the author. As regards (2) we deserve mercy and pity rather than punishment if we perform a bad act in consequence of our ignorance. As regards (1) we are not excused if our ignorance is due to drunkenness or passion that we have brought upon ourselves, or if it is due to our negligence as when we neglect to learn something we ought to have known. Balfour mentions the law as a case in point, but immediately adds that 'a scrupulous and curious knowledge of the law' cannot be demanded of everyone. Boys, soldiers and women are excused if they are ignorant of laws (p. 159) – presumably of some laws only, for even boys, soldiers and women can be expected to know that murder and theft are illegal. In the course of his discussion Aristotle distinguishes between involuntary and non-voluntary acts, and argues that every act done by reason of ignorance is non-voluntary; it is only an act which produces pain and repentance in the agent that is involuntary. This passage led to important medieval discussion on the relation between knowledge and the will, and in this context we find Aquinas spelling out and applying a distinction between antecedent, concomitant and consequent ignorance,[10] by which distinction he is able to display the strength of Aristotle's position. Balfour does not attempt to capitalise on these insights, but it has to be said that in general his *Commentary*, twice the length of the *Nicomachean Ethics*, is a careful exposition and close analysis of the text. An additional merit is that the great panache and elegance of Balfour's style of presentation must have been attractive to students and would have drawn them on to a direct encounter with Aristotle's own text.

Balfour's work is an excellent representative of philosophy in renaissance Scotland, and consideration of its merits prompts the question whether the renaissance was a time of gain or loss for philosophy in Scotland. I think that the answer is 'both'. The loss lies in the fact that valuable advances made by scholastic philosophers in Scotland were not capitalised on, and in most cases were ignored altogether. Yet the abandonment of so many good ideas was in part the outcome of the humanists' drive for the establishment of accurate editions of the Greek and Latin writings of classical antiquity. Identifying Aristotle as *the* philosopher, just as the scholastic philosophers did, post-Mair Scottish philosophers sought (unlike the scholastics) to return to his system and to see it in its pristine state, in Greek, and uncluttered by the accretions of centuries of speculative endeavour. The establishment of the critical editions has to be judged a gain. That said, it is plain that the renaissance Scots who wrote and taught philosophy made no significant advances.

Scots accomplished ground-breaking work during this pre-Enlightenment period, most especially John Napier (1550–1617), whose logarithmic tables permitted advances across a wide range of sciences, while other Scots, such as James Gregory (1638–75), Robert Sibbald (1641–1722) and Archibald Pitcairne (1652–1713), made significant contributions to science. Some theologians, such as Robert Leighton (1611–84), Gilbert Burnet (1643–1715) and Henry Scougal (1650–78), also made their mark. Perhaps the best that can be said as regards philosophy is that it remained in place in the Scottish universities as a discipline that all students had to undertake, and that therefore when the first small stirrings of the Scottish Enlightenment come into view they do so against a cultural background that includes a long tradition of philosophising in Scotland, and a tradition that includes periods of spectacular flourishes when all philosophers in Europe knew the contribution to philosophy that was being made by Scots. The main task of the humanists had been the rehabilitation of the great texts of classical antiquity. Once they had accomplished that task it was hardly possible to philosophise as if the humanist revolution had not taken place, but the next great things that happened in philosophy in Scotland were not writings in the Platonic or the

Aristotelian mode. On the contrary, after small things happened in the classical mould philosophers struck out magnificently, producing great philosophy very different in content from the philosophy of their predecessors in the ancient world. In a number of European countries philosophers responded to the very different world-scene by saying new and sometimes very brilliant things, and the Scottish contribution to this response was immense.

Notes

1. John Durkan, 'John Rutherford and Montaigne', *Bibliothèque d'Humanisme et Renaissance*, 41 (1979): 115–22.
2. See, for example, writings by Mair and Lokert on the important question of the way in which the ordering of terms in a proposition affects the logical properties of the sentence. Their discussions foreshadow in interesting ways modern developments stemming from the presiding genius of modern logic, Gottlob Frege. For the late-medieval discussion see Broadie, *George Lokert*, and Broadie, *Circle of John Mair*.
3. For example, Aristotle discusses two signs of quantity, namely 'all' and 'some', and most scholastic thinkers followed him in this. ('None' can be counted as a third sign of quantity, but it can be defined in terms of 'all' plus negation. That is 'None of the Xs is Y' is equivalent to 'All of the Xs are not Y'). Rutherford, however, also lists 'few' and 'many' as terms indicating quantity. He lists 'often', that is, 'many times', as well. Aristotle gives no account of the way 'few' and 'many' function in the context of inferences.
4. Rutherford, *Commentariorum*, 2nd edn, p. 45.
5. It may be speculated that it was through thinking about the need to write memorable textbooks that the Scottish humanist Alexander Dickson came to make a philosophical examination of memory. The influence of Giordano Bruno's memory theories can be detected in Dickson's writings. See John Durkan, 'Alexander Dickson and STC 6823', *Bibliotheck*, 383 (1962): 183.
6. For the Scots at Leiden see Paul A. G. Dibon, *La philosophie néerlandaise au siècle d'or*. Vol. 1, *L'enseignement philosophique dans les universités à l'époque précartésienne, 1575–1650* (Paris: Elsevier, 1954).
7. Further evidence of his interest in Hebrew is the fact that he presented to George Buchanan a copy of Sebastian Munster's *Dictionarium Hebraicum* (Basel, 1531). Edinburgh University Library has the copy, which contains an autograph inscription 'Georgius Buchananus ex munificentia florentii voluseni'.
8. All translations from Volusenus are my own.
9. Balfour, *Commentarius*, p. 4. All translations from Balfour are my own.
10. Aquinas, *Summa Theologiae*, 1a 2ae, 6, 8c.

CHAPTER 6

Scotland Moves into the Age of Enlightenment

SECTION 1: THREE PHILOSOPHERS

Among the philosophers of the earliest years of the Scottish Enlightenment there are three in particular whom I shall consider in this chapter. Listed in order of publication of their first significant works they are Gershom Carmichael (1672–1729), George Turnbull (1698–1748) and Francis Hutcheson (1694–1746). Hutcheson is sometimes referred to as 'the father of the Scottish Enlightenment'. That he was a major influence on the direction of the Enlightenment in Scotland is not in doubt but it has to be acknowledged that several other thinkers, including Carmichael and Turnbull, were also influential and have strong Enlightenment credentials. If it is thought necessary to invoke parentage on this matter it would therefore be preferable to regard these three thinkers as among the founding fathers of Scottish Enlightenment philosophy.

SECTION 2: GERSHOM CARMICHAEL

Carmichael, the son of a Scottish Presbyterian minister, was a student at Edinburgh University (1687–91) and then taught briefly at St Andrews. Thereafter till his death in 1729 he taught at Glasgow, first as a regent in arts and then as professor of moral philosophy. Carmichael was perhaps the chief conduit to Scotland of the European natural law tradition, a tradition of scientific investigation of human nature with a view to constructing an account of the principles that are morally binding on us. The greatest contributors to the natural law tradition in the seventeenth century were Hugo Grotius (1583–1645), Samuel Pufendorf (1632–94) and John Locke (1632–1704). Their writings were studied in Scotland throughout the Age of Enlightenment and had a major impact on the shaping of moral philosophical thinking in this country. The most recent editors of Carmichael offer several reasons why those writings were found so congenial in Scotland.[1] The seventeenth-century texts on natural law by and large reject the doctrine of divine right of kings and the doctrine of indefeasible hereditary rights, and they argue for the doctrine of a consensual origin of government. Naturally, following the Glorious Revolution of 1688 and the Acts of Union in 1707 by which Scotland and England lost their parliaments and became parts of a single British state, Scots, or at least those who were comfortable with the single parliament and the constitutional monarchy, would find these large aspects of natural law theory congenial. The theory also argued in favour of a natural right to life, liberty, property and self-defence, rights to which almost everyone could assent.

The doctrine of natural law has a complex relation to religion and theology. The greatest medieval exponent of natural law, St Thomas Aquinas (c.1225–74), developed his natural law doctrine within the context of his moral theology. For him natural law, which defines especially the canons of justice that are binding on us, is part of the divine creative act and has to be understood on that basis. The bindingness of the canons is explicable in terms of the fact that the laws are promulgated by God, governor of the universe, whose subjects we are and whose laws therefore we are bound to obey.

There are, however, completely secular versions of natural law, one of which, the earliest to be developed in full detail, was by Hugo Grotius, whose approach was scientific. He started from two facts readily confirmable by experience, namely that we all display self-interest and sociability. Consideration of many kinds of motive reveals them to be traceable to one or other or both of these same features, which suggests that self-interest and sociability are fundamental to us. On this basis Grotius demonstrates the laws that we have to obey if our self-interest and sociability are to be well served. None of his demonstrations requires theological or religious premises and he states explicitly that he has built his theory of natural law without such premises: 'And indeed, all we have now said would take place, though we should even grant, what without the greatest wickedness cannot be granted, that there is no God, or that he takes no care of human affairs.'[2] The secularity of his premises has the advantage that in so far as his demonstration is sound, it should prove acceptable to all who are able to appreciate a sound argument no matter what their religion, and no matter even whether they have one. The history of the development of natural law since the early seventeenth century is one of increasing secularisation. But God might still be centre stage in a particular system of natural law, so long as the justification for affirmations about God's existence, attributes and precepts is based not on an interpretation of a divine revelation but on a rational investigation of nature. Moral philosophy throughout the Scottish Enlightenment wrestled with the problem of the definition of the relation between God and moral precepts. Some accounts, such as Hume's, are totally secular, others less so, and in some, such as Carmichael's, God's presence is ubiquitous.

In the earliest years of the Scottish Enlightenment Carmichael published *Supplements and Observations upon the Two Books of Samuel Pufendorf's* On the Duties of Man and Citizen According to the Law of Nature *Composed for the Use of Students in the Universities.*[3] The greatest natural law theorist in the generation following Grotius's was Samuel Pufendorf, and it was through Carmichael's commentary on Pufendorf that the natural law tradition impacted on Scottish moral philosophy. As a preface to what he himself regards as the first precept of natural law Carmichael writes: 'when God prescribes something to us, He is simply signifying that he requires us to do such and such an action, and regards it, when offered with that intention, as a sign of love and veneration toward him, while failure to perform such actions, and, still worse, commission of the contrary acts, he interprets as an indication of contempt or hatred.' [4] There are, then, sentiments of love and veneration due to God, and on this basis Carmichael distinguishes between immediate and mediate duties, as being those that immediately serve God, or mediately serve him. Our immediate duty is embodied in the first precept of natural law, namely that God is to be worshipped. He seeks from us a sign of love and veneration, and worship is the clearest manifestation of these sentiments.

The second precept, which defines our mediate duties, is: 'each man should promote, so far as it is in his power, the common good of the whole human race, and, so far as this allows, the private good of individuals.'[5] This concerns our 'mediate' duties because indirectly we signify our love and veneration of God by treating his creatures well – almost as if benevolence towards God's creatures is a form of worship. On this basis, Carmichael deploys the distinction between self and others by formulating two subordinate precepts: 'each man should take care to promote his own interest without harming others' and 'sociability is to be cultivated and preserved by every man, so far as in him lies.'[6] These three precepts, concerning duties to God, to self and to others, are the three fundamental precepts of natural law, though, in a sense, they are not equally fundamental since, as Carmichael argues, the precept that God is to be worshipped is prior to and more evident than the precept that one should live sociably with men. Nevertheless the requirement that we cultivate sociability remains a foundation of the well-lived life.

Carmichael, who is critical of many of Pufendorf's teachings, is so of an important aspect of Pufendorf on the cultivation of sociability, for the latter argues that the demand 'that every man must cultivate and preserve sociability so far as he can' is that to which all our duties are subordinate. For Carmichael, such an ordering relation between precepts of natural law is unacceptable because the precept that we worship God is not traceable back to the duty to cultivate sociability.[7] Carmichael holds, on the contrary, that God should always be at the heart of the narrative and the relation in which we creatures stand to him underpins the primacy of the natural law so far as it binds us to act as beings who live our lives towards him. The requirement that we cultivate and preserve sociability cannot precede the laws binding us to behave appropriately in our relation to God.

God is, for example, at the heart of the narrative concerning the duty to cultivate our mind, for performance of this duty requires that we cultivate in ourselves the conviction that God is creator, preserver and governor of the universe and of us. Carmichael criticises Pufendorf for passing too lightly over the subject of cultivation of the mind, and indicates some features that might profitably have been considered by Pufendorf. I shall note salient points, both because of their intrinsic interest and also as permitting cross-reference to Carmichal's successors in the Glasgow chair.

In Carmichael's view due cultivation of the mind involves filling it with sound opinion in respect of our duty; learning how to judge rightly of the objects which commonly stimulate our desires; and accustoming ourselves to control our passions by the norms of rationality. It also involves our acting on the knowledge that we are not superior, any more than we are inferior, to other people in respect of our humanity. The practical implication of this knowledge is plain:

> since sound reason teaches us *to make similar judgments about similar things*, [each person] must permit to others in similar circumstances everything that he claims for himself; and should no more prefer his private convenience to the common good of the human race, than he would privilege the comfort of his smallest limb over the health of his whole body.[8]

Finally, a person with a well-cultivated mind is aware of how little he knows of what the future holds, and responds to this awareness by being neither arrogant at his present prosperous circumstances nor overly anxious about adversities that might lie in the future. This text has a strongly Stoic aspect, found also in Carmichael's injunction that we not be disturbed on account of evils which have befallen us, or which might befall us, due to no fault of ours.[9] Evidently we are not to be 'disturbed' by physical pain or discomfort, but the discomfort that comes from wilful infringement of the moral law, a kind of discomfort thought by Stoic thinkers (though not only Stoic thinkers) to be peculiarly hard to bear, is another matter – though it is to be noted that Carmichael also subscribes to the Stoic notion that virtue is its own reward and vice its own punishment.[10]

In the light of the Stoic tendency here observed in Carmichael, it comes as no surprise to see that, under the heading of 'duty to oneself', he explicitly supports a characteristic Stoic view of anger. He does not express unqualified disapproval of anger, but does note that the problem with anger is that it is very difficult to keep an outburst within just bounds, a fact that makes an outburst a questionable act in relation to natural law since, as he says: 'it must be regarded as one of the things which most of all makes human life unsocial, and has pernicious effects for the human race. Thus we can scarcely be too diligent in restraining our anger.'[11] Thus anger works against sociability, and is to be curbed by a cultivation of the mind under the heading of 'commanding the passions by the norms of reason'.

SECTION 3: GEORGE TURNBULL: *PRINCIPLES OF MORAL PHILOSOPHY*

George Turnbull was born in Alloa, Clackmannanshire, where his father was minister of the Church of Scotland parish church. He entered the Arts Faculty of Edinburgh University in 1711 aged thirteen and proceeded in 1717 to the Faculty of Divinity. At Edinburgh Turnbull was a member of the Rankenian Club, a society composed mostly of young men preparing for the church or the law, who were particularly interested in the ideas of the Third Earl of Shaftesbury, and who wished to create a forum to discuss them.[12] Consonant with the tenor of intellectual liberalism characteristic of the Rankenian Club, Turnbull entered, or at least tried to enter, into correspondence with the Irish freethinker John Toland (1670–1722), who espoused a form of Spinozistic pantheism, a doctrine many of that period were unable to distinguish from atheism.

That Turnbull had had a friendly interest in Toland's philosophy of religion could hardly have been known by the regents of Marischal

College, Aberdeen, when in 1721 it was decided to invite him to become a regent in arts at the college.[13] His task was to take a cohort of students through a three-year cycle of study including mathematics, the natural sciences, moral philosophy and natural theology. On his arrival he inherited a cohort which was about to start the second year of its cycle, and which duly completed the cycle, under Turnbull's tutelage, in 1723. The following cohort (1723–6) included Thomas Reid. At the close of each cycle, when Turnbull presented his students for graduation, he delivered a graduation oration. These orations, *Theses philosophicae de scientiae naturalis cum philosophia morali conjunctione* (*On the unity of natural science and moral philosophy*) (1723) and *Theses academicae de pulcherrima mundi cum materialis tum rationalis constitutione* (*On the very beautiful constitution of the world, both material and rational*) (1726), make it clear that the direction of a most significant feature of Scottish Enlightenment philosophy, namely its acknowledgement of the need to investigate moral philosophy and the nature of mind within an empirical framework of reference, had in effect been set by the early 1720s. Turnbull was the first of many Scots writing on moral philosophy to argue that the experimental method of reasoning must be deployed in the course of investigation of moral subjects. He left Marischal College in 1727, receiving from it an honorary doctorate of laws, the first person on whom the college conferred that degree.

Thereafter he lived for a time in England and latterly in Ulster, where he was appointed rector of the parish of Drumahose after his ordination by the extreme latitudinarian Benjamin Hoadly (1676–1761), Bishop of Winchester.[14] But he also spent many years on the continent, visiting the Netherlands, France, Germany and Italy. These travels gave him extensive experience of the Grand Tour, experience he used to good effect in one of his major works, *A Treatise on Ancient Painting* (1740), on which I shall draw later in this chapter. Turnbull was also employed in effect as a spy, collecting information on exiled Scottish Jacobites.[15]

His writings are mainly on morality, religion and liberal education.[16] The theme of his graduation oration of 1723, the need for moral philosophy to be accepted as a natural science and to be developed with the aid of the same methodology as that employed for the other natural sciences, dominates his chief philosophical work, the two-volumed *The Principles of Moral and Christian Philosophy* (1740).

In the preface to volume one Turnbull declares that aside from 'a few things taken from late writers' the work is the substance of several pneumatological discourses that he had delivered more than twelve years earlier to students of moral philosophy, and he adds that the lectures were delivered at the time of publication of his two 'theses', that is, the orations of 1723 and 1726. Turnbull indicates what he himself regards as his true intellectual context by mentioning some of those who have influenced him. He singles out John Clarke's Boyle lectures,[17] Bishop Berkeley (mainly the *Treatise concerning the Principles of Human Knowledge* (1710)), Lord Shaftesbury's *Characteristicks* (1709, rev. 1711), Bishop Butler's *Analogy of Religion* (1736), Alexander Pope's *An Essay on Man* (1733–4) and Francis Hutcheson – 'one whom I think not inferior to any modern writer on morals in accuracy and perspicuity, but rather superior to almost all'. Though Turnbull is sometimes said to be particularly indebted to Hutcheson, it should be noted that Turnbull's oration of 1723 pre-dates Hutcheson's earliest publication by two years, and it may fairly be supposed that the two men, steeped in the same philosophical-theological canon, reached rather similar conclusions without either having a great influence on the other. To which it has to be added that both had a significant influence on subsequent philosophers of the Scottish Enlightenment. As regards Turnbull's list of influences he might fairly have added Francis Bacon (Lord Verulam), whom he describes as '*sagacissimus Verulam*' (the most wise Verulam), to whose account of proper scientific methodology Turnbull was undoubtedly indebted.

There is good reason to believe that Turnbull was influenced in a substantial way by Shaftesbury. He remarks: 'I cannot express the vast satisfaction, and equal benefit, with which I have often read the Earl of Shaftesbury's *Characteristicks*: a work that must live forever in the esteem of all who delight in moral enquiries. There is in his *Essay on Virtue and Merit* and his *Moral Rhapsody*,[18] a complete system of moral philosophy demonstrated in the strictest manner.'[19] That he felt the effects of Shaftesbury's writings is indicated also by the fact that in the course of the *Principles* he invokes Shaftesbury approvingly on such topics as moral sense, corruption by tyrants, evil as the degeneracy of benevolence, freedom and the arts, innate ideas, Hobbes's doctrine that power is the only principle of life, the relation between public and private good and public and private ill, the need for self-examination, tragedy, the fact that a universal mind can have no malice, and other topics also; the list is long. Shaftesbury's importance to him is further indicated by Turnbull's early membership of the Rankenian Club. Shaftesbury's writings were also the focus of attention of the circle of thinkers who gathered round Lord Molesworth in Dublin, and it is therefore of interest that Turnbull exchanged letters with Molesworth, on the subject of the relation between liberty, education and the need to raise standards in the universities.[20]

The title page of *Principles of Moral Philosophy* (the first volume of *Principles of Moral and Christian Philosophy*) contains a quotation that Turnbull first uses in his graduation oration of 1723, from Sir Isaac Newton's *Opticks*, bk III: 'And if natural philosophy, in all its parts, by pursuing this method, shall at length be perfected, the bounds of moral philosophy will also be enlarged.' On Turnbull's not unreasonable interpretation of this passage, moral philosophy should be placed not outside but within natural philosophy. Natural philosophy is an empirical science, one pursued by the method of observation and experiment, and for Turnbull, as for Newton, human minds, the proper object of study of moral philosophy, are items in nature. Moral philosophers should therefore rely on observation and experiment as their principal means of discovering the powers, affections and operations of the mind. By such means the laws governing the human mind will be laid bare.

Laws of nature are formulated on the basis of observed uniformities in behaviour, but Turnbull believes it possible not only to formulate laws of nature but also to demonstrate their inseparability from a set of values, for the laws play a part in the production of the goodness, beauty and perfection of the natural world. Crucially for Turnbull this is true with respect both to the corporeal world and to the moral world, that is, the world of spirits human and otherwise, and the chief aim of volume one of the *Principles* is the identification of the laws of our human nature and the demonstration that they serve the good both of individuals and of the whole moral system. So far as the laws of nature structure a world that is good and beautiful, they have to be seen as pointing beyond the natural world that they structure to a divinity, a being who has intellect and will, and who also has a providential care for the world he created. The laws are therefore God's instruments in that they constitute the means he has created in order to structure a world that measures up as well as any world could to the goodness of God.

Though the goodness of the world represents God's goodness very imperfectly it represents it better than any other possible created world would do, and it is for this reason that Turnbull repeatedly refers to the world's 'perfection'. Again, though Turnbull is aware of the limits of our intellectual powers as we seek insight into the mind of God, he believes progress in this quest to be possible because we can make discoveries regarding the laws of nature, God's instruments for achieving his intentions in relation to this world. Turnbull's thinking in the *Principles* is therefore in line with that of a number of leading scientists of the period, such as his colleague and friend at Marischal College, the mathematician Colin Maclaurin, who believed that recent scientific discoveries, and particularly those of Newton, constitute the best possible basis on which to form arguments concerning the existence and the attributes of God.[21] Turnbull holds that in this sense natural science spills over into natural theology, or rather that natural theology is one of the facets of natural science, just as natural science spills over into moral philosophy, or rather moral philosophy is one of the facets of natural science. For Turnbull therefore the three apparently disparate disciplines constitute a strong unity.

Turnbull names his first law 'the law of our power', according to which the existence or non-existence of certain things depends on our will. Here he refers to the existence or otherwise of things whether in our minds only or in the outer world, for by an act of will we produce physical artefacts and by an act of will we also have ideas – it is a matter of importance to Turnbull that thoughts are no less subject to our will than are the movements of our limbs. In this sense we have 'dominion' in both the corporeal world and the spiritual. Such dominion is a kind of liberty; having dominion over my limbs I am at liberty to move them, and when I exercise that dominion my limbs move not of their own accord but by my determination. There is a view that liberty and law are incompatible, for law encroaches upon and thereby constrains the scope of liberty, but Turnbull rejects this, and argues that it is only in a world governed by natural laws that beings such as ourselves can be free. His underlying consideration is that a willed act implies both an object at which the agent aims and an act which is the means by which the object is secured. It is necessary to know enough about how the world works to know what has to be done in order to secure the end willed. Such knowledge includes a grasp of the relevant natural laws: 'did not fire gently warm and cruelly burn, according to certain fixed laws ascertainable by us, we could not know how to warm ourselves without burning.'[22] To which he adds that it is by just such an insight into the laws governing the exercise of the mind that we come to acquire much of our knowledge and to contrive our moral improvement. Exercise of our liberty, therefore, involves our using the laws of nature for our own purposes. Because I know that putting myself at a given distance from the fire will warm me, not a greater distance nor a lesser, I exercise my will to get warm by standing at just that distance from the fire. To speak more generally, the laws of corporeal nature are good in so far as they enable us spiritual beings to realise our aims, all of which embody our values – for if we did not see what we aim at as valuable we would not aim at them.

It is the same situation with respect to the moral world. We have dominion over ourselves no less than over things in corporeal nature. We have, for example, dominion over our own thinking in that once a thought comes into our head we have power to determine whether we shall pursue the thought or annihilate it, and we can will to start thinking through a given topic. We are therefore just as free in the inner world as in the outer. Furthermore, in respect of the inner world no less than of the outer, there are laws of nature that we use for our own purposes: 'Thus the knowledge of the passions, and their natural bearings and dependencies encrease our power and skill in governing them, by shewing us how they may be strengthned or diminished; directed to proper objects, or taken off from the pursuit of improper ones.'[23]

Turnbull holds that this 'moral anatomy', that is, the scientific study of the parts, powers and affections of the mind, is not only one part but is the most useful part of 'natural philosophy' rightly understood. The goodness of the natural order is spectacularly evident in regard to our perception of the world on which we act, and Turnbull comments on the fact that by a very early age we have learned sufficient of the laws concerning the magnitude and distance of objects to be able to judge of such things almost instantaneously. Without grasp of the relevant laws we would be hopelessly inefficient at getting about in the world. The goodness of these laws is therefore evident.

A final example of a good law might here be mentioned from among the many that Turnbull spells out. It is the 'law of custom'. The repeated occurrence of a conjunction of two ideas produces a habit of mind by which the subsequent occurrence of either idea draws in its train the other idea. In short, an 'association of ideas' is formed by the mind.[24] This law is as much a law of nature as are any of the laws regarding the corporeal world, and is no less important for us. Without it we could not live as human beings, nor therefore attain the level of culture that we reach, for education is based on our ability to associate ideas one with another so that ideas are available for instant recall.

Since the doctrine of association of ideas plays a major role in Turnbull's philosophy it is important to note an unexpected feature of it. There are qualities which co-exist by nature in virtue of being qualities of one and the same kind of substance. A peach (to take Turnbull's example) has a given taste, smell, colour, shape and texture; in having an idea of a peach these qualities will be represented in the mind. Our idea of a peach is therefore a complex idea representing qualities in various of the sensory modalities. A consequence of repeated perceptions of peaches is that if I shut my eyes and put into my mouth something with a peachy taste I will immediately form a complex idea of an object with the various other qualities that go to make up the fruit. But Turnbull holds, perhaps surprisingly, that within my complex idea of a peach none of the simple ideas adheres to any of the others by association, because the qualities represented by these simple ideas all belong by nature to peaches. That is, they go to make up what a peach is. That the movement of the mind by which one idea draws the others in its train is all but irresistible is irrelevant. Turnbull writes:

> But such supplies [= 'supplementations'], by the imagination to any of our sensible ideas, as intimately as they unite and blend with them, are not called *ideas of association*, because whatever is thus added by the imagination to the perceptions of sense, is a copy of a sensible quality really appertaining to the object perceived.[25]

It may be thought that this aspect of Turnbull's account of association of ideas is unnecessarily restrictive. If by a habit of mind the idea of a peachy colour comes into my mind when I experience a peachy taste or when I form an idea of that taste, then it seems appropriate to say that I associate the taste with the colour, or the colour with the taste. Why should the fact that the colour and the taste are naturally combined in the object be an objection to such associative talk? It cannot simply be the naturalness of the conjunction that makes the difference, since, according to Turnbull, it is by an association of ideas that my thought of an event draws in its train my thought of the cause of the event, and yet the cause is naturally conjoined with its effect. Nevertheless 'association of ideas' is a technical expression in Turnbull's philosophy and has to be treated on that basis. He is free to restrict the expression in the way just described.

Turnbull acknowledges the role that association can play in the production of false judgments and acknowledges also a consequent need to be watchful: 'how can the true values of objects be ascertained, till the ideas of them are scrutinized, and every superadded ingredient by association is separated from the qualities that belong to the thing itself?'[26] This is plainly no small matter, and advice regarding the identification of unsuitable associations lies at the heart of Turnbull's educational theory:

> And indeed it is the chief business of education, if its end be to fit us
> for life, and to teach us to think justly of things, and act well, to inculcate upon youth from their tenderest years, in a way suited to their
> capacity, the necessity of never suffering any ideas that have no
> natural cohesion to be joined by appearances in their understandings:
> or, in general, of never allowing any ideas to be associated in their
> minds, in any other or stronger combination, than what their own
> nature and correspondence gave them.[27]

However, while acknowledging that an inappropriate association of ideas can lead us into error, the whole thrust of Turnbull's writing is towards recognition of the benefits flowing from the routine exercise of mental habits such as association of ideas. Four main areas of benefit may be mentioned.

First, the visibly apparent qualities of a thing change as the thing recedes from us, and we learn to associate visible appearance with distance from the eye. We would not acquire the concept of distance from the eye if it were not for the sense of touch, but having acquired the concept we then learn how to deploy it in response to the purely visual evidence. With the object occupying a smaller and smaller part of our visual field we judge, by the association of ideas, not that the object is diminishing but that it is receding. This association is formed in infancy:

> For how soon, how exceeding quickly do we learn by experience to
> form very ready judgments concerning such laws and connexions in
> the sensible world, as it is absolutely necessary to our well-being, that
> we should early know; or be able to judge of betimes with great readiness, or almost instantaneously? How soon do we learn to judge of
> magnitudes, distances and forms . . .?[28]

Secondly, it is by association of ideas that the thought of an event is likely to draw in its train the idea of its cause or of its effect. Turnbull generalises this point:

> It is, indeed, in consequence of the law of association, that we learn
> any of the connexions of nature; or that any appearance with its
> effects, is not as new to us at all times as at first . . . But what could
> we do, how miserable, how ignorant would we be, without this
> faculty [sc. the faculty for association of ideas]? without it we would
> plainly continue to be in old age, as great novices to the world as we

are in our infancy; as incapable to foresee, and consequently as incapable to direct our conduct.[29]

If we have learned nothing of the regularities of nature, we cannot act in the light of that knowledge, and therefore cannot act at all; for all our acts depend upon our having expectations about the outcome of our proposed acts. Our expectations are formed in consequence of the formation of an association of ideas, and hence in the absence of a faculty of association we cannot act.

Thirdly, without the capacity to form habits we could not act freely even if we could act at all. I am not sure whom Turnbull has in mind when he refers to 'metaphysical janglings there have been about the freedom of our will',[30] but he offers a rather unmetaphysical account of freedom of the will in terms of the formation of habits. For to have a free will is to have a habit, or to be in the habit of, 'thinking well' before one acts, that is, to have a habit of passing the concept of the proposed act before the tribunal of reason and moral conscience, and postponing action until 'reason and moral conscience have pronounced an impartial sentence about them'.[31] Thus, through habituation, desire has come to be associated with a moral imperative, one acknowledged by the agent, to reflect, and in particular to engage in a train of thought leading to a judgment of conscience concerning the propriety of acting to secure the desired object. This sort of habit is to be contrasted with the habit of desultoriness or thoughtlessness, by which, instead of examining the moral credentials of a desire, we hurry into the act. This bad habit is the contrary of the habit of thoughtfulness, termed 'the deliberative temper', which is constituted by our command over ourselves. Self-command, as just expounded, is for Turnbull the essence of freedom of will.

Fourthly, without the exercise of our faculty of association the fine arts could not have their due effect, and therefore would not have been developed. In respect of two of the fine arts Turnbull argues in this way:

> And how, indeed, do poetry or oratory entertain or agitate, or wherein does their chief excellence consist . . . but in associating the ideas, which being assembled together make agreeable, pleasant, charming, well-suited company; in associating ideas which enlighten and set off one another, and by being fitly and closely joined, create great warmth in the mind, or put it into agreeable motion.[32]

There is an issue here as to whether either the intention or the effect of all oratory is to 'create great warmth in the mind, or put it into

agreeable motion', for much oratory seems intended to produce disagreeable, unpleasant emotions, such as fear or rage. But it may be
replied either that Turnbull's reference to 'warmth of mind' encompasses harsh, unpleasant emotions as well as their contraries, or that
the orator who sets out to whip his audience into an ecstasy of anger
does indeed aim to keep them all on his side, that is, agreeing with
him; and therefore, despite the anger that is unleashed by his speech,
there remains in the souls of the listener the agreeable feeling implicit
in their sympathetic response to the orator's words. But putting that
quibble to one side, Turnbull's point is surely unexceptionable, that
the fine arts play heavily upon associations of ideas, not only in the
sense that aesthetically significant associations are spelled out within
the works of creative artists, but also in the sense that creative artists
stimulate in a more or less controlled way associative acts by spectators or audiences, thus shaping their aesthetic responses to the works
of art. Turnbull's position on this matter, therefore, is that but for the
habits of association of ideas it would not be possible for a work of
art to be produced, nor therefore for a work of art to be the object of
aesthetic appreciation. The association of ideas is therefore essential
for the existence of a great swathe of our culture.

   Turnbull focuses on the faculty of association of ideas as necessary
for a good human life. Of course we are sometimes led astray by an
erroneous association, but the faculty is almost always on the side of
the good as enabling us to live well. Turnbull's emphasis on the benefits accruing from the disposition has to be seen in the context of the
broad framework of his philosophy. The disposition to associate ideas
is part of our nature, and it makes its own distinctive contribution to
the fulfilment of God's intention for us, that we flourish as human
beings. We should therefore not allow ourselves to be fixated upon
the fact that the exercise of the disposition leads to what Lord Kames,
in a related context, calls 'a few cross instances'.

SECTION 4: GEORGE TURNBULL: *CHRISTIAN PHILOSOPHY*

I should like now to indicate the main lines of thinking in Turnbull's
Christian Philosophy, volume two of his *Principles of Moral and
Christian Philosophy*. Its overarching concept is that of God's moral
government of the world, a government particularly at work in the
allotment of recompense for our good and evil deeds. The biblical text
that runs as a *Leitmotif* through Turnbull's discussion is: 'Be not
deceived; God is not mocked: for whatsoever a man soweth that shall

he also reap' (Gal. 6:7–8). Turnbull attends to the relationship between this life and the next, and argues that our future state will correspond exactly to our present one by a divine dispensation that is universal in that God does not require to make a separate decision in respect of each person, for he has established a rule or law that governs the outcome for each and every individual on the basis of how each has lived. The situation is therefore exactly as in the natural world. It is by a law established by God that fire heats things and ice cools them and it is by a law likewise established that people are recompensed in due season for their deeds. That is how the system works, and divine providence is to be understood in these terms.

The most troublesome problem for theism concerns the existence of evil, and Turnbull meets it head-on, and in a traditional way, by both acknowledging that there are evils and also insisting that they do not characterise creation as a whole, for they are permitted to exist not for their own sake or because God takes pleasure in them, but because they are the outcome of laws which are designed to produce the best possible world overall. Things which seem to us evil are seen by us from an overly narrow perspective, and if we had 'one united view' the apparent evils would be judged to play a necessary role in the unfolding of a perfect universe.

Among apparent evils are those that befall the virtuous, evils which therefore cannot be seen as a punishment for wrongdoing. But Turnbull has a more ample perspective. For this life is, as he reminds his readers, a time of probation, and the apparent evils that befall us enable us to grow in spiritual and moral strength by the exercise of self-discipline in adversity, and they can therefore even be seen as goods graciously bestowed on us by God, goods that create a space for us within which we can grow towards our perfection. In fact Turnbull insists that we can grow no less by our response to apparent goods than to apparent evils. No less than poverty, prosperity presents us with the opportunity both to enhance our moral substance and to demonstrate our self-discipline. This might seem an unexpected line, but Turnbull's focus on prosperity as a 'means of trial' fits the contemporary suspicion of luxury as a potential cause of moral and spiritual corruption. In that sense, from Turnbull's perspective every circumstance or state in which we find ourselves is good, at least to the extent that it constitutes an opportunity for us to do good and to become better. Whether or not we then do good is something in our power, our power being extensive, and always extensible if only we make the effort to gain more knowledge of the natural world. For such knowledge gives us the power to use nature to make our lives more fully an embodiment of our values.

The concepts of custom and habit, expounded by Turnbull in *The Principles of Moral Philosophy*, are also put to work in *Christian Philosophy*, this time in connection with the thought that recompense in the next life must be appropriate to our virtue or vice in this life. Our moral liberty implies not only knowledge of our circumstances and of natural law, but also a faculty of reason that exercises authority in us in accordance with the dictates of right judgment. Just as it is by repeated acts that bad habits come to exercise power in our souls, so also it is by repeated acts that reason acquires what Turnbull calls its 'rightful power and authority of governing'. 'This', he tells us, 'is the consequence of the law of habits, which renders us capable of improvement to perfection.'[33] Here he is deploying, and perhaps also taking a stage further, the doctrine, developed in *The Principles of Moral Philosophy*, that moral liberty consists in the habit of deliberating prior to acting, and thereby preventing our appetites from hurrying us into action.

The disposition to give reason its head is in accordance with 'the order and perfection in our constitution' or 'our natural make and constitution', and Turnbull concludes that a person so disposed is a 'law to himself', in the sense that he has within himself a principle whose office is to give law to his appetites and affections. As this is how we are when living according to our natural frame it follows that we are then living according to God's intention for us, and hence our constitution is a 'law to itself' in the strict sense of 'law', for it is enacted by God the law-giver when he created our constitution, particularly the mental part of our constitution which Turnbull anatomises in *The Principles of Moral Philosophy*. Here Turnbull moves into quite deep theological waters, but at all times in his handling of these theological themes he is guided by what he himself regards as the light of reason. He argues on the basis of revelation only when the revelation has itself been subjected to critical scrutiny and been shown to be at least consonant with reason and, in many cases, to be an irresistible conclusion from reasonable premises.

Turnbull's *Christian Philosophy* is an exercise in natural, not revealed, theology. This may be why it contains nothing on characteristically Christian doctrines such as the Trinity, the Resurrection and the Transfiguration. But on the other hand Turnbull's title, *Christian Philosophy*, has a lengthy subtitle: *The Christian doctrine concerning God, providence, virtue, and a future state, proved to be agreeable to true philosophy, and to be attended with a truly philo-sophical evidence*, and this subtitle does most of the work on the title page. Since the subtitle tells us what the book really is about, Turnbull can argue that he needs to deploy the doctrines of *The Principles of Moral Philosophy*, but does not need to discuss such concepts as that of the Trinity in order to make out a case for his main thesis, namely, that it is possible to demonstrate the truth of St Paul's declaration: 'Whatsoever a man soweth that shall he reap.'

SECTION 5: GEORGE TURNBULL ON ART

Turnbull's larger works were all written with a view to making a dif-ference to people's lives. In his *Principles of Moral Philosophy* he wanted to indicate ways in which people's behaviour could be better informed with moral principle, and the same is true of his *Christian Philosophy*, whose practical intent is clear on every page. Likewise his magisterial *Observations upon Liberal Education* (1742), which builds upon the *Principles*, presents a comprehensive account of the kind of upbringing that will fit a child for upright citizenship. An important part of that account is also to be found in a further work, *A Treatise on Ancient Painting* (1740), whose title hardly does justice to the content of the book. I should like to end this exposition of Turnbull by noting a doctrine emphasised in both the *Treatise* and the *Observations*.

Turnbull, a regent in arts at Marischal College who then spent some years taking tutees on tours of cultural centres of Europe, was professionally sensitive to the distinction between the grasp of a truth and the presentation of a truth; knowledge of the facts does not imply knowledge of the most appropriate way to present them to the intended audience. The master orator has the right kind of knowl-edge; he is an expert at deploying language to secure the effect he intends. While Turnbull makes these points with respect to what we ordinarily think of as language, he also makes them with respect to a rather more ample concept of language than one that encompasses only conventional languages such as English and Latin. All the fine arts come under this more ample concept; thus sculpture is a lan-guage, so is architecture and so also is painting. A painter can make a point, in painting, and perhaps make it better in painting than he could in his mother tongue. But a speaker aims often to appeal not only to the understanding of the audience but to other faculties as well, in particular, to imagination, emotion and will; and Turnbull believed that a painter can be just as effective at appealing to these other faculties as a speaker of a conventional language can be. Indeed it is appropriate to think of a good painter as an orator of sorts, a master of the language of painting. With these considerations in mind Turnbull invokes the distinction between natural philosophy and moral philosophy, and I shall deal with these two in turn.

A landscape painting is a presentation or representation of a scene in nature. No doubt the painter often tries to give an accurate account of how things appear to him in all their particularity and, so far as he succeeds, the painting is true to the visible appearance of things in their particularity. A spectator who knows that the painting is accurate can therefore learn from the painting something about that piece of nature. But painters are not constrained by the particularity of the scene before them; they can paint what we would all recognise as a landscape, a piece of nature, though the painting does not precisely represent any actual landscape. Even if there is no such scene in the natural world, there could be. As Turnbull puts the point, the view must be 'congruous to nature's laws'.[34] A painter knows how landscapes change under different kinds of cloud cover, how the movement of the sun tracks the change in the quality of the light, how a humid atmosphere affects the light, how the reflection of light from a stretch of water makes a difference to the appearance of the whole scene, and so on. To know these things is to have knowledge of laws of nature and therefore knowledge of the universal. When painters paint on the basis of their grasp of the laws of nature, what they paint may be false to the particular but true to the universal.

Turnbull, who is full of insights regarding the affinities of the various fine arts, writes of poems as 'fictions copied from nature',[35] and this phrase can be applied helpfully to landscape paintings which are true at the level of the universal but not of the particular. A painter, trained to use his eyes and to notice the visible appearance of things, can draw the spectator's attention to possibilities in nature that he might otherwise not have dreamed of. The spectator, looking at the painting, learns something of the universal forms of nature, the laws determining its myriad appearances. By such means landscape paintings can be a vehicle for education in natural science.

The same point can be made about human nature no less than about landscapes, and since these comments are focused on the representation of nature in the fine arts we can start by attending, with Turnbull, to nature in its human manifestation in plays. For there also nature is on display and is false at the level of particularity, but, if the play is good, it is true at the level of universality. The *dramatis personae* may be false representations at the level of particularity for, as a matter of historical fact, no one has ever said or done the things ascribed to the *personae*, and yet the *personae* may be true at the level of universality because they are credible representations of the way in which human beings behave. That is, if the *personae* are not believed in, they must at least be believable. Turnbull's phrase 'fictions copied from nature' is applicable to this type of case. With these points in mind he speaks of plays as 'experiments' or 'samples' of moral truths, that is, truths regarding the operations of the human spirit. They are a way of exploring human nature and they can open our eyes in so far as they make out a good case for the existence of potentialities of the human spirit that we would previously have thought incredible. Turnbull notes the fact that painters and poets are more like philosophers than historians are, for while painters and poets create representations of the universal, the first task of the historian is the representation of the particular, for his first task is to say what actually happened. This is not to deny, nor does Turnbull do so, that the historian is also concerned with the universal, for he says not only what happened but also why it did; he seeks to explain events, and all historical explanation, perhaps all explanation *tout court*, requires recourse to general principles.

We are here on the edge of a theme which is the principal one in the *Treatise on Ancient Painting* and is subsequently revisited in the *Observations*. In the *Treatise* he explores the broad cultural significance of the Grand Tour; his advice on liberal education is especially designed to make a difference to the young 'whose birth and fortunes call upon them to qualify themselves early for public service', and the true purpose of the Grand Tour is to help equip them with knowledge that they will need if they are to fulfil their public role with distinction. In particular, tutors should introduce their charges to paintings which carry strong and appropriate moral content because through the paintings a lesson about morality will be learned. The lesson can be expected to impact directly on behaviour, for a painting can be a powerful piece of rhetoric, representing virtues in such a way as to inspire the spectator to emulate the actions represented, and representing the corresponding vices in dark, sinister tones that will prompt feelings of loathing and disgust towards such actions.

In this respect a painting is much like a speech, able to engage not only the intellect, but also the imagination, the emotions and even the will of the recipient, though a painting has also a certain advantage due to the immediacy of the impact it can have. Speeches take time, in some cases a long time, but a painting can make a massive impact in a second; one glance is often enough to permit the spectator to receive and be moved by a complex message. But the spectator has to know the language of painting, and of course the better he knows it the more responsive he will be to the painting's moral content if it has one. So the tutee on the Grand Tour receives an education in how to look at paintings which are in effect rhetorically strong pieces of reasoning on behalf of a universal moral truth. The tutee will be able to read the painter's exploration of human emotions and moral characters, and will also be motivated to apply the lessons of the painting to his own life. The outcome of his Grand Tour will thus be a morally more mature person, with a well-developed 'philosophical eye', better prepared to take on the role of civic leader, equipped with knowledge of 'mankind and human rights and duties, the best maxims of civil policy and government'.[36]

SECTION 6: FRANCIS HUTCHESON ON THE IDEA OF BEAUTY

Hutcheson's philosophical formation was rich with possibilities. He was born in Drumalig, Ulster, to Ulster Scottish Protestant parents. His father was a minister of the Presbyterian church, as was his grandfather, and in this household young Francis received a traditionalist Scottish Presbyterian upbringing. Outwith the home but still very much within the Ulster Protestant community he received a sound schooling in philosophy, so much so that when he entered Glasgow University as a student in 1711 he was judged to be sufficiently proficient in logic, metaphysics and moral philosophy to go straight into the fourth year of study, which was focused on the natural sciences. In 1712, still at Glasgow University, and following a year's intensive study of the classics, he began his training for the Presbyterian ministry under the tutelage of the professor of sacred theology, John Simson (1667–1740), a man who, despite the express teaching of the Westminster Standards, expressed doubts over whether only those who know Christ can be saved and who also insisted that only revelation that has passed the test of rationality is acceptable. Simson was twice tried for heresy and eventually prohibited from preaching and teaching the Word. There is evidence that Hutcheson was well disposed to several of the doctrines that led to his teacher being found guilty of heresy.[37]

Another of the teachers at Glasgow when Hutcheson arrived was Gershom Carmichael. We should recall that Carmichael's most important work, a commentary on Pufendorf's *On the Duty of Man and Citizen*, was composed for the use of students and was certainly used in Glasgow. Hutcheson seems to have known the work well. He refers to *On the Duty of Man and Citizen* 'which that worthy and ingenious man the late Professor Gershom Carmichael of Glasgow, by far the best commentator on that work, has so supplied [= supplemented] and corrected that the notes are of much more value than the text'. [38] Although he disagreed with Carmichael on a number of issues, and was particularly concerned to distance himself from Carmichael's teaching on moral motivation, Carmichael's preoccupation with the natural law tradition, as it came down through Grotius, Pufendorf and Locke, was duly inherited by Hutcheson and passed on through him to his own philosophical heirs. Hutcheson's election to the Glasgow professoriate was strongly contested by some who thought him theologically unreliable, and there is perhaps a hint of gentle irony in the title of his inaugural lecture: 'De naturali hominum socialitate' – 'The natural sociability of mankind'. It should be added that the title also encapsulates an important part of his predecessor's teaching, a gentle indication of the continuity of philosophical doctrine from Carmichael to Hutcheson.

After his studies at Glasgow Hutcheson returned to Ireland, first to Ulster, and then to Dublin, where he taught at an academy for Presbyterians and other nonconformists, who, as nonconforming, were unable to enrol at the universities of Oxford or Cambridge or at Trinity College, Dublin. He also became involved in the circle that centred on Robert Molesworth. Molesworth, a close friend of Lord Shaftesbury, was a libertarian in matters of both politics and religion. How far he influenced Hutcheson in these areas, and how far Hutcheson was drawn to him because what Molesworth believed was in any case what he already thought, is difficult to say; but Hutcheson seems to have been at home with the radical views of the circle. It was while working in the dissenting academy in Dublin that Hutcheson wrote *An Inquiry into the Original of our Ideas of Beauty and Virtue* (1725),[39] a work comprising two treatises, the first concerning beauty and the second concerning virtue. The formal similarity between the two is in accordance with authorial intention, and I shall comment upon this fact once we have noted the main features of the discussion in each.

Hutcheson, operating within a framework, the 'theory of ideas', that became dominant through the work of Descartes and that was appropriated in due course by John Locke, whose *Essay* Hutcheson studied, spoke of things in the mind termed 'ideas'. We perceive something in the real world and in doing so we are changed, at least to the extent that we thereupon have an idea of the object perceived. Perhaps it is appropriate in some cases to think of the idea as an image of the object, but 'image' hints at visible properties and yet an idea can be of something sensed by hearing, touch, taste or smell. If therefore we take an idea, as many do, to be an image, then the concept of an image must be sufficiently broad to encompass tactile and olfactory images and other sorts as well.

Hutcheson terms some ideas 'sensations', namely those that are produced or 'raised' when we respond perceptually to an external object, and he focuses upon the natural necessity and immediacy of the mental product. That is, if with our well-functioning visual sensory apparatus we stand in front of a dog and look at it, we will thereupon by natural necessity have a visual experience of a dog. Hutcheson writes: 'We find that the Mind in such Cases is passive, and has not Power directly to prevent the Perception or Idea, or to vary it at its Reception, as long as we continue our Bodies in a state fit to be acted upon by the external Object.'[40] In speaking of the mind as passive Hutcheson is attending to the fact that if the will plays a role at all in perception the role is not primary. Of course the will can have an effect on the content of our perceptual experience in the sense that if we will not to look at something or will to look at it for a longer or shorter period the act of will affects that content. But for the will to make a difference the well-functioning sensory apparatus must already be in place, enabling us to perceive the object when our sensory receptor is presented with the appropriate stimuli. Indeed, we are able to exercise voluntary control over our perceptual experience precisely because we know that this is how nature works, for supposing we know that if we now open our eyes we will immediately and necessarily see X, if we think we ought not to look at X then we must will either to keep our eyes shut or at least to avert our gaze when we open them.

Regarding our perceptions, another immediacy that Hutcheson foregrounds is that of the pleasure or pain afforded by many of them. Without our knowing why certain objects please or displease us, they nevertheless affect us in this way, but even if we did know why, this would affect us little or not at all, in that independently of such knowledge we would still find them agreeable or disagreeable. Amongst the pleasures that arise in us immediately and by nature there are those associated with objects that we judge beautiful, and Hutcheson argues that, though we perceive the beauty of all sorts of things accessible by the external senses, it is appropriate to posit a further sense, which he terms an 'internal sense'. For first, people vary widely in their degree of sensitivity to the beauty of different things even where their external senses seem equally efficient, and if it were the external senses that were doing all the work in discovering the beauty of things, why should people with equally efficient external senses not be equally efficient at discerning the beauty of external things? Secondly, a power of sense is clearly at work in the discovery of the beauty of things, for what distinguishes a power of sense is that it operates immediately and purely by natural means in disclosing qualities to us. It is with these considerations in mind that Hutcheson posits an inner sense which is an aesthetic sense.[41] This is not a sense possessed solely by the aesthetically sophisticated person. On Hutcheson's account the inner sense is no less a part of the original frame of our nature than are the senses of sight, hearing and so on. Some may be better at sensing beauty than others are but well-nigh everyone is able to judge some things to be beautiful and some things not to be. Admittedly people disagree on aesthetic matters, but such disagreement, however extensive, is possible only because we all engage in the application of aesthetic categories to things.

Though in all cases we find beautiful things agreeable – they afford us pleasure – there is room for dispute as to Hutcheson's precise conception of the relation between beauty and pleasure. To an extent the issue here might be put in terms of the medieval contrast between realism and nominalism. Where is beauty located? Is it in the object perceived to be beautiful or is it in the mind of the perceiver? In the course of expounding the distinction between absolute (or original) and relative (or comparative) beauty, Hutcheson writes:

> by Absolute or Original Beauty, is not understood any Quality suppos'd to be in the Object, which should of itself be beautiful, without relation to any Mind which perceives it: For Beauty, like other Names of sensible Ideas, properly denotes the Perception of some Mind; so Cold, Hot, Sweet, Bitter, denote the Sensations in our Minds, to which perhaps there is no resemblance in the Objects, which excite these Ideas in us, however we generally imagine that there is something in the Object just like our Perception.[42]

Hutcheson is plainly making use here of the distinction between primary and secondary qualities, between on the one hand those qualities such as size, figure and number which are possessed by things whether or not they are being perceived, and those qualities which are perceived to be what they are because of the particular physiological and chemical make-up of the perceiver. Thus my visual experience of a colour depends no less on the chemistry of the retina than on the physical properties of the pigment of the coloured object. In the foregoing quotation Hutcheson seems to be classing aesthetic qualities as secondary. As the sweetness or bitterness of food depends upon the condition of the taste buds no less than upon the food, so likewise the beauty depends upon the perceiver who is or is not responsive to qualities in the thing perceived. On this basis it seems appropriate to ascribe a form of subjectivism or nominalism to Hutcheson, at least in respect of aesthetic qualities. In so far as they have a location it is surely in the mind of the subject. This interpretation seems supported by Hutcheson's summing up of his position: 'Beauty has always relation to the Sense of some Mind; and when we afterwards shew how generally the Objects which occur to us, are beautiful, we mean that such Objects are agreeable to the Sense of Men.' [43]

There appears here to be a move towards the internalisation of beauty, in the sense that in perceiving something to be beautiful our so perceiving it is identical with our finding the thing agreeable. On this interpretation we cannot perceive something to be beautiful unless we derive pleasure from perceiving it – the feeling wells up. We might go further and say that in a universe in which there were no such welling-up there would be no beauty. There is not in this a narrowly anthropocentric vision, for Hutcheson affirms that there may be other percipient creatures in the universe, beings with senses not constituted as ours are, who delight in things of a quite different form from anything we would find agreeable, and these things would be beautiful to those other creatures.[44] It may also be Hutcheson's view, though I do not know how to demonstrate it, that if *per impossibile* a person could perceive the beauty of a thing but derive absolutely no pleasure from that perception, then that aesthetic experience would be worthless – one might as well not recognise the thing's beauty as recognise it but at the same time be coldly indifferent to it.

It has to be stressed, however, that in Hutcheson's view any creature, human or otherwise, with an aesthetic sensibility must have the power to feel pleasure; and that – to return to our main theme – pleasure, in so far as it is attached to a perception of beauty, is not a product of a judgment of personal advantage. If the pleasure does follow on the heels of a person's judgment to the effect that he will benefit from an object, then the pleasure is quite different in its nature from the pleasure attending a perception of beauty. In short, the perception of beauty is *disinterested*. Something of this thought is already present in Hutcheson's emphasis on the immediacy of the operation of the inner sense. We look at something and a feeling of pleasure thereupon arises – it does not do so on the basis of a conclusion drawn about a benefit we will gain from something. If it did arise on that basis it would not be immediate.

I think that the quality of disinterestedness is also close to the surface in Hutcheson's suggestive statement: 'To make the Pleasures of *Imagination* a constant Source of *Delight*, as they seem intended in the Frame of our Nature, with no hazard of *Pain*, it is necessary to keep the Sense free from foreign *Ideas of Property*, and the *Desire of Distinction*, as much as possible.'[45] The pleasures of imagination here invoked are precisely those that arise in the presence of beauty.[46] The idea of property is 'foreign' to this kind of pleasure since the aesthetic pleasure arises directly and solely from the perception of the object, whereas the proprietor's pleasure at his own object arises at least in part from something outside, namely the spectators' approval of the owner's property. If the spectators approve of the property this gives the owner pleasure, which mingles with the pleasure he derives from his direct pleasure in his property, and if the spectators do not like the object then this casts a shadow over the owner's enjoyment, and may indeed destroy his pleasure in it – so much does the owner depend for his own reaction on the reaction of others. His pleasure in the object is therefore never wholly disinterested – a delight in the object itself – for it is always, at least in part, a delight in the object as *his*. As Hutcheson says: 'he robs himself of his chief Enjoyment if he excludes *Spectators*.'[47]

He makes the same kind of point when, in the same passage, he refers to the necessity of keeping our internal sense free from the 'desire of distinction': 'Where the *Humour of Distinction* is not corrected, our Equals become our Adversaries: The Grandeur of another is our *Misery*, and makes our Enjoyments insipid.'[48] Considerations such as whether our possessions are more distinguished than are our neighbour's are foreign to the question of the real aesthetic value of things, a question best answered by factoring out of the equation any consideration of the kind of interest that comes with ownership. Only if we adopt a disinterested perspective will our judgment measure up to the task of estimating an object's beauty.

In this sense aesthetic judgment requires that the judge secure his freedom. Whatever he judges aesthetically he must judge as if it belongs neither to himself nor to anyone else with whom he is in a relation that could distort his judgment. If the object is a friend's then this might cause him to like it unduly; if an enemy's this might prompt a corresponding dislike. The judge has to factor out all these features of the situation in which a judgment is to be made. His bid for freedom is a clearing of a space between him and the object, so that he can respond to the object and the object alone and is not looking at it through the distorting lens of categories 'foreign' (Hutcheson's term in this context) to the task at hand. The outcome is the pleasure we take in an object where the pleasure is not admixed with, or held in existence by, the pleasure we take in the object's-being-mine or in the object's-being-my-friend's or in the object's-not-being-my-rival's. When I judge I seek to be free from all of these considerations, and therefore disinterestedness is a form of freedom.

Nor is disinterestedness always easily gained, but of course it is right to make the effort. One reason for this is that we owe it to the beautiful object, for a beautiful thing is a bearer of value and it should be valued according to its value. A second reason is that we also owe it to ourselves, for to fail to achieve disinterestedness, or worse to fail to seek it, is to miss an opportunity to be judgmentally free, that is, to secure our autonomy in our judgments concerning the beauty of beautiful things.

The disinterestedness of our aesthetic perceptions is an important feature of Hutcheson's aesthetics, important in itself and for its parallel in his moral theory, and also for the influence that his aesthetic writings would have during the European Enlightenment, particularly for his influence on the aesthetics of Immanuel Kant. It is likely that he also influenced the moral philosophy of Adam Smith. Famously, Smith referred to his former teacher at Glasgow as 'the never to be forgotten Hutcheson'. We shall see later that central to Smith's moral philosophy is the concept of an 'impartial spectator', and it is arguable that he was drawn to this concept at least partly by Hutcheson's attempt to delineate what is in effect an impartial spectator in the field of aesthetics.

There is a case for holding that the disinterestedness of aesthetic perception relates to the shape of the overall argument in the *Inquiry*. Hutcheson deals with aesthetic perception in Treatise I and with moral perception in Treatise II. In the latter treatise he aims to promote the doctrine that we can derive pleasure from the sight of a virtuous act, where the product is in no way a product of our belief that our interest is served by the act. In taking up this position Hutcheson is arguing against philosophers, especially Hobbes and Bernard Mandeville, who believed us to be self-interested all the way through.[49] The fact that our inner sense delivers up perceptions which, by their very nature, are not in the least grounded in considerations of self-interest implies that we are not after all self-interested all the way through. This does not mean that moral perceptions must be like aesthetic ones in being disinterested, but once it is demonstrated that self-interest is not fundamental to all our judgments this opens up the prospect that our moral perceptions are, at least sometimes, not shaped by self-interest. We are capable of disinterested judgment in the aesthetic sphere, so why not also in the moral?

Although in one respect Hutcheson's focus is on the internality of beauty, a question remains as to what it is on the outside to which we respond by perceiving it as beautiful. He affirms: 'The Figures which excite in us the Ideas of Beauty, seem to be those in which there is Uniformity amidst Variety.' He adds: 'where the Uniformity of Bodys is equal, the Beauty is as the Variety; and where the Variety is equal, the Beauty is as the Uniformity.'[50] He offers examples which do not do his thesis any favours, for he tells us that we find a square more beautiful than an equilateral triangle because though they are equally uniform the square has greater variety; and that for the same reason a cube is more beautiful than a regular pyramid. These examples fail to persuade, not only because they leave us wondering in what sense a square has more variety than an equilateral triangle. It may be that what Hutcheson has in mind is a pair of extremes which are equally far from prompting the requisite feeling of pleasure. On the one hand there is extreme uniformity and on the other an object that seems chaotic so that there is no evident principle of unity or uniformity. In both cases the likely affective response is boredom; the object is simply of no aesthetic interest.

Hutcheson is not saying or implying that in ascribing beauty to an external thing its beauty is nothing but its uniformity amidst variety. There could be uniformity amidst variety in a world in which there were no minds (if there could be a world in which there were no minds), but without minds there would be no one to find pleasure in the uniformity amidst variety, and there would therefore, on Hutcheson's account, be no beauty in that world.

Hutcheson, as already noted, gives a range of examples of uniformity amidst variety, and I should like to mention a further example, one that merits particular attention given that the Scottish Enlightenment was noteworthy for its historiographical accomplishments, by Hume among others, no less than for its philosophical. Writing of the 'beauty of history' Hutcheson affirms:

> Every one knows how dull a Study it is to read over a Collection of Gazettes, which shall perhaps relate all the same Events with the Historian: The superior Pleasure then of History must arise, like that of Poetry, from the Manners; as when we see a Character well drawn, wherein we find the secret Causes of a great Diversity of seemingly inconsistent Actions; or an Interest of State laid open, or an artful View nicely unfolded, the Execution of which influences very different and opposite Actions, as the Circumstances may alter.[51]

A collection of gazettes merely lists external events and therefore holds less interest and pleasure than does well-written history, which lists the external events in the context of a narrative within which we are told not only what happened but also why it happened, not just what people did but what their motives and intentions were. Once we have an account of the inner aspect of a person's actions we can see that many apparently disparate actions, that had previously seemed to add up to a rather chaotic fragment of a life, are in fact systematically related parts of a single plan of action. For this reason Hutcheson refers to a 'character *well drawn*'. What is at issue here is not what happened but the historian's mode of presentation of what happened. The narrative, unlike the gazette's list, has a much tighter uniformity amidst diversity and therefore is found more agreeable than the bare list of external events. In short, the historical narrative has greater beauty.

Yet granted that well-nigh everyone has an inner sense, granted also that a thing's uniformity amidst diversity raises in us the idea of the thing's beauty, and granted finally that it is not difficult to recognise uniformity amidst diversity, then it seems problematic that there should be such disagreement between people on aesthetic matters and no less problematic that one person can find something first agreeable and then disagreeable even though there has been no perceptible change in the thing. Hutcheson responds by deploying Locke's notion of association of ideas.[52] Associations of ideas are habits of thought by which an idea of an X comes to draw an idea of a Y in its train. A child's nurse tells the child stories of wicked spirits that come out after dark, and thereafter the child associates the dark hours with wicked spirits and is afraid to go out at night. Regarding the power of association to affect what we find agreeable and disagreeable, Hutcheson concurs: 'We know how agreeable a very wild Country may be to any Person who has spent the chearful Days of his Youth in it, and how disagreeable very beautiful Places may be, if they were the Scenes of his Misery.'[53]

There is a question regarding how much aesthetic disagreement there really is, and Hutcheson contributes a thought towards a possible answer:

> But there does not seem to be any Ground to believe such a Diversity in human Minds, as that the same simple Idea or Perception should give pleasure to one and pain to another, or to the same Person at different times; not to say that it seems a Contradiction, that the same simple Idea should do so.[54]

It is hard to know how to assess this claim. Hutcheson seems to hold that if two people are having the same identical simple perceptual experience – perhaps they are listening to the same single musical note (assuming that to be an example of a simple idea) – then, so long as their perception is not distorted by associated ideas, the two people will find the experience equally agreeable or equally disagreeable. It is not clear what the evidence is that supports Hutcheson's claim. He seems to imply that the claim is a logical truth – that is at least the implication of his claim that its denial is a contradiction, but he does not say why it would be a contradiction.

Hutcheson's claim that associations can distort the perception of beauty is perhaps plausible, but there is need for more discussion on this matter than we find in Hutcheson. The development of associations of ideas is essential if, as regards any art work, we are to be in a position to pass an aesthetic judgment worth attending to. Our knowledge and experience concerning the history of artistic forms – painting, literature, music – make all the difference to the quality of our judgments. Our educated judgment of a Bartók quartet involves bringing to bear a substantial body of associated ideas relating to matters integral to the tradition out of which the work grew. Without this background set of associations we would be listening to the quartet as we listen to someone speaking an unknown tongue.

All this is not to suggest that aesthetic sensibility is reducible, with little if any remainder, to the disposition to associate, though this is the position to which Archibald Alison was drawn late in the Scottish Enlightenment,[55] for we might well agree with Hutcheson's claim that our sense of beauty is natural to us, from which it seems to follow that we are capable of making aesthetic judgments antecedent to any associated ideas that might be factored into the judgment. What I am speaking about here is not what is necessary if we are to make aesthetic judgments but instead what is necessary if we are to make aesthetic judgments that are not so ill informed as to be value-less; the additional material required is a substantial battery of associated ideas. Yet Hutcheson's focus is largely, almost entirely, on associations that distort our perceptions of beauty, with almost nothing on the kinds of associations of ideas that enhance our perceptions. On this matter he is in opposition to Turnbull, who, as we noted, places emphasis on the benefits for us of our capacity for forming associations of ideas, whereas Hutcheson is consonant with Locke, who saw little good and much harmfulness in that same capacity.

Section 7: Francis Hutcheson on the idea of virtue

Hutcheson does not confine his application of the term 'beauty' to works of art; he uses it in reference to natural phenomena and he also deploys it in his moral philosophy, for he holds that virtue has a sort of beauty – call it a moral beauty – and in holding this he does not stray far (if at all) from the concept of beauty that he deploys in writing about aesthetics. It is perhaps stretching a point to say that his moral theory is contained within his aesthetic (or indeed the converse); perhaps better to say that they are two intimately related parts of a single doctrine about human sense perception.

As a first move towards demonstrating the similarity between aesthetic and moral perception, I should like to focus on the fact that for Hutcheson things which we perceive to be good, whether naturally good (such as health), or aesthetically (such as beauty, sublimity and grandeur), or morally (such as justice, courage and temperance), all prompt in us a pleasure that necessarily accompanies the perception of their goodness. In each case the pleasure arises unbidden and immediately. The perception of the goodness also (if it is something additional to the pleasure) is likewise immediate. The will plays no part and neither does reason.

To describe the situation more cautiously: we may allow that the will and reason contribute in many ways to our moral education so that through them our moral perceptions become more sophisticated, sensitive or refined – more 'perceptive'. But unless we first had moral perceptions that were immediate, there could not thereafter be a role for reason and will to play in making us more perceptive. We have to be perceptive by nature if we are to become more perceptive. Closely related to this is the fact that unless there are some things that by their nature and by our nature immediately delight us, such as kindly acts, or that immediately revolt us, such as acts of wanton brutality, we neither are nor can become moral agents. Our nature would not have fitted us for the tasks of moral agency any more than a person would be fitted for the task of seeing if he did not have eyes. This parallel between perception of visible and of moral qualities is not fortuitous: Hutcheson holds that each of us has a moral sense which is part of the original frame or constitution of our nature; the moral sense has to be in place if we are to be morally educable.

At the start of the *Essay on the Nature and Conduct of the Passions* Hutcheson augments his list of senses. There are, first, the five external senses; secondly, the internal sense by which aesthetic qualities are perceived; thirdly, a public sense which is defined as 'our Determination to be pleased with the *Happiness* of others, and to be uneasy at their *Misery*'; fourthly, the moral sense by which we perceive virtue or vice in ourselves or others; and fifthly, a sense of honour by which we are pleased at the approbation or gratitude of others, and shamed by their dislike or resentment at injuries done by us.[56] Hutcheson retains here his model of external senses and the immediacy of their action. We no sooner open our eyes than we see something – our will is not engaged; likewise no sooner do we see others happy than a feeling (Hutcheson sometimes says a 'perception') of pleasure wells up in us. It is immediate; we do not calculate that their happiness will somehow benefit us. In fact, given the immediacy of our response, we cannot have calculated at all. Since the happiness of others is felt by us to be a good we are therefore motivated to promote their happiness and correspondingly to relieve their distress. To will the happiness of others and to do so for their sake is to be benevolent. If we can act benevolently then the doctrine of psychological egoism, promoted by Thomas Hobbes and Bernard Mandeville, must be false. Hutcheson does not deny that a person can act selfishly, or from an exclusively self-interested motive; what he denies is the claim that everyone acts solely from an exclusively self-interested motive. A major part of his opposition to the egoistic doctrine is that it leaves no room for virtue, since it leaves no room for benevolence, and for Hutcheson benevolence is *the* moral motive.

He writes:

> If we examine all the Actions which are counted amiable any where, and enquire into the Grounds upon which they are approv'd, we shall find, that in the Opinion of the Person who approves them, they always appear as Benevolent, or flowing from Love of others, and a Study of their Happiness, whether the Approver be one of the Persons belov'd, or profited, or not.[57]

It might be, as Mandeville argued in *The Fable of the Bees*, that everyone's acting selfishly would result in public benefit, and that everyone's acting benevolently would have the same outcome. It might even be, as Mandeville thought, that everyone's acting selfishly would bring more benefit to society, for he held that a society of the virtuous would not make progress in respect of the things that make people happy. But the beneficial outcome of selfishness would not confer a kind of delayed virtuousness on the selfish action. Hutcheson holds that if everyone acts selfishly then no one acts virtuously, no matter the outcomes of the acts. For it is precisely on the motive that the moral status of the act depends, and the only motive that can ground virtue is benevolence. Self-interest cannot serve as such a ground.

Hutcheson deploys several arguments to educate our intuitions on this matter. Among them are the following. Some people who lived in the distant past are judged by us to have been virtuous although it is implausible to suppose that we now derive any benefit from their acts. Psychological egoists might reply to this that we who judge virtuous the person who lived in the distant past do so because we imagine ourselves as of his time and place and imagine ourselves as beneficiaries of his acts. But Hutcheson resists this move, because if the past person was a miser and if we imagined ourselves as his heir and therefore as the beneficiaries of his miserliness, we would not judge him to have been virtuous however much benefit we imagine ourselves to have derived, for we simply do not think miserliness a virtue.

A further argument is the empirical fact that sight of people in distress prompts us immediately to move to help them, and this points to a 'natural, kind Instinct' in us. It is true that Hobbes holds, to the contrary, that the supposedly natural, kind instinct has a self-interested element, for the explanation for our helpful response to the distress of others is that sight of their distress prompts in us a like suffering and we have to do something to relieve our own suffering. But Hutcheson argues against this on the grounds that it is incompatible with what we know about human beings. For first, if the sight of the distress of others gives us pain it would make as much sense to avert our gaze, go away, think about something else, as to move to help them, and yet we do not turn away. On the contrary we seek to know more so that we can target our help more effectively. Secondly, suppose God gave us a choice between either giving help to those in distress or blotting them and their distress from our minds, we would not choose to have knowledge of the distress blotted out, but would instead choose to help – which is exactly what would be expected if we were motivated by benevolence but not if motivated by self-interest or self-love.

In our discussion of the inner sense we attended to the question of what it is in an object that prompts us to judge the object beautiful, and we noted Hutcheson's response: 'The Figures which excite in us the Ideas of Beauty, seem to be those in which there is Uniformity amidst Variety . . . [W]here the Uniformity of Bodys is equal, the Beauty is as the Variety; and where the Variety is equal, the Beauty is as the Uniformity.' A corresponding question can be asked about the moral sense: what is it in an act that prompts us to judge it virtuous or morally beautiful? The short answer, as already observed, is that it is motivated by benevolence. But Hutcheson seeks greater precision; he writes: 'that Action is best, which procures the greatest Happiness for the greatest Number; and that, worst, which, in like manner, occasions Misery.' This is qualified by his adjacent comment that, as regards the moral quality of an action:

> in equal Degrees of Happiness, expected to proceed from the Action, the Virtue is in proportion to the Number of Persons to whom the Happiness shall extend; (and here the Dignity, or moral Importance of Persons, may compensate Numbers) and in equal Numbers, the Virtue is as the Quantity of the Happiness, or natural Good.[58]

There is an impressive agreement in form between Hutcheson's account of the two values, beauty and virtue. In the case of each value he takes two variables: as regards beauty they are (1) uniformity and variety, and as regards virtue they are (2) happiness and number of people. And in each case he affirms that if either variable is held constant then an increase in the other variable implies an increase in the value; and a diminution in either variable implies a diminution in the value. It is unlikely that Hutcheson's exposition of the two values contains this formal similarity by accident, for, as already indicated, both values are in a sense aesthetic, at least in the broad sense that he is writing about two forms of one thing, beauty, on the one hand the aesthetic (in the narrow sense) and on the other the moral, and it need not be surprising that different forms of the one thing, beauty, should have significant formal similarities.

Hutcheson's promotion of the concept of a moral sense prompted attacks on him from the direction of rationalism. Gilbert Burnet, on behalf of the rationalist cause, was quick to respond to the *Inquiry* and in a series of letters in the *London Journal* he and Hutcheson argued over the merits of the doctrine of moral sense.[59]

Burnet's first reason for opposing the doctrine of moral sense is that the senses can lead us into errorful judgment, and therefore a proper standard for morals cannot be found in sense. It is, believes Burnett, only reason that can be a proper standard. In addition, Hutcheson's focus on the role of the feeling of approbation in our perception of moral goodness is inappropriate because there still arises the question of what it is that makes the approbation reasonable. Surely, argues Burnett, it is because we have a reason for judging a given act to be morally good that we approve of the act. The judgment must come first and, since the judgment must be based upon some reason that we have, the true ground of the approbation is reason, not sense.

In response to Burnet's argument concerning the fact that senses can mislead, Hutcheson concedes the claim in respect of the external senses, and agrees also that the moral sense can mislead. But he points out that we have ways of correcting misleading external sense perceptions (for example, using the data of one sense to correct a judgment based on the data of another sense) so that the senses do not mislead us as frequently as they might, and he adds that though the moral sense likewise can mislead us, we have ways of correcting its misleading perceptions. Such corrections do not always deliver up the reliabilities, indeed the certainties, characteristic of mathematics; but Hutcheson does not in any case think that in the common life we are always afforded the luxury of such certainty in respect of morality. The nearest we can approach to certainty is by the application of the tactics commonly deployed to correct the deliverances of the moral sense. This move weakens, even if it does not destroy, Burnet's case for saying that there has to be a standard – agreement with reason – by which the deliverances of moral sense are to be judged.

Burnet's second argument, concerning the need to ground moral approbation on reason rather than on moral sense, leads Hutcheson into a series of points thought now to be characteristically Humean, though Hutcheson's exposition predates Hume's by fifteen years. Moral approbation moves us to act, and in that sense is practical.

If reason is not practical in this sense, then it cannot be the ground of moral approbation. The question at issue therefore, and the one addressed by Hutcheson, is whether reason can be practical in the sense that from within its own resources it is able to motivate us or (in his terminology) 'excite us to action', and he proposes to respond to this question on the basis of his account of reason as our '*Power of finding out true Propositions*' and of his account of reasonableness as '*Conformity to true Propositions, or to Truth*'.[60] These definitions open up the prospect of an account of the reasonableness of an action as 'conformity of an action to a true proposition', but as Hutcheson argues, that account does not enable us to separate out the virtuous from the vicious and therefore cannot justify identifying virtue with reason. The act of preserving property conforms to the truth that preservation of property encourages industry, and the act of theft conforms to the truth that robbery discourages industry. Preserving property is a virtuous act, and stealing is a vicious act. Both acts are conformable to a truth, and therefore even if conforming to a truth is the mark of a reasonable act it is certainly not the mark of a virtuous one. Hence, *contra* Gilbert Burnet, it is unreasonable to cite reason as the standard of virtue.[61]

Hutcheson does not make an issue of the fact that we speak of acts as 'reasonable', but he does maintain that there are two kinds of reason, and the question is whether the contribution of either kind could of itself render an act virtuous. The two kinds are 'exciting reason' and 'justifying reason'. The former motivates the agent to act; for example, the reason the luxurious person pursues wealth is that it enables him to purchase pleasures. The latter kind serves as a ground of approbation of an act; for example, the reason for approving of a person risking her life in a just war is that such behaviour tends to protect our fellow-citizens. However, Hutcheson's *Illustrations upon the Moral Sense* has as a main thrust the doctrine that the fact that we have reasons for actions, whichever kind the reasons might be, does not support the rationalist, anti-moral-sense position, for of the two kinds of reasons for action that Hutcheson identifies, those of the exciting kind presuppose instincts and affections, and those of the justifying kind presuppose a moral sense.[62] In neither case therefore is reason in the driving seat; it neither excites us to act nor prompts us to approve of what has been, or might yet be, done. This is a crucial doctrine of Hutcheson's, and I shall now probe it.

Regarding exciting reasons, we have ends that we desire, and we can and do reason both about the most effective means to achieve a given end and also which end we should aim for when it turns out that all of them cannot be achieved at the same time, though all at that time are making a moral demand on us. Such reasoning takes place in the context of an antecedent desire, and the question therefore is whether an exciting reason can move us if there is not some antecedent desire in place. Hutcheson's answer is in the negative. Desires set the agenda for our practical reasoning; remove desires and we shall not think to do anything nor therefore reason about what to do.

Regarding justifying reasons, the fact that a given act is the most efficient means available to us to attain a given end would not justify performance of the act unless of course the end were justified. The end might be justified on the grounds that through it we can gain access to a further end, but at some point we have to justify an end in itself and not in terms of something beyond it. For Hutcheson therefore the issue concerns ends that are ultimate, and his contention is that we can justify our pursuit of a given ultimate end solely by reference to an unmediated insight into its rightness. That is to say, at some point in the chain of justificatory reasons there must be recourse to a deliverance of the moral sense, for otherwise every justification would be provisional, a holding operation while we sought justification for some further end, which itself would require justification in its turn in a process that would be never-ending unless the moral sense were invoked. Moral rationalism therefore is unable to give a satisfactory account of fundamental features of morality.

These same features can, however, be satisfactorily accommodated within Hutcheson's accounts of the affective or emotional life and the faculty of moral sense, accounts according to which we have a moral sense which both judges motives and motivational dispositions to be on the side of virtue or of vice, and gives rise to feelings of approval and of disapproval in the presence respectively of virtues and vices – though it should be stressed that for Hutcheson the worth of the acts or characters of those being judged is not reducible to the judge's affective state of approval or disapproval. We approve or disapprove of a value that is truly predicable of something in reality, something that would truly have that value whether we approved of the thing or not. To that extent it is appropriate to classify Hutcheson as a moral realist in addition to being a moral sense theorist.

All this mental apparatus is ascribed by Hutcheson to the workings of nature. Our moral sense is part of the original frame or constitution of our nature, by which constitution our approval and disapproval arise by nature; and virtues, primarily the virtue of benevolence, are no less part of our nature. It is true that reason enables us to make countless modifications, large and small, within these cognitive and affective operations, but reason would have nothing to do in respect of our practical life did we not by nature possess this cognitively and affectively rich constitution.

A major element in this picture is human nature as naturally virtuous in the sense that the original frame of our nature includes benevolence, a disposition to wish happiness for others and to wish it for their sake and not for our own. In addition, Hutcheson rejects the idea that vice is in any way a part of our nature:

> For though certain parts of our nature, certain desires, carry us into many vices in the corrupt state of things in which we find ourselves, yet when we contemplate the whole fabric of human nature, disordered and corrupt though it be, and the different parts of our human nature, in particular the social and kindly . . . affections and that moral sense which we may also call natural conscience, we see clearly that vices are not natural to our nature.[63]

Hutcheson's position is remarkable, given its contrast with the kind of Calvinist Christianity, prevalent in seventeenth- and early-eighteenth-century Scotland, that places heavy emphasis on the Fall and on our consequent depravity.[64] The problem is that if preachers ignore the fact that we have kind and generous affections by nature and instead focus on the Fall and on our depravity, this must affect the image that we have of ourselves and of each other. We will see not only ourselves but also everyone else as wicked and, since we treat people in accordance with our image of them, if we think everyone is wicked we will treat them as wicked. If the bad news about our wickedness is hammered home by our preachers and is consequently built into our responses to each other, then we will tend to behave in such a way as to confirm this theologically driven stereotype.

On this view, a certain reading of Calvinism is dangerous to morality and, on this view, during the early decades of the eighteenth century the kirk, which policed morality in Scotland, preached virtue but did so within the context of a theology that worked against the very virtue that the kirk sought to inculcate; the minister's preaching of the word was accomplished in such a manner as to add to the obstacles confronting his flock in their attempt to live by the word. Hutcheson is especially sensitive to this paradoxical situation, and at the same time he holds that virtue has to be defended at all costs, and that the Calvinism which he inherited has to be revised to ensure that it is not in conflict with its own express objective of strengthening the virtue of the faithful.

We should here recall also Hutcheson's refutations of psychological egoism. For the position just outlined regarding the danger posed for morality by a certain kind of Calvinism is also posed, on Hutcheson's view, by philosophies that argue that self-love or self-interest are at the base of all our motives. He writes: 'many have been discourag'd from all Attempts of cultivating *kind generous Affections* in themselves, by a previous Notion that there are no such Affections in Nature, and that all Pretence to them was only *Dissimulation, Affectation*, or at best some *unnatural Enthusiasm*.'[65] This 'previous notion' was thought by Hutcheson to be the central insight of both Hobbes and Mandeville, and his determination to refute their philosophies seems to have been fuelled as much by his belief in their dangerousness for moral practice as by his belief in the sheer error-fulness of the doctrines. It is, therefore, not just our concept of virtue that needs to be protected but our practice of virtue. Those who can speak out warmly in its cause should do so.

Amongst those whom Hutcheson would wish to charge with the noble task of speaking warmly in the cause of virtue are the professors of moral philosophy at Scotland's five universities, St Andrews, Glasgow, Edinburgh, King's College and Marischal College, Aberdeen. Their lecturing had to be a kind of preaching, a carefully slanted exercise in rhetoric in which the lecturer has to take a leaf out of the note-book of the poets. It is in the light of Hutcheson's concerns about a practical tension within the Calvinism he inherited that we have to read the following interesting passage:

> Where we are studying to raise any Desire, or Admiration of an Object really beautiful, we are not content with a bare Narration, but endeavour, if we can, to present the Object it self, or the most lively Image of it. And hence the Epic Poem, or Tragedy, gives a vastly greater Pleasure than the Writings of Philosophers, tho both aim at recommending Virtue. The representing the Actions themselves, if the Representation be judicious, natural, and lively, will make us admire the Good, and detest the Vitious, the Inhuman, the Treacherous and Cruel, by means of our moral Sense, without any Reflections of the Poet to guide our Sentiments.[66]

Hutcheson is here suggesting that a certain aspect of moral philosophy lecturing should aspire to the condition of poetry. Not that the lectures should simply be poetry, for though the poet neither offers, nor needs to offer, reflections of his own on the subject of virtue, the moral philosophy professor must of course reflect on that subject. And what he should reflect on is stated by Hutcheson with due clarity in the *Inquiry*:

> Now the principal Business of the moral Philosopher is to shew, from solid Reasons, 'That universal Benevolence tends to the Happiness of the Benevolent, either from the Pleasures of Reflection, Honour, natural Tendency to engage the good Offices of Men, upon whose Aid we must depend for our Happiness in this World; or from the Sanctions of divine Laws discover'd to us by the Constitution of the Universe.'[67]

The *Inquiry* also contains a note of caution in this regarding the professor's powers of persuasion: 'But Virtue it self, or good Dispositions of Mind, are not directly taught, or produc'd by Instruction; they must be originally implanted in our Nature, by its great Author; and afterwards strengthen'd and confirm'd by our own Cultivation.'[68] One of the ways by which we may become cultivated in matters of virtue is to listen to the moral philosophy professor who is himself cultivated not only in matters of virtue but also, as we have just noted, in matters of poetic skill. The latter feature is as important as the former in a moral philosophy professor. Hutcheson's *Essay* further emphasises the role of the study of morals as a means to the practice of morality:

> The Pursuits of the *Learned* have often as much Folly in them as any others, when Studies are not valued according to their *Use in Life*, or the real Pleasures they contain, but only for the *Difficulty* and *Obscurity*, and consequently the *Rarity* and *Distinction*. Nay, an abuse may be made of the most noble and manly Studies, even of *Morals*, *Politicks*, and *Religion* itself, if our Admiration and Desire terminate upon the *Knowledge* itself, and not upon the Possession of the *Dispositions* and *Affections* inculcated in these studies.[69]

Hutcheson believes that where the study of morals does not result in good moral practice the study is, if not totally valueless, then at least of far less value than it would otherwise be, for it is precisely at the inculcation in moral practice that the professor's teaching should aim – the theory should be for the sake of practice.

It is in the light of these considerations that we have to understand one of the defining moments in the history of the moral philosophy chairs in Scotland, the rejection of David Hume's application for the Edinburgh chair. Hutcheson advised that the application be rejected, arguing that Hume lacked warmth in the cause of virtue. Hume speaks of philosophers of a certain kind who

> paint [virtue] in the most amiable colours; borrowing all helps from poetry and eloquence, and treating their subject in an easy and obvious manner, and such as is best fitted to please the imagination, and engage the affections . . . They make us *feel* the difference between vice and virtue; they excite and regulate our sentiments; and so they can but bend our hearts to the love of probity and true honour, they think, that they have fully attained the end of all their labours.[70]

Hume here describes a kind of philosophising of which Hutcheson strongly approves, a philosophising that aims to produce moral improvement in the audience. But Hume describes his own style of philosophy as that of an anatomist, not a painter. By giving pride of place to the 'anatomical' style of moral philosophy, not the painterly, Hume sets himself up as a likely target for the criticism that he lacks warmth in the cause of virtue.[71]

Notes

1. Carmichael, *Natural Rights*, eds Moore and Silverthorne, pp. ix–x (hereinafter *Natural Rights*).
2. Hugo Grotius, *The Rights of War and Peace*, Book 1, ed. Richard Tuck (Indianapolis, IN: Liberty Fund, 2005), p. 89.
3. First edn Glasgow, 1718; 2nd edn Edinburgh, 1724. Substantial passages of the 2nd edn are translated in *Natural Rights*.
4. *Natural Rights*, p. 46.
5. Ibid. p. 48.
6. Ibid. pp. 48, 49.
7. Ibid. p. 348.
8. Ibid. p. 60.
9. Ibid. p. 61.
10. Ibid. p. 24 (where fn. 8 provides a number of Stoic sources).
11. Ibid. p. 65.
12. For information on this very interesting club see M. A. Stewart, 'Berkeley and the Rankenian Club', in D. Berman (ed.), *George Berkeley: Essays and Replies* (Dublin: Irish Academy Press in assoc. with Hermathena, 1986), pp. 25–45. Among the members were William Wishart (c.1692–1753) (later principal of Edinburgh University), John Stevenson (1695–1775) (later professor of logic at Edinburgh), Colin Maclaurin (1698–1746) (later professor of mathematic at Edinburgh), John Pringle (1707–82) (later professor of moral philosophy at Edinburgh and later still president of the Royal Society of

London), Sir Alexander Dick (1703–85) (later president of the Royal College of Physicians) and Alexander Boswell of Auchinleck (1707–82) (later a Lord of Session and father of James Boswell).

13. He does mention Toland in the Graduation Oration of 1723, but his purpose there is to tar Toland, along with Hobbes and Spinoza, with the brush of atheism and materialism.

14. His steps towards ordination were facilitated by Arthur Ashley Sykes, a latitudinarian thinker who strongly advocated a rationalist form of Protestantism. At times his stance bears a passing resemblance to David Hume's. See Sykes's discussion of miracles in his *The Principles and Connexion of Natural and Revealed Religion* (London, 1740).

15. For information on his time in Italy see Wood, 'George Turnbull'.

16. For the last of these three, see his *Observations upon Liberal Education*; also *A Treatise on Ancient Painting* (London, 1740).

17. John Clarke (1682–1757) delivered the lectures in 1719 and 1720. They were published under the titles *An Enquiry into the Cause and Origin of Evil* (London, 1720) and *An Enquiry into the Cause and Origin of Moral Evil* (London, 1721).

18. 'An inquiry concerning virtue and merit' and 'The moralists, a philosophical rhapsody' are in Shaftesbury's *Characteristics*. See Klein edition, pp. 163–230 and pp. 231–338 respectively.

19. Turnbull, *Principles*, ed. Broadie, p. 13 (hereinafter *PMCP*).

20. M. A. Stewart, 'George Turnbull and educational reform', in Carter and Pittock (eds), *Aberdeen and the Enlightenment*, pp. 95–103.

21. Maclaurin, *Account of Sir Isaac Newton's Philosophical Discoveries*, ch. 1.

22. *PMCP*, vol. 1, p. 58.

23. Ibid. vol. 1, p. 71.

24. The locus classicus for eighteenth-century discussions of associationism is John Locke, *Essay Concerning Human Understanding*, bk II, ch. XXXIII. Another major source is Joseph Addison's series of essays on the pleasures of the imagination, published as nos. 411–21 in Addison and Steele, *The Spectator*, ed. Bond, vol. 3, pp. 535–82.

25. *PMCP*, vol. 1, p. 122.

26. Ibid. vol. 1, pp. 124–5.

27. Ibid. vol. 2, p. 708.

28. Ibid. vol. 1, p. 79.

29. Ibid. vol. 1, pp. 126–7.

30. Ibid. vol. 1, p. 139.

31. Ibid. vol. 1, p. 139.

32. Ibid. vol. 1, p. 131.

33. Ibid. vol. 2, p. 669.

34. Turnbull, *Observations*, p. 397.

35. Ibid. p. 392.

36. Ibid. p. 396.
37. See Skoczylas, *Mr Simson's Knotty Case*.
38. Hutcheson, *Philosophiae Moralis*, p. i.
39. Three further editions of the book appeared in Hutcheson's lifetime, in 1726, 1729 and 1738. Several issues of the fourth edition appeared in 1738, and the relations between them are complex.
40. Hutcheson, *Inquiry*, ed. Leidhold, p. 19 (hereinafter *Inquiry*).
41. This was not the first time the notion of a sense of beauty was posited. It is, notably, in the writings of Anthony Ashley Cooper, Third Earl of Shaftesbury, a philosopher Hutcheson admired. See for example Shaftesbury, *Inquiry concerning Virtue or Merit*, bk. I, pt. II, sect. 3, one of the treatises collected in his *Characteristicks*.
42. *Inquiry*, p. 27.
43. Ibid. p. 28.
44. Ibid. p. 28.
45. Hutcheson, *An Essay on the Nature and Conduct of the Passions and Affections*, ed. Garrett, p. 114 (hereinafter *Essay*).
46. Hutcheson's source here is Addison's essays on the pleasures of the imagination.
47. *Essay*, p. 114.
48. Ibid. p. 115.
49. Thomas Hobbes, *Leviathan*, ed. Richard Tuck (Cambridge: Cambridge University Press, 1991), esp. pt I; Bernard Mandeville, *The Fable of the Bees: Or, Private Vices, Publick Benefits*, 2 vols, ed. F. B. Kaye (Indianapolis, IN: Liberty Fund, 1988), passim.
50. *Inquiry*, pp. 28–9.
51. Ibid. p. 65.
52. Locke, *Essay*, bk. II, ch. 33.
53. *Inquiry*, p. 69.
54. Ibid. p. 22.
55. Alison, *Essays on the Nature and Principles of Taste*. Alison's position had already been adumbrated by Joseph Priestley in his *Course of Lectures in Oratory and Criticism* (London, 1777).
56. *Essay*, pp. 17–18.
57. *Inquiry*, p. 116.
58. Ibid. p. 125.
59. The arguments of the letters are re-presented in *Essay*. The exchange of letters, which originally took place in the *London Journal*, 10 April to 15 December 1725, is to be found in *Letters Between the Late Mr. Gilbert Burnet, and Mr. Hutcheson*.
60. *Essay*, p. 137.
61. Ibid. pp. 137–8.
62. Ibid. p. 138. Hutcheson takes his distinction between exciting and justifying reasons from Grotius, *De jure belli et pacis*, II.I.I, who himself

quotes the Roman writers Polibius and Livy as sources for the distinction.

63. 'The natural sociability of mankind', in Hutcheson, *Logic*, p. 199.
64. These elements were prominent before this period and are still present, but my concern here is with the early part of the Scottish Enlightenment.
65. *Essay*, pp. 3–4.
66. *Inquiry*, p. 173.
67. Ibid. p. 178.
68. Ibid. p. 178.
69. *Essay*, p. 115.
70. Hume, *Enquiry Concerning Human Understanding*, I.1, p. 87.
71. It should be noted that Hume affirms that anatomy is useful to the painter, for the painter of the human form is better placed for the task if knowing the inward structure, the position of the muscles, the 'fabric of the bones' and so on. Hume, *Enquiry*, I.5, p. 90.

CHAPTER 7

David Hume

SECTION 1: A PORTRAIT OF HUME

David Hume was born in Edinburgh on 26 April 1711. He came, as he reports, 'of a good family, both by father and mother'.[1] His father was a kinsman of the Earl of Home[2] and his mother was the daughter of Sir David Falconer, president of the College of Justice. David was two years old when his father died. Thereafter he and his elder brother John and elder sister Katherine were raised by their mother partly at the family estate, Ninewells, near Chirnside in the Scottish Borders, and partly in Edinburgh.

Hume's studies at Edinburgh University probably began at the start of the 1721–2 session.[3] It is likely that in his first year he studied Latin, proceeding in his second year to Greek, in his third to logic and metaphysics and in his fourth to natural philosophy. His third-year lectures are thought to have included a form of Calvinist scholasticism, while in the fourth year Hume was exposed to Robert Boyle's experimental physics and Newtonian mechanics, optics and astronomy.

Hume left the university in 1725. He did not graduate but did continue his intensive reading of both the classics and philosophy. In a letter to a physician he reported a consequence of this industry:

> After much Study, & Reflection on this, at last, when I was about 18 Years of Age, there seem'd to be open'd up to me a new Scene of Thought, which transported me beyond Measure, & made me, with an Ardor natural to young men, throw up every other Pleasure or Business to apply entirely to it. The Law, which was the Business I design'd to follow, appear'd nauseous to me, & I cou'd think of no other way of pushing my Fortune in the World, but that of a Scholar & Philosopher.[4]

Whatever may have been the content of Hume's 'new scene of thought', and its content is a matter for speculation, he shortly thereafter suffered a serious breakdown in health, partly physical and partly mental, from which he did not recover for several years.

In 1734 he went to Bristol, where he was employed briefly by a merchant, before travelling on to France, staying briefly at Paris and Rheims before going on to the village of La Flèche in Anjou near the Jesuit college at which Descartes had been educated. During his three years in France he drafted the *Treatise of Human Nature*. Books I and II appeared in 1739 and book III the following year. The work, which was published anonymously, was not on the whole well received, though Hume seriously understated its immediate impact when he wrote: 'Never literary attempt was more unfortunate than my Treatise of Human Nature. It fell *dead-born from the press*, without reaching such distinction, as even to excite a murmur among the zealots.'[5]

The first volume of Hume's *Essays Moral and Political* appeared in 1741, followed one year later by volume two. The essays cover political topics such as freedom of the press and the idea of politics as a science, though there is also an essay 'Of superstition and enthusiasm', his first published writing on religion, and he includes a set of four essays on philosophical types, the Epicurean, the Stoic, the Platonist and the sceptic.

In 1745 Hume was a candidate for the chair of moral philosophy at Edinburgh. Hutcheson, who turned down an invitation to take the chair, opposed Hume's candidacy, as did a committee of divines who rejected his candidacy 'on account of his principles'. The professor of moral philosophy had to teach the truth of Christianity and according to a rather common perception in the kirk that noble task could not safely be left to Hume.[6] In that same year Hume went south to act as tutor to the Marquis of Annandale and was therefore not in Scotland during the 1745 Jacobite uprising.

Thereafter for a period Hume was secretary to General James St Clair, first when the general prepared to take a force to Canada, then when the fleet sailed to the Brittany coast to lay seige to Lorient, and finally when he accompanied the general on an embassy to Vienna and Turin. None of these three activities counted for much in the course of history (the sailing to Canada was aborted, the seige of Lorient was lifted when the French were about to surrender, and St Clair's embassies were overtaken by the Peace of Aix-la-Chapelle), but during this period a fourth activity, writing and rewriting, counted for a great deal, for in 1748 Hume published both a second edition of his *Essays* and also his *Philosophical Essays concerning*

Human Understanding, a title replaced in the 1756 edition by *An Enquiry concerning Human Understanding*. In 1751 a further set of writings was published, *An Enquiry concerning the Principles of Morals*, 'which', affirmed Hume, 'in my own opinion (who ought not to judge on that subject), is of all my writings, historical, philosophical, or literary, incomparably the best'.[7]

During that same year the question of a university chair for Hume was again raised. The moral philosophy chair at Glasgow had become vacant, and Adam Smith, who occupied the university's chair of logic and rhetoric, evidently thought to move to the moral philosophy chair, thus creating a vacancy in the logic and rhetoric chair that could be filled by Hume. But again there were insurmountable ecclesiastical obstacles and Hume's candidacy came to nothing.[8] Soon after, however, he was offered, and accepted, the librarianship of the Library of the Faculty of Advocates in Edinburgh. The post left him ample time to write. In 1757 appeared his *Four Dissertations* (including *The Natural History of Religion*), and during the period 1754–62 he published his six-volume *History of England*, the work for which he was best known during his lifetime.

From 1763 to 1765 Hume worked at the British Embassy in Paris, first as personal secretary to the embassador, the Earl of Hertford, then as embassy secretary and finally as chargé d'affaires. It was a period of intense social activity. He was received at court, he attended several salons and met most if not all of the leading intellectuals then in Paris, such as D'Alembert, Diderot, Baron d'Holbach, Turgot and Helvétius. He was also on friendly terms with some of the women who were major players in the French Enlightenment, such as Madame Geoffrin, Madame de l'Espinasse, the Marquise du Deffand, and especially the Comtesse de Boufflers, to whom Hume felt a close attachment to the end, as witness the moving farewell he sent her as he was dying. A further acquaintance, one who caused Hume much pain and little pleasure, was Rousseau. Hume tried to help Rousseau, who was then in trouble with the French authorities, by finding him a refuge in England and also by seeking out funds, but relations quickly turned sour, with Rousseau, who was seriously paranoid, claiming that Hume was a member of a conspiracy against him.

In 1767 Hume was appointed under-secretary to the Northern Department, a post that committed him to doing little more than drafting letters for government ministers, though in 1767 he did also draft the annual letter from the throne that was delivered to the kirk's governing body, the General Assembly. In 1769 he retired to

Edinburgh, and died there on 25 August 1776. Some days before he died he finished revising a work that had been on his mind from the early 1750s if not before, the *Dialogues concerning Natural Religion*. He had been advised not to publish it in view of its apparently anti-religious stance, and he had first thought in terms of leaving it to Adam Smith to publish it for him, but in the end he requested that his publisher William Strahan publish the *Dialogues*, failing whom the charge would fall to Hume's nephew, also named David Hume. His nephew duly complied in 1779.

Hume, a convivial man, belonged to many clubs and had many friends, and he was widely mourned. Adam Smith wrote a moving tribute to him, ending with the words: 'Upon the whole, I have always considered him, both in his lifetime, and since his death, as approaching as nearly to the idea of a perfectly wise and virtuous man, as perhaps the nature of human frailty will permit.'[9]

Section 2: Impressions and ideas

The *Treatise of Human Nature*[10] is a long work, divided into three 'books' devoted successively to the understanding, to the passions and to morals. Books covering these fields were rather common in Hume's day, and in general a book covering those three fields would also have quite a lot to say about religion. The *Treatise* is, however, notably quiet on that subject, not completely silent but almost so, and when it does deal with religion it does not do so in such a way as to imply the author's endorsement of any religious doctrine, such as, say, the existence of God. There is in fact a good deal in the *Treatise* that might easily seem incompatible with rational belief in God, and unsurprisingly it was widely thought that Hume was an atheist.

Treatise book I is entitled 'Of the understanding'. On that topic Hume reappeared in print nine years later with his *Philosophical Essays concerning Human Understanding* (1748) (whose title, as we saw, would change in 1756 to *An Enquiry concerning Human Understanding*). The account of the understanding in the *Enquiry* does not precisely match that in the *Treatise*, and some of the differences will be noted below, but for the present I shall focus on the account in the *Treatise*.

The term 'sceptic' might imply a certain negativity. If it does it would be misleading as applied to Hume's philosophy as a whole, since his philosophy has a strongly affirmative character, implied by the subtitle of the book: 'being an attempt to introduce the experimental method of reasoning into moral subjects'. The experimental method, described in detail by Francis Bacon, is the scientific way to probe the workings of nature, and Hume proposes in his treatise of 'human nature' to consider human beings as parts of nature, and therefore as appropriate subjects for investigation by means of the method which has proved most effective in the investigation of nature. The experimental method had been used with spectacular success by both Sir Isaac Newton and Robert Boyle, and Hume's subtitle signals his use of the same scientific method in his investigation of 'moral subjects', that is, subjects relating to the human mind, particularly to fundamental human beliefs, to passions and the moral life. There is not much negativity in the scientific work of Newton and Boyle except in so far as they remove errors from their path, explicitly or otherwise, while en route to their own positive accounts of the workings of nature, and exactly the same can be said of Hume as he clears errors out of the way, explicitly or otherwise, while en route to his positive account of the workings of human nature.

Hume's starting point is the fact, if it be one, that human experiences or, as he terms them, 'perceptions of the human mind' are the immediate objects of the mind. Descartes taught this doctrine, and by the time of John Locke it had become an orthodoxy. However, the doctrine is used by Hume as the premiss of an argument leading to conclusions that Descartes and Locke would assuredly have rejected. To take one example, if we start with perceptions, which are mental entities, things existing 'in the mind', and we hold them, and only them, to be the immediate objects of the mind, then a question arises as to how we come to be certain that there are objects which are not in the mind, objects which therefore can be grasped, if at all, only indirectly. Surely there are such objects – is not the material world composed of such things? If our grasp of them is indirect, then what is the further step, beyond our apprehension of the perceptions in the mind, that has to be taken if we are to come by a belief in the existence of external things? On a common and readily defensible interpretation of the *Treatise*, Hume seeks to argue that the concept of an entity which lies outside the mind is a good deal more problematic than his predecessors had realised. In a sense of 'sceptical' that we shall explore, he finds himself drawn to a scepticism regarding such entities.

As a start, we should note that perceptions are held to be of two kinds: impressions and ideas. The distinction is based on ordinary experience: we see something and later recall it; we hear a sound and later recall it; and so on through the five external sensory modalities.

The same distinction can be made in respect of our feelings and emotions; we undergo an agonising experience and later in the imagination bring the pain to mind. In the case of each of these pairs of perceptions, the second perception, called an 'idea', is a copy of the first, which is an 'impression'.

An impression is said to differ from the resembling idea in two ways. First, the impression has greater liveliness, forcefulness or vivacity, and secondly, the idea is an effect of the impression. This picture is quickly modified, however, in the light of the fact that in certain heightened mental states the liveliness of our ideas may approach that of our impressions, and on the other hand an impression may be so faint that we cannot be sure whether it is an impression or an idea, whether for example we really did see a brief twinkle of light in the darkness or whether it was a figment of our imagination, or whether in a frightened and nervous state in solitude in the dark we really did hear a footstep or whether our imagination had conjured it up. Hume's recognition that there are such cases does not prompt him to withdraw the claim that degree of liveliness is a sound criterion for distinguishing between impressions and ideas, and this suggests that the claim has the status of a well-founded empirical generalisation. It is the conclusion of a scientific consideration of human nature, an application of the experimental method of reasoning. Hume has found that our impressions are, in the vast majority of cases, livelier than our ideas, and the generalisation is therefore empirically well founded – though this way of putting the matter should lead us to wonder how we know that a given very weak impression *is* an impression and not an idea.

As regards the causal dependence of ideas on impressions, a distinction has to be made, between the simple and the complex. Not all our ideas are copies of preceding impressions, for some of my complex ideas are the work of my imagination. I have never seen anything that the image in my mind resembles nor ever heard a real performance of the tune running through my mind; the image is my own invention as is the tune, but Hume argues that though the complex image might be my own invention it is composed of parts which cannot be so. The idea of the tartan I have just thought up might resemble no tartan in the real world, but the colours of my newly imagined tartan are not themselves newly imagined. I could not mentally arrange reds, greens and yellows in that way unless I had previously seen those colours. Likewise, Mozart's creativity does not involve creating the notes of which his compositions are composed.

He had to hear C natural sounding in the real world to have an idea what it sounds like. Consequently the principle, known as the 'copy principle', that ideas are copies of antecedent impressions requires qualification. It holds for all simple ideas but not for all complex ideas. I can imagine the taste of a plate of carrots and turnips though I have never actually eaten these two vegetables together, but I cannot imagine what the combination of them tastes like if I have never actually tasted one or other of these vegetables. The copy principle as applied to simple ideas is reached by the experimental method of reasoning. Hume is commending the application of the method to the copy principle when he invites his reader to run over as many examples as he pleases and see for himself that his simple ideas are copies of simple impressions. Anyone who rejects the copy principle should, *qua* scientist, do so only on the basis of the discovery of a simple idea resembling no antecedent impression. Hume expresses certainty that no such exception to the principle will be found.[11] His certainty does not imply that he thinks that the principle is not after all empirically grounded, and therefore defeasible as are all empirically grounded principles. It implies instead that though Hume accepts the defeasibility of the principle, he thinks that there are so many pieces of evidence tending to confirm the principle that, in the absence of any disconfirmation, he is entitled to feel confidence that the principle holds in all cases. The principle, therefore, is unequivocally empirical, despite Hume's certainty that exceptions will not be found.

Further evidence that Hume regards it as an empirical principle is to be found in the fact that he supports the principle with the empirical observation that a person born blind or deaf cannot form visual ideas (in particular, ideas of the various colours) or auditory ideas (ideas of the various sounds), an observation which is more general than, but of the same form as, the point made earlier, that a person who has never tasted a carrot will not be able to form an idea of that particular taste (assuming, of course, that only carrots taste like carrots).

However, having denied that there are exceptions to the copy principle he then provides one. If we cannot have an idea of blue unless we have already had an impression of the colour, we cannot have an idea of a given shade of blue unless we have antecedently had an impression of that shade. Suppose a person to have seen all shades of blue save one and that he is presented with a spectrum of the shades of blue from the lightest to the darkest, with a blank where that missing shade would have been. Hume asks whether the person could form an idea of the missing shade and replies that few would deny that he could. From which he draws a conclusion:

> this may serve as a proof, that the simple ideas are not always deriv'd from the correspondent impressions; tho' the instance is so particular and singular, that 'tis scarce worth our observing, and does not merit that for it alone we shou'd alter our general maxim.[12]

Hume indicates thereby that the singularity of his counter-example implies he is justified in not withdrawing the copy principle. Yet it can be argued that the counter-example is not singular. For, first, if an idea can be formed of one missing shade of blue then it can be formed of several. Secondly, if this is true of blue then it is true of the other colours also. Thirdly, it is also true in respect of other sensory modalities, in particular those of which it makes sense to speak about the impressions in the modality being placed in a spectrum, whether auditory, gustatory, olfactory or tactile. Perhaps all such feelings can be placed in spectra, but it is certain that sounds can, from low pitch to high and from quiet to loud. Thus, to employ the form of the model Hume used, a person who had heard sounds at other pitches but not at middle C might well be able to form an idea of the missing note if presented with notes at the other pitches. This indicates that the missing shade of blue is not singular after all.

Commentators have responded in a variety of ways to Hume's singular exception to the copy principle. It might be that Hume should have said that the spectator could indeed form an idea of the missing shade but that his copy principle concerns simple ideas only whereas the idea formed of the missing shade of blue is in fact a complex idea, being an amalgam of the shades flanking the blank in the spectrum.

Secondly, it might be said that the idea of the missing shade of blue is indeed simple but that this fact is of no great significance for his philosophy, for the role of the copy principle is to enable Hume to reject the claim that we can form a specific collection of simple ideas, all of them in heavy use by earlier philosophers, and none of them reachable by means of some spectrum that contains a judiciously placed blank. That is, Hume can with equanimity concede the missing shade of blue, for the concession bears little philosophical cost.

A third approach is to say that Hume is in error in setting up his spectrum of blue. He surely assumes there to be a finite number of discrete shades of blue, for the spectrum is said to contain all the shades of blue 'excepting one'. Yet it may be that shades of blue form a continuum from lightest to darkest, in the sense that there are no two shades of blue so close to each other that there are not other shades lying between them. In which case the blank in the spectrum shown to the spectator would not be filled uniquely by a given impression; it would be filled by an indefinitely large number.

There is something to be said for (and against) the various responses, but what does seem clear in the midst of this much-debated issue is that here again Hume is faithful to his role of the scientist applying the experimental method of reasoning to moral subjects. That he is willing even to contemplate the possibility of exceptions to the copy principle demonstrates that the principle has the status of a well-founded empirical generalisation. It is founded on the large number of confirmatory cases and is theoretically defeasible. In this respect Hume is faithful to his commitment to 'introduce the experimental method of resoning into moral subjects'.

But it is questionable whether he is faithful to the experimental method of reasoning in identifying an exception to the copy principle and thereupon proceeding as if he had found no exception. Though Hume has been described as the 'Newton of the moral sciences' one can hardly imagine Newton, Boyle or other major figures of the recently established Royal Society taking a Humean attitude to counter-examples. Hume declares the copy principle to be the 'first principle' of his science of human nature, and it is first both in being the first enunciated and in bearing the weight of all the rest of the *Treatise*. The equivalent for Newton would perhaps be his law of gravity, and it is unthinkable that had he discovered a counter-example to his law he would thereafter have disregarded the counter-example on the grounds that it was singular. On the contrary he would have investigated it with a view either to demonstrating that it was only a seeming, not a real, counter-example, or to finessing his law in the light of the counter-example.

Hume identifies his doctrine embodied in the copy principle with the doctrine that there are no innate ideas. In reaction against a long tradition, Locke had argued that we do not have ideas that are not derived from experience, whether external sensory experience or experience of the kind that we have by reflection on our own bodily states and mental acts, and Hume holds that his own arguments in support of the copy principle are also arguments in support of the rejection of innate ideas. What of those ideas that have been, or that might be, thought innate, such as the ideas of space, of power, or of the necessary connection between cause and effect? Hume's view is that either the ideas are empty, lacking content because they lack an experiential basis, or they do after all have a content because they do have such a basis. It is with this in mind that he unfolds the programme of the *Treatise*. He considers ideas, such as those of space, time, power, causality, externality, self-identity, justice, and enquires into the impressions of which these are the ideas. In the case of all of these ideas he finds the relevant impressions, though not where many people might have thought to look for them, and he demonstrates thereby that the ideas are not innate.

Hume's acceptance of the fact that we can form an idea of a shade of blue of which we have not had prior visual experience leads to an unexpected conclusion. For if an innate idea is one which is not a copy of an antecedently grasped impression, then the idea of the missing shade of blue is, after all, an innate idea, and in that case Hume's position must be that while the doctrine that there are no innate ideas is supported by countless confirmatory experiences, it is nevertheless false, not merely defeasible but defeated, since the idea of the missing shade of blue is incompatible with it.

It might be supposed that since impressions are antecedent to ideas, Hume's enquiry into 'moral subjects', that is, the human mind, will begin with a consideration of philosophically significant impressions and will thereafter proceed to a consideration of ideas, but Hume has good reason to proceed in the opposite direction. Impressions are of two kinds, those of sensation and of reflection. The former are such as arise from the exercise of our external sensory receptors and also our sensations of hunger, thirst, and bodily pleasures and pains. Hume has almost nothing to say about the origin of such impressions, for he is a philosopher analysing the mind and its contents; he is not a physiologist or anatomist. The impressions of sensation give rise to their corresponding ideas, and these ideas in their turn, such as ideas of pleasurable or painful sensations, give rise to new impressions, of desire and aversion, of hope and fear, which in appropriate circumstances give rise to the whole array of emotions or passions. All these latter impressions are impressions of reflection, and they are in large measure a product of ideas. Hume, not being a physiologist or anatomist, has nothing to tell us about the origin of impressions of sensation, but as a philosopher he has a good deal to say about impressions of reflection, and since the latter arise largely from ideas his philosophical enquiry will begin with ideas and proceed thereafter to impressions of reflection.

Amongst our ideas are those of memory and imagination. At many points in the *Treatise* the difference between these two kinds or 'species' of idea is crucial. Two are identified. The first is that ideas of memory have greater liveliness or vivacity and ideas of imagination less. The ideas of memory are 'much more lively and strong', and they flow into the mind in a 'forceful manner' whereas ideas of imagination are 'faint and languid'. Hume may be presumed to be thinking here of complex ideas only, for in the case of simple ideas, apart from singular cases such as the missing shade of blue, all ideas are ideas of memory. As regards complex ideas there is a further distinction. The memory is tied down to an ordering of its simple parts which reflects precisely the ordering of the parts in the corresponding antecedent impression, whereas an idea of imagination may not, in respect of the ordering of its simple parts, correspond to any antecedent impression, for we can order and reorder simple ideas at will. On this basis, Hume formulates as a second principle of the science of human nature: 'the liberty of the imagination to transpose and change its ideas'. (The first principle is the copy principle.)

Hume's third principle relates to the question why we have our ideas, whether of memory or of imagination, when we do, and his answer is that they occur not randomly but in a rather orderly or rule-governed way. He identifies three rules, which he discovers neither accidentally nor by a priori reasoning but instead by the experimental method. Hume considers a large number of cases of ideas joined in the mind and can find only these three rules of conjunction or association: given an idea of an object X in the mind of person P, the next idea which occurs to P, an idea of Y, is likely to be united with X in P's mind if (1) X and Y resemble each other, or (2) P has perceived X and Y next to each other in space or time, or (3) P believes X to be either a cause of Y or an effect of Y. Hume describes the tendency for one idea to be associated with another in the mind as 'a gentle force, which commonly prevails'[13] and he speaks of it also as 'a kind of ATTRACTION, which in the mental world will be found to have as extraordinary effects as in the natural, and to show itself in as many and as various forms'.[14] Hume does not mention Newton's name in his account of the association of ideas, but it is plain that he has him in mind. We are being told that ideas attract each other in somewhat the same way that, in Newtonian mechanics, all particles of matter are in a relation of mutual attraction, and to this extent the Newtonian picture has been appropriated as a kind of metaphor for the mind and its operations.

Hume was particularly pleased by his theory of the association of ideas. In the *Abstract* of the *Treatise* that he published anonymously shortly after the perceived failure of the *Treatise*, he writes: 'if any thing can entitle the author to so glorious a name as that of an *inventor*, 'tis the use he makes of the principle of the association of ideas, which enters into most of his philosophy.' For reasons which will shortly become clear he adds that the three principles of association 'are really *to us* the cement of the universe, and all the operations of the mind must, in a great measure, depend on them'.[15] Resemblance, contiguity and causation are not the only forms of relation that Hume deals with; the relations of identity, of contrariety, of proportion of quantity and of degree of quality are also in his list, and at least one of them, that of identity, is in due course investigated in depth.

Before leaving Hume's exposition of the basic features of ideas and their corresponding impressions, a further element should be mentioned. If I have an idea which corresponds to some actual impression then the idea must have a content which in some respect is also the content of the impression. Here, however, a problem arises – what if the impression is a perfectly coherent experience but the idea is incoherent? How can it be an idea of that impression? Examples of such cases are easily found. I have an idea of a triangle, not of any triangle in particular but of a triangle-as-such – we may suppose that a geometer wishing to prove a theorem about triangles-as-such has an idea of a triangle-as-such. His idea is one that corresponds to every triangle in the world, whether the real-world triangle is equilateral or not, right-angled or not, and so on. If the geometer's idea corresponds to a real equilateral triangle then the idea must surely be of such a triangle, and if that same idea corresponds to a non-equilateral triangle then his idea must also be of a non-equilateral triangle. But this idea of a triangle which is both equilateral and non-equilateral, and which will also be both a right-angled triangle and a non-right-angled triangle, is incoherent. It is in effect self-contradictory. How can such an idea correspond to any impression?

The idea of a triangle-as-such that I have described as incoherent is in Hume's day commonly termed 'general' since it applies generally to all triangles. It is also termed 'abstract' because of the common view that in order to be able to function as a generally applicable idea it must be formed by abstraction from ideas that are exact copies of particular triangles. We do have ideas which are abstract and general in the sense that they are equally applicable to disparate things which, however disparate, are all of the same sort. How is this possible?

This is one of the perennial problems of philosophy, and Hume's way forward is to appropriate the answer given by George

Berkeley[16] and to add further substance to that answer. Hume agrees
with Berkeley that the idea of a triangle cannot lack the determinacy
possessed by every triangle. An idea, any idea, is as particular as are
the things of which it is an idea, so an idea of a triangle will in fact
be of an equilateral triangle or it will be of a non-equilateral triangle; it cannot be of both and it cannot be of neither. But there is a
term 'triangle' with which I can truthfully answer the question
'What is it of which you are now entertaining an idea?', no matter
what kind of triangle it is that I am then thinking of. This means that
there is annexed to every particular idea of a triangle a term which
is abstract and general in that it is equally applicable to any triangle
whatsoever. This is true of all common nouns. Hume assumes that
every idea has the same sort of particularity as is possessed by every
impression, and that an idea is general not in virtue of any element
within the idea but in virtue of the nature of the term which is
annexed to the idea. The term is general in the sense that it is predicable truly of many different things, things which may differ from
each other in all sorts of ways but which are nevertheless things of
the same sort. What sort? The sort is given by the term annexed to
the ideas.

Hume next proceeds to a consideration of two ideas, those of space
and time,[17] each philosophically more significant than is the idea of a
triangle, and raises the question of what the impression is that corresponds to each of these ideas. Hume argues that there is no simple
impression of space or of time of which the ideas are copies. His solution regarding space is based on the fact that we derive our idea of
space from the senses of sight and touch; our complex visual or tactile
impression is the origin of our idea of space. It is an idea of *this* particular space, that is, of the extension of *this* particular object of
sensory perception. We also have ideas of other particular spaces,
ideas whose origins lie in different visual or tactile impressions. We
use a general term 'space'. When this general term is annexed to a particular idea of a space the idea can then be termed an abstract or
general idea of space, but it is general not because that particular idea
is general but because to that particular idea of a space there has been
annexed the general term 'space'.

Hume's account of the origin of our idea of time has much the same
form, but the starting point is an impression of a succession of events.
Such particular impressions give rise to the particular idea of this time
and the idea of this other time and so on. We use a term 'time' which
is general in being truly predicable of each of these particular times

and of every other possible time also. When this general term is annexed to a particular idea of a time, the idea can then be termed an abstract or general idea of time, where, again, it is general not because that particular idea is general (which of course it cannot be if it is particular) but because to the particular idea of a time there has been annexed the general term 'time'.

We learn here something of Hume's method. The routes from our ideas of space and time to the corresponding impressions imply that there is not any one impression of which our idea of space or of time is an idea. Although the copy principle might at first sight seem to afford us hope that we can demonstrate that an idea has content if we can locate the impression of which the idea is an idea, Hume's applications of the copy principle to the cases of space and time show that the content of an idea can in some cases not be demonstrated without twists and turns. The path, while real enough, may be anything but direct.

SECTION 3: CAUSATION

In this and the following two sections attention will be paid to three ideas: first the idea of the necessary connection between a cause and its effect, then that of the external world and finally that of the self. Hume's aim is to find their origin in our impressions. He has no doubt that we have these ideas, for we all believe that there exists in reality something corresponding to them, and in *Treatise* 1.3 and 1.4 he seeks to give an account of the origin of each of these ideas. If the copy principle is correct their origin must be, or at least include, impressions. The story would be easily told if each of these three ideas were simple, but in fact Hume believes them all to be highly complex and to be grounded in a multiplicity of impressions, ideas and principles of association.

Let us look first at the idea of a necessary connection between a cause and its effect. Hume devotes greatest space to this relation because of the prominent role it plays in our ordinary reasoning about what there is in the world. On seeing a given event C (or 'on having a visual impression of C'), we not only form an idea of C and, by association, an idea of some event that we judge C to cause, but we also believe that the second event just mentioned is about to happen. Likewise by association we reason backward from a present impression of E to a judgment that C had happened. So association by cause and effect permits us to argue both from a present impression to a future existent (an effect) and from a present impression to a previous existent (a cause). What permits such inferences?

For the answer, we need to probe the idea of causation, and an example would help the process. Hume's is that of a billiard ball striking another. B1 hits B2 whereupon B2 moves. This would be seen by everyone as a case of causation, a case in which B2 moved be*cause* B1 hit it. Two features are immediately noted by Hume. First, B1 and B2 are spatially contiguous when B1 causes B2 to move. Secondly, B1's colliding with B2 is antecedent to B2's moving, though this second feature may not be as evident as the first. But against those who might think that there is a simultaneity here, Hume argues that if a cause and its effect are simultaneous then in every chain of causes and effects (and no one doubts that there are such chains) the start of the chain would be simultaneous with the final effect, and that is certainly not according to our experience.

Spatial contiguity and temporal antecedence cannot be the whole story, for by themselves they would not explain our natural tendency to reason from an event to its effect. The further element in the picture is expressed by 'must'. The effect does not follow as a mere accident or happenstance; it must happen, there is a necessary connection between the cause and its effect, and this prompts the question: what is the impression corresponding to the idea of 'must' or of 'necessary connection'? Is the impression visual, tactile, auditory or what?

In the *Abstract* of the *Treatise* Hume considers the development of Adam's mental powers.[18] Had Adam never before seen things collide he would not have known that if B1 were to strike B2, B2 would thereupon move. Such knowledge comes only with experience, not with experience of just a single instance but of several. When Adam first sees B1 hit B2, for all he knows B2 will turn into a butterfly or will vanish or will continue to lie in exactly the same position. Nor even, if these are the first moments after his creation, will he have any reason to suppose that there is any connection between B1's colliding with B2 and anything whatever happening because of the collision. Before he learns that things happen because other things have happened, Adam has to have perceived repeated sequences of events. What happens as a result of such perception of constant conjunctions is that Adam acquires a habit of mind by which, on having an impression of the collision, he forms an expectation that B2 will move; he will infer the future motion of B2 from the present collision of B1 with B2.

Since he *infers* B2's future motion from a present impression, on seeing the collision he *believes* that B2 will thereupon move. Hume holds that this is a suitable use of the term 'believe' and offers an account of belief that fits his narrative well. The idea we form of the movement of B2 has a vivacity greater than that normally possessed by ideas of imagination. This is due to the idea's close association with the present impression of the cause that prompts us to have that idea. The idea is enlivened by the impression. This is not exactly a transference of liveliness, in so far as 'transference' implies that the liveliness of the impression is to some degree diminished; it is more a case of communication of liveliness, as a light-source communicates its light, without loss of light, to everything that is illuminated by it. It is with these considerations in mind that Hume defines belief as 'a lively idea related to or associated with a present impression'.[19]

There is in this account of the nature of belief a pointer to a general feature of Hume's philosophy: the tendency to downplay the role of reason or intellect in our lives and to emphasise the role of sentiment or passion. When the process of causal 'reasoning' produces a belief, the reasoning process is primarily accounted for in terms not of an intellectual insight but of a product of a habit or custom of the mind that is itself produced by the sheer repetition of sequences of impressions. We do not have to think hard, we hardly have to think at all, to reason causally. Hume is therefore presenting a causal psychological account of the process, and what is delivered by the process is a belief, something which differs from an idea of imagination by virtue of its degree of liveliness or vivacity. But the liveliness of the belief and therefore the belief itself are, according to Hume, something that we *feel*.[20] Causal reasoning proceeds by the exercise of a mental habit whose existence has a purely psychological explanation, and it concludes in a sentiment or feeling. In this sense causal reasoning, which is a dominant feature of the common life, is heavily on the side of sentiment.

Where in all this is the 'necessity' of the causal relation? The answer lies in the determination of the mind, once the mental habit has been established, to expect the second event when we have an impression of the first. On perceiving the cause, the process of causal inference is well-nigh unstoppable; we immediately expect the effect, and feel this determination of the mind as necessitated. This feeling of necessity is then projected onto the world and is read as a feature of the relation between the first event and the second in the causal sequence, though in reality what is out there in the real world is simply the pair of events related by spatial contiguity and by the temporal ordering of earlier and later. Hume has therefore tracked down the impression which corresponds to the idea of the necessary

connection between a cause and its effect. The idea of necessary connection is not bogus or a sham; it is contentful, and Hume's narrative
concerning the elements involved in the process of causal inference
provides us with the content.

It should be said, however, that in the history of philosophy
Hume's narrative has sometimes been misrepresented, and for a
reason that is perhaps understandable. We all believe there to be a
necessary connection between a cause and its effect, and if the cause
and the effect are both out there in the real world then the obvious
thing to say about the necessity of the necessary connection is that it
too must be out there as a feature of the relation of these two external things or events. However, the whole thrust of Hume's argument
is towards a denial of the seemingly self-evident belief that the necessity of the relation must be where the relation is and that the relation
must be where the relation's termini, the cause and its effect, are.

Hume's formulations of the nature of causation permit at least two
interpretations, one focused on what we find outside in the real world
and the other focused on the contribution made by the human mind
looking out on the world. According to one interpretation, what are
actually out there in the real world that correspond to our idea of
causation are pairs of events that are related by constant conjunction,
where the conjunction is dual, consisting of spatial contiguity and of
temporal priority and posteriority. According to the other interpretation the necessity of the connection between cause and effect is essential to any causal sequence; it is what makes it a causal sequence. On
this account causality is inseparable from the fact that we make causal
inferences, so that there is no causation if there is no causal inference.
The human mind cannot be kept out of the picture, least of all in
respect of Hume's narrative.

It is not necessary here to adjudicate between these alternatives,
though it has to be said that we must surely give priority to the internal side of the narrative if we lend particular weight to Hume's statement: 'There is a NECESSARY CONNEXION to be taken into
consideration; and that relation is of much greater importance, than
any of the other two above-mention'd [namely contiguity and temporal succession].'[21] However, there are other passages which emphasise contiguity and temporal succession. I am not persuaded it is
important to settle the issue. Hume's is a compelling analysis in which
due attention is paid both to the external and to the internal features
of the situation in which a causal inference is drawn. In Hume's judgment both types of feature are necessary elements in the analysis; in

effect he holds that causal necessity is a constitutive part of the real world only in so far as we have so constituted the world that it is constituted by such necessity. And we could not so constitute it if we were not habit-forming creatures incapable of perceiving frequently iterated sequences without forming well-nigh irresistible expectations. In an uninhabited world which featured constant conjunctions there would be no necessary connections because there would be no causal inferences in it.

There are different ways of describing Hume's accomplishment in his discussion of causation. One would focus on his contribution to psychology, in particular on what has to be in place to make possible the formation of beliefs about causal connections. A second would focus on his contribution to metaphysics. We believe both that causal relations exist out there and that things related as cause to effect are connected by necessity. Though we might be clear about the mode of existence of the cause and of the effect – at least we could perhaps tell a story about their materiality, spatiality and temporality – a question would remain about the mode of existence of the necessity of the relation. That is a metaphysical question and, as we have seen, Hume answers it by saying that it exists as an impression of reflection, a felt determination of the mind.

This answer points to a way in which Hume might be classed in relation to at least one of the great principles of division among philosophers. During our discussion of Duns Scotus on the subject of universals we drew a distinction between realists and nominalists, and noted that those philosophers who hold that universals are, at least primarily, in the real world and are mind-independent, or to an extent are mind-independent, are realists, and that those who hold that universals are only in the mind, and are mind-dependent, are nominalists. We acknowledged that there was a spectrum of views, and not just two homogeneous schools, and found that Scotus could be located on the realist side of the spectrum, though only just. Exactly the same distinction, and spectrum, can be invoked in respect of causal necessity. It is possible to argue, as we did above, that when the cause and the effect are both out there in the real world, then the necessary connection between them, and therefore the necessity itself, must be out there as a feature of the relation of these two external things or events. This is a claim on the side of realism. But Hume rejects this claim and holds instead that contrary to our naive intuitions on this matter the necessity is to be located in the determination of the mind. It is on the inside, and seems outside solely because we project it onto the world and do this inadvertently as it were, without even noticing that we are engaged in such a stupendous act. It is evident that in respect of his teaching on causal necessity Hume's position is firmly in the nominalist camp.

SECTION 4: THE EXTERNAL WORLD

We turn now to Hume's discussion of the external world, the world of material bodies, and begin with the observation that in our examination of necessary connection it was assumed that there was indeed a real world out there, and a question arose as to whether the necessity of the connection between cause and effect was located in that same world in which were located material causes and their effect. The discussion did not include investigation of the credentials of the assumption about the real world itself – for it is surely 'out there' in a way that is so obvious that it would seem utterly strange to wonder whether it might possibly not be. But Hume is prepared to go where his arguments take him, however strange the intellectual territory in which he might find himself.

It is important to know precisely what the big question is that Hume asks regarding external bodies, for if the question is misunderstood the answer is likely to be also. Hume does not challenge the belief that there is an external world, a world of material bodies. That there are, Hume holds, is something that we all take for granted, but a question may reasonably be raised concerning how we come by the belief. The big question for Hume therefore concerns not the existence of bodies but the formation of our belief in them,[22] because of the nature of the elements out of which he constructs his system. Impressions and ideas last only for micro-seconds or perhaps minutes. We shut our eyes and all visual impressions cease; we change the direction of our gaze and one visual impression is thereupon replaced by another; we think about something, then about something else, and in the process one idea is replaced by another. All the building blocks of our experience are transitory or ephemeral. But if all the things with which we are directly acquainted are ephemeral, how do we come to believe in the existence of bodies that last far longer than do any of our perceptions? Through the exercise of which faculty of the mind do we come by our belief in the existence of bodies? Is it the senses, reason, the imagination? In Hume's view no other faculty has any claim to serious consideration. It must be one of, or a combination of, these three.

It cannot be the senses, or at least the senses alone, that deliver our belief in external bodies, and this for at least two reasons. First, by the exercise of the senses we have sensory impressions, and in so far as they are impressions they have a very brief time span. Secondly, impressions are, as we would now say, 'mind-dependent'. They last only as long as does our consciousness of them, and indeed there may be nothing more to them than our consciousness of them. But external bodies are just that – external. They are mind-independent, able to continue existing even when not being perceived.

If the senses cannot by themselves ground our belief in an external world, can reason do so? But how? And even if there is such an explanation, how many people know what it is? If few people know it, then its existence cannot explain why everyone believes there to be an external world. Hence the cause of our belief in the external world cannot be the exercise of the faculty of reason.

By elimination therefore the faculty that is doing the work must be the imagination. This is Hume's conclusion, and much of his discussion concerning the continuity and distinctness of the world is taken up with an examination of the role of imagination in the formation of our belief in continuing, distinct things. Hume's discussion focuses especially on the fact that many temporal series of impressions display both a constancy and a coherence to which the imagination responds in a manner dictated by its nature. This manner is a consequence of the tendency of imagination to form habits in response to the perceived constancy and coherence of our impressions. The habits turn out to be all-important in the formation of our belief in the external world.

Hume's examples are helpful. I look out at mountains, houses and trees and my looking produces in me various visual impressions. I look away or shut my eyes, and when I look again the impressions I have are exactly the same. This is characteristic of impressions of objects to which we ascribe external existence. Although each impression we have of the mountain is a different impression, nevertheless on account of the constancy of the series of impressions we ascribe external existence to the mountain. This is not the only kind of case of ascription of externality; we often make such ascriptions even where there is change, even considerable change, in the impressions that form the temporal series. I have an impression of a fire. I leave the room and return an hour later and the impression is perceptibly different. I leave and return again and there are only ashes in the grate. Yet I have no hesitation in ascribing externality to the fire. In this case there is no constancy in the single series – no two impressions in the series are alike. Yet the series as a whole resembles many other series of impressions, for we have often seen a fire at its brightest and then seen it diminish and finally seen it reduced to ashes. So while there is no constancy in the individual series there is a constancy in the series themselves, what we might call a constancy of change. Such constancy is termed 'coherence' by Hume.

Perceptions which have the kind of constancy we find in our successive impressions lead to a change in the mind in that it engages in what Adam Smith was later to describe in a happy phrase as a 'career of the imagination'. Having been presented with an earlier impression in the series the imagination goes careering along forming ideas, in an orderly way, of impressions at later positions in the sequence. Hume compares this process to a galley: 'the imagination, when set into any train of thinking, is apt to continue, even when its object fails it, and like a galley put in motion by the oars, carries on its course without any new impulse'.[23]

Hume provides a more complex example: I hear a noise which is indistinguishable from that of a door creaking on its hinges. My imagination then proceeds along a familiar path, for the idea of the door of my study comes to mind, and then that of my porter opening the door, and then that of the stairs leading to the door. Out of a brief sound I thus construct a complex idea which confers sense on the sound. Why believe the door exists? It is because I have often watched-and-heard the door creak open and I therefore associate the perception of the opening door with the perception of a creak. If I hear the creak while not looking at the door, I can make the auditory perception most agreeable to past experience by supposing the door to have been opened. Likewise I have routinely climbed stairs to enter by that door, and the impression of the creak is therefore made most agreeable to past experience if I associate it with the stairs. And so on. The imagination enables us to produce a coherent picture out of utterly disparate impressions. Our minds are discomforted by incoherence; that is an original quality of human nature. The outcome of this striving for mental comfort is that we form a picture, which is agreeable to us, of a state of affairs consisting hardly at all of impressions and almost entirely of ideas supplied by the imagination in its search for a coherent image. Each of us has many such images, some nested in others, and the largest is that of the world of the perceiver, a world which is largely the product of the perceiver's imagination. Central to Hume's concept of this image is the fact that the image is achieved on the assumption that things are in place whether we have impressions of them or not. Motivated by the need to make sense of our perceptions, that is, to find a way in which they appear coherent, we are drawn to the belief that our world can get along without us and that for most of the time it does exactly that.

Hume starts his philosophy with perceptions, purely mental existences which by their nature can have no being outside the mind. A question arises for him as to how, if our point of departure is inside the mind, we manage to reach the 'real world' outside. His solution is in effect that we do not get outside. He does not deny that there is a real world; his question, as we noted at the start of this discussion, relates to belief formation: 'What causes induce us to believe in the existence of body?' In response he invokes principles of operation of the mind by which we construct a world and suppose it to be a world which continues to exist whether we are perceiving it or not. It is noteworthy that Hume refers to the world thus constructed as a 'fiction'.[24] A novelist uses his imagination and produces a work of fiction. Hume thinks that we all produce such a work though on a vastly larger scale than the novelist, and that we believe in the product of our imagination more than the novelist believes in his novel.

Some might say that if the world exists as a product of the imagination then it does not really exist, but Hume would no doubt reply that impressions have no representative function. There was a view – some think it was held by Locke – that impressions of sensation (or, rather, that the elements that Hume called 'impressions of sensation') represent to the mind the things in the external world that the impressions are impressions *of*. But Hume does not think that if there is a sensory impression of an X there must be two things in play: first, the impression, which is an item in the mind, and secondly an external X, that the impression is an impression of. There is instead one thing, namely the impression-of-an-X, which is 'of an X' in virtue of being the kind of impression it is, not in virtue of its relation to something else that is in no way part of, or an aspect of, the impression. Herein is a major contrast between impressions and ideas. An idea does have a representative function – it represents an impression in virtue of being a copy of it; but the impression of which the idea is a copy is not itself a copy of anything.

SECTION 5: PERSONAL IDENTITY

We turn now to Hume's account of personal identity, the identity of the self; and we should by now be prepared for the shape of the question principally in focus. Regarding the necessary connection between a cause and its effect, the issue for Hume is not the justification for our belief in such a connection but rather the route by which the belief comes to be formed. Likewise regarding our belief in the existence of a distinct and continuing world, the issue for Hume is not the justification for our belief in such a world but rather the route by which the belief comes to be formed. So likewise, in dealing with personal identity, the issue for Hume is not the justification for our belief in the existence of our self, something that continues unchangeably throughout our lives, but rather the route by which the belief comes to be formed.

We might suppose that the route starts at an impression that we each have of our self, an impression that we can each vouch for by introspection. However, Hume in scientific mode reports that he has never had such an impression, that when he looks within he finds only an ever-changing array of particular impressions and ideas and nothing whatever that is constant throughout the introspection. In any case he cannot, merely on the basis of inner observation, vouch for there being a continuous and unchangeable something throughout his life, for he is not always observing what is occurring within, not to mention that he sometimes falls asleep and wakes up with the belief that he is the same person as the one that fell asleep. Nor does Hume think that anyone else is better placed to vouch, on the basis of experience, for the existence of a continuing, unchangeable self. But, to invoke the copy principle, if all that inner observation reveals is a swirling mass of perceptions and no constancy within the mass, what is the impression of which our idea of the self is a copy?

Hume offers a simile: 'The mind is a kind of theatre, where several perceptions successively make their appearance; pass, re-pass, glide away, and mingle in an infinite variety of postures and situations.'[25] However, he immediately modifies the simile: 'They are the successive perceptions only, that constitute the mind; nor have we the most distant notion of the place, where these scenes are represented, or of the materials, of which it is compos'd.' In short, rather than think of a theatre in which there is a performance, we are to think away the theatre and instead think only of the performance. The performance is what the mind is. In the light of these considerations Hume states that the mind is 'nothing but a bundle or collection of different perceptions, which succeed each other with an inconceivable rapidity, and are in a perpetual flux and movement'. Why then believe there to be a continuous and unchanging self? Most of Hume's discussion of self-identity is devoted to this question.

We are, each of us, still the same person at the end of a period of time as we were at the start of it, and this despite all the changes to which we have been subject. Hume wants to know what it is in virtue of which we ascribe a continuing sameness or identity to ourselves, given that we are in a constant state of change. Identity or sameness is to be contrasted with diversity or difference. Yet the action of the imagination when we contemplate something that is invariant for a period may not feel any different from its action when we contemplate a series of things which are closely related, particularly if they are related by the associative principles of resemblance, contiguity or causation. Hume writes:

> The relation facilitates the transition of the mind from one object to another, and renders its passage as smooth as if it contemplated one continu'd object. This resemblance is the cause of the confusion and mistake, and makes us substitute the notion of identity, instead of that of related objects.[26]

When this confusion occurs the result is the ascription of identity to what is truly a diversity, and the identity is therefore 'feigned' (Hume's term) and is a 'fiction' created by the imagination. The externality of causal necessity is a fiction, so is the distinct and continuing existence of bodies, and now Hume uses the term 'fiction' of identity also.[27] Identity is diversity worked on by the imagination.

Before dealing with identity of the self Hume provides examples of identity of other sorts of thing. If a piece of a mountain becomes detached and falls off, nobody thinks that there is a different mountain in that place. Likewise if a ship has been repaired many times over the years, it is still considered to be the same ship even though few of the parts it now has were present in the ship when it was first constructed. A fully mature oak is considered to be the same tree as the sapling from which it grew even though not one particle of matter in the mature tree was in the sapling. In each case there is an easy transition of the imagination from the object at one stage in its history to the object at another stage, and this very ease of transition tends to prompt in us the belief that there is really something, one and the same identical thing, that is invariant through the diversity.

In spelling out the role of the principles of association in the process by which a belief in personal identity is formed, association by contiguity may safely be excluded since a mind now is not contiguous with that mind at an earlier time. But association by resemblance and by causation plays a significant role. To consider resemblance first: that the mind at one time resembles the mind at another time is inevitable given the exercise of the faculty of memory, for in remembering we form an idea of a previous perception. This facilitates the transition of the imagination from consideration of the mind at one stage in its history to another, and thus produces a feeling of continuity and therefore of the mind at the later stage being the same mind as at the earlier stage. This implies that the faculty of memory contributes to the production of the identity of the mind through time by producing resembling perceptions at different times.

The associative principle of causation contributes hardly less than does resemblance to the production and maintenance of the fiction of personal identity. The mind is a system of perceptions linked by causation. Impressions produce in us their corresponding ideas which prompt other ideas to appear. There is no smoother transition that the imagination can make than that from one idea to another that is linked to the first by causation. Each stage of the mind seems linked to another stage by causation and the mind, contemplating a slice of its own history, moves with greatest ease from one stage to the next when the principles of resemblance and causation are both in operation. How can the mind not be 'the same again' when we consider its history and perceive such a tight unity between the stages, so tight a unity that 'identity' is surely the best way to describe it? We read identity into the mind, an identity that is a product of the imagination.

It is in just the same sort of way that we feel the determination of the mind to expect the second event in a causal sequence when we have an impression of the first, and read that feeling into the relation between cause and effect in terms of the 'necessity' of the connection between the two; and likewise we construct a coherent picture out of the swirl of our impressions and ideas, and read that coherence in terms of distinct and continuing objects. The imagination therefore is the faculty responsible for the formation of our beliefs about causality, externality and personal identity. Philosophical analysis thus delivers the conclusion that the things in this world of which we are most certain are all works of fiction in the sense in which novels are works of fiction, with this difference, that people suspend belief when they read novels.

The imagination is good at producing fictions and at causing us to believe in them, but philosophical systems are themselves works of imagination and a question therefore arises concerning whether Hume's philosophy implies that his own philosophy is a work of fiction. At the end of the first book of the *Treatise* Hume reports that he is in despair: 'When I turn my eye inward, I find nothing but doubt and ignorance.'[28] What removes the feeling of despair is not a countervailing argument but nature itself:

> I dine, I play a game of back-gammon, I converse, and am merry with my friends; and when after three or four hour's amusement, I wou'd return to these speculations, they appear so cold, and strain'd, and ridiculous, that I cannot find in my heart to enter into them any farther.[29]

We shall see that Hume's sociability wins out against the despair induced by his scepticism, but to appreciate the significance of the victory of his sociability it is necessary to take the measure of the scepticism about the powers of the mind to find arguments in support of our very strongest beliefs about the world, concerning causation, the continuing external world, and personal identity. Such scepticism would perhaps be easily livable with if the beliefs continued to have some claim to being true despite the demonstration that the intellect is not up to the job of providing adequate support for them, but Hume's arguments are directed to the conclusion that necessary connection, externality and self-identity are fictions.

Yet he does not stop philosophising. One reason for this is that nature asserts itself in the very activity of doing philosophy, for it is our nature to pose philosophical questions about human nature and to try to answer them. Philosophy is also, as Hume argues, a precious resource in the fight against superstition, and however little prospect there may be of stamping out such a pernicious religious disposition, we must do what we can to fight the good fight. So Hume moves forward, carrying with him in his philosophical baggage the apparatus of impressions, ideas and principles of association, and also the beliefs that we have that are well-nigh universal amongst us human beings, beliefs without which we would be wholly incapable of taking our place in human society, such as the belief that each of us is a self among selves and is not a solitary self trapped in a solipsistic world of one's own creation.

SECTION 6: PASSION AND ITS SLAVE

Our role as a self among selves is nowhere more clearly expounded than in Hume's discussion of sympathy. Having studied the faculty of understanding, he turns in book two of the *Treatise* to an investigation of the affective life, the life of the passions, such as the 'direct' passions of desire, aversion, grief and joy, and the 'indirect' passions such as pride, humility, love and hate.[30] Pride and humility (or shame) are not possible except on the assumption of a social context. We take pride in things that we value highly and that are more or less closely related to ourselves. Our virtue, beauty and riches (Hume's examples) are causes of pride, and the object of the pride is ourself, the person to whom the valued things are more or less closely related, to which Hume adds that such causes 'have little influence, when not seconded by the opinions and sentiments of others'.[31] If our peer group disapprove of an act we have performed we might all the same be proud of what we have done, but their disapproval is likely to dampen our pride and may in fact destroy it. Likewise, if they approve greatly then our pride, if weak at first, might be greatly enhanced by their response. That is an original quality of human nature; that we are beings of such a kind as to be affected in such a way by the sentiments and opinions of others is not to be explained, we just have to accept that we are like that. Hume undertakes to analyse this brute fact about us. Part of his analysis focuses on the fact that we have a mechanism by which we can gain an idea of the sentiment or opinion that another has about us, and can thereby come to have much the same sentiment or opinion. The mechanism is termed 'sympathy'.

Sympathy is neither a passion nor an opinion but is instead a means by which passions and opinions that others have are communicated to ourself and enlivened. Hume's model of this communication is as follows: I perceive a person A engaged in some act, one which I recognise as expressing a given sentiment. An element in my recognition of his sentiment is my idea of that very sentiment. Like A, I too am a human being. I have an impression of myself (or 'my self'), and the liveliness of this impression affects my idea of the other's sentiment to the extent that the idea is itself so enlivened as to become an impression. That is, my idea of the sentiment that the other is undergoing becomes a sentiment that I am undergoing. It is in that sense that the mechanism of sympathy is a mechanism of communication by which a sentiment is shared.

The bare humanity of the other is sufficient for the mechanism to operate, but there are other things that facilitate the communication of sentiments, and here Hume deploys his associative psychology. In fact the associative psychology has already been invoked, for the fact that the other is a human being means that the spectator who sympathises bears a resemblance to the other. Hume's point is that the greater the resemblance the stronger is the disposition to enliven into an impression the idea of the sentiment of the other. Thus we are more likely to share fully the sentiment of someone who resembles us in respect of, say, nationality, religion or musical taste than someone very distant from us in these respects, and the closer the resemblance the stronger the disposition.

As regards contiguity, we will sympathise more fully with someone who is geographically close to us than with someone in a remote part of the world. As regards the associative principle of causation, the fact that someone is a close blood relative (one of the kinds of causal relations cited by Hume) means that we are likely to sympathise more easily and more fully with their sentiments, from which it follows that sympathy is a principle of partiality to this extent, that we sympathise more easily and more fully with loved ones than with complete strangers. One effect of this partiality is that the approval of some people has a greater effect on our sentiments of pride and shame. If I am proud of some act I have performed and a total stranger from an alien culture disapproves of the act this is less likely to shake my pride than is the total disapproval of someone I love. By the same token their approval is less likely to enhance or intensify my pride than is the approval of a loved one. Likewise disapproval by someone close is more likely to produce or intensify shame in me.

It is evident that though there is a massive shift in the context of the narrative of the *Treatise* from the first to the second book, nevertheless much remains. The self considered in abstraction from society is replaced by the social self, but the psychological machinery constructed at the start of the *Treatise* remains intact and is a major element in the narrative. It might be thought that the *Treatise* is broken-backed to the extent that the first book is sceptical about the self and the two subsequent books take it for granted, but it can be said, first, that book one does not deny the existence of the self, if by 'self' is meant the bundle of impressions and ideas that we find when we introspect; and secondly, that the self which is at issue when attention is directed to the passions and the mechanism of sympathy is that same self as in book one, but assumed to be in society and interacting with other selves resembling it in a thousand ways.

Much of our interacting with others takes the form of freely performed acts, and Hume provides an analysis of our freedom or liberty of action. To this we now turn, taking into the discussion central features of the Humean philosophy that we have already considered, including most especially the fact that Hume considered his philosophy of human nature to be empirical science, a product of the 'experimental method of reasoning'. Human nature is being investigated on the assumption that it is appropriate to study it by means of the methodology appropriate to the scientific investigation of nature, but the methodology has the form it has in the light of the belief that there is a uniformity in nature and that this uniformity is expressible in terms of law-like statements which enable us to test predictions. For Hume, this holds whether we are talking about human nature or animal nature or botanical nature and so on. Examples of such uniformities in respect of human nature are the three principles of association of ideas, and the exercise of the mechanism of sympathy. But to claim such uniformities in respect of human nature is to prompt a worrying line of thought. Hume writes: ''Tis universally acknowledg'd, that the operations of external bodies are necessary, and that in the communication of their motion, in their attraction, and mutual cohesion, there are not the least traces of indifference or liberty.'[32] Are we to conclude that there is not the least trace of indifference or liberty in the case of human nature also, that we are no less necessitated in our behaviour than are particles of matter? Hume's answer is 'yes'.

Philosophers dealing with the question of our liberty or necessitation routinely invoke the will as the faculty by which free acts become possible, but Hume has very little to say about the will. He gives what may seem to be a definition of it: 'by the *will*, I mean nothing but *the internal impression we feel and are conscious of, when we knowingly give rise to any new motion of our body, or new perception of our mind*.'[33] This is not in fact a definition if by definition is meant an analysis of the impression, for Hume thinks that the impression that he calls will is simple and therefore not analysable. However, Hume believes that the will is not the appropriate place to start if we wish to be clear about the sense, if any, in which we act freely. He proposes instead to start with his account of causation, an account which involves two main elements, namely a constant conjunction and a determination of the mind to expect an event of a given kind when faced with an impression of a given kind, and he regards as empirical the question whether causal determination is a feature of human acts. So he engages in a scientifically motivated observation of human beings and reports his findings:

> Whether we consider mankind according to difference of sexes, ages, governments, conditions, or methods of education; the same uniformity and regular operation of natural principles are discernible. Like

causes still produce like effects; in the same manner as in the mutual action of the elements and powers of nature . . . The skin, pores, muscles, and nerves of a day-labourer are different from those of a man of quality: So are his sentiments, actions and manners. The different stations of life influence the whole fabric, external and internal; and these different stations arise necessarily, because uniformly, from the necessary and uniform principles of human nature.[34]

In short, Hume finds in the domain of human behaviour the very features that lead us to find causal necessity in other domains, and concludes that our behviour is causally necessitated. Nor do our ordinary judgments of people contradict this conclusion. We do indeed find people's behaviour predictable, and the better we know somone the more accurate we are at predicting how they will act in a given circumstance. We have observed constant conjunctions of such a kind as: 'Whenever X is in circumstance C he performs act A.' The repeated observation of the sequence produces in us a habit of mind by which we are determined to expect X to perform act of kind A when we see him again in circumstance C. It is true that we cannot always predict what people do, and that sometimes indeed they surprise us, but this does not prove that humans are not like the rest of nature in respect of causality. Sometimes dead matter surprises us too, and on such occasions we are likely to suppose ourselves to have inadequate knowledge of the circumstances. Why not say therefore that when the person's behaviour surprises us there is something in the situation that we have not taken into account?

It may be argued that there is introspective evidence which works against the conclusion that we are not 'really' free, for when we act we 'feel' free. However, Hume rejects this line of argument:

> We may imagine we feel a liberty within ourselves; but a spectator can commonly infer our actions from our motives and character; and even where he cannot, he concludes in general, that he might, were he perfectly acquainted with every circumstance of our situation and temper, and the most secret springs of our complexion and disposition.[35]

In this response Hume privileges the spectator's perspective over the agent's. Hume's justification for this is his belief that the spectator's judgment has a firmer scientific basis, for it is based on far more information of the relevant sort than is the agent's, who is depending principally on the single fact that he has a feeling of liberty and is in all probability ignoring, because he is ignorant of, all the evidence available to the spectator concerning the agent's uniformity of behaviour in the past. Hence when the single feeling of the agent is contrasted with the extensive knowledge that the spectator has, based on his own observations of the agent's past behaviour, it is clear that science would come down on the side of the spectator's judgment as against the agent's. Hume is a scientist, and he therefore regards himself as justified in privileging the spectator's judgment.

This not to say that it is inappropriate to deploy the term 'liberty' in speaking of our acts, but it becomes necessary to say what is meant by 'liberty' in this context. Hume invokes a medieval distinction between the 'liberty of *spontaneity*' and the 'liberty of *indifference*', or 'betwixt that which is oppos'd to violence, and that which means a negation of necessity and causes'.[36] The latter form of liberty is absolutely to be ruled out, for the reasons we have already considered, but the liberty which is 'oppos'd to violence' is a liberty the agent has in so far as he acts in accordance with his desires and values and not because of some force that is exerted on him. In invoking liberty of spontaneity Hume evidently wishes to exclude cases where a person is coerced, or where a bodily illness causes limbs to go into spasm; if we act without such forms of constraint then our acts are free. Yet it is a freedom within a deterministic framework.

While many would find this an unpalatable doctrine, Hume believes that all of us agree with it in practice, as witness the fact that governments legislate knowing that the sanctions for law-breaking will be sufficient to ensure that most of the citizens will be law-abiding most of the time. Army officers give commands knowing that their subordinates will obey. A person acts on a friend's promise knowing very well that the promise will be kept. Occasionally the prediction turns out false, but predictions are made in the first place because we recognise the predictability of people even if we also recognise that we lack perfect knowledge, knowledge that would be sufficient to ensure that all our predictions about people's behaviour would be correct.

Earlier, in noting Hume's account of the will as *'the internal impression we feel and are conscious of, when we knowingly give rise to any new motion of our body, or new perception of our mind'*, we observed that Hume appears to have in mind a causal chain which includes (1) a desire and a belief jointly causing (2) a volition which causes (3) a willed act. I should like here to attend to this causal chain since it concerns Hume's account of motivation.

Hume was heir to a dispute almost as old as philosophy concerning motives to action, and especially he inherited a doctrine according to which the faculties of reason and of emotion (or passion or sentiment) can each supply us with a motive which is by itself able to move us. Reason can move us to act, so also can sentiment, and we are virtuous to the extent that we are motivated by reason and vicious to the extent that we are motivated by sentiment.

Hume's major contribution to this territory starts with the fact that reasoning is of two kinds, one a priori and deductive, such as is found in mathematics and logic, and the other empirical and inductive, such as is found in causal inference. The deductive kind cannot by itself motivate us. A trader, given a ten-euro note for a six-euro article, deduces that the correct change is four euros, but his deduction does not in itself motivate him to do anything, and certainly does not motivate him to hand over four euros. If he does, it is because he wants to deal honestly with his customer. But the desire has to be in place, and in that case it is the desire that motivates him to secure a given end, and reason is deployed in an instrumental way to give due direction to the will to ensure that the desired goal is reached. Likewise, wishing to make coffee I reason that if I switch on the kettle I will have to hand a supply of hot of water such as I need, so I switch on the kettle. The inference would not have moved me to act had I not wanted to make coffee. In neither kind of case therefore does reason move me to act; it is desire that does that, and indeed on this account it is desire that motivates the reasoning process. From this it follows that reason by itself is, in Hume's term, 'inert'; passion (or sentiment or emotion) motivates. Hume holds that not only can reason not motivate the will, it cannot even 'oppose passion in the direction of the will'. The explanation for this is that a passion can be stopped from moving us to act only if there is in place something else that moves us in a contrary way. But reason does not by itself move us at all, and hence cannot oppose a passion.

These several positions are summed up by Hume: 'Reason is, and ought only to be the slave of the passions, and can never pretend to any other office than to serve and obey them.'[37] It is tempting to see Hume as writing off reason as motivationally insignificant, but that would be wrong. While the life of slaves is dependent on the will of their master, their master is no less dependent on his slaves and cannot function without them. Their relation is therefore one of mutual dependence. The relation between passion and reason is likewise one of mutual dependence. A human agent who desires X is helpless if reason has absolutely no input into the question of how X is to be achieved; and reason is blind if it is provided with no end or purpose for acting. Any account of human motivation must assign a place to both. Reason without passion does not know where to go and passion without reason does not know how to get there.

The sharply different functions of reason and passion are to the fore when Hume turns to the question of the origin of the moral distinctions that we make. Hume holds that virtue and vice exist and that we can no more deny their reality than we can deny the reality of the necessary connection between a cause and its effect, or the reality of continuing distinct bodies. But he wishes to know the origin of these ideas, and his approach is the same as in the other cases just mentioned – he searches out the impressions that correspond to the ideas. His approach is to consider the role played by reason and by passion or sentiment in our production of moral judgments. Reason must be considered if only because there was a school of philosophy, the rationalist, which held that our moral concepts and judgments owe everything to reason. We have already noted that on Hume's analysis reason is inert in the sense that it cannot by itself move us to act; we must have a goal in mind. By contrast, a moral judgment to the effect that we ought to produce A motivates us to produce A. If reason cannot by itself motivate us to do anything and moral judgments can, then reason cannot by itself produce moral judgments.

Hume believes that we are motivated by sentiments or passions, for we are prompted to act by love, hate, curiosity, jealousy, and so on. Suppose I hate my neighbour because he practises the trumpet at dead of night and thereby prevents me sleeping. This sentiment does not count as moral disapproval of the agent, because the hate is based solely on my assessment of his act so far as the act conflicts with my own interests. But if I abstract from those interests and consider his act as being unneighbourly in relation not merely to me but to all his neighbours, and if I also abstract from the here and now, and consider how his behaviour would affect people in different eras and in different parts of the world, and if I still find that his behaviour produces in me disagreeable feelings; then my disapproval is moral.[38] The hate that started this process is not the sentiment of moral disapproval that ended the process, for a good deal of modification had to go on in the direction of considering the other's act from the general point of view. I may continue to hate the person whose trumpet playing is keeping me awake, but that sentiment of hate is not the sentiment of moral disapproval which I also feel. The hate is directed to *that* individual; the moral disapproval, on the other hand, is directed to the *character*, or to a character trait, of the agent being judged. A character trait has a certain universality, for there is no limit to the number of people who could have it. So moral disapproval is not a form, even a very calm form, of hate, notwithstanding the fact that it has its origin in hate according to Hume. And, by the same token, moral approval is not a form, even a very calm form, of the sentiment of love, notwithstanding the fact that moral approval has its origin in love.

The character traits that prompt in us the sentiment of moral approval are the various virtues, of which some are classed by Hume as natural and some as artificial. Among the former are generosity, clemency and humanity. A person acting on such a virtue is motivated to perform each of his naturally virtuous acts by the good that will thereby accrue to others. Thus, for example, each act of generosity is aimed at the good of the person on whom the agent acts. The artificial virtues are quite otherwise. Among them are justice, promise-keeping, allegiance to government, treaty-keeping and chastity, though justice is the artificial virtue on which Hume chiefly focuses. Of course justice is a virtue. The motive for just acts is the good of others, and those who recognise that an act is a product of the agent's just disposition will approve of the act. But it is characteristic of a just act that the agent might perform it though knowing that he will not benefit the recipient of the act, and a spectator may not any the less morally approve of the act despite knowing that the person being acted on will not benefit and might even be harmed.

Hume offers examples: 'Judges take from a poor man to give to a rich; they bestow on the dissolute the labour of the industrious; and put into the hands of the vicious the means of harming both themselves and others.'[39] Why do they do it? Hume continues: 'The whole scheme, however, of law and justice is advantageous to the society and to every individual; and 'twas with a view to this advantage, that men, by their voluntary conventions, establish'd it.' Justice is a system of laws of such a content that if everyone obeyed them then everyone in society would be better off than they would be if there were no laws for people to obey. The outcome is that on occasion an act is performed in obedience to the law despite the fact that had the agent been acting from a natural virtue such as humanity he would not have dreamed of performing the act demanded by justice.

That the artificial virtues do on occasion, and perhaps rather often, cut vertically across the natural ones is a poignant reminder of our plight, living as we do in conditions of relative scarcity of resources. There is not so much of everything that anybody could gather up their fill without thereby depriving others of something that they need, so rules arise which give content to the concept of property. If something is yours then the fact that I want it or even need it does not imply my entitlement to take it; since it is yours I cannot make use of it except by your permission. If I take it without your permission then I have acted unjustly even though you have no need of that property and I must have it for the sake of my physical well-being. Civilised living is dependent upon the existence of laws and upon our attendant recognition of our obligation to obey them. A society whose members live under the rule of law is materially far stronger, and can advance culturally far beyond a society which lacks such a system.

SECTION 7: THE STANDARD OF TASTE

In his investigation of moral judgment and the moral life Hume returns repeatedly to the problem of the role of reason and its relation to sentiment or passion, and he encapsulates his solution in the affirmation: 'Reason is the slave of the passions.' Likewise in discussing our aesthetic judgments he investigates the relative roles of reason and sentiment, and in this context also he could have deployed the affirmation: 'Reason is the slave of the passions' in summation of his solution. Hume had intended to include in the *Treatise* material on 'criticism', a field which includes the nature of aesthetic judgment, but for reasons unknown he eventually abandoned the idea. However, he subsequently published several essays in which issues relating to criticism were investigated, and it may be surmised that these essays contain ideas originally intended for the *Treatise*.[40] At any rate, the main points of the essays articulate closely with the *Treatise* and hardly, if at all, conflict with it.

There is wide disagreement in matters of taste, perhaps even wider than is at first apparent, when account is taken of the fact that many agreements regarding taste are in fact agreements about the meaning of terms. For example, all agree, as how could we not, that beauty and elegance are fine things and that ugliness and ungainliness are not, yet not all agree about which things are beautiful, which things are elegant. Nevertheless, no one, unless perhaps a philosopher in the grip of a theory, thinks that anyone's judgment of taste is as good as anyone else's; we believe some judgments to be right, namely our own, and others, those incompatible with ours, to be wrong. We may even believe that the aesthetic judgments of many people are not to be taken seriously. What then are the conditions that a person has to satisfy if his judgment is to be taken seriously on matters of taste? In his seminal essay 'Of the standard of taste'[41] Hume discusses five qualities possessed by a good critic, a person whose judgment should be taken seriously.

First is a delicacy of the imagination that is analogous to the delicacy of physical taste. Hume illustrates this with a tale from Don Quixote regarding two men, with a reputation as wine tasters, who both sample the wine in a hogshead. One likes the wine except, he says, for the slight taste of leather that he detects and the other also likes it except, he says, for its slight taste of iron. They are mocked by bystanders but when the hogshead is emptied a leather thong with a key on it is found at the bottom. These two men had such refined palates that they tasted everything that was there to be tasted and they could also distinguish the separate ingredients. A critic whose judgment is to be taken seriously must likewise be able to distinguish good qualities in a work of art that others might easily miss, and he would be able to argue persuasively for a work by pointing out these features that spectators or audience might otherwise miss.

Second is a record of practice, of attending again and again to a given work and to other works by the same writer or composer or painter. Such experience has a natural tendency to produce in us more exact, refined feelings. Those whose feelings have been thus educated are more likely to produce judgments of taste that are worth listening to, and to be able to use arguments effectively to persuade others of the merit of a work.

Third is a record of making comparisons. To know what is good and what bad we need to have surveyed the field; what we judge to be good we so judge because we think it better than the things we judge to be less good among the objects that we have surveyed. All judgments of taste, if they are to be well informed, must rest in part on such comparisons with other objects of the same kind; it is only by comparison that we become sensitised to what is there. We come to notice and to distinguish things whose subtlety or fineness mean that at first they will escape our view.

Fourth is freedom from prejudice. In assessing an object we must factor out our relation to the creator of the work. Our friendship or enmity should be of no consequence in the judgment of taste; if it becomes of consequence it distorts or corrupts the judgment. So, adds Hume, I must consider myself as 'a man in general' and should forget my 'individual being'. This precisely parallels his doctrine of the need for the general point of view in judgments of morals.

Finally, good sense is required. For example, it is needed in judging whether the characters in a work of fiction are portrayed with due consistency. Do they speak and act as such a character would? Do the different *dramatis personae* respond to each other as one would expect? In short, has the author produced something which is, if not true, at least credible? Good sense is our guide in answering such questions.

With these criteria we can identify a 'good critic', and the criteria have the advantage that they concern matters of fact and are empirically verifiable. Certainly criteria two to five can be checked empirically, and likewise the first, delicacy of sentiment. A good critic is especially sensitive to the features of a work of art that make it pleasing. What sorts of features are these? Hume replies that they are features found in great works, ones that have stood the test of centuries, if not millennia. The *Illiad* and the *Aeneid* have them, and a person blessed with delicacy of sentiment will notice these features, even if they are only barely present in other works and even if they have to compete with other, louder, brasher qualities. The great works that have stood the test of time play a major role in Hume's account of the judgment of taste. The great works are unquestionably good – for while other works have come and gone as fashion has changed, these have gone on giving pleasure through the centuries – and other works might reasonably be thought good if they have been judged good by a good critic.

SECTION 8: THE *TREATISE* AND THE *ENQUIRIES*

It is not clear for how long Hume remained satisfied with the *Treatise of Human Nature*, but that he came to have doubts about it is evidenced by the fact that he subsequently published two works, the *Enquiry Concerning Human Understanding* (EHU), which is a substantially revised version of book one of the *Treatise*, and the *Enquiry Concerning the Principles of Morals* (EPM), which is a substantially revised version of book three. Some of the differences between the *Treatise* and the two later works should here be noted.

First, there is no sustained discussion of religion in the *Treatise*, and this despite the fact that the book as a whole is cast in such a form that his contemporaries would reasonably have expected to find just such a discussion there. On the other hand, two sections of *EHU* are on religious topics, and this despite the fact that the form of *EHU* would not prompt in contemporaries the same lively expectation that it would contain substantial material on religion. Next, the *Treatise* is replete with associationist doctrines, and yet they receive rather little mention in either *Enquiry*, this despite the fact that, as will be recalled, Hume had said in the anonymous *Abstract*: 'if any thing can entitle the author to so glorious name as that of an *inventor*, 'tis the use he makes of the principle of the association of ideas, which enters into most of his philosophy.' For example, the *Treatise*'s discussion of sympathy is heavily associationist and yet the doctrine of sympathy in *EPM* is shorn of associationism. A further difference is that the heavy scepticism of the *Treatise* is hardly present in either *Enquiry*. Arguments for the claim that the external world is a fiction do not put in an appearance in *EHU* where external bodies are discussed, and there is no trace in either *Enquiry* of Hume's lengthy investigation of personal identity. Likewise the important distinction between natural and artificial virtues is not put to work in *EPM*. On the other hand, some of Hume's doctrines in the *Treatise* reappear in the *Enquiries* with new material added, for example in the discussions on causation and freedom of the will.

There is room for dispute concerning whether the omissions of significant parts of the *Treatise* (including almost the whole of book two) are due to his wish to make his philosophy more palatable or whether he changed his mind on major issues. Each position is implied by several strong statements of Hume's. Beyond giving the above list of areas where modification occurred I shall, with one exception, not enter into this territory. The exception concerns religion. However, this area is particularly problematic because it is known that he originally intended to include material on religion in the *Treatise*. Writing to Henry Home in December 1737, Hume enclosed a piece entitled *Reasonings concerning Miracles*, 'which I once thought of publishing with the rest, [namely in the *Treatise*] but which I am afraid will give too much offence, even as the world is disposed at present'.[42] Hume also composed an early piece on evil, in which he expounds the view that the existence of evil implies that nature does not proceed in fulfilment of a morally motivated plan, and this latter piece may also have been written originally for the *Treatise*.[43] These two pieces aside, there seem to be no other writings by Hume on religion that would have been to hand when he prepared the final version of the *Treatise* for publication. It may fairly be speculated that it was a redraft of *Reasonings concerning Miracles* that appeared as section 10, 'Of miracles', in *EHU*.

SECTION 9: HUME 'THE GREAT INFIDEL'

By the mid-1730s Hume was writing on religion, and he continued to write on it till his dying days. So strong was this abiding concern and so deeply philosophical was his engagement that the desire to resolve the questions at issue may well have been the single most powerful driving force of his philosophy.

Hume approaches the field of religious belief with two large questions: what are the psychological causes of our believing religious claims, and by what arguments can the beliefs be supported? The first question concerns the process of belief formation, and he answers it in terms of features of our psychological nature that make religious beliefs well-nigh irresistible given our physical circumstances. The second question is answered in terms of the logical merits and demerits of arguments for the existence of God, and in particular for the existence of a God who has a given set of moral and other attributes. Hume will seek to demonstrate both that reason is not up to the task of delivering sound arguments in support of our religious beliefs and also that the beliefs are in place almost solely on account of features of our sentimental or passionate nature. Hume's sentimentalist, anti-rationalist stance, evident elsewhere in his philosophy, is no less evident in his work on religion. Of his two great writings on religion, the *Natural History of Religion* (1757) spells out the sentimentalist strand of his thinking and the *Dialogues concerning Natural Religion* (1779) spell out the anti-rationalist strand. Both writings fall within the project defined by the subtitle of the *Treatise*: 'being an attempt to introduce the experimental method of reasoning into moral subjects'. The fact that we believe in God counts as a 'moral subject', as indeed do all our acts of belief, given the broad sense of 'moral' with which Hume was working, and it is the experimental method that is at issue throughout; for starting from empirical facts Hume proceeds, by deployment of a plausible empirical psychological model, to a set of empirical conclusions. Regarding the *Natural History*, the question at issue is one for empirical psychology concerning the features of the human mind that cause us to have our beliefs. Regarding the *Dialogues*, the question at issue concerns the empirical evidence for divine existence and for the divinity's having particular attributes, especially moral ones. Thus the *Dialogues* start from broad features of the world we experience and discuss how far we can go towards establishing the existence of a divinity responsible for what we experience.

In the *Natural History* Hume argues that our psychological machinery, part of the frame of our nature, works on our fears and anxieties prompted by our circumstances, and produces a belief in invisible spirits or powers who control fear-inducing events in our environment; in short, by means of our own imaginative activity we come to believe in gods. Hume's account of our belief in the external world provides a suggestive parallel. We note his words in *Treatise* 1.4.2: 'We may well ask, *What causes induce us to believe in the existence of body?* but 'tis in vain to ask, *Whether there be body or not?* That is a point, which we must take for granted in all our reasonings.' In *The Natural History* he could well have written: 'We may well ask, *What causes induce us to believe in the existence of a god?* but 'tis in vain to ask, *Whether there be a god or not?* That is a point, which we must take for granted in all our reasonings.' Indeed, the distinction between the latter two questions is implicit in the opening sentence of the *Natural History*, where Hume affirms that with regard to religion there are two questions which challenge our attention: 'that concerning its foundation in reason, and that concerning its origin in human nature'. The answer to the first is given immediately: 'The whole frame of nature bespeaks an intelligent author; and no rational enquirer can, after serious reflection, suspend his belief a moment with regard to the primary principles of genuine Theism and Religion.'[44] So, as with the question whether there is body, the answer he now gives is an immediate if equivocal 'yes', equivocal because in the *Dialogues* Hume seeks to show that reason's attempt to establish the existence and the attributes of God highlights reason's frailty in this area. To deal with the second question, '*What causes induce us to believe in the existence of God?*', the *Natural History* offers a detailed answer – one, however, which explains why we would believe in a god whether or not any god existed, which is to say that our belief in God can get along just as well even if there is in reality no God.

Hume was familiar with histories of religion by divines who treated the Bible as testimony by reliable witnesses, and in the *Enquiry Concerning Human Understanding* section 10 he enquires into this type of argument, focusing on the question of the criteria that have to be satisfied if a person is to be judged a credible witness. He does not raise the question whether miracles actually occurred. The question instead remains entirely within the realms of empirical scientific enquiry – how to measure the quality of testimony; and he replies that the testimony that supports the laws of nature is so great that no testimony for a miracle can be sufficient to outweigh that for the law of nature with which the alleged miracle is in conflict. Likewise, in the *Natural History*, Hume is not interested in whether a particular religious belief is true but instead he asks why any religious belief should ever have arisen. Again, therefore, the truth of the belief is not at issue; instead at issue is a purely natural event, namely someone's believing something.

There is, however, an important difference between the case of belief in the external world and belief in a god or gods, namely the fact that Hume ascribes the belief in gods to secondary principles of our nature rather than to primary principles such as those that underpin our belief in the external world. Nevertheless, he clearly thinks that the secondary principles in question have very deep roots as is implied by the fact that religious belief is almost universal in the human race. It is evident from these remarks that the *Natural History* is a further step in the programme of the *Treatise*, and it is easy to suppose that had Hume been minded to include in the *Treatise* a part on religion the *Natural History* would have fitted easily into that expanded work.

Hume holds that there are sufficient hard empirical facts to justify the conclusion that the historical starting point of religion is polytheism. For first, there is the 'clear testimony of history'. We do not have records of the earliest period of the human race, but 'the most ancient records' that we do have show those earliest recorded people to have been polytheists. Hume conjectures that earlier peoples were more ignorant and barbarous than later peoples; he adds the premiss that polytheism is error and monotheism truth, and concludes that the human race could not have accepted the truth of monotheism when they were more ignorant and barbarous and then accepted the error of polytheism in the earliest historically recorded times – there is a natural progress by which we rise gradually from the inferior to the superior.

A doubt should be registered regarding Hume's argument. In the *Natural History* section 11 Hume reveals that he regards polytheism as morally superior to monotheism in that, as tending to inclusivity, polytheism promotes the virtue of tolerance whereas monotheism, as tending to exclusivity, promotes intolerance. In that case, if polytheism were the first religion on the scene, then, as regards the virtue of tolerance, the morally superior preceded the morally inferior – which is not at all according to Hume's claim that there is a natural progress of human thought by which we rise gradually from the inferior to the superior.

However, Hume thinks that there is also another kind of evidence for the historical priority of polytheism, namely the practices of present 'barbarous nations' – the 'savage tribes of America, Africa and Asia' – all of whom are polytheists, worshippers of idols. The unstated premiss here is that if present-day primitive peoples, and other primitive peoples in recorded history, are polytheistic then peoples prior to recorded history must also have been polytheistic. This argument is not water-tight, but it is not intended as more than a persuasive argument from analogy. Modern primitives are, after all, not quite like earlier primitives for, by definition, they belong to a line with a longer cultural history, and may in theory have reached their polytheism by a quite complex route that included religious beliefs that were not polytheistic. Nevertheless, there clearly are quite close similarities between the primitive peoples of the earliest recorded history and of recent recorded history, and that is all that Hume needs as a basis for his conjecture about the earliest peoples.

There are at least two kinds of religion, 'popular' and 'philosophical'. The former are the kind that most people profess: Buddhism, Hinduism, Islam and so on. Philosophical religion is the kind that arises from philosophical insights about the universe, particularly as regards its orderliness. Popular religions, on the contrary, have their origin in the perception of the disorderliness of things. Hume has in mind the fact that sometimes the weather helps us to flourish and sometimes it is destructive, sometimes rivers deliver up food and sometimes they inundate and destroy, and so on. In the face of this disorder, we bring to bear a human tendency to personalise the principles of change. We know ourselves as agents, that is, intelligent and active beings, and we naturally read the helpful natural events and the calamitous ones as products of beings who are like us except that they are more powerful and are invisible. These invisible powers are to be feared, and the natural human response is the same as our natural response to humans whom also we fear, namely, to appease them.

As there are divisions of labour among humans so we have a natural tendency to suppose such divisions among the invisible powers; and in this way there arises the idea of a multiplicity of gods, with the different gods identified by their different functions or areas of activity. In time monotheism arises, not through philosophical insight but from the gradual development of an especial fear of one of the gods. Through that fear, people declare him to be the only god, the only one from whom we may, through due appeasement, receive benefit. The motivation for this acceptance of the one god is the fear of the evils that will befall those who do not acknowledge his oneness.

In an important passage Hume speaks of a flux and reflux of polytheism and monotheism.[45] He has in mind a movement by which the god of monotheism becomes intellectually so hard to grasp that intermediaries are invented in order to fill the gap that used to be filled by a number of gods, and, since the intermediaries could not fulfil their function unless they were divine, polytheism is reintroduced. For Hume these are the opening stages in an oscillatory process.

It is appropriate to wonder whether we would fare equally well (or equally badly) under polytheism and monotheism, and on this matter Hume suggests that had we a choice we would be wise to choose polytheism, not because it is so good but because it is less awful, its chief mitigating feature being its tolerance. On the whole each polytheistic sect tolerates the rites of all the others, for there is a fundamental compatibility of beliefs and practices. As contrasted with the 'tolerating spirit of idolaters',[46] monotheism is intolerant because each sect thinks that it alone has grasped the truth and that it is entitled not to tolerate the beliefs and practices of those errorful people who are outwith the sect. There are, as Hume acknowledges, some monotheistic societies which are tolerant on matters of religion, and here he has in mind Britain and the Low Countries; but he accounts for this in terms of the spirit of liberty and tolerance motivating the civil magistrates rather than the spirit motivating the clergy.

The *Natural History* provides a case for the claim that religion would be a dominant feature of our lives whether or not any religious claims were true. Hence the fact (if it be a fact) that almost everyone has some religious belief is not evidence, strong or weak, for the existence of a god or gods. Whether there is a good argument for the existence of gods is not a question addressed in the *Natural History*. It is in the *Dialogues concerning Natural Religion* that the question of the rational, as opposed to the psychological, basis of religious belief is foregrounded.

One of the *personae* of the *Dialogues*, Cleanthes (who has 'an accurate philosophical turn' according to Pamphilus, who relates the conversation), presents a version of the design argument for the existence of God. The argument notes that the adaptation of means to ends is to be found in nature, and that such adaptation in nature 'resembles exactly, though it much exceeds' such adaptations in human artefacts. Where the effects closely resemble each other, there, 'by all the rules of analogy', the causes must also resemble each other. Like us, therefore, the artificer of nature must have thought, wisdom and intelligence, though on a proportionally greater scale, matching the relative grandeur of nature.[47]

To this argument Philo (to whom Pamphilus attributes a 'careless scepticism') responds with two related criticisms. First, Cleanthes is envisaging God as a certain kind of human being, even if one vastly greater than we creatures are. Secondly, if the divine artificer is like us in having thought, wisdom and intelligence, then the question of the source of means-ends order in the world has merely been set back a step rather than answered. For we ourselves in respect of our minds have an orderliness of precisely the kind whose existence is to be explained, and if the divine artificer's mind has that kind of orderliness then his is no less in need of explanation. Hence the quasi-human nature of the divine artificer invoked by Cleanthes merely serves to reintroduce the problem it was invoked to solve.

In any case, is it necessary to look outside the natural world for an explanation for why the world is as it is? We know of many principles, physical, chemical, vegetative and so on, which determine how things come to be as they are, and these principles separately or combined, and without a further, external principle, might produce a universe in which there are means-ends adaptations. To this consideration Philo adds that, so far as we know, we have access to only a tiny corner of the world and should not be seeking to explain everything in terms of just one of the principles of change that happens to be moderately well understood by us. As Philo puts this crucial point: 'What peculiar privilege has this little agitation of the brain which we call thought, that we must thus make it the model of the whole universe?'[48] Since Philo has in mind Cleanthes' anthropomorphic account of God, there is here a quite particular concern expressed, namely the fact that of the perhaps countless principles of change in the universe Cleanthes has opted to explain the appearance of the whole world in terms of a principle that lies within ourselves, our own intelligence. Of course, we are well placed to talk only about what lies within our experience, but then we should remain aware of the limits of our experience and of the inadequacy of our reason when we seek to deploy it beyond our experience.

If we suppose, however, that God exists, a question may be raised concerning the rational grounds for ascribing to him justice, mercy, benevolence and other attributes routinely ascribed to him. Philo wishes to learn whether these various claims are justified. It is the suffering in the world that concerns him. If God does indeed have the moral attributes ascribed to him this surely has empirical implications. If it does not, then how, if at all, are we to understand claims regarding God's providential concern for us?

Cleanthes affirms that there is a preponderance of pleasure over pain in the world, and Hume produces two heartfelt responses. The first is to impress us with the harsh reality that needs to be squared with the existence of a good God:

> Admitting your position, replied PHILO, which yet is extremely doubtful, you must, at the same time, allow, that, if pain be less frequent than pleasure, it is infinitely more violent and durable. One hour of it is often able to outweigh a day, a week, a month of our common insipid enjoyments: And how many days, weeks, and months are passed by several in the most acute torments . . . But pain often, Good God, how often! rises to torture and agony; and the longer it continues, it becomes still more genuine agony and torture.[49]

This powerful piece of rhetoric hints at a rejection of the doctrine that God has providential concern for his creatures, and indeed suggests that God is indifferent to our existence, for otherwise, as a morally perfect being, he would surely do something to prevent or at least to relieve the unbearable pain of his creatures.

The second response makes a logical point on the basis of this harsh reality. Philo affirms to Cleanthes:

> But allowing you, what never will be believed; at least, what you never possibly can prove, that animal, or at least, human happiness, in this life, exceeds its misery; you have yet done nothing: For this is not, by any means, what we expect from infinite power, infinite wisdom, and infinite goodness. Why is there any misery at all in the world?[50]

Not by God's intention, since he is perfectly benevolent; nor contrary to his intention, since he is almighty. Is he then a God of indifference?

The position that Philo has staked out against Cleanthes is in fact stronger than so far indicated, for even if by some philosophical magic Cleanthes can demonstrate that the suffering in the world is somehow compatible with the divine moral attributes of benevolence and of providential concern for his creatures, Cleanthes will not have done enough, for the question is not merely one of compatibility. Cleanthes, like Philo, is deploying the 'experimental method of reasoning'. Both men are starting from empirically ascertainable facts. Philo says that these are not the facts that you would expect in a world governed by a benevolent God who has providential concern for his creatures. Cleanthes must demonstrate, on the basis of the empirical facts, that God does indeed have the moral attributes he ascribes to him. But if we restrict ourselves to the empirical facts, and do not have resort to revelation, Cleanthes seems to confront an impossible task, for in arguing from effect to cause we must not attribute to the cause more than is necessary to explain the effect, and therefore in arguing from a world which contains much good and much evil it is not logically permissible to conclude that the cause of the world has the moral perfections that Cleanthes ascribes to God.

What conclusion is to be drawn? The dying Hume, still preoccupied with questions of religion, wrote the following:

> If the whole of natural theology, as some people seem to maintain, resolves itself into one simple, though somewhat ambiguous, at least undefined proposition, *that the cause or causes of order in the universe probably bear some remote analogy to human intelligence*: If this proposition be not capable of extension, variation, or more particular explication: If it afford no inference that affects human life, or can be the source of any action or forbearance: If the analogy, imperfect as it is, can be carried no farther than to the human intelligence; and cannot be transferred, with any appearance of probability, to the other qualities of the mind: If this really be the case, what can the most inquisitive, contemplative, and religious man do more than give a plain, philosophical assent to the proposition, as often as it occurs: and believe that the arguments, on which it is established, exceed the objections which lie against it?[51]

How to characterise Hume's stance? Hume affirms: 'A wise man, therefore, proportions his belief to the evidence.'[52] On that basis, Hume is at least committed to moral atheism, for he holds that there is no evidence that there is a God who has the moral attributes ascribed to him by the religious, no evidence therefore that there is a benevolent God with providential concern for us. What we are left with is a cause of order in the universe which probably has some remote analogy to human intelligence. The existence of this cause has no implication whatever for the way we either do or should behave. It cannot be a ground of moral virtue, nor of religious practices, such as prayer or ministration of the sacraments. We are left therefore, at most, with something that is remotely similar to human intelligence but is in practice valueless. If one can be a deist by believing that the universe possesses a cause of order that has some remote analogy to human intelligence, then Hume is a deist. But if so then he is a deist of the most etiolated possible kind. Hume speaks about a 'mitigated scepticism' possessed by those reflective enough to recognise 'the universal perplexity and confusion, which is inherent in human nature'. Hume, the most mitigated of mitigated sceptics, concludes that: 'In general, there is a degree of doubt, and caution, and modesty, which, in all kinds of scrutiny and decision, ought for ever to accompany a just reasoner.'[53] A closely related version of this form of mitigated scepticism prompts us to 'the limitation of our enquiries to such subjects as are best adapted to the narrow capacity of human understanding', by which, he tells us, he means that we should confine ourselves, in our reasoning, to the 'common life' and to such subjects as fall under daily practice and experience. Other topics can be left to the 'embellishment of poets and orators, or to the arts of priests and politicians'.[54]

Via the *persona* of Philo, he has argued for a form of deism that is totally shorn of religious significance. In a sense the victim of the argument of the *Dialogues* is the faculty of reason itself, for reason is cross-examined to determine whether it is up to the task of delivering substantive truths on God, and all the arguments point to the conclusion that reason cannot deliver. For in the realm of religion it is seeking to operate beyond the bounds of experience, and it cannot succeed in such an enterprise. To borrow a phrase from Immanuel Kant, reason operating beyond experience is like a bird flapping its wings in the void. To classify Hume as an 'atheist' *tout court* would be a step too far. Nevertheless, application of the 'experimental method of reasoning' to the concept of God as a providential being who has due concern for his creatures reveals no evidence whatever of the existence of such a being. If there were a justification for religion it could only be the pragmatic one that those who are religious are demonstrably on the side of morality and civic virtue. But Hume looks at the behaviour of religious communities and finds no grounds for such a justification.

Notes

1. See Hume, *My Own Life*, reprinted in Hume, *Essays*, ed. Miller, p. xxxii (hereinafter *Essays*).
2. Hume's family spelled their name 'Home'. It was at some point during his thirties that Hume himself changed the spelling of his name to 'Hume'.
3. The numeral 2 written beside Hume's signature in the Greek professor's matriculation register on 27 February 1723 indicates that he was then in his second year of attendance.
4. Hume, *Letters*, ed. Greig, letter 3, vol. 1, p. 13.
5. Hume, *My Own Life*, in *Essays*, p. xxxiv.
6. M. A. Stewart, *The Kirk and the Infidel* (Inaugural Lecture) (Lancaster: Lancaster University Press, 1994).

7. Hume, *My Own Life*, in *Essays*, p. xxxvi.

8. R. L. Emerson, 'The "affair" at Edinburgh and the "project" at Glasgow: the politics of Hume's attempts to become a professor', in Stewart and Wright (eds), *Hume and Hume's Connexions*, pp. 1–22.

9. Hume, *Letters*, vol. 2, p. 452 (in letter dated 9 November 1776, from Smith to William Strahan).

10. The most widely available edition of *A Treatise of Human Nature* is that by L. A. Selby-Bigge, but I have chosen to use the recently published critical edition by David F. Norton and Mary Norton. All page references are to this edition (hereinafter *Treatise*). For those without access to the Norton edition I have also used the standard 'book, part, section' way of referencing passages.

11. *Treatise*, 1.1.1, p. 8.

12. Ibid. 1.1.1, p. 10.

13. Ibid. 1.1.4, p. 12.

14. Ibid. 1.1.4, p. 14.

15. Ibid. *Abstract*, pp. 416–17.

16. Berkeley, *A Treatise Concerning the Principles of Human Knowledge* (London, 1710), Introduction, sects 6–20, and Berkeley, *A New Theory of Vision* (London, 1709), sects 122–5.

17. These are the subject of *Treatise*, 1.2.

18. *Treatise*, Abstract, p. 410.

19. *Treatise*, 1.3.5, p. 67.

20. 'An idea assented to *feels* different from a fictitious idea, that the fancy alone presents to us . . . it [namely belief] is something *felt* by the mind, which distinguishes the ideas of the judgment from the fictions of the imagination' (*Treatise*, 1.3.7, p. 68). Cf *Enquiry Concerning Human Understanding*, ed. Beauchamp, V.II, p. 124 (hereafter *EHU*): 'the difference between *fiction* and *belief* lies in some sentiment or feeling, which is annexed to the latter, not to the former'. In this last-mentioned passage Hume has in mind the difference in vividness and liveliness between fictions and beliefs.

21. *Treatise*, 1.3.2, p. 55.

22. Ibid. 1.4.2, p. 125. The full answer is developed through 1.4.2: 'Of scepticism with regard to the senses'.

23. Ibid. 1.4.2, p. 132.

24. Ibid. 1.4.2, pp. 133, 136, 138.

25. Ibid. 1.4.6, p. 165.

26. Ibid. 1.4.6, p. 166.

27. Ibid. 1.4.6, p. 166. See also p. 169: 'The identity, which we ascribe to the mind of man, is only a fictitious one, and of a like kind with that which we ascribe to vegetables and animal bodies.'

28. Ibid. 1.4.7, p. 172.

29. Ibid. 1.4.7, p. 175.

30. Direct passions are 'such as arise immediately from good or evil, from pain or pleasure'. The indirect passions likewise arise from good and evil, from pleasure and pain, but not directly, for they also require the exercise of the associative principles of resemblance, contiguity and causation. See *Treatise*, 2.1.1, p. 182.
31. Ibid. 2.1.11, p. 206.
32. Ibid. 2.3.1, p. 257.
33. Ibid. 2.3.1, p. 257.
34. Ibid. 2.3.1, pp. 258–9.
35. Ibid. 2.3.2, pp. 262–3.
36. Ibid. 2.3.2, p. 262.
37. Ibid. 2.3.3, p. 266.
38. Ibid. 3.1.2, p. 303.
39. Ibid. 3.3.1, p. 370.
40. See especially 'Of the delicacy of taste and passion', 'Of eloquence', 'Of tragedy', 'Of the standard of taste' and 'Of refinement in the arts', in Hume, *Essays*.
41. *Essays*, pp. 226–49.
42. Hume, *Letters*, vol. 1. p. 24.
43. M. A. Stewart, 'An early fragment on evil', in Stewart and Wright (eds), *Hume and Hume's Connexions*, pp. 160–70.
44. Hume, *Principal Writings*, ed. Gaskin, p. 134.
45. Ibid. pp. 158ff.
46. Ibid. p.161.
47. Ibid. p. 45.
48. Ibid. p. 50.
49. Ibid. p. 102.
50. Ibid. p. 103.
51. Ibid. p. 129.
52. *EHU*, X.I, p. 170.
53. Ibid. XII.III, p. 208.
54. Ibid. XII.III, p. 208.

CHAPTER 8

Adam Smith

SECTION 1: A PORTRAIT OF ADAM SMITH

Smith was born in Kirkcaldy, Fife, in 1723.[1] His father, also named Adam Smith, an Edinburgh lawyer and later comptroller of customs at Kirkcaldy, died shortly before his son was born, and young Adam was brought up by his mother Margaret Douglas (d. 1784), to whom he remained devoted and with whom he lived for much the greater part of his life.

Smith learned Latin at his school in Kirkcaldy and then at the age of fourteen went up to Glasgow University, where his subjects were Latin, Greek, mathematics, science and philosophy. Thereafter he remembered with affection his Glasgow teacher, the 'never to be forgotten Dr Hutcheson', and also spoke very respectfully of another Glasgow professor, the mathematician Robert Simson. Writing of Simpson and of the Edinburgh mathematician Matthew Stewart (father of the philosopher Dugald Stewart), he affirmed that they were 'the two greatest mathematicians that I ever have had the honour to be known to' and added that they were 'the two greatest [mathematicians] that have lived in my time'.[2] These references are important as indicating Smith's early and lasting interest in science including the mathematical sciences. He was not a practising scientist and made no significant contribution to mathematics, physics or the other natural sciences, but he wrote with real sophistication about the philosophical dimension of the great scientific enterprise of western Europe.

After three years at Glasgow he won an exhibition (a scholarship) to Balliol College, Oxford, where he read widely in science, particularly physics and astronomy, as well as in moral philosophy and metaphysics, particularly the classical authors and philosophers of seventeenth- and eighteenth-century Britain and France. He was not complimentary about the education then available at Oxford, but he derived immense educational benefit from his six years there in view of his self-imposed programme of study. It was almost certainly during those years that he drafted his *History of Astronomy*, a work that required detailed knowledge of Newtonian mechanics and mathematics as well as a deep understanding of pre-Newtonian systems of astronomy.[3] Thereafter Smith remained close to science and to scientists, to the extent that the executors of his will were two of the greatest scientists of the age, his long-standing friends Joseph Black and James Hutton.

In 1746, after six years at Balliol, he left Oxford and returned to Kirkcaldy, where after two years he received, through the good offices of Henry Hume, an invitation to deliver a course of lectures on rhetoric in Edinburgh. This was to be a public course, not one delivered under the auspices of the university. It was delivered in 1748 and in the following two years also. When therefore in 1751 the chair of logic and rhetoric at Glasgow University became available Smith applied as someone experienced in teaching at least one of the disciplines represented by the chair. The application was successful and he began lecturing on rhetoric in Glasgow. There is an extant copy of a set of student notes of the Glasgow lectures on rhetoric,[4] though there is no known copy of the Edinburgh lectures.

A year after taking up the chair of logic and rhetoric, Smith moved to the chair of moral philosophy that had just become available, and thus became a successor to his 'never to be forgotten Dr Hutcheson'. He remained in post until 1764. During those years he lectured in the mornings on natural theology (including the existence and attributes of God), ethics, natural jurisprudence and political economy. There have come down to us no writings by Smith on natural theology, though such indications as we have from his writings and from the student notes of his lectures suggest that he was not a Christian and leave open the question whether he was in any significant sense a believer in a deity. To become professor of moral philosophy Smith had to sign the Westminster Confessions and to undertake to lead the students in prayer each morning. It is reported that he sought exemption from the latter and that the request was turned down. What is to be made of the fact that he was prepared to sign the Calvinist doctrine that lays out in detail what the Church of Scotland stands for is not clear, though by Smith's time the signature may have meant no more than does our own 'yours faithfully' or 'yours sincerely' at the end of a letter. In which context it may be recalled that Hume, who was certainly not a Christian and arguably was at most a deist of the most attenuated sort, showed himself willing to sign that same Calvinist document when he applied for the logic and rhetoric chair at Glasgow.

Smith's lectures on ethics transmogrified into his first masterpiece, *The Theory of Moral Sentiments*, which appeared in 1759 and went through five further editions during the author's lifetime, with particularly significant changes made to the second edition (1761) and the sixth (1790). The lectures on jurisprudence and on political economy eventually transmogrified into Smith's other masterpiece, *An Inquiry into the Nature and Causes of the Wealth of Nations* (1776), of which five editions appeared during the author's lifetime. There are also extant sets of student reports on Smith's lectures on jurisprudence,[5] covering among many other topics the development of the law concerning property and the attendant 'stadial theory' of human development according to which there are four stages in the natural (even if not certain) progress of human beings from the life of the hunter-gatherer, to that of the herdsman, to that of the farmer, to that of members of a commercial society.

By the time of Smith's arrival at the Glasgow chair he and Hume had become close friends, and on publication of the *Theory of Moral Sentiments* Hume wrote to him about the book: 'Charles Townshend, who passes for the cleverest Fellow in England, is so taken with the Performance, that he said to Oswald [of Dunnikier] he wou'd put the Duke of Buccleugh under the Authors Care, and woud endeavour to make it worth his while to accept of that Charge.'[6] Townshend's recent marriage to Lady Dalkeith had made him stepfather to her three children, one of whom was Henry Scott, Third Duke of Buccleuch. Townshend, later famous as the chancellor of the exchequer whose policy on colonial taxation led to the Boston Tea Party, was as good as his word. Late in 1763 Smith received an invitation to act as tutor to the third duke on the Grand Tour. He accepted and early in the following year went to France with the seventeen-year-old duke. They visited Paris, Montpellier and Geneva, though they spent most of their time in Toulouse. It was a fruitful time for the tutor, who took the opportunity to meet many of the leading participants of the French Enlightenment, including Voltaire, Helvétius, Turgot and Quesnay. He had meantime also taken under his wing the third duke's younger brother Hew, who not long after fell ill and died. Smith returned to England with the body in late 1766 and shortly thereafter returned to Kirkcaldy to continue work on the *Wealth of Nations*, which had occupied him since his days in the moral philosophy chair at Glasgow. It was finally published in 1776. Hume, by then a very sick man, read it and sent Smith warm congratulations.

The *Wealth of Nations* is a work of political economy, a discipline different in subject matter and character from the modern, highly mathematical discipline of econometrics. Political economy investigates the behaviour of *Homo economicus* within a political context; questions relating to justice are either on or not far below the surface. For Smith economic acts are also assessible in moral terms, and economic policy is bad policy if it has morally unacceptable consequences. An example should make the point. Regarding the activity of government Smith says that there are three areas that are a government's concern and for which it should pay, namely, defence of the realm, administration of justice, and public works and institutions that private citizens will not on the whole pay for but which have to be in place, including education. The *Wealth of Nations* is based on the principle of division of labour, and Smith was aware of the dangers posed by the principle if carried too far, as it is sure to be. A person who has a minute task to perform and has to perform it ten thousand times a day will become intellectually, morally and spiritually damaged. Smith argues that the proper response, to be paid for by the government, is to set up a system of schooling that will protect the workers, a schooling that includes reading, writing, arithmetic and the more sublime principles of science. It is also stipulated that the schooling should be compulsory. An impressive feature of the *Wealth of Nations* is precisely that Smith anticipates potential moral problems arising from the systematic application of otherwise sound economic practice, and works out in advance the solution to the moral problem with a view to building the solution into the social fabric before the damage is done.

Some months after the publication of the *Wealth of Nations* Smith's closest friend, Hume, died. We noted in the preceding chapter Smith's moving tribute to him: 'Upon the whole, I have always considered him, both in his lifetime and since his death, as approaching as nearly to the idea of a perfectly wise and virtuous man, as perhaps the nature of human frailty will permit.' Since Hume had a reputation as an atheist the tribute brought a vitriolic response, which prompted a brief, sad comment from Smith: 'A single, and as I thought a very harmless Sheet of paper, which I happened to Write concerning the death of our late friend Mr Hume, brought upon me ten times more abuse than the very violent attack I had made upon the whole commercial system of Great Britain.'[7]

In 1778 Smith began work as a commissioner of the Customs Board in Edinburgh, with the task of overseeing the collection of import duties and the prevention of smuggling. This entailed his moving to Edinburgh, where he remained for the last twelve years of his life, having previously spent practically all his life in Kirkcaldy, Glasgow and Oxford. In Edinburgh he was, with Joseph Black and James Hutton, a founder member of the Oyster Club, and in 1783 was a founder member of the Royal Society of Edinburgh. In 1787 he was elected Lord Rector of Glasgow University. His response was fulsome:

> No man can owe greater obligations to a Society than I do to the University of Glasgow . . . The period of thirteen years which I spent as a member of that society I remember as by far the most useful, and, therefore, as by far the happiest and most honourable period of my life.[8]

Shortly before his death Smith told Joseph Black and James Hutton that, aside from certain papers that he specified, he wished all his volumes of manuscripts destroyed without examination. They complied. Smith died on 17 July 1790 and was buried in the Canongate churchyard in Edinburgh. Black and Hutton then published an edition of the papers that they had been asked not to destroy, Smith's *Essays on Philosophical Subjects* (1795), which included some of his earliest thoughts, on the history of astronomy, and some of his last, on aesthetics.

Section 2: Spectatorship and sympathy – Smith's context

In the *Theory of Moral Sentiments* the concept of the spectator takes centre stage. The concept had already been deployed by both Hutcheson and Hume, and it is plausible to see Smith's writings on the spectator as a development of the work of his older colleagues. The urge to relate spectatorship to morality is understandable. To know whether I have acted well or not, I must consult others who are spectators of my action, for if I consult only myself, and if, as is likely, my judgment is affected by my self-love or self-interest, the judgment will be a distortion of the truth.

Both Hutcheson and Hume thought along those lines. Hutcheson maintains that the concept of a spectator, and here he clearly has in mind the disinterested or impartial spectator, is part of the concept of the 'amiability or loveliness of a virtue'. He writes:

> Virtue is then called Amiable or Lovely, from its raising Good-will or Love in Spectators toward the Agent; and not from the Agent's perceiving the virtuous Temper to be advantageous to him, or desiring to

obtain it under that View. A virtuous Temper is called Good or Beatifick . . . from this, that every Spectator is persuaded that the reflex Acts of the virtuous Agent upon his own Temper will give him the highest Pleasures.[9]

There is plainly a sense in which, for Hutcheson, the spectator's judgment has priority over the agent's.

The spectator is again invoked in Hutcheson's discussion of merit or worthiness or reward, for he suggests that 'Rewardable' denotes 'That Quality of Actions which would make a Spectator approve a superior Nature, when he conferred Happiness on the Agent, and disapprove that Superior, who inflicted Misery on the Agent, or punished him'.[10] Here also Hutcheson prioritises the spectator's judgment as against that of the agent observed because the spectator's perspective has a claim to disinterestedness or impartiality. More than a decade before Hume's *Treatise* was published, therefore, and about three decades before the first edition of the *Theory of Moral Sentiments*, seeds of the characteristically Smithian concept of the impartial spectator had already been sown by Smith's teacher.

In outline, at least, Hume's position was close to Hutcheson's. Hume distinguishes between terms such as 'enemy' and 'antagonist', with which a person 'is understood . . . to express sentiments, peculiar to himself', and terms such as 'vicious' and 'depraved', with which he 'expresses sentiments, in which, he expects, all his audience are to concur with him. He must here, therefore, depart from his private and particular situation, and must choose a point of view, common to him with others.'[11] Here therefore the distinctive feature of moral terms is that their use implies a perspective shared with others, one that is not self-interested but impartial. So again the spectator's perspective is prioritised. This feature of Hume's moral theory is underlined when he gives as a definition of 'virtue': *'whatever mental action or quality gives to a spectator the pleasing sentiment of approbation'*.[12]

The concept of sympathy, no less than that of the spectator, was firmly on the moral philosophical agenda in the Scottish Enlightenment before Smith took up his chair at Glasgow, and again Hutcheson and Hume were major players. Hutcheson deployed the fact of sympathy as a crucial part of his anti-Hobbesian doctrine that benevolence is natural to us human beings. By sympathy or compassion

we are dispos'd to study the Interest of others, without any Views of private Advantage . . . Every Mortal is made uneasy by any grievous

> Misery he sees another involv'd in, unless the Person be imagin'd evil, in a moral Sense: Nay, it is almost impossible for us to be unmov'd, even in that Case.[13]

But while Smith, and indeed Hume, would accept this position, they must have seen that Hutcheson's teachings on sympathy left a great deal of work to be done, and in particular that he does not tell us in detail what he takes sympathy to be. Hume and Smith provide details. I considered Hume's position in Chapter 7, so shall simply highlight certain features of Hume's account here in order to provide a basis for cross-reference to Smith.

Although Hume occasionally uses 'sympathy' to refer to a feeling, the whole weight of his exposition is on sympathy as a principle of communication of feelings and opinions. Since as a result of the communication the spectator might share the agent's feeling of dismay or joy, and so on, Humean 'sympathy' is not the same thing as compassion or pity. The spectator observes in the agent's face, voice or behaviour qualities that he takes to signify a given passion or feeling, and in doing so he forms an idea of that feeling. 'This idea is presently converted into an impression, and acquires such a degree of force and vivacity, as to become the very passion itself, and produce an equal emotion, as any original affection.'[14] If the spectator does not believe the agent to have a given passion then he does not sympathise with the agent, for Humean sympathy is a principle of communication by which the spectator comes to have a passion that he believes the agent to have, and he comes to have it because of this belief.

Hume's doctrine of sympathy is rejected by Smith, who holds that it is possible for a spectator sympathetically to have a passion that he does not believe the agent to have, or even that he knows the agent cannot have. On seeing an agent suffer, we spectators form in our imagination a copy of such 'impressions of our own senses' as we have experienced when we have been in a situation of the kind the agent is in. We 'form some idea of his sensations' and even feel something 'which, though weaker in degree, is not altogether unlike them', and we do this by means of the imaginative experiment of placing ourselves in the agent's circumstance: 'we enter as it were into his body, and become in some measure the same person with him'.[15] This last point, that we 'become in some measure the same person with' the agent, is a crucial part of the case that can be made in defence against any claim that Smith's is essentially a 'selfish' system, 'selfish' given that the baseline in the formation of a moral judgment about a person's attitude or behaviour is how *I* would feel if *I* were in that person's shoes.[16] For Smith stresses that in sympathising, the spectator imagines not being himself in the agent's situation but being the *agent* in that situation: 'But though sympathy is very properly said to arise from an imaginary change of situations with the person principally concerned, yet this imaginary change is not supposed to happen to me in my own person and character, but in that of the person with whom I sympathize.' If I sympathetically grieve with you in your bereavement my 'grief . . . is entirely upon your account, and not in the least upon my own. It is not, therefore, in the least selfish.'[17] I do not mean to imply that this can be taken as an effective rebuttal of the charge of selfishness, but only to claim that Smith was aware of the likelihood of an attack from that direction and believed that he had an effective defence.

Delight or happiness, just as much as pity or compassion, could arise by Smithian sympathy. Thus in the *Lectures on Rhetoric and Belles Lettres* Smith deals with the historian's power to produce a wide range of sympathetic responses in the reader: 'We enter into their [namely, human beings'] misfortunes, grieve when they grieve, rejoice when they rejoice, and in a word feel for them in some respect as if we ourselves were in the same condition.'[18] Smith reserves the term 'sympathy' for 'our fellow-feeling for any passion whatever', and emphasises the fact that he is extending the scope of the term. 'Sympathy' is therefore to be understood no less as a technical term in Smith's system than it is in Hume's, and misunderstandings arise when this fact is not taken into account.

In its ordinary sense sympathy is one feeling or emotion among many and resembles pity or compassion. But as Smith uses 'sympathy' the spectator's anger would count as sympathy *qua* fellow-feeling with the agent's anger, and his joy, *qua* fellow-feeling with the agent's joy, would likewise count as sympathy. It is therefore more appropriate to think of sympathy as an adverbial modification of a given feeling, for the term indicates the *way* in which the spectator has the feeling – he has it *sympathetically*. It is the way he is angry, or is joyful, and so on. Hence Smithian sympathy has a kind of universality that has to be contrasted with the singularity of each feeling.

On this basis it is easy to resolve the so-called 'Adam Smith problem'. It is alleged that Smith's two masterpieces are mutually incompatible, that the *Theory of Moral Sentiments* is based on the motive of sympathy and the *Wealth of Nations* on the motive of self-interest. It is not at issue that self-interest is the main motive assumed in the *Wealth of Nations*:

> Give me that which I want, and you shall have this which you want . . . it is in this manner that we obtain from one another the far greater part of those good offices which we stand in need of. It is not from the benevolence of the butcher, the brewer, or the baker, that we expect our dinner, but from their regard to their own interest.[19]

Might the two books simply contradict each other? Yet in 1762, a year after the second edition of the *Theory of Moral Sentiments* and five years before the third, Smith was lecturing on the material that grew into the *Wealth of Nations*.[20] The economic theory was being developed therefore within the context of a moral theory that goes wide and deep, a context that carries the message that an economic theory has to be developed within a moral philosophical framework. It is incredible that Smith should forget his moral theory while expounding his economic ideas, and incredible also that he should not forget the moral theory but instead simply fail to notice the contradiction. H. T. Buckle's solution is that our nature has two aspects, one sympathetic, the other selfish, and that in the *Theory of Moral Sentiments* Smith investigates one, in the *Wealth of Nations* the other.[21] But Buckle's interpretation and solution are mistaken, for Smithian sympathy is not the motive for moral action nor indeed is it a motive at all, and therefore it cannot be a motive that excludes the motive of self-interest.[22]

That sympathy has a universality not possessed by the particular feelings is a claim that can also be made of sympathy in the Humean sense, in that if the spectator has a given feeling as a result of the operation of the mechanism of sympathy, the feeling he has is the one he believes the agent to have, no matter what that feeling is. Consequently merely to know that the spectator sympathises is not to know the spectator's feeling, but only to know the way he came by the feeling. Hume uses the term 'sympathy' to refer both to the sympathetic feeling and also to the mechanism by which the feeling is generated. The same is true of Smith.

Smith's account of sympathy seems at first very Humean, including his vocabulary, which invokes a contrast between the *impressions* of the spectator's senses and the *idea* that the spectator forms of the agent's feelings. Nevertheless a feature of sympathy to which Smith frequently refers seems not to be part of Hume's account: 'By the imagination we place ourselves in his [namely, the agent's] situation', and sympathy 'does not arise so much from the view of the passion, as from that of the situation which excites it'.[23] Arguably Smith has Hume in his sights. On Hume's account sympathy arises from the spectator's view of the agent's passion, and he does not discuss the agent's situation. All that we learn is that the spectator's perception of signs of the agent's passion results in the same passion in the spectator; the impression causes an idea of the agent's passion, and the spectator's idea of the agent's passion becomes so enlivened as to be a passion in the spectator. But emphasis on the agent's situation leads Smith to attach less significance to the spectator's perception of the agent's passion in the formation of the spectator's sympathetic feeling. Indeed emphasis on the agent's situation leads Smith to say that the spectator may sympathise with the agent even though he, the spectator, does not have the same feeling as the agent. This is plainly a departure from Hume's position.

Smith deploys some examples of sympathy that fit well the Humean prescription: 'Upon some occasions sympathy may seem to arise merely from the view of a certain emotion in another person . . . Grief and joy, for example, strongly expressed in the look and gestures of any one, at once affect the spectator with some degree of a like painful or agreeable emotion.'[24] Here there is a progression from the spectator's impression to his idea of the agent's passion, and thence to that same passion in the spectator. Smith does not here mention the intermediate idea, but he had previously told us[25] that it is via an idea of the agent's passion that the spectator himself comes to have the passion. But he adds immediately that what is true of grief and joy does not hold universally, and in effect Smith thereby criticises Hume for treating passions such as grief and joy as typical of all passions when in fact they are exceptions. Expression of anger is not sufficient to arouse sympathy; we also need to know the situation of the angry person, in particular the causal factors of his anger. But if we know the situation of those with whom he is angry, the situation being the violence to which they have been exposed by the enraged person, we are if anything inclined to sympathise with them instead. Indeed for Smith knowledge of the situation plays a role even in the case of grief and joy, for the expressions of those passions suggest to us the general idea of some good or ill fortune that has befallen the agent, and without this concept of the agent's situation the spectator would not sympathise with him. But sympathy with a grieving person would not, even if accompanied with this general idea, lead to much sorrow, for the agent's lamentations 'create rather a curiosity to inquire into his situation . . . than any actual sympathy that is very sensible'.[26] It is therefore demonstrable that knowledge of the situation is factored into Smith's account of sympathy.

The agent's own feelings often play a correspondingly insignificant role, and in some cases can play no role at all in view of the fact that the agent does not have the feeling that the spectator has sympathetically for the agent. Smith gives two examples of a sympathetic feeling which does not correspond to the agent's own. The first concerns the agent who has lost his reason. The spectator's sympathetic feeling of sorrow for the agent is not matched by the agent's own feeling, for he is happy, unaware of the tragedy that has befallen him. The spectator considers how he himself would feel were he reduced to the same unhappy situation, and in this imaginative experiment the idea of the agent's situation plays a large role whereas the idea of the agent's feelings has a role only in the sense that the happiness of the agent is itself evidence of his tragedy. The second example is the spectator's sympathy for the dead. Here the spectator has sympathetic feelings which are plainly not matched by the agent's. Once again Smith invokes the agent's situation, emphasising the fact that the spectator comes to sympathise by imagining himself in the agent's situation, and imagining how he himself would feel if so placed.

These examples provide a clue to the correct interpretation of Smith's statement that 'sympathy' may 'without much impropriety' be made use of to denote 'our fellow-feeling for any passion whatever'. 'Fellow-feeling' here does not imply that two people have feelings of the same kind. In ordinary usage my fellow-feeling for you is my commiserating with your sorrow and my rejoicing at your joy, and in this respect Smithian sympathy is even less like sympathy ordinarily understood than is Humean sympathy, for in the case of the latter a sympathetic feeling is a fellow-feeling at least in the sense that it is shared – spectator and agent both have it.

What the spectator does that results in his sympathetic feeling is indicated by several phrases. 'We enter as it were into his [namely, the agent's] body'; we 'become in some measure the same person with him'; 'it is by changing places in fancy with the sufferer'; the spectator, by 'bringing the case home to himself', imagines what should be the sentiments of the sufferer; 'we put ourselves in his case'. These expressions indicate the strangeness of Smith's concept of sympathy with the dead, but the concept, in respect of that example, works hard for Smith. He writes of the 'illusion of the imagination' from which 'arises one of the most important principles in human nature, the dread of death, the great poison to the happiness, but the great restraint upon the injustice of mankind, which, while it afflicts and mortifies the individual, guards and protects the society.'[27]

In the phrase 'we enter as it were into his body', the 'as it were' has to be given due weight, as has 'in some measure' in 'we become in some measure the same person'. Even where the spectator shares the agent's feeling, the spectator's feeling is significantly different in that it is a product of an imaginative act that not only brought the feeling into existence but also sustains it. His sympathetic suffering is due not to his being in the situation he sees the agent in but to his being sympathetic. He only imagines how he would feel if he had suffered the bereavement or insult that the agent suffered, and hence the imaginative act 'excites some degree of the same emotion, in proportion to the vivacity or dulness of the conception'.[28]

Smith recognises that this difference is of practical importance:

> What they [the spectators] feel, will, indeed, always be, in some respects, different from what he [the agent] feels, and compassion can never be exactly the same with original sorrow; because the secret consciousness that the change of situations, from which the sympathetic sentiment arises, is but imaginary, not only lowers it in degree, but, in some measure, varies it in kind, and gives it a quite different modification.[29]

Though imperfect, the correspondence is, however, 'sufficient for the harmony of society' and 'this is all that is wanted or required'.

Section 3: Sympathy and pleasure

Smith believes that though some cases of sympathising are explicable in terms of purely natural causation, many are not. His starting point is the fact (as Smith believes it to be) that sympathy always gives pleasure. He holds that 'nothing pleases us more than to observe in other men a fellow-feeling with all the emotions of our own breast'.[30] Awareness of the spectator's sympathy brings relief to the suffering agent by admixing with the original suffering the pleasure afforded by the sympathy; and the spectator's sympathetic joy enhances or heightens the happy agent's joy by adding the pleasure afforded by his awareness of the spectator's sympathy. It seems to be pleasure that links sympathy with approval or approbation. We learn that for the spectator to approve of the agent's feeling is for him to observe that he sympathises with the agent, and for him to disapprove is to observe that he does not sympathise,[31] in which case approbation should perhaps be classed as a judgment, *contra* Hume, for whom it is a feeling. It should be added that Smith's position appears to be revised shortly thereafter when he speaks of approbation not as an observation but as a feeling: 'This last emotion, in which the sentiment of approbation properly consists, is alway agreeable and delightful.'[32] But so far as a settled doctrine is discernible it is that approbation is not a sentiment but an observation or judgment.

Disagreement motivates us to see whether it can be smoothed out, as if by nature we find it disagreeable to disagree. It may be hard work for a spectator to modify his sentiments so that they agree with the agent's; he must 'endeavour, as much as he can, to put himself in the situation of the other'; he must 'strive to render as perfect as possible, that imaginary change of situation upon which his sympathy is founded';[33] his 'natural feeling of his own distress, his own natural view of his own situation, presses hard upon him, and he cannot, without a very great effort, fix his attention upon that of the impartial spectator'.[34] On one interpretation Smith's awareness of the effort we may have to make to secure agreement, or at least to determine whether agreement is possible, is what led him to emphasise the pleasure associated with sympathy.[35] In brief, if we know that the effort will bring reward in the form of pleasure, or enhanced pleasure, we are motivated to make the effort. However, though this is part of the explanation of our willingness to make the effort, another part, one perhaps more significant for Smith, relates to considerations of fairness to the agent. Whatever love of our neighbour may be it is at least a willingness to make the effort to see things from our neighbour's point of view, and Smith sees this as a Christian stance, though plainly it also involves the Stoic virtue of self-command, a virtue on which elsewhere Smith places great emphasis. Nevertheless, whether or not the duty to exercise this Christian-*cum*-Stoic virtue is a major part of the motivation for the exercise of our sympathetic imagination, Smith does insist on the close relation between pleasure and sympathy.

Smith's position contrasts interestingly with that of Hume, who also attends to the relation between sympathy and pleasure. Hume accounts for sympathy in terms of natural causation and the principles of association of impressions and of ideas, whereas Smith stresses the role of will as against nature. Perhaps the spectator does not naturally sympathise with the agent, and it is by will rather than by nature that he seeks a way to iron out the disagreement. Hume, no less than Smith, writes of the process by which we modify sympathetic feelings,[36] and indeed such processes of modification are essential to Hume's account of the genesis of moral judgment. But Smith factors these modifications into the process of sympathy itself whereas Hume takes them to occur after operation of the mechanism of sympathy.

A distinction is made by Smith in order to deal with a criticism famously made by Hume:

> I wish you had more particularly and fully prov'd, that all kinds of Sympathy are necessarily Agreeable. This is the Hinge of your System, & yet you only mention the Matter cursorily in p. 20.[37] Now it woud appear that there is a disagreeable Sympathy, as well as an agreeable: And indeed, as the Sympathetic Passion is a reflex Image of the principal, it must partake of its Qualities, & be painful where that is so. Indeed, *when we converse with a man with whom we can entirely sympathize*, that is, where there is a warm & intimate Friendship, the cordial openness of such a Commerce overpowers the Pain of a disagreeable Sympathy, and renders the whole Movement agreeable. But in ordinary Cases, this cannot have place. An ill-humord Fellow; a man tir'd & disgusted with every thing, always *ennuié*; sickly, complaining, embarass'd; such a one throws an evident Damp on Company, which I suppose wou'd be accounted for by Sympathy; and yet is disagreeable. It is always thought a difficult Problem to account for the Pleasure, receivd from the Tears & Grief & Sympathy of Tragedy; which woud not be the Case, if all Sympathy was agreeable. An Hospital woud be a more entertaining Place than a Ball.[38]

Two years after receipt of Hume's letter, Smith used the second edition of the *Theory of Moral Sentiments* as the vehicle for his reply:

> I answer, that in the sentiment of approbation there are two things to be taken notice of; first, the sympathetic passion of the spectator; and, secondly, the emotion which arises from his observing the perfect coincidence between this sympathetic passion in himself, and the original passion in the person principally concerned. This last emotion, in which the sentiment of approbation properly consists, is always agreeable and delightful. The other may either be agreeable or disagreeable, according to the nature of the original passion, whose features it must always, in some measure, retain.[39]

This distinction is evidently justified; there is surely a difference between the feeling that the spectator has that is the 'reflex Image' of the agent's, and the spectator's feeling that arises from his observation of the perfect coincidence of his feeling with that of the agent. But Smith's claim to have 'entirely discomfitted' Hume[40] is almost certainly false. Smith's rebuttal begs the question whether observation of agreement gives rise to an agreeable feeling. Smith states that it does, but Hume has already said that 'in ordinary Cases, this cannot have Place'. By implication Hume is accusing Smith of treating an exceptional case as if it is typical of all cases. The exceptional case is that in which a person sympathises with a friend, when it might well be that the spectator's observation of agreement of feeling with his friend, the agent, gives rise to pleasure, but in the case of friendship a good deal of baggage comes along within the relationship which might easily explain why sympathy is associated with pleasure. What Hume wants to know is what is to be said of cases in which the spectator is not a friend of the agent and perhaps indeed dislikes him. On Hume's view Smith silently assumes that the agent is indeed a friend, though it is precisely in this kind of case that an argument is required, not just an assumption.

Smith cannot be right in saying that the emotion which arises from observation of the agreement in feelings is *always* agreeable, if Hume is right regarding his example of the '*ennuié*' who 'throws an evident Damp on Company'. Hume plainly believes that the issue can be settled by empirical means, and Smith would surely agree. He is not simply stipulating usage for the term 'sympathy'; he is telling us how things are, and must say what is wrong with Hume's counter-example. Nor is Smith's case defended effectively by pointing out that his concept of sympathy is significantly different from the one Hume develops in the *Treatise*. For first, Hume would not make the methodologically flawed move of attacking Smith's account of sympathy on the basis of a concept of sympathy that is not Smith's, and secondly, it is in any case difficult to see how Smith, even on his own terms, can deal plausibly with Hume's counter-example.

In this dispute something important is at stake: our motivation to strive for coincidence of feeling. I turn now to this striving and therefore to Smith's discussions of propriety, impropriety, merit and demerit, and his account of the impartial spectator. The systematic relations between propriety and impropriety on the one side and merit and demerit on the other are expounded in detail in the *Theory of Moral Sentiments*.

SECTION 4: SYMPATHY AND MORAL CATEGORIES

The natural desire to approve and be approved of has the consequence that sympathy must be able to operate within a dynamic social context. Where a spectator's immediate reaction to an agent is not one of approval, he may not let the matter rest there. Hume's distinction between an agent who is a friend and one who is not is pertinent here, for the spectator's natural tendency may be to leave his disapproval in place if the agent is an enemy or at least not a friend, for in general it is easier to think ill of one's enemies than to think well of them, but if a friend's behaviour prompts an immediate reaction of disapproval the spectator's natural tendency is to wonder whether the agent's behaviour was as inappropriate as at first it seemed. If in the latter case the spectator will naturally move to see whether the disagreement can be ironed out; in the former case he will move (if at all) in the light of the moral injunction to be fair. In both cases, however, his tactic is the same – by an exercise of informed imagination to fit himself as well as he can into the situation of the agent and see whether there are features of that situation that he overlooked initially. The spectator's question 'What is he seeing that I am failing to see?' can therefore lead to a change not only in his perspective but also in his feelings.

Smith provides telling examples of a spectator asking himself this question. He considers the case in which we no longer derive amusement from a book or poem but take pleasure in reading the work to another person: 'we consider all the ideas which it presents rather in the light in which they appear to him, than in that in which they appear to ourselves, and we are amused by sympathy with his amusement which thus enlivens our own.'[41] Likewise in reacting to the agent's display of feeling, where those are not the feelings that the spectator approves of or thinks appropriate, the spectator probes the agent's intentions, motives and beliefs by putting himself in the agent's shoes and looking at the world from that new perspective. The spectator might then decide that he would have acted in the same way, and his disapproval of the agent's act might then be replaced by approval.

The spectator *qua* moral agent has the ability to effect a change in the person whom he observes by revealing to the person his reaction to him. One reason for the spectator's ability is the agent's desire to be approved of. For while the spectator seeks to approve, the agent seeks his approval, and if he thinks that he may be judged to have feelings which are excessive (or deficient) in relation to his situation he will engage in an exercise that corresponds to the spectator's, that is, he will seek to see his own situation through the eyes of the spectator, and he might then for the first time grasp the real significance of previously noted features of his situation. In the light of these new perceptions, gained by an exercise of his creative imagination, his feelings will naturally change, probably towards conformity with the feelings of the spectator. Disagreement in feeling will be transformed into agreement, and in effect each will come to sympathise with the other. Sympathy will be mutual. This hints at Smith's famous sequence 'truck, barter and exchange' in the *Wealth of Nations*.[42] Two people meet, disagree about the worth of the goods on offer; they haggle, with each edging the other closer to his own valuation; they reach an agreement and the exchange is effected. So also do spectator and agent interact.

It is possible to interpret the spectator's judgment of the propriety of the agent's sentiment as the spectator's approval of the agent's sentiment or alternatively as an intellectual act in conformity with that approval, but either way it is a product of interaction between spectator and agent. Smith, however, devotes as much attention to a trilateral relation, between a spectator, an agent who acts upon someone, and the person who is acted upon, to whom I shall refer as the 'recipient'. The recipient's response to the agent's act may be of several kinds. Smith focuses upon two: a grateful and a resentful.

Where the spectator judges the recipient's gratitude to be proper or appropriate he approves of the agent's act as meritorious, or worthy of reward. Where he judges the recipient's resentment proper or appropriate he disapproves of the agent's act as demeritorious, or worthy of punishment. Judgments of merit or demerit concerning a person's act are therefore made on the basis of an antecedent judgment concerning the propriety or impropriety of another person's reaction to that act. Sympathy underlies all these judgments, for in the cases just mentioned the spectator has direct sympathy with the affections and motives of the agent, and indirect sympathy with the recipient's gratitude, or judging the agent's behaviour improper the spectator has indirect sympathy with the recipient's resentment.[43]

In these various cases we have supposed the recipient to have the feeling in question, whether of gratitude or resentment. However, the spectator's belief about what the recipient actually feels about the agent is not important for the spectator's judgment concerning the merit and demerit of the agent. The recipient may, for whatever reason, resent an act that was kindly intentioned and in all other ways admirable, and the spectator, knowing the situation better than the recipient, puts himself imaginatively in the shoes of the recipient while taking with him into this spectatorial role information about the agent's behaviour that the recipient lacks. The spectator judges that in the recipient's situation he would be grateful for the agent's act, and on that basis he approves of the agent's act and judges it meritorious.

Here the spectator regards himself as a better (because better-informed) spectator of the agent's act than the recipient is.

In respect of judgments of merit and demerit, therefore, though Smith sets up a model of three people, the three differ regarding the weight that has to be assigned to their work. The recipient does almost nothing. He is acted on by the agent, but apart from that he is no more than a place-holder for the spectator, who will imaginatively occupy that place and make a judgment concerning merit or demerit on the basis of his conception of how he would respond to the agent if he were in the place of the recipient, and who does not judge on the basis of the actual reaction of the recipient, who might approve of the agent's act or disapprove or be indifferent.

SECTION 5: THE IMPARTIAL SPECTATOR

There is a real person into whose shoes the spectator imaginatively places himself when forming judgments of propriety or merit of the acts of others, but in the case to which I now turn there seems not to be. How is a person to know what to think of his own acts? Commonly when a spectator judges another person he has the advantage of disinterest but may lack requisite information, and the creative imagination has to rectify the lack, but in judging himself he has, or may be presumed to have, the information but has to overcome self-love or self-interest. He does this by imagining a spectator, an *other* who observes him at a distance. Distance creates the possibility of disinterest or impartiality, but if the spectator is the creature of the agent's own imagination how is disinterest achieved?

Is it the voice of society, the representative of established social attitudes? Occasionally in the first edition of the *Theory of Moral Sentiments* Smith comes close to saying this, and in a letter to Smith, Sir Gilbert Elliot[44] interprets him in that way. The second edition makes it clear that this is not the role of the impartial spectator, for the latter can, and sometimes does, speak against established social attitudes; or, as Smith puts the matter in his reply to Elliot: 'real magnanimity and conscious virtue can support itselfe under the disapprobation of all mankind.'[45] The impartial spectator cannot simply be a repository of social opinion, nor is it possible to reduce the judgment of the impartial spectator to the judgment of society even where those two judgments coincide. Nevertheless, were it not for our discovery that while we observe and judge other people, they observe and judge us, we would not form the idea of an impartial spectator.

The impartial spectator is the product of an act of imagination, and hence in one sense is not a real spectator who has the merit of being impartial but an ideal spectator, one that exists as an idea. Smith sanctions this terminology.[46] In another sense the impartial spectator is indeed real, for it is no other than the agent who is imagining it into existence.

The impartial spectator is the key to Smith's account of the faculty of conscience:

> The all-wise Author of Nature has, in this manner, taught man to respect the sentiments and judgments of his brethren . . . But though man has, in this manner, been rendered the immediate judge of mankind, he has been rendered so only in the first instance; and an appeal lies from his sentence to a much higher tribunal, to the tribunal of their own consciences, to that of the supposed impartial and well-informed spectator, to that of the man within the breast, the great judge and arbiter of their conduct. The jurisdictions of those two tribunals are founded upon principles which, though in some respects resembling and akin, are, however, in reality different and distinct. The jurisdiction of the man without, is founded altogether in the desire of actual praise, and in the aversion to actual blame. The jurisdiction of the man within, is founded altogether in the desire of praise-worthiness, and in the aversion to blame-worthiness.[47]

By whatever means the impartial spectator, considered as our conscience, comes into being, it is not a member of society.

This interpretation of the relation between the agent and the impartial spectator has an implication for the question of how many impartial spectators there are. Following Smith, commentators speak about *the* impartial spectator, and I have followed this practice, but sometimes Smith uses the indefinite article, and sometimes he refers to *every* impartial spectator: '[Gratitude and resentment] seem proper and are approved of, when the heart of every impartial spectator entirely sympathizes with them, when every indifferent bystander entirely enters into, and goes along with them.'[48] We have to be on our guard. It is probable that the reference to 'every indifferent by-stander' is not to the impartial spectator, understood as a product of our imagination, but to real live witnesses, and neither can it be ruled out that in this case the reference to an 'impartial spectator' is also to a real live by-stander. But even if we think of the impartial spectator as being merely a product of our imagination, it might still be said that there are many impartial spectators, for each person creates his own.

As a creature of the imagination the impartial spectator has just as much information about what is to be judged as the agent has, for the creature must be just as well informed as its creator. Where the agent has information about his own situation that is not possessed by the external spectators, 'the great demigod within the breast' is better placed than are external spectators to make a judgment about the propriety of his behaviour. So the agent asks himself what the judgment of the external spectators would be if they knew what he knows. In this way the agent tries to see his own situation in a disinterested way, while at the same time benefiting from the level of information that he himself has.

However, even if the agent is better informed than the spectators, he may still be failing to note features in his situation that would make all the difference to his judgment about his own acts and attitudes, but the information he has is all that is available to the impartial spectator, whose judgment therefore is not indefeasible. We can therefore never say definitively that the impartial spectator's judgment is true, and every such judgment is therefore no more than a holding operation. There are two standards that we can apply in judging our character and conduct. One is the idea of exact propriety and perfection, and the other is the idea of such an approximation to propriety as is commonly attained in the world. The wise and virtuous man, we are told, directs his principal attention to the first of these standards:

> There exists in the mind of every man, an idea of this kind, gradually formed from his observations upon the character and conduct both of himself and of other people. It is the slow, gradual, and progressive work of the great demigod within the breast, the great judge and arbiter of conduct . . . Every day some feature is improved; every day some blemish is corrected.[49]

Plainly Smith acknowledges that the demigod within the breast is fallible. But there is one particular form of fallibility to which the impartial spectator is subject, namely that arising from moral luck.[50]

Smith begins with the fact (if it be one) that however proper and beneficent may be a person's intention, if he fails to produce the intended effect his merit will seem imperfect. Smiths continues:

> Nor is this irregularity of sentiment felt only by those who are immediately affected by the consequences of any action. It is felt, in some measure, even by the impartial spectator . . . if, between the friend who fails and the friend who succeeds, all other circumstances are

equal, there will, even in the noblest and the best mind, be some little difference of affection in favour of him who succeeds.[51]

Since Smith describes this 'irregularity of sentiment' as 'unjust' he must think that the impartial spectator can pass unjust judgment. Later he notes the case of a person who, without any ill intention, harms another, but apologises to the sufferer: 'This task would surely never be imposed upon him, did not even the impartial spectator feel some indulgence for what may be regarded as the unjust resentment of that other.'[52] If the impartial spectator feels some indulgence for what may be regarded as the unjust resentment of the other, he must have some sympathy for that unjust resentment, and hence is sympathising unjustly. This is evidence that the impartial spectator, already noted to be imperfect in being no better informed than the creator-agent, also possesses at least one moral flaw.

We should therefore grant that despite Smith's reference to 'the judgment of the ideal man within the breast',[53] the doctrine of the impartial spectator is not a version of the so-called 'ideal observer theory'. The impartial spectator is not ideal, but is instead the best that we can manage, a best that is constrained by limited information admixed with error and by an affective nature that can yield to pressure from outside forces. The impartial spectator is not God, but only a demigod. Smith affirms that sometimes 'this demigod within the breast appears, like the demigods of the poets, though partly of immortal, yet partly too of mortal extraction'. He has in mind the case where the demigod becomes fearful and hesitant in judgment in response to a fearsome clamour of real spectators who violently proclaim a judgment which is contrary to the one that the impartial spectator would have passed. Then our only recourse is to the all-seeing judge of the world 'whose judgments can never be perverted',[54] as contrasted with the human impartial spectator. God, therefore, is the impartial spectator of the universe, infinitely better placed than the humanly created spectator who is only imperfectly informed and liable to bow to social pressures.

Sir Gilbert Elliot had asked whether the impartial spectator's judgment is anything other than a reflection of an actual attitude of society. Smith replied that it is indeed other, but here acknowledges that social attitudes can be hard to resist. It may be added that aside from this possibly malign influence of real external spectators, they can also have a benign influence by prompting the impartial spectator to spectate: 'The man within the breast, the abstract and ideal spectator of our sentiments and conduct, requires often to be awakened and put in mind of his duty, by the presence of the real spectator.'[55]

Second- and third-person moral judgments seem easier to make, on Smith's account, than do first-person moral judgments. In the former cases the spectator need do no more than imagine himself in the shoes of the agent, and observe an agreement, or lack of agreement, between the way he himself would feel or behave in that situation and the way the agent actually does feel or behave. Where there is agreement the spectator approves; where there is disagreement the spectator disapproves, or at least does not approve, of the agent's feelings or behaviour. A more complex story needs to be told in the case of first-person judgments, for there the agent has to imagine himself as an impartial spectator of his feelings or acts, and has to note the impartial spectator's agreement or otherwise with the agent's feelings or acts. If he agrees then the agent morally approves of his own acts; if not then not.

Section 6: Smith's moral naturalism

The concept of conscience is reached by a direct route that starts with the idea of the human agent as a spectator of other people's behaviour. It progresses to the idea of the spectator as not only a judge but also a person aware that he is being judged. His awareness of the gaze of others prompts a response. He considers first whether what he is doing will gain praise, and then finds that praise does not satisfy him if he is unworthy of it. So he examines his acts and attitudes in order to decide not whether they will be praised but whether they are praiseworthy. In the light of countless observations of the kinds of act that we have regarded as praiseworthy, we form general moral rules. It is an important feature of Smith's moral theory that the rules are not reached on the basis of calculations of the utility of obedience but instead are reached by means of an induction from our previous impartial approvals. In due course we revere these rules and act out of reverence for them. They underpin society: 'Without this sacred regard to general rules, there is no man whose conduct can be much depended upon. It is this which constitutes the most essential difference between a man of principle and honour and a worthless fellow.'[56] It is true that the term 'sacred' carries overtones of the divine but, aside from that deployment of the term, what has just been said concerning the formulation of moral rules is entirely naturalistic.

There is therefore a question to be raised concerning the proper way to interpret Smith's assertion that moral rules are laws of God. There is good reason to think that it is to be understood principally as conventional eighteenth-century rhetoric and does not imply that there is a God. As evidence for this I note that according to Smith we do not come by all our individual moral judgments by applying the rules, for we come by the rules via our individual moral judgments, and the materials deployed by Smith in his account of those judgments are none of them religious or theological.

While most commentators have held that Smith's account of the process by which the impartial spectator or conscience comes into being does not require the theological framework that Smith lightly sketches,[57] a few have disagreed.[58] God is certainly invoked at several points in the exposition of the role of the impartial spectator, but the fact that humbled and afflicted man can find consolation in an appeal to God does not contribute to an enrichment of the concept of the impartial spectator. True, it makes the point that the impartial spectator has the limitations of a human being, but that point had previously been made in some detail without God being invoked. And an atheist or agnostic would not on that account have a concept of the impartial spectator different from that of a person who finds consolation in an appeal to a yet higher tribunal. This is not to say that the theodicy is nothing but a rhetorical device within the *Theory of Moral Sentiments*, for Smith sees belief in a just God to be a *natural* phenomenon, and he is interested in the question of how such a belief stands in relation to the moral categories with which we operate. He does, however, hold that a person can operate with a set of moral categories, such as propriety, impropriety, merit, demerit, duty and moral rules, without holding those categories in a synthetic unity with categories of a religious or theological sort. It is therefore possible to see Smith as seeking to demonstrate that a theory of moral sentiments, one sufficient to accommodate the moral framework within which most of us operate, can be developed without recourse to theological materials. The interpretative problem is, however, a live one.

Section 7: Justice and the other virtues

We all believe that there are moral rules, and that virtue is on the side of obeying them and vice on the side of infringing them, but in some cases, perhaps most, it is difficult to find a formulation for the rules that does not run into immediate trouble. Smith discusses the case of gratitude in an attempt to tease out the rules for grateful behaviour, and finds that questions loom.[59] If your benefactor visited you during your illness, does the obligation of gratitude require that you visit him during his? If so, then should you spend as much time with him as he did with you? If he lent you money when you needed it, do you lend him now that he is in need? If so, then as much as he lent you, or as much as he needs? If he lent you all of the small sum that you required, are you now bound in gratitude to lend him all of the large sum that he needs? And for how long? And so on. The problem is not that as recipients of a beneficent act we have trouble knowing how to express our gratitude, for we may know very well how to express it. Nor even is it that we do not know how to formulate rough-and-ready rules. It is instead that we do not know how to formulate detailed, practical rules that can withstand the sort of questions that have just been listed. Such rules as we do manage to formulate are, in Smith's phrase, 'loose, vague, and indeterminate'.[60] The same might be said of other virtues – Smith mentions prudence, courage, charity, generosity, humanity, hospitability and magnanimity, whose rules are likewise 'loose, vague and indeterminate', though again ignorance of, or at least total inability to formulate, precise and accurate rules does not seem an obstacle to people being virtuous in these ways.

In contrast with all other virtues, there are precise and accurate rules of justice which are of such a nature as to exclude latitude. To take Smith's example, if I owe someone ten pounds to be returned on a given day then justice requires that on that day I return ten pounds to him. There is no room here for modification or refinement. Having agreed to return the sum on that day, I do not have moral latitude to wonder whether nine pounds ninety-nine pence will do as well (for after all what difference could a penny make?) nor to wonder whether the day after the appointed day will do as well (for after all it is only one day later). Nor may I argue that since my creditor is rich and I am poor I would be more justified in not repaying the debt than he would be in forcing me to repay. Smith speaks plainly on this kind of manoeuvring: 'A man often becomes a villain the moment he begins, even in his own heart, to chicane in this manner.'[61]

Smith's distinction between justice and all the other virtues prompts him to make a parallel distinction between grammarians and critics. Grammarians, that is, writers who investigate what it is that constitutes the grammaticality of well-formed sentences, formulate detailed, precise and accurate rules for the construction of such sentences. Critics, that is, writers who investigate what it is that constitutes the beauty, sublimity, elegance, stylishness and related virtues of buildings, paintings, musical compositions and so on, give not 'certain and infallible directions' for the achievement of these artistic virtues, but instead 'a general idea of the perfection we ought to aim at'.[62] The distinction between the two kinds of virtue and the distinction between grammarians and critics suggests to Smith a way of characterising the role of moral philosophers, namely that when on the topic of justice they should write in the manner of grammarians and when on the topic of the other virtues they should write in the manner of critics. It seems evident that Smith regards himself as accomplishing precisely this task in the *Theory of Moral Sentiments*.

But he does not believe that the practice of all moral philosophers has accorded with this prescription, for many have written only as grammarians and others only as critics. Smith tells us that some, including all the ancient moralists, have treated of justice in the manner of the critic. In the case of each virtue they have analysed the sentiments of the heart on which the virtue is founded, the feeling that constitutes the essence of the virtue, be the virtue humanity, justice or generosity, and so on, and have analysed the general tenor of conduct of the agent motivated by the virtue. But this approach, focused on the motivating sentiments, the feelings that people have for each other, results not in certain and infallible directions for conduct but rather in models for us to emulate, 'a general idea of the perfection we ought to aim at', pictures of exemplary generosity, humanity or courage, say, combined with exhortations to us to try our utmost to live up to them.

Other moralists, amongst whom are natural jurisprudentialists and casuists, seek to formulate exact and precise rules for our conduct in every circumstance of our behaviour. These two groups are mutually distinct in their conception of the kind of case with which they have to deal. Let us suppose two persons who are 'creditor' and 'debtor' (not Smith's terms) in relation to a given obligation; the creditor is the one to whom the obligation is due and the debtor the one who owes him the obligation. The jurisprudentialist focuses on the creditor and asks what a judge or arbiter, to whom the creditor has submitted his case, ought to oblige the debtor to suffer or to perform. In part the question here is not what the adjudication ought to be, given the actual law of the land, but instead what the law ought to be, given that such an adjudication would accord with natural justice.

As against this kind of case, the casuist focuses on the debtor and asks what he should consider himself bound to do out of regard for the general rules of justice, and from 'the most conscientious dread, either of wronging his neighbour, or of violating the integrity of his own character'.[63] Plainly the natural jurisprudentialist and the casuist have different tasks. The former formulates rules for the guidance of a judge, the latter lays down rules to be followed by a good man. The two sets of rules are different in this respect also, that obedience to rules of the first set warrants a different outcome from obedience to rules of the second. The outcome in the first case should be no more, or less, than avoidance of punishment; the outcome in the latter should be entitlement to praise because of the exactness and 'scrupulous delicacy' of the debtor's behaviour, an exactness and scrupulosity that have motivated the debtor to go above and beyond what could fairly be demanded of him by the law. Smith gives the example of a highwayman who has, by threat, extracted a promise from a traveller to surrender to him a given sum of money to be delivered at a later date. Wherein lies the traveller's obligation? Natural jurisprudence affirms unequivocally that the traveller is under no obligation to surrender the sum since the highwayman has no entitlement to constrain the traveller to surrender it. He has no such entitlement because a promise made under extreme threat does not bind the promisee.

In contrast casuistical responses to the same question have been mutually incompatible. If the traveller aims to act out of regard for the general rules of justice, and from 'the most conscientious dread, either of wronging his neighbour, or of violating the integrity of his own character', what is he to do? Smith reports that some casuistical responses, including those of Pufendorf, Barbeyrac and Hutcheson, have been to the effect that the traveller should not regard himself as bound to keep his promise. Others, including St Augustine and Jean La Placette, have been of the contrary view, that having made a promise, even if under threat, some blame is incurred if the promise is disregarded. Smith evidently agrees with this latter judgment. He affirms: 'whenever such promises are violated, though for the most necessary reasons, it is always with some degree of dishonour to the person who made them . . . no man, I imagine, who has gone through an adventure of this kind would be fond of telling the story.'[64]

Smith's position appears to be not that promises are not to be broken lightly, nor even that they are not to be broken at all, but that though in extreme circumstances they may be broken, a conscientious person, suffused with a fear of violating his own integrity, would not break a promise without anguish at his act, even if the promise had been extracted from him by the direst threats. The anguish indicates that the person believed himself to be doing something wrong, even if he recognised that what he was doing was also, from another legitimate point of view, defensible. Smith would evidently sympathise with the person's anguish, which he would hardly do if he sided with the position of the natural jurisprudentialists. The latter would say that the highwayman was not entitled, in natural law, to force the traveller to keep his promise, and that therefore, so far as natural law is concerned, there is no obligation on the traveller to keep it. Hence, he had no good reason to anguish over his decision not to keep his promise.

However, such sympathy as we have for the traveller's anguish should not be allowed to mask the fact that we are unable to formulate with any precision the rules at issue. Suppose the traveller had promised to deliver a sum which was in fact so large that it would beggar his family, or suppose that it were not large but that it would probably be used for criminal purposes, and so on. There are countless variables and there is no prospect of formulating the rules that the traveller could profitably consult in trying to decide what to do in the light of his promise. Natural law is so much simpler – a promise made under threat does not put the promisee under an obligation to deliver.

Textbooks on the art of casuistry were an outgrowth of the work of priest-confessors. Believers came to their confessors with cases of conscience, especially regarding highly detailed matters of justice, chastity and veracity: was what they had thought to be a delicate sense of justice an exercise in scrupulosity? Had what they had thought graceful and relaxed behaviour in fact been a licentious act? Had what they had thought to be a proper sense of the need to keep a secret in fact been a willingness to engage in sheer deceit? Smith does not think that such questions are not worth asking; on the contrary it is obvious that sometimes they are questions of the greatest importance, since the answer might indicate that the agent has behaved badly towards another person to whom therefore he must discharge an obligation of reparation. But Smith thinks that casuists are wrong in the way they go about answering such questions, for in answering them they write as grammarians and not as critics. He affirms: 'With regard to all such matters, what would hold good in any one case would scarce do so exactly in any other, and what constitutes the propriety and happiness of behaviour varies in every case with the smallest variety of situation. Books of casuistry, therefore, are generally as useless as they are commonly tiresome.'[65] The problem is that the questions asked are not hypothetical; they are asked in respect of a single real act by a conscience-stricken individual and have to be answered in respect of that act in its existential situation. But it is a matter of fine and delicate judgment which elements or features of the situation are morally relevant, and there is also a question concerning the relative weighting of those elements or features. What is relevant in the *casus conscientiae* may indeed be of such a nature that in effect the act that prompts the crisis of conscience is unique, in which case it is unclear in what way it would be helpful to be told of a rule that had, or had not, been infringed. Smith sums up: 'It may be said in general of the works of the casuists that they attempted, to no purpose, to direct by precise rules what it belongs to feeling and sentiment only to judge of.'[66] Casuistry should therefore be banished from the field of moral philosophy, which therefore must have only two parts: ethics and jurisprudence. The *Theory of Moral Sentiments*, with its detailed description of the virtues provided on the basis of the analysis of the concepts of sympathy and the impartial spectator, is written, as appropriate, in the manner sometimes of the grammarian and sometimes of the critic.

SECTION 8: SCIENTIFIC PROGRESS

Scientific papers are as clear an exercise in discursive reason as is possible. In effect a scientific paper contains a set of premises to which rules of inference are applied, and a conclusion is then drawn; we read of nothing except observations, experiments, and the implications of these. It might seem that the contrast with Smithian morality could not be greater; in science reason is in the driving seat and in morality it is sentiment.

But Smith would reject the claim that in science it is reason that is in the driving seat. Or at least he would insist on a distinction between scientific papers and what the scientist does in order to be in a position to write his papers. The scientist's sentiments are not in sight in his paper; he does not announce how he feels about anything. Everything about the paper directs the reader towards phenomena out there in the natural world and towards what follows from what has been observed. Yet the paper is the product of human acts, for the scientist did something in writing the paper and he did something in order to be in a position to write it. It is pertinent to ask why both these acts were performed. Writing a scientific paper is not a negligible or trivial act, in which case it has to be supposed that writing it mattered to the scientist; he must have been motivated. Since the writing embodied a value of the scientist's the paper is, in Smithian terms, the expression of a sentiment, however impersonal may be the style of composition. So the paper is a product of both reason and sentiment. Sentiment by itself would not be enough, for without reason there would have been no content to the paper, and reason would not have been enough, for without sentiment there would have been no motivation for the scientist to translate the ideas from his head into the public domain.

Prior to the writing there had to be the scientific research, and, for Smith, this also must have been motivated by something. Since there is no motivation without sentiment, a sentiment must be invoked as at least partial explanation. Smith focuses on a particular aspect of this last point. His thoughts are in his early work, the *History of Astronomy*, or to give the work its full and much more revealing title, *The Principles which lead and direct Philosophical Enquiries; Illustrated by the History of Astronomy*. These philosophical enquiries are enquiries into natural philosophy, that is, physics, astronomy and the other sciences of nature. Smith does not propose to do natural philosophy, though he will report on astronomical findings. Instead he aims to unpack the principles that 'lead and direct' the natural philosophers, and in particular he will offer an account of the psychology of scientific discovery. Three principles are identified as leading and directing the natural philosopher; they are surprise, wonder and admiration.

It is the unexpected that prompts the sentiment of surprise. When the expected happens we react with a sentiment appropriate to the event, and since the event is expected the attendant sentiment comes upon us without violence or suddenness. We must have previously had an idea of the event, and Smith holds that the idea must then have been attended by that same emotion though at a lower level of intensity. The contrary happens when the event is unexpected. There is an abrupt change in the mind; a sentiment appropriate to the new event is suddenly present without, so to say, the ground having been prepared. This new sentiment is the sentiment of surprise. There is no one sentiment that is the sentiment of surprise; the unexpected can be met with joy, anger, grief, hope or fear, and so on. What makes each of these a sentiment of surprise is the violent and sudden change in the mind when the emotion arises in response to the event and to the event's unexpectedness.[67] The sentiment of surprise is therefore universal in the domain of sentiments, for a sentiment of any kind whatever could be felt in surprise mode. In this respect surprise may be classed with Smithian sympathy, for the latter is universal in that any sentiment could be felt sympathetically. Hence I argued earlier that sympathy is best understood not so much as a particular kind of sentiment but rather as an adverbial modification of a sentiment. There is reason to hold that the same thing is true of Smithian surprise, which is best understood as indicating the manner in which a given sentiment enters the mind. As we are joyful or distressed sympathetically so we are joyful or distressed surprisedly when the sentiment suddenly arises in response to the unexpected.

Surprise is rarely if ever the end of the story, for we are naturally minded to ask questions regarding things that have taken us by surprise. Smith discusses two kinds of case. We observe resemblances between things and classify things in the light of their resemblance; then we see something that defies our powers of classification, something 'quite new and singular', say a duck-billed platypus. We try to answer the question: 'What kind of thing is it?' Inquisitiveness motivates us because of its sentimental component – the wanting that is implicit in it along with the intellectual component that is the content of the question. Smith describes this first stage after surprise as 'wonder', as in the phrases 'I wonder why' and 'I wonder how'. In this sense an object is wonderful if it fills us with wonder at what it is.

Smith also discusses a second cause for wonderment in which the Humean content is unmistakable. It concerns familiar sequences of events. In our experience events of type A have always been followed immediately by events of type B; an association of ideas is therefore formed. We find it increasingly difficult to imagine A without the idea of A drawing in its train the idea of B. Smith speaks about the habit as becoming 'more and more rivetted and confirmed'.[68] The ideas fall in with 'the natural career of the imagination'. That is, the imagination careers along, on tramlines of its own making, following particular sequences of ideas for no other reason than that it is in the habit of following those sequences. When such a habit of thought is set up, it is unlikely that the person will think to question the sequence. Sheer familiarity with the order of events is an obstacle to asking why it is that B happens when A happens.

Then something goes wrong. A happens and is followed not by B but by C. The imagination careering along is stopped dead in its tracks as a gap opens up, a B-shaped space but no B. The surprise at the non-appearance of B prompts the question why C happened when B should have. Surprise has thus engendered wonder, as to why C rather than B came next, and the imagination naturally entertains the hypothesis that there is an invisible chain between A and C. The search is then on to determine the constituents of the invisible chain. Smith adds a complicating factor to this picture of observed customary sequences. Some people are more sensitive than others; a musician has a 'nicer ear' than others and, unlike the majority, will notice that a singer has drifted fractionally out of tune. Smith believes that real scientists have a 'nicer ear' for things in nature that call for explanation. Every time I have hit a tennis ball against a brick wall it has bounced back. Familiarity has set my mind on tramlines. But I'm not a scientist. A real scientist knows that many substances would not bounce off a brick wall, that some would go right through and others would simply fall to the ground, and he wonders about the properties of the ball and of the wall that ensure that they behave as they do. Real scientists look for answers to questions that others do not even think to ask, and they are able to do this because they have been educated into a sensitivity about sequences in nature. Smith writes: 'the more practised thought of a philosopher [i.e. natural philosopher], who has spent his whole life in the study of the connecting principles of nature, will often feel an interval betwixt two objects, which, to more careless observers, seem very strictly conjoined.'[69]

Success is to be measured in psychological terms. Philosophy, 'the science of the connecting principles of nature',[70] seeks

> to introduce order into this chaos of jarring and discordant appearances, to allay this tumult of the imagination, and to restore it, when it surveys the great revolutions of the universe, to that tone of tranquillity and composure, which is both most agreeable in itself, and most suitable to its nature.[71]

Science is therefore on the side of peace of mind, and the great virtue of Newton's *Principia Mathematica* is to have gone furthest in the direction of showing us how we may be protected from the tumult of the imagination. He brought physics to 'that summit of perfection to which it is at present supposed to have arrived, and to which, indeed, it has equally been supposed to have arrived in almost all former times'.[72] The holding back is evident here. It is true that Smith later affirms of Newton: 'His system, however, now prevails over all opposition, and has advanced to the acquisition of the most universal empire that was ever established in philosophy.' It is 'the greatest discovery that ever was made by man'.[73] Nevertheless, Smith notes that Newton's physics is at the summit of perfection at which the discipline is 'at present supposed to have arrived', and that in former times former systems have also received the accolade of being at the summit of perfection. This does not imply that his words are not a ringing endorsement of Newton's achievement, but they are instead a recognition that all achievements in empirical science are defeasible. Another system might yet prevail over Newton's.

Newton's *Principia*, which is itself a product of surprise and wonder, prompts us to a third sentiment: admiration, in this case of the natural world. To borrow a phrase from Hutcheson's aesthetics, Newton has discovered a 'unity amidst diversity', and the spectacle of nature seems yet more magnificent, the phenomena awesome in their coherence. Smith's comment has a modern ring:

> Let us examine, therefore, all the different systems of nature, which, in these western parts of the world, the only parts of whose history we know any thing, have successively been adopted by the learned and ingenious; and, without regarding their absurdity or probability, their agreement or inconsistency with truth and reality, let us consider them only in that particular point of view which belongs to our subject; and content ourselves with inquiring how far each of them was fitted to sooth the imagination, and to render the theatre of nature a more coherent, and therefore a more magnificent spectacle, than otherwise it would have appeared to be.[74]

Smith does not go quite so far as to separate the scientific enterprise of the western world from questions of truth, for he explicitly restricts his comments to 'the particular point of view which belongs to our subject', namely 'the principles which lead and direct philosophical enquiries'. But he makes it clear that these principles concern not truth and reality, but the soothing of the imagination. Evidently the ultimate aim of science is not the theoretical one of reaching the truth, but the practical one of bringing calm to an agitated mind. Nor even is the intermediate goal one of truth; it is, as Smith says, to render the theatre of nature a more coherent spectacle than otherwise it appears to be.

The spirit of Hume hovers over this part of Smith's project: 'Reason is, and ought only to be the slave of the passions, and can never pretend to any other office than to serve and obey them.'[75] Smith holds that peace of mind is a psychological imperative comparable to the biological imperatives for food and warmth. The desire for peace of mind and an end to agitation and tumult motivates a good deal of what we do, and his thesis in the *History of Astronomy* is that one of the things it motivates is our science. There could not be a more spectacular example of reason as the slave of the passions.

The Age of Enlightenment has been called the Age of Reason, and it has been seen as in opposition to the Middle Ages, during which belief was based not on rational insight but on respect or reverence for authority. In the light of Smith's analysis of the psychology of scientific discovery it is evident that this account of the Age of Enlightenment is not plain sailing. That is, Smith did not lose sight of the fact that science is produced by scientists, human beings who, in the ways that matter most, are much like all other human beings, and the principles of action that characterise all of us characterise scientists too. The *Theory of Moral Sentiments* makes it clear that sentiment is in the driving seat in respect of human motivation and that even our most elevated moral motives have a sentimental base. Extending his perspective to the western scientific enterprise, Smith concludes that, for all the rhetoric of scientific papers, sentiment cannot be kept out of science. The western scientific enterprise is a march of reason but it is a march of reason to the drum beat of sentiment.

Section 9: Morality, science and art

We observed in the last section that on Smith's analysis the sentiments of surprise, wonder and admiration are basic to science. These three sentiments have a pleasing orderliness in so far as they concern the beginning, middle and end of an activity; and they also have a pleasing familiarity, for it is a sequence that we all live through perhaps many times daily – we are surprised at something, we wonder what the explanation is for what surprised us, and we are relieved to discover the explanation. But if that sequence of sentiments is so common, it might be expected to feature in Smith's writings on other aspects of human activity, and in fact it is also present in his accounts of both morality and art.

As regards morality it is easy to see that the sequence is busy in the *Theory of Moral Sentiments* even before the three sentiments are explicitly invoked in that work.[76] Sympathy, of course, is involved. In Section 2 I expounded the concept of sympathy in terms of our seeing an agent suffer and thereupon forming in our imagination 'some idea of his sensations' and feeling something 'which, though weaker in degree, is not altogether unlike them'. We accomplish this by means of the imaginative experiment of placing ourselves in the agent's circumstance. Often enough we do this without being prompted into it by something odd about the agent's behaviour, but not always. It is common enough to be surprised by someone's behaviour, and then straightaway we are launched on the sequence of surprise, wonder and admiration, for the 'natural career of the imagination' has been stopped in its tracks. We are discomforted by the failure of the customary to happen, and we wonder why it has failed to. One way forward is to make the first move that the sympathetic spectator makes – we put ourselves in the shoes of the other and try to see his situation as he sees it. By this measure we look at his act through fresh eyes and are likely to see things that previously we had simply missed, and perhaps discover that after all his act made perfectly good sense and was perhaps an ingenious solution to a problem that we did not even know he was facing. In that case our wonder might be followed by admiration for what he did. This example fits (though not uniquely) the case that Smith considers in which the harmony of feeling between an agent and us arises because the sentiments of the agent have led and directed our own. We discover that in forming his sentiments the agent 'appears to have attended to many things which we had overlooked, and to have adjusted them to all the various circumstances of their objects'.[77]

Smith had a long-standing interest in the fine arts. He lectured on rhetoric and belles lettres while a professor in Glasgow, made comments on the fine arts in both the *Theory of Moral Sentiments* and the *Wealth of Nations*, and delivered lectures on the subject in the 1770s and 1780s. Smith entitled one manuscript 'Of the nature of that imitation which takes place in what are called the imitative arts'.[78] He does not believe that all art works are imitative, but some certainly are, most obviously painting and sculpture, and some arguably are not, such as, in Smith's view, certain kinds of music. Some imitations please and some do not. A painting that is so like the object painted as to deceive spectators into thinking it *is* the object is not any the more pleasing for being so accurate a representation; on the contrary spectators, who at first are 'surprised' (Smith's word) by the work, then judge it 'insipid and tiresome' once they have seen through the deception. Great visual works of art, according to Smith, not only are not deceptive in this way but in fact are incompatible with being deceptive, for we cannot look at them without seeing that they are works of art. There must then be a perceptible disparity between such works and their object.

As to what causes our pleasure in art works, Smith is clear that accurate representation of a beautiful object is not a major factor, for dull or humdrum or even downright ugly things can be the subject of pleasing paintings. Instead he focuses on the disparity between the kind of object that the art work is and the kind that the subject of the art work is. He writes that the pleasure derived from looking at a painting or sculpture

> is founded altogether upon our wonder at seeing an object of one kind represent so well an object of a very different kind, and upon our admiration of the art which surmounts so happily that disparity which Nature had established between them . . . We wonder and are amazed at the effect; and we are pleased ourselves, and happy to find that we can comprehend, in some measure, how that wonderful effect is produced.[79]

As regards disparity, Smith has in mind especially that between a three-dimensional object and the two-dimensional representation of it on a flat canvas, and the disparity between a marble statue and the subject it represents. The latter disparity is of course less than the former since the statue, like its object, is three-dimensional. Given that the disparity between a painting and its three-dimensional subject is greater than that between a statue and its object, more ingenuity has to go into the painting than into the sculpture, and this very ingenuity is itself an important cause of the pleasure we take in the art work: 'Even in the meanest subjects we can often trace with pleasure the ingenious means by which Painting surmounts this disparity. But we cannot do this in Statuary, because the disparity not being so great, the means do not appear so ingenious.'[80]

We are amazed at a painting, we wonder at it, we see how the painter has overcome the problem caused by the non-two-dimensional nature of the object, and we admire the art which has surmounted that disparity. The parallel with Smith's account of the psychology of scientific discovery is evident in respect both of conceptual content and of technical vocabulary. But there is one significant difference that Smith emphasises, namely that the fine art work bears indications of the way in which the artist succeeded in overcoming the disparity he had to overcome, whereas natural phenomena bear no such indications in themselves. One does not have to be a trained artist to see, even if only roughly, how the artist secured the effect he aimed at:

> The eye, even of an unskilful spectator, immediately discerns, in some measure, how it is that a certain modification of figure in Statuary, and of brighter and darker colours in Painting, can represent, with so much truth and vivacity, the actions, passions, and behaviour of men, as well as a great variety of other objects.[81]

But natural phenomena are quite otherwise. The eye of an unskilful spectator would never see how the eliptical path of the planets is produced. Scientific knowledge requires the application of scientific methodology, and those not skilled in such application will not produce answers to scientific questions. But that aside, the similarity between the scientific case and the artistic is impressive. Smith's application of the ordered triple 'surprise/wonder/admiration' to his moral theory, to his theory of scientific discovery and to his account of the imitative arts points to a significant degree of unity among elements that might otherwise be supposed mutually disparate.

Notes

1. The fullest modern biography of Smith is Ross, *Life of Adam Smith*. See also Buchan, *Adam Smith*, and Rae, *Life of Adam Smith*.
2. Smith, *Theory of Moral Sentiments*, eds Raphael and Macfie, p. 124 (hereinafter *TMS*).
3. *History of Astronomy*, in Smith, *Essays on Philosophical Subjects*, eds Wightman, Bryce and Ross, pp. 31–105 (hereinafter *EPS*).
4. Smith, *Lectures on Rhetoric and Belles Lettres*, ed. Bryce (hereinafter *LRBL*).
5. Smith, *Lectures on Jurisprudence*, eds Meek, Raphael and Stein.
6. Smith, *Correspondence*, eds Mossner and Ross, 2nd edn, p. 36 (hereinafter *Correspondence*).
7. Ibid. p. 251.
8. Ibid. pp. 308–9.
9. Hutcheson, *Inquiry*, ed. Leidhold, p. 218, a passage added in the 3rd edn of 1729. The reflex acts here invoked are the agent's acts of *reflecting* upon his temper, for Hutcheson is concerned to make the anti-Hobbesian claim that while there is indeed a close relation between virtue and pleasure, the pleasure is being considered not as a cause of the virtuous temper, but as an effect, in the agent, of his awareness of the virtuousness of his temper. Nevertheless Hutcheson is not content to refer only to the agent. For discussion of Hutcheson on 'reflex acts' or 'reflection' see Alexander Broadie, 'Francis Hutcheson on connoisseurship and the role of reflection', *British Journal for the History of Philosophy* (forthcoming, 2009).
10. Hutcheson, *Essay*, p. 182.
11. Hume, *Enquiry Concerning the Principles of Morals*, IX.I, p. 148 (hereinafter *EPM*).
12. Ibid. app. I, p. 160.
13. Hutcheson, *Inquiry*, p. 159.
14. Hume, *Treatise*, 2.1.1, p. 206.

15. *TMS*, I.i.1.2.
16. This was in fact a line of attack developed by Thomas Reid. See J. C. Stewart-Robertson and David F. Norton, 'Thomas Reid on Adam Smith's theory of morals', *Journal of the History of Ideas*, 41 (1980): 381–98, and 45 (1984): 309–21.
17. *TMS*, VII.iii.1.4. Cf. Charles L. Griswold, *Adam Smith and the Virtues of Enlightenment* (Cambridge: Cambridge University Press, 1999), pp. 90–6.
18. *LRBL*, p. 90.
19. Smith, *An Inquiry into the Nature and Causes of the Wealth of Nations*, eds Campbell, Skinner and Todd, pp. 26–7 (hereinafter *WN*).
20. *TMS*, editors' introduction, pp. 38–9. Cf. Ross, *Life of Adam Smith*, pp. 122–3.
21. H. T. Buckle, *History of Civilization in England*, 2 vols (London: Parker, 1861), vol. 2, ch. 6.
22. There is a large literature on this topic. See *TMS*, editors' introduction, pp. 20–4; Laurence Dickey, 'Historicizing the "Adam Smith problem": conceptual, historiographical, and textual issues', *Journal of Modern History*, 58 (1986): 579–609.
23. *TMS*, I.i.1.2 and 10. See Haakonssen, *The Science of a Legislator*, pp. 46–9, for discussion of the significance of these statements.
24. *TMS*, I.i.1.6.
25. Ibid. I.i.1.2.
26. Ibid. I.i.1.9.
27. Ibid. I.i.1.13.
28. Ibid. I.i.1.2.
29. Ibid. I.i.4.7. Cf. *TMS*, I.i.4.7: 'The thought of their [sc. the spectators'] own safety, the thought that they themselves are not really the sufferers, continually intrudes itself upon them; and . . . hinders them from conceiving any thing that approaches to the same degree of violence.'
30. Ibid. I.i.2.1.
31. Ibid. I.i.3.1.
32. Ibid. I.iii.1.9, note.
33. Ibid. I.i.4.6.
34. Ibid. III.3.28.
35. See Eugene Heath, 'The commerce of sympathy: Adam Smith on the emergence of morals', *Journal of the History of Philosophy*, 33 (1995): 447–66.
36. *EPM*, pp. 227–8.
37. Hume here indicates *TMS*, I.i.2.6: 'As the person who is principally interested in any event is pleased with our sympathy, and hurt by the want of it, so we, too, seem to be pleased when we are able to sympathize with him, and to be hurt when we are unable to do so. We run not only to congratulate the successful, but to condole with the afflicted.'

38. Hume, *Letters*, vol. 1, pp. 311–14, at 313. The letter is dated 28 July 1759, some three months after the publication of the first edition of *TMS*.
39. *TMS*, I.iii.1.9, note.
40. In a letter to Gilbert Elliot, dated 10 October 1759. See *Correspondence*, p. 49. For discussion on these matters see David R. Raynor, 'Hume's Abstract of Adam Smith's *Theory of Moral Sentiments*', *Journal of the History of Philosophy*, 22 (1984): 51–79. Simon Blackburn also sides with Hume against Smith on this matter. See his *Ruling Passions: A Theory of Practical Reasoning* (Oxford: Clarendon Press, 1998), pp. 202–4, esp. fn. 6.
41. *TMS*, I.i.2.2. In a variation on this idea in the *LRBL*, p. 90, Smith notes that it is possible to read a tragedy repeatedly without the play palling, and this despite suspense being essential to the play. His explanation is that though the play is not new to us the events, as they unfold, are new to the *dramatis personae*, and we readers put ourselves in their shoes and see events unfolding through their eyes. They do not know what will happen and so, in imagination, neither do we.
42. *WN*, p. 25.
43. *TMS*, II.i.5.1–2.
44. Smith's friend Sir Gilbert Elliot (1693–1766) was a legislator (MP 1722–6) and a lawyer (appointed lord commissioner of justiciary in 1733 and lord justice-clerk in 1763).
45. For discussion of this change in emphasis between publication of the first and second editions see D. D. Raphael, 'The impartial spectator', in Skinner and Wilson (eds), *Essays on Adam Smith*, esp. pp. 90–1; also Raphael and Macfie, 'Introduction', in *TMS*, pp. 15–17. Smith's reply to Elliot is the letter (*Correspondence*, letter 40) referred to earlier, in which he claimed to have 'entirely discomfitted' Hume.
46. Cf. *TMS*, III.3.26: 'not only the judgment of the ideal man within the breast, but that of the real spectators who might happen to be present, would be entirely overlooked and disregarded.' We shall see that the impartial spectator is not ideal in the sense of being perfect in respect of his judgments.
47. *TMS*, III.2.31–2.
48. Ibid. II.i.2.2.
49. Ibid. VI.iii.25.
50. Smith's discussion of the relation between luck and the moral sentiments is in the section 'Of the influence of fortune upon the sentiments of mankind, with regard to the merit or demerit of actions', *TMS*, pp. 92–108. For helpful comment on Smith on moral luck see Griswold, *Adam Smith and the Virtues of Enlightenment*, pp. 240–4.
51. *TMS*, II.iii.2.2.
52. Ibid. II.iii.2.10.

53. Ibid. III.3.26.
54. Ibid. III.2.33.
55. Ibid. III.3.38.
56. Ibid. III.5.2.
57. See especially A. L. Macfie, *The Individual in Society: Papers on Adam Smith* (London: Allen & Unwin, 1967), ch. 6; Haakonssen, *The Science of a Legislator*, pp. 74–9.
58. Richard A. Kleer, 'Final causes in Adam Smith's *Theory of Moral Sentiments*', *Journal of the History of Philosophy*, 33 (1995): 275–300.
59. *TMS*, III.6.9.
60. Ibid. VII.iv.1.
61. Ibid. III.6.10.
62. Ibid. VII.iv.1.
63. Ibid. VII.iv.8.
64. Ibid. VII.iv.13.
65. Ibid. VII.iv.33.
66. Ibid. VII.iv.33.
67. *EPS*, p. 35.
68. Ibid. p. 41.
69. Ibid. p. 45.
70. Ibid. p. 45.
71. Ibid. pp. 45–6.
72. Ibid. p. 46.
73. Ibid. pp. 104–5.
74. Ibid. p. 46.
75. Hume, *Treatise*, 2.3.3, p. 266.
76. *TMS*, I.i.4.3. See also I.ii.1.12 and IV.2.8. There is room to doubt that the three terms have the same sense in these locations as the one assigned in the *History of Astronomy*, but this terminological point is of no great significance. What is significant here is the fact that it is easy to construct *TMS*-type cases that fit perfectly what Smith says in the *History of Astronomy*.
77. *TMS*, I.i.4.3.
78. *EPS*, pp. 176–213. It is a matter for speculation whether pp. 210–13 had been intended by Smith to be published as a final part of the 'Imitative Arts'. Black and Hutton took the decision to append those last four pages to the essay.
79. Ibid. p. 185.
80. Ibid. p. 186.
81. Ibid. p. 185.

CHAPTER 9

The Scottish School of Common Sense Philosophy

SECTION 1: COMMON SENSE AND ITS CRITERIA

Famously Hume said of his *Treatise of Human Nature*: 'It fell *dead-born from the press*, without reaching such distinction, as even to excite a murmur among the zealots.'[1] Yet Reid wrote in the dedication to his *Inquiry into the Human Mind on the Principles of Common Sense*:

> I never thought of calling in question the principles commonly received with regard to the human understanding, until the *Treatise of human nature* was published, in the year 1739. The ingenious author of that treatise, upon the principles of Locke, who was no sceptic, hath built a system of scepticism, which leaves no ground to believe any one thing rather than its contrary. His reasoning appeared to me to be just: there was therefore a necessity to call in question the principles upon which it was founded, or to admit the conclusion.[2]

Evidently Hume's report on the immediate fate of the *Treatise* was misleading; indeed once the work was published it was quite difficult to do philosophy in Scotland without an eye on what Hume had said. In 1763 Reid wrote to Hume in these terms:

> Your Friendly Adversaries Drs Campbel & Gerard as well as Dr Gregory return their Compliments to you respectfully. A little Philosophical Society here of which all the three are members, is much indebted to you for its Entertainment. . . . If you write no more in morals politicks or metaphysicks, I am affraid we shall be at a loss for Subjects.[3]

Reid here mentions several members of the Aberdeen Philosophical Society (the Wise Club), a club heavily committed to the philosophy of common sense, a philosophy whose highest expression is to be found in Reid's three masterpieces, the *Inquiry into the Human Mind*, the *Essays on the Intellectual Powers of Man* and the *Essays on the Active Powers of the Human Mind*, and though common sense philosophy did not arise solely as a response to the *Treatise*, Hume's great work was undoubtedly a major stimulus to developments in that school. I call it a school, and it has been customary to call it that and to see it as having a rather wide membership clustered round Reid. Herein lies a significant distinction between Hume and Reid, for though Hume's philosophy was the subject of intense research by Scottish philosophers, nothing remotely describable as a school formed round his philosophy. Many philosophers appropriated some of Hume's ideas and one great philosopher, Adam Smith, was close to what may be termed a Humean way of thinking, but all this falls far short of saying that a school formed round Hume's philosophy. Besides Thomas Reid, the Scottish school of common sense philosophy has commonly been taken to include George Campbell, James Beattie, David Fordyce, James Oswald, Lord Monboddo, Dugald Stewart, Adam Ferguson, Alexander Gerard, Lord Kames, John Millar and Thomas Brown.

Many others also have been claimed for the school, but it has to be said that the greater the number of those who are included in the school the more restricted is the sense of the term 'common sense'. Here I shall mention some few ingredients that are arguably central to the common sense philosophy, assuming it to have a centre, and shall then indicate some consequent problems concerning the question of membership of the school.

First, common sense philosophers subscribe to a set of common sense principles which lie at the base of any recognisably human belief system and are therefore well-nigh universal among human beings. They cannot be proved, for whoever would seek to prove them would have to presuppose them, and whoever understands a proof (if there be one) and accepts it must likewise be presupposing those same principles. These principles are normally characterised as part of the original constitution of our nature, and therefore we cannot be taught them, for they have already to be in place in us if we are to be educable.

Secondly, in consequence of the belief that common sense principles are grounded in the original constitution of our nature, common sense philosophers reject Humean scepticism, believing that it implies a denial of one or other of these principles. Whether that rejection is based on a correct understanding of the kind of scepticism that Hume embraces is a separate issue.

Thirdly, and consequent upon the second criterion, members of the school of common sense philosophy believe in a providential God, creator of the natural world and therefore of us and of our mental powers. In the writings of members of the school there are countless references to the intentions of 'our maker' in giving us the powers that we have, and while it might be possible to salvage much of the philosophy if God is written out of the script, the remnant, even if large, would still have a very different character or personality, and arguably would be too far removed from the paradigm cases of common sense philosophy to count as a philosophy of that genre.

Fourthly, common sense philosophers use a Baconian or Newtonian methodology and see themselves as entitled to employ that methodology because they are studying human nature in the light of the belief that we human beings are part of the natural world. The subtitle of Hume's *Treatise*, '*being an attempt to introduce the experimental method of reasoning into moral subjects*', would not give the common sense school qualms. They all considered that they were applying the experimental method of reasoning to moral subjects.

Fifthly, but still within the realm of scientific methodology, great emphasis was placed by the common sense philosophers on the place of consciousness in our lives and in philosophy. It is noteworthy that the first principle of common sense listed by Reid in his *Essays on the Intellectual Powers* is couched in these terms:

> I shall take it for granted, that I *think*, that I *remember*, that I *reason*, and, in general, that I really perform all those operations of mind of which I am conscious. The operations of our minds are attended with consciousness; and this consciousness is the evidence, the only evidence which we have or can have of their existence.[4]

Among the acts of mind are sensations, remembrances, deliberations, desires, hopes, decisions, and it is only by consciousness that we know of them. A philosopher wishing to say something philosophical about such acts must therefore be conscious of them. But that is not sufficient; reflection, consisting in close attention to an object, is also required. By means of it 'we survey it [namely, the object] on all sides, and form such judgments about it as appear to be just and true'.[5] Reflection therefore requires scrutiny, investigation, an enquiry into the object. We find repeatedly that common sense philosophers give considerable weight to the deliverances of consciousness, especially when the deliverances are the product of reflection.

There is room for discussion and dispute about the distinctive features of a common sense philosophy. The question is largely, if not entirely, an empirical one to be resolved by looking to see what collection of doctrines marks out at least the majority of those called 'common sense philosophers'. The five that I have mentioned can all be shown to be widespread among those commonly regarded as members of the common sense school, and I shall work with this list of criteria while acknowledging that the list is contestable. I wish to consider whether some philosophers, commonly perceived to be of the common sense variety, satisfy the criteria; I shall argue that they perhaps do not, and shall hold that this should come as no surprise, for the concept of a common sense philosopher is vague at the edges (as are all empirical concepts) and therefore allows room for unresolvable dispute as to whether certain proposed cases do or do not fall under the concept. However, everyone agrees that Thomas Reid is quintessentially a common sense philosopher, and I shall therefore begin by discussing his work.

SECTION 2: A PORTRAIT OF THOMAS REID

Thomas Reid's mother Margaret was a Gregory, a family important on the Scottish intellectual scene, particularly the scientific, during the seventeenth and eighteenth centuries. She had three brothers, all professors of mathematics, David at Edinburgh and Oxford, James at Edinburgh (as his brother's immediate successor), and Charles at St Andrews (to be followed by his son David). Her uncle James Gregory had been professor of mathematics at St Andrews and Edinburgh, several other members of the family were professors of medicine at Scottish universities, and in Chapter 5 mention was made of a seventeenth-century Gregory, James, who did significant innovative work on the reflecting telescope. These points regarding the Gregory family are important here because there is good evidence that the family's scientific achievements are a major feature of Reid's self-image. Largely on the testimony of his pupil and friend Dugald Stewart, Reid is standardly presented as a philosopher and nothing more than a philosopher, but he was in fact as much a scientist as a philosopher. Reference to his seventeenth-century ancestor prompts recollection of Reid's own activities in the field of astronomy, and we shall observe later that he was also an accomplished, perhaps brilliant mathematician. Furthermore, his science impacted directly on his philosophy, as we shall notice when we come to consider his development of a geometric model that may be termed, though anachronistically, non-Euclidean.

Reid's father, Lewis Reid, was a minister of the kirk in Strachan, Kincardineshire, when Thomas was born on 26 April 1710. Thomas's religious context impacted on his career no less than did his scientific context. He was a committed member of the kirk; the kirk's belief system was also his; and he produced a philosophy that sat comfortably with his beliefs. It should be no surprise that among his present-day admirers are philosophers of the reformed persuasion, particularly in America but also in Europe, who see Reid's philosophy, and especially his theory of knowledge, as providing strong underpinning to reformed theology.[6] In 1723 Reid went up to Marischal College, Aberdeen, where first he studied Greek under Thomas Blackwell the younger, and then philosophy, including Pufendorf, Locke, Shaftesbury and the English deist tradition, under George Turnbull, who also taught his cohort of students mathematics and the natural sciences. Here we may recall that Turnbull had been an early member of the Rankenian Club, where he had imbibed the ideas of Shaftesbury and of English deism. He had also sought contact with the freethinking Toland, who espoused a position many thought atheistic, but while it is doubtful that Turnbull spoke kindly of Toland to his students he would have spoken very respectfully about Shaftesbury. He would also have taught them the virtue of treating the philosophy of mind as one of the natural sciences, as Newton had recommended; and as regards the methodology that was to be considered appropriate, Turnbull would have told Reid and his fellow-students that Francis Bacon was a precious source of ideas.[7]

Reid graduated master of arts in 1726 and proceeded to the study of divinity, first under Thomas Blackwell the elder and then under James Chalmers. In the early 1730s he had a series of jobs, as clerk to the presbytery of Kincardine O'Neil (the parish whose school Reid had attended) and as a preacher there; then for three years from 1733 he was librarian of Marischal College.

Reid only twice left Scotland, once to go to the south of England in 1736 in the company of his friend the distinguished mathematician John Stewart, and once in 1740 to London to marry his cousin Elizabeth, daughter of his uncle George Reid, though while in London he also attended a meeting of the Royal Society, in whose *Philosophical Transactions* his first published work[8] would appear in 1748. On the 1736 visit Reid and Stewart went to Oxford, where Reid's uncle David Gregory occupied the mathematics chair, and to Cambridge, where they met Nicholas Saunderson, the professor of mathematics who, in virtue of his mastery of geometry despite his blindness, figures significantly in Reid's first great work, *An Inquiry into the Human Mind on the Principles of Common Sense.*

In 1737 Reid became minister of New Machar in Aberdeenshire, and stayed in that post until 1751, during which time he benefited from the presence nearby of George Campbell (1719–96) and Alexander Gerard (1728–95), both of whom were to become significant figures on the Scottish philosophical scene, both of them Aberdeen professors. In terms of religion and ecclesiastical politics, no less than of philosophy, the three men were close, in so far as all were members of that loose alliance known as the 'moderate party' in the kirk. During those New Machar years the three discussed philosophy, and Reid worked on the mathematical and physical sciences, dedicating himself especially to Newton's writings. Among the leading philosophers of eighteenth-century Scotland (here I include Hutcheson, Hume, Smith, Kames, Ferguson and Stewart), Reid was the most accomplished practitioner of mathematics and the natural sciences.

In 1751 Reid was elected regent at King's College, Aberdeen, and taught four cohorts of students the full cycle of arts subjects, each cycle three years in duration. The subjects he covered included mathematics, the natural sciences, pneumatology (or philosophy of mind), ethics, politics, natural theology and rhetoric, by modern standards an extraordinary range of subjects. But in the eighteenth century it was standard work for regents in arts in Scotland (and for their students) and is a rather distant descendant of the medieval university curriculum of the seven liberal arts, namely the *trivium* of grammar, logic and rhetoric, and the *quadrivium* of arithmetic, geometry, astronomy and music. The wide span of the regent's work is reflected in the range of subjects dealt with in Aberdeen's Wise Club, of which Reid was a founder-member. Others who figure in its activities are John Gregory, David Skene, Alexander Gerard, James Beattie, George Campbell, Robert Traill and James Dunbar.[9] To this club Reid read several papers that later appeared in his first major work; presentations by other members of the society would also appear in print, for example, parts of George Campbell's *Philosophy of Rhetoric* and *Dissertation on Miracles*.

The Wise Club devoted time to Hume's philosophy, and several of its members, including Alexander Gerard and George Campbell, published lengthy criticism of him. Then there was Reid's *Inquiry into the Human Mind*, of which Hume had seen a draft. The book, containing both a powerful attack on the theory of ideas in the versions developed by John Locke, George Berkeley[10] and Hume, and also an exposition and defence of an alternative philosophy of perception, immediately attracted strongly favourable attention in Scotland, including at Glasgow University, whose chair of moral philosophy had recently been vacated by Adam Smith.

In May 1764 Reid was elected to the moral philosophy chair, which he occupied until his death thirty-two years later. Reid's professorship at Glasgow was a different kind of post from his regentship at Aberdeen. Though in Glasgow he had some latitude regarding the contents of his 'public lectures', there were tight limits; in particular he could not cover logic and rhetoric since there was a professor of logic and rhetoric (James Clow,[11] who was followed during Reid's professorship by George Jardine[12]). Reid gave public lectures daily for a course that dealt with pneumatology, ethics (including natural jurisprudence) and politics, with most time devoted to pneumatology. The pneumatology lectures dealt with the human mind, in particular our intellectual and active powers, and the existence and mind of God. Reid also delivered 'private lectures' three times a week to an advanced class on the culture (that is, the cultivation) of the mind, in which he spoke on logic and rhetoric as well as on the fine arts, and much of the area that he covered in these lectures is represented in his later publications. Some of his ideas on logic saw the light of day due to a commission from his friend Henry Home, raised to the bench with the title of Lord Kames, a man who never occupied an academic post but with whom Reid had countless conversations about the arts and sciences. Reid and his family were regular guests at Kames's family seat at Blair Drummond. He refers to one such visit in a letter of 31 October 1767: 'I passed eight Days lately with Lord Kaims at Blair Drummond . . . I have been labouring at Barbara Celarent for three weeks bygone.'[13] This is the first intimation we have of Kames's invitation to Reid to write 'A brief account of Aristotle's logic, with remarks', a work that eventually appeared as an appendix to Kames's *Sketches of the History of Man* (1774).

In 1780 Reid, by then seventy years old, withdrew from his teaching duties, seemingly in consequence of increasing deafness, and left his assistant Archibald Arthur to do the teaching in his place. Reid, having retired neither from his chair nor from philosophy, dedicated himself to preparing for publication a large unitary work, which Kames termed Reid's '*Opus Magnum*'.[14] Rather late in the process, perhaps as late as 1784, Reid decided that the work should be divided into two, the first on the intellectual, and the second on the active, powers, giving as his reason the fact that he was uncertain that he would live long enough to publish the essays on the active powers. In the course of his immense task he received extensive comment from his kinsman James Gregory and from Dugald Stewart, who are the joint dedicatees of the *Essays on the Intellectual Powers* (1785).[15] In their labour of appraisal and correction they were joined by Lord Kames, who revised the text 'more than once, as far as it was carried, before his death [in 1782]'. The *Essays on the Active Powers* appeared in 1788. These two large volumes are a product of the lectures that Reid delivered both at Glasgow, to his classes on pneumatology and ethics, and also at King's College, Aberdeen; he also incorporated revised versions of lectures to the Wise Club in Aberdeen and the Glasgow Literary Society.

As Humean scepticism was the philosophical issue that most concerned Reid in his earlier years, so in his latter years the philosophical issue that seems most to have concerned him was materialism, particularly in the version of Joseph Priestley. But while he wrote a good deal on this issue he did not publish any of these writings, perhaps because he was not fully satisfied with the effectiveness of his rebuttal of Priestley.[16]

Circa 1794 Reid wrote for Sir John Sinclair an account of Glasgow University that was eventually published posthumously in 1799 in the final volume of Sinclair's twenty-one-volume *Statistical Account of Scotland*.

Reid was never an ivory-towered academic. He spent fourteen years as a parish minister and thereafter on a number of occasions he represented his university, first King's College and then Glasgow, at the annual meeting of the General Assembly of the Church of Scotland. Late in life he was a founder-member of the Glasgow Society of the Sons of Ministers of the Church of Scotland.[17] At a time when the anti-slavery movement was gathering momentum Reid wrote to his cousin James Gregory:

> Our University has sent a petition to the House of Commons, in favour of the African slaves. I hope yours will not be the last in this humane design; and that the Clergy of Scotland will likewise join in it. I comfort my grey hairs with the thoughts that the world is growing better, having long resolved to resist the common sentiment of old age, that it is always growing worse.[18]

He was also committed to penal reform, and in particular gave strong support to the penal reformer John Howard.[19] Likewise he had strong views on both the American and the French Revolutions. Thus in summer 1791 he wrote to a friend:

Some few here think or affect to think, that to be a Friend to the Revolution of France is to be an Enemy to the Constitution of Britain, or at least to its present Administration. I know the contrary to be true in my self, & verily believe that most of my Acquaintance who Rejoice in that Revolution agree with me in this.[20]

Reid died on 7 October 1796, four years after his wife Elizabeth. Of their nine children he was survived by just one, Martha, wife of Gershom Carmichael's son.

SECTION 3: AN ANATOMY OF THE MIND – METHODOLOGICAL PRELIMINARIES

'All that we know of the body, is owing to anatomical dissection and observation, and it must be by an anatomy of the mind that we can discover its powers and principles.'[21] In this sentence Reid declares the topic of the three books he published and also hints at the methodology implied; the topic is the powers and principles of the mind, and the approach is that of the empirical scientist. The approach is the Newtonian method, precisely that commended by his teacher George Turnbull, though Reid knew that Newton had not invented it. In a letter to Dugald Stewart, Reid wrote: 'Did not his [namely Bacon's] Novum Organum give birth to the Art of Induction? . . . it is too little known that the Spirit of Newton and Locke descended from the Loins of Lord Bacon.' [22]

The art of induction was developed in part as a positive phase in a movement in logic whose negative phase was an attack on Aristotle's theory of the demonstrative syllogism. Bacon objected to the syllogistic theory on the grounds that it is useless for the purposes of empirical science and that what is required instead is a method that involves collecting data, by experiment and observation, and formulating general rules that can both accommodate the observations and be used to make successful predictions. As to what was wrong with the Aristotelian syllogism, Reid discusses the matter in his 'Brief account of Aristotle's logic, with remarks', and makes clear that for him a logic should have 'utility' and that its utility is to be measured by the extent to which the logic enables us to advance from what is known to what is unknown, but with a valid Aristotelian syllogism no such progress is made. Given that every dog is an animal and that every spaniel is a dog it may validly be concluded that every spaniel is an animal, but the fact that every spaniel is an animal is 'virtually contained' in the premisses and does not constitute a discovery, in Reid's view.[23] What Reid wants to know is how the premisses are reached. Is it not by seeing a great many dogs and seeing that they are all animals, and by seeing no counter-examples, and likewise with the discovery that all spaniels are dogs? But this is not a method of discovery that is articulated in the Aristotelian syllogistic logic. What Reid finds in Bacon is a logic of scientific discovery, an inductive logic, by which we move up from observed singular instances to generalisations, and then, by way of prediction, down from the generalisations to new singular instances. This is the method that Reid aims to deploy in his anatomical investigations of the mind. It is a consequence of this, and one welcomed by Reid, that his conclusions about the powers and principles of the mind are empirically testable.

All scientific projects face obstacles that are consequent upon their subject matter. The anatomy of the mind is no different, and Reid spells out some of the obstacles. First there is the fact that the only mind which the anatomist can examine 'with any degree of accuracy and distinctness' is his own, for it is only to his own that he has direct access. In Reid's metaphor, his is the only mind that 'he can look into';[24] he has access to all other minds only indirectly, by external signs which he interprets in the light of what he knows about his own mind as a result of his direct access to it. All this is in contrast to the physical anatomist who has direct access to many bodies, not only his own, and who is therefore able to acquire a much larger database before constructing his inductive arguments about the nature of human bodies.

Secondly, while there are some powers (Reid terms them 'faculties'[25]) which are original and natural to us, such as our powers of sensory perception, whose existence is not a product of human culture or cultivation, other powers develop in us only as a result of the impact on us of our human culture. I can speak English because I was brought up in an anglophone community; I can play the flute because someone taught me. As a result of the different environments to which we are exposed, combined with our native differences, the mind of each person displays significant variations from that of other people and, as Reid concludes: 'such a prodigious diversity of minds must make it extremely difficult to discover the common principles of the species.'[26]

Thirdly, by the time the anatomist of mind begins his scientific study he faces a problem at least as great as that faced by the chemist, who has to analyse something which may be the product of processes of composition, dissolution, evaporation and sublimation, all carried out in an order that would have to be discovered, and upon an initial set of materials whose nature has to be discovered. Likewise with the mind, where some of the processes may be rational but most are instinctual, habitual, associative and so on, thus creating immense obstacles to a scientific determination of the fundamentals of the mind.

Fourthly, from earliest infancy we acquire the habit of attending to the objects of sense perception, things in the outer world, and hardly at all to things in the inner world unless they force themselves upon us by their pleasantness or painfulness. Attention directed inwards therefore requires us to work against a long and strongly established habit of mind.

Fifthly, many mental acts are intentional in their nature in the sense that they are directed to an object, as for example to remember is to remember something, to see is to see something, to be angry is to be angry at something; and the something is always other than the act itself. Naturally when so engaged we attend not to the act but to its object, and it requires an effort to attend to the act, to which it should be added that in many cases the object sustains the operation, with the result that the transference of attention from the object annihilates the act; if I am angry at something and take the opportunity of the anger to investigate the state of being angry rather than what I am angry at, the anger itself will subside because what prompts the anger has disappeared from sight. There is plainly a methodological problem concerning how to attend to an intentional act that vanishes when it becomes the object of attention.[27]

Sixthly, we have a problem due to the sheer rapidity of succession of what we need to study, our thoughts and feelings, in general the operations of the mind with their infinitely diverse contents. Indeed, things that had best stay still if we are to have a good look at them come and go so fast that we can often hardly be sure that they were ever there.

Finally, the anatomist of the mind has a problem about presentation of his findings. Descartes, Malebranche, Locke, Berkeley, Hutcheson, Hume and many other philosophers had adopted the doctrine, Reid's philosophical *bête noir*, known as the 'theory of ideas', and had appropriated familiar terminology, such as 'thought', 'impression' and 'idea', to express their doctrines. Since, however, they gave these appropriated terms a sense that could not be deduced from a knowledge of common usage, this creates a problem for other philosophers who wish to use ordinary terms with their ordinary meanings. In short, their very language had been spoiled for them by the theorists of ideas.

SECTION 4: AN ANATOMY OF THE MIND – INTELLECTUAL POWERS

Reid does not undertake a definition of 'mind', but he says enough to indicate what he is writing about: 'By the *mind* of a man, we understand that in him which thinks, remembers, reasons, wills.'[28] That is all we learn but it is enough; Reid identifies mind not by what it is but by what it does. Implicitly we learn what it *is*, for mind is that principle in us in virtue of which we are able to engage in such acts as thinking, remembering, reasoning and willing. What it is about us that permits us to engage in such acts we are not told; Reid's whole focus on the mind is instead on the mind's acts and the powers that we must ascribe to it in virtue of our being able to perform such acts. But it is already plain that something, even if only at a high level of abstraction, can be said about the nature of mind, for if mind is to be identified by its acts then it is being conceived of as an agent. This indicates the metaphysical territory Reid is traversing. If in the scientific investigation of mind the fundamental relation to be probed is that of an agent to its acts then the relation is not that of a substance to its accidents, properties or qualities, nor is it that of a container to its contents. The philosophy that Reid constructs on the basis of this insight has both a negative and a positive aspect. Negatively, it is an attack on the theory of ideas, and it is to this attack that I shall now turn, beginning with a brief consideration of the point, made earlier, that the theorists of ideas appropriated terms in common currency and put those terms to uncommon use.

Chief amongst the contested terms is that of 'idea'. Locke used the term to signify 'whatsoever is the object of the understanding when a man thinks'.[29] Hume's term 'perception' seems to have the same significance as Locke's 'idea', though, as noted in Chapter 7, Hume considered perceptions as of two kinds: 'impressions', which are perceptions on their first appearance in the soul, and 'ideas', which are faint copies of impressions. In each case Reid understands Locke and Hume to be speaking about a mental entity, whether 'idea' or 'perception', which is itself an object of thought, and the only direct object of thought.

Reid refuses to fall into line with linguistic decrees. To have an idea about some external object X is not, in his view, to be thinking about a mental entity; it is instead to be thinking about external object X; it is to be remembering it, imagining it, conceiving it or reasoning about it, but in each case it is the external object X itself that is the object of the mental act, and not the idea of the object. But if to have an idea of X is to be thinking about X, then to have an idea is to be engaged in a mental act by which something, whether in the mind or outside it, is grasped. In this sense, which is the sense Reid derives from common linguistic practice, 'idea' is to be understood in terms of a mental act that can be just as easily directed to the external world as to anything in the mind. The idea is not the object of thought but is the mental act by which an object is grasped. It is Reid's contention that the theory of ideas conflates these two things, and places the object of the mental act in the mind when it is only the act itself that must be located in the mind.

In discussing Hume's account of the association of ideas, I said that Hume's model of the mind is Newtonian in that he in effect invites us to consider the mind in terms of a mental space within which mental particles and clusters of particles (simple ideas and complex ideas) gravitate towards, or 'attract', each other with discernible regularity, that is, they exhibit law-like behaviour. On this interpretation of Hume he has appropriated the Newtonian picture as a metaphor for the mind and its operations. Reid, who understood Hume in these terms, responds by saying that Hume's position is based on a misunderstanding of the metaphysical status of our ideas; ideas are not mental particles attracting each other by a mental form of gravitation; instead they are acts of an agent whose action may just as easily be directed to the outer world as to the inner. In either case, the idea is not the object of thought. If an idea is, as Locke says, 'whatsoever is the object of the understanding, when a man thinks' then, as Reid holds, there are no ideas. Of course Reid thinks that there are ideas, but that they are not what Locke says they are. It is on this basis that Reid accuses the theorists of ideas of distorting ordinary linguistic practices and thereby queering the linguistic pitch for other philosophers. One reason for the distortion is that they are seeking to understand the mind on an analogy with matter, when in fact mind is too unlike matter for the analogy to have any worth. Reid is not in general hostile to analogical reasoning, and indeed is full of praise for Bishop Butler's use of it: 'I know no Author who has made a more just and a more happy use of [analogical] reasoning, than Bishop BUTLER, in his Analogy of Religion, Natural and Revealed, to the Constitution and Course of Nature.'[30] Nevertheless he acknowledges that it can yield probable conclusions at best, never certainties, and he also thinks that it can at worst yield conclusions that are valueless, as in the case of attempts to model mind on the analogy of matter.[31]

One distinction between mind and matter that Reid stresses from first to last is that mind is essentially active, something which thinks, imagines, intuits, conceives, remembers, anticipates, deliberates and so on – it is always doing something – whereas matter is essentially passive, for the behaviour of every particle is determined very precisely by the balance of forces operating on it. Newtonian dynamics presupposes the passivity of particles; they don't have a mind of their own, unlike us. Reasoning analogically from the behaviour of matter to our behaviour is therefore almost certain to fail.

It is because it is plain to experience that mind is profoundly unlike matter in its modes of operation that Reid, as a good empirical scientist, resists the temptation to use the one as a model for the other. He proceeds on the basis of observation and duly reports that we operate in accordance with given principles which are undeniable but which cannot be proved because we need to assume those very principles if we are to prove anything at all. These 'first principles' or 'principles of common sense' are discovered empirically by a consideration of languages, and of our behaviour, and of our reaction to those who deny those principles. Nowhere does Reid produce what he declares to be a complete list of such principles, nor could he do so without coming into conflict with his avowedly empirical approach to their identification; and just as the scientist's conclusions are always defeasible, since he can never rule out the possibility that new discoveries will be made which will imply that his account is incomplete or is plain wrong, so also an empirical scientist's conclusions about human nature will always, and for the same reasons, be likewise defeasible.

Among Reid's principles of common sense are the following. First, we really do perform all the mental operations of which we are conscious. Reid employs 'consciousness' as a technical term to refer to our awareness of specifically internal acts and events and not at all of things that occur in the physical world; I am conscious of my thoughts, memories, reasonings, pleasures and pains, but not of the desk I sit at or the painting on the wall. The objects of consciousness cannot not exist while we are conscious of them; if I am conscious of a pain then the pain exists, and for me my consciousness of my pain is the sole evidence I either have or even can have that the pain exists. Likewise if I am conscious of thinking then I have conclusive evidence of the existence of the thoughts. Reid's emphasis, however, is not on the actual existence of something, but on the persuasiveness of the evi-

dence. As he puts the point: 'Every man finds himself under a necessity of believing what consciousness testifies.'[32] By the original constitution of our nature we believe the deliverances of consciousness.
It is not that no one can deny such deliverances but that anyone who
denies them in all seriousness is insane, and the remedy lies with
medical science, not with philosophy.

Secondly, we know our past experiences by memory as we know
our present mental operations by consciousness. It is not at issue that
our memory can deliver false testimony about the past; of course it
can. Reid attends instead to the necessity we find ourselves under to
believe what memory tells us. While it is not impossible that anyone
should deny that memory delivers reliable testimony concerning our
past, anyone who in all seriousness does deny this is insane, and the
remedy, if there is one, must be medical. It cannot be philosophical,
for if a person is not prepared to trust his memory, then he is not prepared to trust it when it tells him at any given moment what the premisses are that have so far been presented to him in the philosophical
argument against his position. Indeed, for someone who truly dis-
trusts his memory, how by the middle of a sentence addressed to him
can he know what he had heard at the start of it?

Thirdly, the thoughts that each of us is conscious of are thoughts
that a thinking agent has, a thinking agent that each of us terms
'myself' or 'my mind'. Of this thinking agent each of us is convinced
that it has a continuing identity that stretches back as far as our
memory takes us. Someone who doubts that he has a continuing identity can hardly be argued out of his doubt, for the argument would be
directed at him, and would therefore presuppose a continuing person
at whom the argument is directed. Yet it is precisely this continuing
person whose existence is doubted by the person who needs to be
argued out of his doubt. Once again Reid thinks that the doubter's
problem is medical:

> Every man of a sound mind finds himself under a necessity of believ-
> ing his own identity, and continued existence. The conviction of this
> is immediate and irresistible; and if he should lose this conviction, it
> would be a certain proof of insanity, which is not to be remedied by
> reasoning.[33]

Fourthly, Reid attends to things whose existence we do not doubt
and which presuppose things beyond themselves whose existence also
cannot be doubted. Reid has two kinds of case in mind. First, there
are kinds of things perceived immediately by sensory perception, such

as hardness, softness, figure, colour and so on, all of which we judge to be qualities of a thing, a subject, which has them. That is, qualities are judged to be incomplete in themselves in that any quality is always a quality *of an* X in which it inheres and without which the quality could not itself exist. In somewhat the same way acts or operations presuppose an agent that performs them; thinking presupposes a thinker and speaking presupposes a speaker. To deny that qualities are of things qualified and that acts are performed by agents is to deny principles of common sense.

What justifies the claim that the aforementioned principles of common sense are indeed common to all people or at least to all of sound mind? First is the fact, as Reid believes it to be, that our behaviour implies our acceptance of the principles. We all act on the assumption that, for example, our memory is on the whole a reliable instrument for delivering up truths about the past, and that we are not momentary existences but on the contrary have a past existence that continues through the present and into the future. That we are remorseful about past behaviour and make plans to atone for our misconduct demonstrates that we believe in ourselves as continuing existences. The belief shows up in our behaviour every hour of our waking lives.

As well as the behavioural evidence there is the linguistic evidence, which Reid repeatedly invokes. The underlying insight is that our linguistic practices reflect our beliefs about the world and that if there are beliefs that we all share they will be reflected in our languages; universal features of language will indicate universal beliefs about the world. That is the order: we have certain linguistic practices because we experience the world as we do; it is not that we experience the world as we do because of our linguistic practices. Reid writes:

> Language is the express image and picture of human thoughts; and, from the picture, we may often draw very certain conclusions with regard to the original. We find in all languages the same parts of speech, nouns substantive and adjective, verbs active and passive, varied according to the tenses of past, present and future; we find adverbs, prepositions, and conjunctions. There are general rules of syntax common to all languages. This uniformity in the structure of language, shows a certain degree of uniformity in those notions upon which the structure of language is grounded.[34]

In justification of his claim that certain beliefs are common sense, in his technical sense of the term, he therefore undertakes to parade universals of language. Thus we read:

> In all ages, and in all languages, ancient and modern, the various modes of thinking have been expressed by words of active significa-tion, such as seeing, hearing, reasoning, willing, and the like. It seems therefore to be the natural judgment of mankind, that the mind is active in its various ways of thinking; and for this reason they are called its operations, and are expressed by active verbs.[35]

Reid then affirms that most operations of the mind are expressed by active transitive verbs, and adds:

> And we know, that, in all languages, such verbs require a thing or person, which is the agent, and a noun following in an oblique case, which is the object. Whence it is evident, that all mankind, both those who have contrived language, and those who use it with understand-ing, have distinguished these three things as different, to wit, the oper-ations of the mind, which are expressed by active verbs, the mind itself, which is the nominative to those verbs, and the object, which is, in the oblique case, governed by them.[36]

One more example should suffice:

> All languages have a plural number in many of their nouns; from which we may infer, that all men have notions, not of individual things only, but of attributes, or things which are common to many individuals; for no individual can have a plural number.[37]

It is not clear whether Reid's conclusions overreach his methodol-ogy on the matter of universals of language. He had a reading knowl-edge of three languages, perhaps four, but that of course is a hopelessly inadequate basis for drawing conclusions about all lan-guages. There were available to him scholarly writings on languages far removed from English, French and Latin[38] but, whatever his knowledge of those writings, he never provides the kinds of detailed evidence that is needed in justification of his claims concerning fea-tures, most of them syntactical, said to be present in all languages. There will be further comment on this point later in the chapter in the context of specific claims about all languages.

The first of Reid's masterpieces, his *Inquiry into the Human Mind*, is an investigation into our faculty of sensory perception, and in the *Essays on the Intellectual Powers* the first of the powers investigated is that of sensory perception (the others being memory, conception, abstraction, judgment and reasoning). In this section on Reid on the intellectual powers I shall focus on his theory of perception, dealing first with perception in general and then turning to visual perception in order to note a major achievement of Reid's.

Sensory perception contains three elements or aspects, namely conception, judgment and sensation. As regards conception, we cannot perceive an object without forming a conception of it. As regards visual perception, the greater the distance or the feebler the light the less distinct the conception of the object, other things being equal. That last qualification has to be added since two people perceiving the same object at the same time and from more or less the same position may form very different conceptions of it, for one may know a great deal about such objects and will therefore form a rich concept of it, whereas the other, knowing far less about such objects, will form a much thinner concept of it though he sees it just as well as his neighbour does.[39]

As regards the place of judgment in perception, Reid holds that the faculty of sense perception is a faculty of judgment, for in perceiving something we form an irresistible conviction of and belief in its existence, and the belief is itself part of the perception. Of course some perceptions are very faint. Is that really a star in the sky at sunset? Is that really a ship on the horizon? But if we do indeed take ourselves to be perceiving an X, then we must believe that what we perceive exists, and if we are in doubt whether there is an X there then we must doubt whether we are perceiving an X there.

The third element in perception is sensation. This is often, perhaps almost always, an elusive feature of our experiencing of the world in that there are often large obstacles to our attending to our sensations. Some sensations are unproblematic; we can easily focus on them and sometimes they are so attention-demanding that we can hardly focus on anything else. For example, when we feel a pain it can be difficult not to attend to it. This case provides Reid with an example of the occasional unhelpfulness of language as an indicator of our beliefs about reality. 'I see a tree' and 'I feel a pain' are the same grammatical shape but logically they are different. The tree I am looking at does not depend for its existence on the perceptual operation by which I see the tree; I do not believe that if I stop looking at it it will cease to exist; but the pain does depend for its existence on my feeling it. While I feel a pain the pain exists and the moment I cease to feel it it ceases to exist. Rather than say that the feeling and the pain are two separate things, it is better to say that the pain is the form that the feeling takes, whereas it is appropriate to say that the seeing and the tree are two different things, one the mental operation of seeing and the other the tree which is the object of the seeing, but which is not any the less real a tree when it ceases to be the object of a perceptual act.

Most mental acts have objects – this is a favourite theme of Reid's. We do not just perceive; we perceive something. We do not just love; we love something. But the feeling which is a pain does not have an object. The pain might, and no doubt does, have a cause, say a physical injury. But causes and objects are different sorts of things and in relation to the same mental act may not coincide – the cause of my anger may be a bad day at the office but the object of my anger, that at whom or which it is directed, may be my partner's mildly irritating behaviour once I have returned home. In the case of pain caused by physical injury the lesion is no more than the cause of the feeling. The feeling itself, which is a sensation, has no object. In fact it is Reid's contention that no sensation has an object, but it may be difficult to accept this contention because in many, perhaps most, cases sensations are parts of complex acts that do have objects. Among examples of this are our acts of sensory perception. Reid holds that Hume conflated sensation and perception, and did so to the detriment of his philosophy, but Reid also holds that attention to our linguistic practice in this matter will be of little help since the distinction hardly shows up in our linguistic practice – nor is there any reason why it should, because for ordinary purposes there is no need for us to mark the distinction between sensation and perception. Since the distinction is philosophically important as marking a major point of weakness in the theory of ideas, we should note Reid's position.

In smelling a rose I have a sensation, an agreeable one of the scent of the rose. This olfactory sensation is in me in that I am the subject of it, the person who has the sensation. The sensation depends on me for its existence; I cease to smell the rose and the smell of the rose, considered as a sensation, thereby ceases to exist, for there is nothing more to the sensation than my having it. The cause of my sensation, which is the rose or more particularly some feature of its chemical make-up, may continue to exist when I move out of olfactory range of the flower, but the cause of my sensation is not the sensation itself. Nevertheless, and here is the linguistic point that Reid focuses on, the cause of the olfactory sensation is called 'the smell of the rose', for the flower has a certain fragrance whether anyone smells it or not.

Hence there are two answers to the question: 'Where is the smell of the rose?' One is 'It is in the person who has the olfactory sensation' and the other is 'It is in the rose which causes the sensation'; 'smell' has a different sense in the two cases. Smell, considered as a sensation, can exist only in a sentient being, but a flower is not, so far as we know, a sentient being, and if it were the point would still remain that it is not in virtue of its sentience that it is here being said to have a smell; it has a smell in the same sense in which smoke from a log fire has a smell.

It has to be concluded that the phrase 'smell of the rose' refers to two things that are not only really distinct but also that do not in any way resemble each other – for sensations, existing, and able to exist, only in the mind of a sentient being, are utterly unlike bits of chemistry, which are in no way modifications or operations of a mind. The olfactory sensation no more resembles the chemical cause in the rose than my pain resembles the leg injury that causes it. The same may be said of the relation between sensations of other kinds and their causes; for example, sensations of warmth and cold, of softness and hardness, of loudness and quiet. The sensation of warmth, which is a feeling, can exist only in a sentient being and only for as long as the sentient being is feeling it. But that same sensation is caused by something external, say a fire, and the fire, as a physical thing, cannot exist in a mind.

If the relation of a sensation to the object of the perceptual act is not one of resemblance, then what is it? Reid's short answer is that it is the relation of a natural sign to its significate. The notion of a natural sign works hard in Reid's philosophy; he identifies three sorts. First, the relation between a natural sign and its significate is established by nature but discovered by observation and experiment. Where two things are related as cause to effect in nature, the former is a natural sign of the latter; the relation between the two phenomena is natural but it is by experience that we learn to read the cause as a sign of the effect. The whole project of natural science is taken up with the empirical task of determining what is a natural sign of what. Secondly, the relation between a natural sign and its significate is established by nature and is, in Reid's words, 'discovered to us by a natural principle, without reasoning or experience'.[40] His examples include our recognition of the significance of an angry countenance, of a smile, of various modulations of the voice. Infants do not need to be taught what these mean; they know by the original constitution of their nature. Thirdly, in Reid's words: 'though we never before had any notion or conception of the things signified, [the natural signs] do suggest it, or conjure it up, as it were, by a natural kind of magic, and at once give us a conception, and create a belief of it'.[41] Sensations are in this sense natural signs of external things. Our sensations prompt us 'by a natural kind of magic' to conceive these external things and to believe in their existence.

It is plain that without our sensations we could not have the kind of awareness of the external world that we do have. Nevertheless in the case of most of our perceptual acts the sensations that are part of them do not force themselves on our attention, for, to speak generally, it is not in our sensations that we are interested but in what our sensations signify. The sensation of heat signifies the heat of the fire, and this is information about the fire that is of practical interest to us. As regards our lack of attention to our sensations the situation is much the same as that regarding the font-type and font-size used in a book. We can read to the bottom of a page and take in the meaning of everything on the page, yet be unable to report what the print looked like because we had simply not attended to it. So long as it was easy to read, the print had done its job. If the print is delightful or ugly we will notice it, and then it is an obstacle to the primary purpose of the print, which is to signify the thought of the author. Likewise with sensations. Sometimes they are agreeable or disagreeable and we notice them for that reason, but most often they are neither and then they can perform their usual role of signifying something external.

Reid does not underestimate the problem of attending to our sensations, and speaks at times of the work of many years that he dedicated to focusing on them. It is our nature to be aware of the outer world; we have to live in it, to act on it and react to it. Attention to the inner things that need to take place for the outer awareness to occur would be a distraction from, and an obstacle to, the all-important task of making a success of living in the world. But Reid is engaged in the scientific task of describing human nature, and he has therefore to analyse our perceptual acts and to comment on the elements, such as sensation, that his analysis discloses. He finds sensations to be associated with all the sensory modalities, including sight. As with the other senses, there are visual sensations that flit by and in most cases leave no trace of their passage. Reid trained himself to notice the sensations associated with sight, and he did so not for practical purposes but because he needed sound empirical support for the claim that visual sensation and visual perception are mutually distinct, even though philosophers have standardly failed to notice that there are differences between them, one of them being that perception, unlike sensation, includes a judgment about the existence of things in the outer world, and the other being that sensation, unlike perception, is not directed to an object, and especially is not directed outward to an object in the external world.

The sensory modality to which Reid paid closest attention in the *Inquiry* is that of sight, and I should like here to comment on a prominent feature of his discussion, namely his account of the surprisingly large extent of the knowledge that a blind person can have of what we suppose to be specifically visible aspects of the world. Paradoxically the hero of Reid's extensive discussion on sight is a blind geometer, and the person whom Reid evidently had in mind was Dr Nicholas Saunderson, whose blindness did not prevent him occupying with great distinction the Lucasian chair of mathematics at Cambridge.

The relation of sign to significate and the problem we have in attending to signs are prominent in Reid's discussion of sight, especially in connection with his distinction between two sorts of magnitude: real magnitude and apparent (or visible) magnitude. The real magnitude of an object is measured in terms of its length, how many centimetres or kilometres long it is. Its apparent or visible magnitude is measured in terms of the angle formed by two lines drawn to the eye from the extremities of the object. Thus while I am now sitting at my desk the apparent width of my desk is seventy degrees of my field of vision, since that is the angle at my eye formed by two lines drawn to the eye from the left and the right extremities of the desk.[42] The real width is two metres. For Reid real magnitude is possessed by objects-*qua*-tangible, and apparent magnitude is possessed by objects-*qua*-visible.

The rhetorical force of 'real' as opposed to 'apparent' is important here, as implying an order of value implicit in Reid's doctrine that, by the original constitution of our nature, we treat the visibly apparent as a sign of the tangibly real. The visible appearance of things has value for us, not in its own right, but as a sign for us of the things in the real world; and it is these real things, the significates of visible appearances, that we value. They are things we can manipulate, things with which we can interact causally, things, finally, we can depend upon to be there when we are not observing them. In virtue of qualities or features of visible appearances, we can affirm that there really exist out there things which present such an appearance to the eye, and we can read off from the visible appearances the qualities that the things out there really have.

Visible appearances are fleeting existences, yet without them we could not judge, using our eyes, what really is in the world. Reid affirms that the people, perhaps the only people, who make a proper study of visible appearances are painters; the rest of us are so interested in the significates of those appearances, the things out there and their qualities, that we could scarcely be persuaded of the existence of the signs, the visible appearances themselves. But painters scrutinise visible appearances, for it is the visible appearance of things that is rendered in paint.[43] I shall now consider some of the main points Reid makes regarding the art of painting what we see.

The fact that two objects in a painter's line of vision are really the same size does not mean that he will represent them with images that are the same size, for one of the objects might be further from the painter than the other is, and the further object will be rendered by a smaller image. The reason for the painter's practice is that he is representing apparent, not real, magnitude. He is painting what he sees, not what he knows – he knows that the objects are the same size, but they are different in respect of apparent magnitude, so the corresponding patches of paint are different sizes, this being a standard way to represent relative distance. But apparent magnitude cannot be the only basis for a judgment of relative distance by sight. If we know, of two things, that they are the same height, then if the apparent height of one is one tenth that of the other, we can deduce that it is ten times the distance; but if we have no idea whether they are the same height or not then the apparent difference in height might be due to the fact that though they are equidistant from us one is in reality one tenth the height of the other. Hence, evidence based solely on apparent magnitude needs to be augmented.

Another kind of evidence considered by Reid concerns the colours and inner shapes of the object. I look at a nearby tree and see the individual leaves, the pale brown twigs and the dark brown bark, all these things distinctly visible, but as I walk away from the tree there is a gradual degradation of these visible details, first a blurring of the contours of the leaves and the twigs, and thereafter only an impression of a greenish-brown mass. Increasing distance therefore is accompanied not only by diminished apparent magnitude but also by degradation of colours and figures. We are not accustomed to attend to these changes because we are interested in knowing how far away something is, and the diminished apparent magnitude and the degradation of colour are natural signs of greater distance. We attend to the significate, not to the sign, but the painter must analyse the differences made to the quality of the visible appearance by varying distances. Reid sums up:

> But the masters in painting know how, by the degradation of the colour, and the confusion of the minute parts, figures, which are upon

the same canvas, and at the same distance from the eye, may be made
to represent objects which are at the most unequal distances. They
know how to make the objects appear to be of the same colour, by
making their pictures really of different colours, according to their
distances or shades.[44]

The painter knows that the more distant tree contains many shades
of green and of brown, and that it has other colours too, but he paints
what he sees and what he sees is a greenish-brown blur.

Reid adds an observation concerning the way a painter should represent the quality of light. He attends to a point made by Bishop
Berkeley and taken up by the mathematician Robert Smith.[45] The
quality of light differs in different countries because the purity of the
air is different; the greater the purity the greater the distance at which
details can be seen. Italy has a purer air than the Netherlands, and the
painters of the two countries can be expected therefore to represent
in a slightly different way the distance of distant objects. Reid reports
that this is a commonly assigned reason why Italian painters give a
more lively colour to the sky than do Flemish ones, and he then argues
that since the air of Italy is purer the country's painters should give
'less degradation of the colours, and less indistinctness of the minute
parts, in the representation of very distant objects'.[46] Elsewhere Reid
writes: 'the appearances of the same colour are so various and change-
able, according to the different modifications of the light, of the
medium, and of the eye, that language could not afford names for
them.'[47] As light conditions vary, therefore, so also do visible appearances. Yet the real objects are the same, with the same colours, the
same figures, and so on. It is the visible appearances that the painter
renders on canvas without being detached from reality, for visible
appearances are signs of real objects, and we know how to read these
signs.

Among visible properties a distinction is to be made between
colours and the visible properties that admit of geometrical analysis.
That the colours of a body appear to us in the way they do is, in
Reid's view, inexplicable to us except by saying that it is according to
the divine intention in creating our faculties, but Reid holds that the
geometric properties of things are another matter, for given the real
geometric properties of things we can calculate what their visible
appearance must be. For example, knowing that X is a flat disk we
can demonstrate that if it is parallel to the eye it will appear circular;
that if it is then placed at an oblique angle to the eye it will appear as

an ellipse, and that if it is placed perpendicular to the eye it will appear as a straight line. It can also be demonstrated that as the object recedes from the eye the apparent magnitude of the object diminishes and that when the object is ten times the distance the angle subtended at the eye has diminished to a tenth of its earlier size, which is to say that the apparent magnitude has diminished to a tenth of its earlier size.

These facts all concern the 'visible figure' as contrasted with the 'real figure' of a body. The visible figure of a body consists of the position of the various parts of the body in their relation to the eye, and the real figure consists of the position of the various parts in relation to each other. As regards the visible figure, in most cases this changes as the external body's position in relation to the eye changes. Reid argues that the relation between these two kinds of figure is something that a blind geometer can understand perfectly well. He can understand that, as a flat disk which is parallel to the eye is then tilted, its visible or apparent figure must change from a circle to an ellipse and then to a straight line, and as it continues to rotate in the same direction it again becomes an ellipse and in due course a circle.

Regarding distance from the eye, Reid adopts a position, which by his day was common currency, that we learn distance from the eye not by sight alone but by sight combined with touch. From our earliest days we are handling things, holding them at arm's length, bringing them closer to the eye, noticing that their apparent magnitude diminishes as we place them at arm's length and increases as we bring them to our face. Reid holds that these early activities, which might appear utterly inconsequential, are amongst the most important things in a person's education, because they establish in the child a concept of the distance of a thing from the eye and also teach it what the visible signs are by which distance from the eye can be known. Thus, although it is with the aid of the sense of touch that we initially learn that things are at a distance from the eye, in time we learn how to tell, without the help of touch, that something is at a distance. In all cases we are learning what the significates are of certain visible appearances, and of such slight importance to us are the signs in themselves and of such great importance to us are the significates that, in Reid's language, we acquire a confirmed and inveterate habit of inattention to the signs; 'their passage is so quick, and so familiar, that it is absolutely unheeded; nor do they leave any footsteps of themselves, either in the memory or imagination'.[48] In taking further the question of the relation between sign and significate, which is my immediate purpose here, I wish to focus particularly on the visible figure of objects, an aspect a blind geometer can learn about in great detail – and indeed can think about in a creatively productive way. My question concerns the relation between visible figure and tangible figure. It is especially geometry that deals with the figures of external objects, and a question therefore arises as to whether the geometry of visibles is the same as the geometry of tangibles.

Euclid's geometry, a subject of nearly lifelong interest to Reid,[49] includes diagrams of straight lines, triangles, squares and so on to enable us to grasp more clearly both the sense of the theorems and the stages of the proofs. Since the diagrams are visual aids their presence surely implies that the geometry is a geometry of visible figures. Reid does not question the fact that Euclid's theorems do indeed follow from the postulates and axioms, though over a period of many years he was uneasy about the lack of intuitive obviousness of the postulate that affirmed that through any given point just one line can be drawn that is parallel to a given line. No doubt the lack of intuitive obviousness of the postulate was one element in Reid's openness to the possibility of a geometry that was not Euclid's.

Reid proceeds by imagining a being who is no more than an eye and whose perceptual knowledge of the world is therefore solely visual, and who is therefore bereft of information concerning the distance that anything might be from the eye. The eye is at the centre of a hollow sphere. Since the eye has no concept of distance from itself it has no concept of one object being further from the eye than another object is, nor a concept of an object approaching the eye or receding from it. An object approaching the eye in a straight line can therefore appear to the eye to increase in size but cannot be interpreted as remaining the same size but approaching. An object going behind a larger object and re-emerging at the other side cannot be interpreted as doing what I have just described, for the eye has no conception of a body interposed between the eye and a body, since such a concept implies the concept of distance from the eye. Instead the eye must suppose that the body ceases to be and that sometime later a similar body appears on the other side of the larger body. It is plain that the eye, in the middle of a three-dimensional world, can have no concept of three-dimensionality. The world of visual appearance is solely two-dimensional.

Reid describes the geometry of this two-dimensional world. Let us suppose a line that starts at the north pole of the hollow sphere and proceeds down a longitudinal line on the inner surface of the sphere. To the eye the line is straight. The line proceeds, still visibly straight, towards the south pole. It then continues visibly straight in a northerly direction to the north pole, its point of departure. It is a visibly straight line from start to finish and yet it ends where it started. Its behaviour is un-Euclidean since on Euclid's concept of a straight line, such a line, however far projected, will not coincide with itself.

Let us now suppose that a line starts somewhere on the equator of the hollow sphere and proceeds along the equator. The eye must perceive this as a straight line. Again let us suppose that the line proceeds the full length of its 360-degree journey, so that its point of arrival coincides with its point of departure. It is a visibly straight line and therefore, if its geometry were Euclidean, it could not coincide with itself however far it were projected. In addition, on its journey round the equator it twice cuts the line previously traced from north pole to south and back again. Hence we are speaking of two lines which are straight and yet which cross each other at two points. This also is un-Euclidean since according to Euclid two straight lines can cross each other at most once. Within the model Reid has set up there are countless theorems that are incompatible with Euclid.

If Euclidean geometry is not that of visible space then of what is it the geometry? Reid's answer is that it is the geometry of tangible space – the space of real things, not of visible appearances – and in his view the geometry of visibles had not previously been developed because visible appearances are ephemera, passing fleetingly through the mind and leaving no trace. They affect us only so far as they function as signs of real things, and then, as already noted, it is the real things that hold our attention – as they held Euclid's. One curious feature of Reid's geometry of visibles is that it could have been developed in all its detail by a blind geometer, yet this geometry has the potential to give us an endlessly rich account of visible figure.

An important element in the geometry of visibles has particular philosophical significance as enabling Reid to attack a prominent argument presented by Hume in support of his account (the Humean account) of what is immediately present to the mind when we perceive something. What is at issue is whether what we immediately perceive is the external object itself or is an image of the object. Hume represents the beliefs of ordinary, non-reflective people as follows: 'This very table, which we see white, and which we feel hard, is believed to exist, independent of our perception, and to be something external to our mind, which perceives it. Our presence bestows not being on it: Our absence does not annihilate it.'[50] He then argues against this non-reflective view; his doctrine is that nothing can ever be present to the mind but an image or perception, and the senses are only the inlets through which these images are conveyed. He gives an example of an image, on the basis of which he constructs an argument: 'The table, which we see, seems to diminish, as we remove farther from it: But the real table, which exists independent of us, suffers no alteration: It was, therefore, nothing but its image, which was present to the mind.'[51]

Against this argument Reid invokes his distinction between real and apparent magnitude. The table seems to diminish as we move away from it, that is, its apparent magnitude diminishes; it occupies a smaller proportion of our visual field. The real table does not diminish as we move away from it, that is, its real magnitude does not diminish. Whereas Hume concludes that it is therefore not the real table that we see, he should draw the opposite conclusion. It is mathematically demonstrable that as we move away from a real table its apparent magnitude must diminish, and that is in fact exactly what happens – it looks smaller as we walk away from it. In that case the fact that it looks smaller cannot be evidence that it is not the real table we are looking at. Reid's reply therefore is that by due application of the distinction between real and apparent magnitude the common sense view is not only not undermined but is in fact confirmed.

Reid believes that if the common sense of mankind is in conflict with a received philosophical doctrine then the burden of proof lies not with common sense but with the philosophers. On the question of whether we directly perceive external objects or instead directly perceive only images, Reid sides with common sense, which affirms that our senses give us direct access to objects in the external world, and he wonders what argument anti-common sense philosophers, such as Hume, present in support of their contrary position. Reid finds in Hume's writings only one argument in support of the contrary position, and since this argument is now shown to be flawed, Reid holds that the philosophers have yet to discharge their burden and that he therefore remains entitled to dwell with common sense.

Section 5: An anatomy of the mind – active powers

Let us now consider principles of common sense so far as they concern ourselves as agents, beings who freely act on the world, and the most important such principle is this: 'That we are efficient causes in our deliberate and voluntary actions.'[52] Packed into this proposition are several elements which will emerge in due course, but at its heart is the concept of ourselves as having not just a will but also power over our will. That we will does not by itself make us an efficient cause; to be such a cause we require also control of our will. Reid holds that such control requires a faculty of understanding by which we are able to consider our various motives for acting, but whatever act we perform after considering those motives it was no less open to us not to perform it; this openness is at the heart of the matter. An act is not in my control unless whether I perform it or not is in my control. If I cannot not perform it then not performing it is not in my control, and if I am necessitated to perform it then again it is not in my control whether I perform it – for I cannot not. Power, therefore, implies not necessitation to act but liberty to act or not to act. If they are not both open to me then I am powerless in relation to each of them.

Reid writes: 'By the *Liberty of a Moral Agent*, I understand, *a power over the determinations of his own Will*.'[53] Since the claim that we have moral liberty is a first principle of common sense, it cannot be proved, and yet Reid does undertake to show that we have moral liberty. This may look odd, but it has to be remembered that Reid does not think that principles of common sense are pieces of mindless prejudice. He holds that 'there are certain ways of reasoning even about them, by which those that are just and solid may be confirmed, and those that are false may be detected'.[54] He has in mind such ways of reasoning as the following.

(1) If a person rejects one first principle of common sense and accepts another then he is guilty of inconsistency, for the two principles have the same basis. For example, someone who rejects the testimony of sense or of memory but accepts that of consciousness is guilty of inconsistency, for these faculties are 'all equally the gifts of Nature'. (2) '[T]he consent of ages and nations, of the learned and unlearned, ought to have great authority with regard to first principles, where every man is a competent judge.' Reid is quick to add that this is not a matter of counting votes and of thinking that something must be true if it has received the most votes; instead it is a matter of respecting a practice engaged in by everyone, including scientists, people who are in general particularly wary of arguments from authority. A mathematician who has constructed a new theory may find no fault in it but will still submit his discovery to the judgment of fellow-mathematicians, and will feel more confident in his own

judgment if theirs agrees with his. If most members of his peer group are arrayed against his theory the onus is then on the mathematician to persuade them that they are wrong to reject his work. Reid is saying that this is no less true of someone who denies a principle of common sense, except that in this latter case he has not only mathematicians but all human beings (perhaps excepting a few sceptical philosophers) arrayed against him. It is psychologically very difficult to be indifferent to the judgment of one's peer group, nor is there any virtue in such indifference. (3) If an opinion is so necessary for the conduct of life that not to believe it leads us into countless absurdities in practice, it may be taken for a first principle of common sense.[55]

In the light of these considerations – and of others also deployed by Reid – he feels free to seek rational support for the common sense principle that we have moral liberty. I shall briefly note three closely related pieces of rational support provided by Reid.

First, as regards many types of act that we all perform and have performed for as long as we have had a faculty of reason, acts such as deliberating about what to do, forming a resolution, making a promise, blaming oneself for a wrong use of power, all such imply that we have power over our will. For example, our deliberations about what to do are undertaken with a view to choosing in the light of our deliberations. This is not to say that we must choose in line with the judgment of what would be the best thing to do, for we might say no to it, even if to say no would be a stupid response.

This is not a direct proof that we have control over our will and therefore have moral liberty; it is only a proof that a practice that everyone engages in, and that we have all engaged in once we have a developed faculty of will, implies that we believe that we have power over our will. It is a belief that must already be in place by the time we start exercising our reason, thus opening up the possibility that the belief is itself part of the original constitution of our nature, in which case the belief would be a first principle of common sense. In addition, to reject the belief would be a practical absurdity, for whoever rejects it is hopelessly compromised by the fact that his very deliberations constitute an implicit affirmation of the belief he purports to reject. It makes no sense to deliberate if we think we have no control over whether or not we act on the outcome of the deliberation.

These points can be made equally about forming a resolution, making a promise, and blaming oneself. For to resolve to do something does not make sense unless on the assumption that it is in our power to will to do what we have resolved. In making a promise we set up in the recipient an expectation that we shall indeed do as we promised. Finally in this series, blaming oneself presupposes moral liberty, for blame presupposes the actual wrong use of power and the possible right use of it, and therefore presupposes that prior to the act that attracted the blame the agent was open both to the action he did perform and to some other action that he might have performed (and should have) but failed to. Again this does not prove that we have moral liberty, but it does place in a logically compromising position anyone who denies that we have such liberty and yet also suffers at times from remorse.

A second piece of rational support provided by Reid for the principle that we have moral liberty is in territory adjacent to that just discussed. Everyone believes that we have moral obligations and that we are accountable for our actions when we discharge those obligations and also when we fail to discharge them. But if we lack moral liberty we are not accountable for our actions. That we have moral liberty follows therefore from a universal belief that we all have moral obligations.

A third piece of rational support provided by Reid is that a person's possession of moral liberty is presupposed by the fact that 'he is capable of carrying on, wisely and prudently, a system of conduct, which he has before conceived in his mind, and resolved to prosecute'.[56] If he does not in fact have power over his will, and if his acts are the effect of some other cause acting on him so that he himself is necessitated to go through the physical motions which suggest wisdom and prudence, then his behaviour is deceptive. The fact that he is necessitated means that he may not in fact have either conceived the plan or resolved to prosecute it. Hence if his acts count as evidence that he has wisdom and prudence they must also count as evidence that he has moral liberty. Since it is the same evidence, it follows that whoever denies that we have moral liberty has to face up to the implication that we are in no position to endorse the claim that people are wise and prudent. This, as with the previous arguments, is not intended to be a demonstration of our moral liberty. It is instead an argument to the effect that whoever denies that we have moral liberty thereby burdens himself with intellectual commitments that he will probably be loath to shoulder.

The necessitarian might of course, in the interest of intellectual honesty, be prepared to shoulder the burdens in question because he believes that the arguments in favour of the necessitarian doctrine are undefeated. Reid therefore undertakes to point up weaknesses in some of the supporting arguments. In introducing his discussion Reid ascribes several arguments to necessitarians. In sequence: (1) every deliberate action has a motive. If there is only one motive then it must determine the agent; if there are contrary motives the strongest prevails. (2) To reason from men's motives to their actions is a form of causal reasoning. Since any action caused by motives is determined, a free action must be motiveless and must therefore be a mere caprice. Furthermore if we are free, and therefore uncaused in our acts, rewards and punishments cannot cause us to act and we must therefore be ungovernable. Since we are not in general capricious in our acts and since we are plainly responsive to rewards and punishments, it follows that the necessitarian wins the argument.[57]

The concept of a motive bears a good deal of weight in this line of argument, and Reid replies by acknowledging the manifest fact that we are indeed influenced by motives, and by arguing for the claim that their influence is much like that of recommendations or advice or even exhortation, and therefore falls far short of necessitation. However, a plausible explanation for the fact that a given motive does not in fact determine our will is that there was also a contrary motive in place and that the contrary one was the stronger and therefore prevailed. In a closely related context Reid invokes the law of material nature: 'That every motion and change of motion, is proportional to the force impressed, and in the direction of that force', and he offers for inspection a corresponding law for intelligent beings: 'Every action, or change of action, in an intelligent being, is proportional to the force of motives impressed, and in the direction of that force.'[58] This is precisely the sort of law suggested by the idea that where contrary motives are in play it is always the strongest that prevails. Reid's response is to analyse the concept of 'strongest motive', for until we know the criteria for relative strength of motives we cannot say whether the strongest always prevails. In some cases it is easy; as Reid says, a bribe of a thousand pounds is a stronger motive than one of a hundred. But where the contrary motives are hardly commensurable, such as health versus wealth, or good reputation versus political power, it is not clear how relative strengths are to be compared.

Some have said that it is always the strongest that prevails and have deployed the metaphor of a weighing-scale in support of their claim. Motives are, it is said, like weights placed on a balance. But the metaphor, complains Reid, is in effect incompatible with human agency since the stronger motive (= heavier weight) would leave the person with nothing to do other than respond to the motive by acting in the direction dictated by it. For a human being to be like a balance fits perfectly the necessitarian's picture of us; but why choose that metaphor? Reid himself suggests a different one: 'Contrary motives may very properly be compared to advocates pleading the opposite sides of a cause at the bar. It would be very weak reasoning to say, that such an advocate is the most powerful pleader, because sentence was given on his side.'[59] It is, after all, not the advocate but the judge who passes judgment, and in the case of motives it is the agent who determines what will be done. He does so, no doubt, in the light of the various motives in play, but it is he who is the determinant, not the motives.

At this point Reid makes a crucial distinction: that between animal motives and rational motives, motives addressed to the animal or to the rational parts of our nature. We can measure animal motives by the extent of the effort we need to make if we are to resist them, and the feeling of resistance that is required is the 'animal test for strength of motive'. If two animal motives are mutually contrary then the stronger is the one requiring greater effort if it is to be resisted. Reid speculates that in the case of non-human animals the strongest motive always prevails, for they seem not to have the self-command that is required if a weaker animal motive is to prevail over a stronger.

But we humans do not necessarily obey the dictate of our strongest animal motive, as witness the fact that though hungry we will not in general eat food that is to hand if it belongs to someone else. In most cases, though not all, the rational motive of justice will prevail over the animal motive of hunger. So the strongest animal motive may not prevail, and the strongest rational motive also may not prevail. What conclusion should we draw regarding the necessitarian position? To follow Reid on this matter: if we have moral liberty over the actions in our power, we will often be in a position to choose between those acts that afford us present pleasures at a cost of real harm in the future and other acts that afford us a more distant greater good though perhaps at the cost of present harm. What will we do? On the whole the foolish will use their liberty to opt for the present pleasures while on the whole the wise will opt for the greater but more distant good. Since this is what will happen if we really do have moral liberty, the fact that that is how in general we actually behave cannot be a good reason for adopting the necessitarian position. Let us therefore move forward on the basis of the proposition that we agents make judgments and determine our will in the light of our judgments; in acting wisely we determine our will in accordance with our wise judgment. On this matter Reid is thinking principally about our moral judgments, and I should like here to open up his concept of a moral judgment.

Reid, a successor of Hutcheson in the chair of moral philosophy at Glasgow, is content to use the Hutchesonian terminology of moral sense, but his concept of moral sense is different for, as against Hutcheson, he regards moral sense as a faculty of judgment. In this respect moral sense is like the faculties of sensory perception. In perceiving something I judge it to exist and to have given qualities. Just to have the sensation is insufficient for perception; in the absence of the judgment of present existence I might be imagining the thing to exist or be conceiving it, but not perceiving it. To take the opposite case, merely to be judging the thing to exist is insufficient for perceiving, which requires also the mental act of sensation. This account by Reid of what is involved in perception applies no less to moral sense than to the outer senses, and is sufficient to establish his divergence from Hutcheson; and also from Hume, whose dictum that 'Morality, therefore, is more properly felt than judg'd of'[60] is plainly contradicted by the concept of moral sense just sketched.

A judgment is 'a determination of the understanding, with regard to what is true, or false, or dubious'.[61] What makes a moral judgment true or false? Reid tells us that the form of the answer is the same as for sense-perceptual judgments:

> every judgment is, in its own nature, true or false; and, though it depends upon the fabric of a mind, whether it have such a judgment or not, it depends not upon that fabric whether the judgment be true or not. A true judgment will be true, whatever be the fabric of the mind; but a particular structure and fabric is necessary, in order to our perceiving that truth.[62]

As to what it is that makes the judgment true, Reid argues, partly on the linguistic evidence, that it is the obvious thing. In judging that a person's act was wicked or was kindly I ascribe wickedness or kindliness to the act as qualities of the act.

Granted that judgment is one element in the exercise of our moral sense, a second is conception. We require moral conceptions for moral judgments just as we require perceptual sensory conceptions for judgments of outer sense: 'by our moral faculty, we have both the original conceptions of right and wrong in conduct, of merit and demerit, and the original judgments that this conduct is right, that is wrong; that this character has worth, that demerit.'[63] We should not assume that Reid believed that we form moral judgments by putting together such items as conceptions. In the course of an attack on the theory of ideas he writes:

> without some degree of judgment, we can form no accurate and distinct notions of things; so that, one province of judgment is, to aid us in forming clear and distinct conceptions of things, which are the only fit materials for reasoning. This will probably appear to be a paradox to Philosophers, who have always considered the formation of ideas of every kind as belonging to simple apprehension; and that the sole province of judgment is to put them together in affirmative or negative propositions.[64]

The implication of this appears to be that we cannot reach clear and distinct moral concepts without first making moral judgments.

We reach a third element in the exercising of our moral sense: 'Our moral judgments are not like those we form in speculative matters, dry and unaffecting, but, from their nature, are necessarily accompanied with affections and feelings.'[65] Just as judgments are prior to the conceptions which are integral to them so also they are prior to the affections and feelings which accompany them: 'in most of the operations of mind in which judgment or belief is combined with feeling, the feeling is the consequence of the judgment, and is regulated by it.'[66] Thus the feeling wells up because of the antecedent judgment; it is not that the judgment is formed in the light of the feeling. Reid's position is plainly at odds with Humean sentimentalism.

Since moral judgment is antecedent to moral feeling, that is, to the feeling caused by the judgment, it is appropriate to wonder what purpose is served by the feeling. Is the judgment not enough? I shall argue that Reid believes the feeling accompanying moral judgment to be necessary if the object which is being morally judged is to be *valued*. In support of this claim I should like to continue a quotation from the previous paragraph: 'we approve of good actions, and disapprove of bad; and this approbation and disapprobation, when we analyse it, appears to include, not only a moral judgment of the action, but some affection, favourable or unfavourable, towards the agent, and some feeling in ourselves.'[67]

Reid adds a detail: 'In the approbation of a good action, therefore, there is feeling indeed, but there is also esteem of the agent; and both the feeling and the esteem depend upon the judgment we form of his conduct.'[68] There are then dry and unaffecting judgments and there are judgments of morality. Morality is not solely a matter of judgment but also one of affective response to the moral values of morally valuable things. Our judging that an act is morally good is not in itself our valuing the act; morally to value the act is to feel esteem for the agent and also feel pleasure at the performance. Reid makes clear his sense of the importance of the affective dimension of moral sense when he writes: 'Nor can we conceive a greater depravity in the heart of man, than it would be to see and acknowledge worth without feeling any respect to it; or to see and acknowledge the highest worthlessness without any degree of dislike and indignation.'[69]

Earlier we noted that sense perception involves a tripartite division into sensation, conception and judgment. The same division is to be found in moral sense, but in the case of moral sense we move from judgment and conception to feeling (a kind of sensation). There remains, however, an underlying unity in that for Reid, who is concerned to defend a realist position in respect both of the external world and of morality, a faculty of sense, whether outer or moral, is essentially a faculty of judgment, where judgment is a radically different kind of thing from sensation or feeling.

SECTION 6: AN ANATOMY OF THE MIND – THE FINE ARTS

In the preceding section I commented on the unity of Reid's teaching on sensory perception and moral sense. I should like to point to a further display of unity in Reid's thought, namely the unity of his accounts of moral sense and taste, where the latter is understood as: 'That power of the mind by which we are capable of discerning and relishing the beauties of Nature, and whatever is excellent in the fine arts'.[70] We have an aesthetic sense which is a faculty of judgment by which we judge a given quality, one of beauty, grandeur or sublimity, and so on, to be presently existent in some object.

There also occur, in company with the judgment, both a sensation, which is a feeling of pleasure or pain that arises in response to our perception of the quality, and a conception of the quality to which the feeling is a response. The feeling is in the spectator and the quality is in the object. Reid deplores what he terms a 'fashion in philosophy' by which things external to us are held to be internal, a fashion which cuts significantly across linguistic practice. Hume argued that one of the things that is in fact internal to us is the sentiment of beauty, a construal of the location of beauty that, for Hume, holds as a philosophical truth despite the natural human tendency to project the quality of beauty onto outer things and to read the outer world as if beauty is in it. Reid parades Hume's thesis on the internality of beauty before the tribunal of common sense and rules the thesis absurd, partly on the linguistic evidence, for we predicate beauty and grandeur of outer things, not of ourselves. Why, after all, do I say that the garden is beautiful if not because I judge the garden to possess the quality of beauty? The syntax of the sentence makes clear the speaker's judgment of where the beauty is located. As Reid adds:

> No reason can be given why all mankind should express themselves thus, but that they believe what they say. It is therefore contrary to the universal sense of mankind, expressed by their language, that beauty is not really in the object, but is merely a feeling in the person who is said to perceive it.[71]

We can therefore allow both that it is on account of a feature of our constitution that we are able to perceive the aesthetic quality in a thing, and that the aesthetic quality is really in the thing judged.

Reid affirms: 'Our judgment of beauty is not indeed a dry and unaffecting judgment, like that of a mathematical or metaphysical truth. By the constitution of our nature, it is accompanied with an agreeable feeling or emotion, for which we have no other name but the sense of beauty.'[72] The relation of accompaniment is an important feature of Reid's philosophy of mind. In his discussion of the relation between a sign and its significate Reid discusses the sort of case in which the relation is established by nature and is 'discovered to us by a natural principle, without reasoning or experience'.[73] Among his examples are our grasp of the meaning of a sad or an angry countenance, of a smile, and of various modulations of the voice. Babies do not need to be taught the meaning of such signs; by the original constitution of their nature they understand them perfectly well. Reid believes that these natural signs are the basis of the fine arts, that music developed from the human voice, and that acting likewise capitalises on our natural grasp of voice modulation, of countenance and bodily posture and movement.

Let us say, then, that some of the external expressions of our emotions take the form they do because of the original constitution of our nature and that it is likewise by our original constitution that we know how to read these natural signs. Reid writes:

> Nature has established a connexion between the Disposition of the Mind and the Sound of the Voice. And Nature teaches all Men to discern the one in some degree by perceiving the other. Now every thing which is signified or expressed by Sound may be expressed by Music. This Expression is the capital thing in all Compositions of

> Music, and this evidently depends upon those connections between Sound & thought between things Sensible & things intellectual.[74]

Reid speaks here in particular of the relation between natural signs and music, but what he says is equally applicable to other fine arts, and is equally applied by him to them.

We find in these ideas the concept of 'expression' holding centre stage; but we need to be clear about what is being said to express what if we are to understand the sense in which Reid's philosophy of art is an expressionist doctrine. Reid does not take the view that an art work expresses a given emotion in the sense that it is a work that tends to produce that emotion in the spectator or audience, nor does it express a given emotion in the sense that its creator was expressing that emotion when he created the work. Reid's point is instead anchored in the concept of a natural sign; the creative artist knows what the natural signs are that express given emotions and is good at representing them in his works.

This is not to say that there is not an immense element of convention built over and round the natural signs, but the conventional element in an art form could not serve its purpose if there were not a natural basis on which to establish the significance of conventional signs of the emotions. We are, or become, adept at perceiving the significance of the signs provided by the creative artist. We listeners can perceive their significance without ourselves having the same emotion as that signified by the music, and the composer knows how to write music which has that emotional significance even though he himself is not then and there experiencing that same emotion. So the listener listens to a piece of music, discerns its excellence, judges it to be excellent, and relishes the work, that is, has an agreeable feeling as he listens to it.

It should be said that Reid also holds a position which may be incompatible with this doctrine but which may instead be understood to provide greater depth to it. This further position is that the aesthetic properties of a work are 'really' in the mind of the creator, that the grandeur or sublimity of a work is really the grandeur or sublimity of the creative artist and that these properties are only figuratively predicated of the work itself.[75] There is room for doubt as to whether Reid's doctrine on the reality of aesthetic properties in a work of art is compatible with his claim that the grandeur of a work is figuratively in the work and really in the mind of its creator. But whether it is or not, Reid's writing on natural signs and their application to the fine arts and to the expressiveness of works of art constitutes a major contribution to the philosophy of art in the eighteenth century.[76]

Henry Home (1696–1782), who assumed the title Lord Kames in 1752 when appointed lord of session, was born in the Scottish borders in the village of Kames, close to Duns, the birthplace of John Duns Scotus. He trained as a lawyer and became prominent through his role as defence counsel in the trial of Captain John Porteous in 1736.[77] Kames published several legal books including his *Remarkable Decisions of the Court of Session from 1716 to 1728* (1728) and his *Principles of Equity* (1760), the latter work highly regarded by his contemporaries. He also composed several philosophical works, of which perhaps the most important is his *Essays on the Principles of Morality and Natural Religion* (1751), though his philosophical bent is also manifest in many of his writings on law and in his writings on taste and on history, especially his *Sketches of the History of Man* (1774), where a number of the sketches, such as the one entitled 'Patriotism', are deeply philosophical.

Kames belonged to several societies, including the Select Society, of which he was a founder-member, and he was close to a number of prominent literati, including Hume, Smith and James Boswell. In addition to philosophy and the law Kames also had a lively interest in land improvement and agriculture. In 1766 his wife inherited Blair Drummond near Stirling, and Kames worked with others to turn the vast tract of mossy bog around Blair Drummond into good agricultural land.

Kames remained intellectually active to the very end of his long life. In his last years he was consulted by Thomas Reid on the ever-growing manuscript of the *Essays on the Intellectual Powers*, and in the dedication to that work Reid writes movingly of his old friend:

> It would be ingratitude to a man whose memory I most highly respect, not to mention my obligations to the late Lord KAMES for the concern he was pleased to take in this Work . . . It is difficult to say whether that worthy man was more eminent in active life or in speculation. Very rare, surely, have been the instances where the talents for both were united in so eminent a degree.[78]

The two men were philosophically rather close, as witness Kames's invitation to Reid to write a sketch on Aristotle's logic for Kames's

Sketches for the History of Man, as well as Reid's invitation to Kames to turn his formidable critical powers to the task of revising parts of the *Essays on the Intellectual Powers*. How close the two men were philosophically is an interesting question to which I shall now turn. I shall attend in particular to a doctrine of Kames's that appears to cut sharply across a central theme of the common sense philosophy of Reid.

The first edition of Kames's *Essays on the Principles of Morality and Natural Religion*, which appeared anonymously in 1751, contains a remarkable essay entitled 'Liberty and necessity'. For the second, and still anonymous, edition in 1758 Kames extensively revised the essay, in the process replacing its most shocking feature with an alternative line that nevertheless had the power to upset the upsettable, and the third edition, with the troublesome essay again revised, appeared in 1779. While it was common practice in the eighteenth century for authors to publish anonymously there was particular reason for Kames to refrain from proclaiming his authorship of the first two editions. He must have known that his book would raise a storm and could hardly have been surprised at the consequent attempt, made in 1751, to have him excommunicated. I shall deal with the first edition before moving on to the third, the last one published in his lifetime.

In essay three, 'Liberty and necessity', Kames attends to the extent to which, in both the theoretical and the practical dimensions of our lives, we are governed by error. Kames held that by the original constitution of our nature we form concepts that are well suited to the mode of life for which God has created us; certain of these concepts do not correspond to what Kames calls 'the philosophic truth of things' or 'the real truth',[79] and in that sense they may be termed 'deceitful'. But 'strict philosophic truth' is not the only thing of value in the world; something else of value is the provision we have for fulfilling the proper purposes of our life, and if we are deceived by these concepts let this be tempered by the fact that they enable us to live properly.

Among the concepts are those of secondary qualities, the smells, tastes, tactile properties, sounds and colours of things, all of which were thought not really to reside in outer things as qualities of them, for in reality they are a product of the interaction between outer things and our sensory reception apparatus. So the colour of an outer thing is not really as it appears to be, for the outer thing cannot in itself really have a colour at all. Instead, as Kames believes, the thing has constituent parts each of a given size and location, and as a result of these physical features the thing appears to us to have a colour, though if we affirm that it really has one or that the colour is really in the thing then strictly speaking our affirmation is false. Colour is therefore 'a sort of romance and illusion', for the existence of colours in outer things is a fiction.

Nevertheless, though a fiction, it is not one that harms us but is instead a provision of nature that leaves us better provided for than we would be if we had to deal with the 'strictest truth of things'. Seeing things as having colours enables us to act more efficiently in and on the world. Kames sums this up: 'Our perceptions some times, are less accommodating to the truth of things, than to the end for which our senses are designed.'[80] The claim that our natural powers by their nature deceive us has the implication that God is a deceiver, for he is the author of our nature and therefore of the deception to which we are naturally subjected. Of course, as Kames points out, as well as having a faculty of sense perception, which systematically deceives us, we have also been given a faculty of reason, by which we can discover the deception. But, as Kames well appreciates, even if philosophers can discover the deception, they are very few as compared with humankind as a whole. His chief response therefore is that the deception has to be set against the benefit, which is great and is indicative of God's benevolence towards us. Yet God is the God of truth and therefore cannot be a deceiver. Plainly there is a problem here, and I shall return to it later, after dealing with the other, yet more spectacular example of deception to which Kames attends, concerning the practical rather than theoretical dimension of our lives, ourselves as agents rather than as spectators.

We display what appears to be inconsistency in our judgments about human acts. We reason on the basis of the known motives of others and sometimes predict their future acts with certainty because we know what is motivating them. The context of this kind of prediction is the pair of beliefs that we all have (1) that motives are causes and (2) that the acts that are effects of an agent's motives follow necessarily from those motives just as every effect follows necessarily from its cause. Granted also the claim, which is accepted by Kames, that all human acts are performed on the basis of a motive, there follows the doctrine of necessitarianism: that every human act is necessitated by the agent's motives. Yet our moral judgments seem incompatible with necessitarianism. A judgment that agent X acted shamefully implies that X both had the power to do other than he did and also ought to have done otherwise; we think he was free to do otherwise and that therefore his act was not necessary. The agent's feeling that he is free is no less real and no less a ground of conviction than is our feeling that agents are necessitated by their motives.

Often, uncertain as to what to do, an agent deliberates, and while deliberating he may have no idea what he will do; he has competing motives and has to weigh them. Then what? Kames's answer is that there emerges a winner, some motive that is stronger than all the others and that therefore has a stronger influence on the agent than do all the other motives. Kames elucidates: 'it is involved in the very idea of the strongest motive, that it must have the strongest effect in determining the mind. This can no more be doubted of, than that, in a balance, the greater weight must turn the scale.'[81] Kames returns repeatedly to the metaphor of a balance on which material objects are weighed to determine which is heavier. If indeed motives relate to the power of deliberation as physical objects relate to a balance or scales and if, as Kames believes, we always act from motives, it follows that we will act on the strongest or weightiest motive, and the indolent person who weighs motives and in the end does nothing is no counter-example, for he is plainly motivated by indolence as his strongest motive.

On this account there seems no room for real liberty, notwithstanding (1) our acknowledgement that we feel free in respect of our future actions while deliberating about what to do; (2) the fact that in blaming others for having acted shamelessly we judge that they could and should have done otherwise and therefore could not have been necessitated to do what they did; and (3) the fact that our ascription of liberty to ourselves and others is a product of the original constitution of our nature. The underlying philosophical insight at work here is this: liberty, when understood as something in opposition to moral necessity, implies a power in us to act without any motive or to act against all motives or, as Kames formulates the concept:

> a power of acting without any view, purpose or design, and even of
> acting in contradiction to our own desires and aversions, or to all our
> principles of action; which power, besides that no man was ever con-
> scious of it, seems to be an absurdity altogether inconsistent with a
> rational nature.[82]

On this matter Kames's position is barely, if at, distinguishable from Hume's. If motives did not necessitate then, as Kames affirms, nothing would bind or fix a man and hence no man could be depended upon. Liberty, as so conceived, is unbounded and arbitrary and could only 'deform and unhinge the whole human constitution'.[83] Kames concludes: 'Let us fairly own that the truth of things is on the side of necessity.' But if that is where the truth lies and yet we are constitutionally committed to the belief that we are free, it follows that our creator so created us that we are systematically deceived.

Kames's *Essays* had scarcely been published when a move was made to excommunicate him. Hume, writing to his friend Michael Ramsay, asked:

> Have you seen our Friend Harrys Essays? They are well wrote; and are an unusual instance of an obliging method of answering a Book. Philosophers must judge of the question; but the Clergy have already decided it, & say he is as bad as me. Nay some affirm him to be worse, as much as a treacherous friend is worse than an open Enemy.'[84]

Leading the charge against Kames's *Essays* was George Anderson, whose arguments at times resemble arguments that common sense philosophers were later to make their own: 'We feel, and are conscious, that we are free agents; and therefore we are actually and in truth and reality such: or consciousness is no foundation of any truth, or certainty; no, not of our own being.'[85]

Kames's defence is this: 'it was necessary for man to be formed, with such feelings and notions of contingency, as would fit him for the part he has to act.'[86] The part we have been allotted is that of the moral agent, a part which cannot be fulfilled unless we suppose the future both to be open to us as we start our deliberations and also to be determined by us as a result of the choices we make in the light of those deliberations. This defence is the same in form as his response to the problem caused by the fact that we ascribe secondary qualities to outer things when they are in fact a product of the interaction between outer things and our sensory receptors and exist in us, not in the outer things.

We are therefore endowed by nature with a feeling of liberty, a feeling that we are really open to contraries, so that whatever we do we could in that moment and in those circumstances have done something else. From which it follows that though we always act on a false supposition, if that false supposition were removed from our constitution the notion of accountability for actions would have no place in our conceptual map of reality, and hence we could not consider ourselves or others appropriate recipients of praise or blame, nor could we be susceptible to pangs of remorse.

In the light of these considerations let us return to the issue whether it is an imperfection in God that he cannot establish virtue among humankind except on a delusive foundation. The short answer is that, in Kames's view, consistency is as much a virtue in action as it is in thought and that there is therefore no virtue in contradiction whether in action or in thought. For God to create us as free beings living in a wholly deterministic world would be for him to do something contradictory and therefore imperfect. God wished to introduce morally virtuous beings into the world, for a world not containing such beings would be less good than it could be; so he did the best thing possible given both his wish and the fact that his acts will have the perfection of consistency – he created beings who, though not free, by nature feel free.

This doctrine tells us something about where Kames stands in relation to the philosophy of common sense, for on at least one central issue he is at odds with a characteristic feature of it, namely its privileging of consciousness as a faculty whose deliverances are reliable. Reid attaches special importance to the deliverances of consciousness and reflection; he affirms that the operations of the mind are known not by sense but by consciousness, 'the authority of which is as certain and as irresistible as that of sense', and adds that consciousness as such is not sufficient for we must also attend to the objects of consciousness and reflect upon them with care, including feelings, among them the feeling of freedom of which we are conscious when we exert ourselves as agents acting on the world.

Some of the feelings revealed by consciousness are part of the original constitution of our nature, given us by a providential God, and are wholly trustworthy. As Reid affirms repeatedly, any proof of the untrustworthiness of any original principle of our nature must be a proof of the untrustworthiness of every such principle. If therefore we are not entitled to trust our feeling of freedom then neither are we entitled to trust our powers of sensory perception, of reason or even of consciousness. We have seen that Kames holds that on the matter of the reality of liberty there are two perspectives; that of the first person, who feels himself to be free to do or not to do an act which is the object of his deliberation, and that of the third person, who looks out upon other people and finds them dependable. The better we know them, the better we know what motivates them, and the better, in consequence, we are able to predict how they will behave. This last is the scientific view, the one privileged no less by Kames than by Hume. But for Reid, as for other common sense philosophers, such as Beattie, we cannot deny the trustworthiness of the feeling of freedom without implicitly denying the trustworthiness of the other faculties, such as the faculty of reason when it is engaged in the process of scientific reasoning by which we draw the conclusion that the feeling of freedom is untrustworthy.

By the third edition of the *Essays on the Principles of Morality and Natural Religion* in 1779 Kames has fully repudiated his view that the original constitution of our nature includes a deceitful principle. He does not deny that we are deceived into thinking that our acts are free in the sense that we have the power to act against our motives. His point is that the belief that we are free in this way is 'a delusion of passion, not of nature'. Kames uses the feeling of remorse to illustrate the point.[87] Yielding to a passion we perform a shameful act and then acknowledge that we could have and ought to have restrained the passion, even though at the time of the act we were unconscious of a power to restrain it. Kames contends that the notion of a restraining power constantly attends remorse and that our notion of such a power never comes alone but is always accompanied by a passion, where the passion produces the delusive notion of a restraining power. The indignation of a spectator is likewise gratified by the thought that the agent could have restrained himself. On the other hand, where recollection of some act we have performed does not prompt remorse in us we give no thought to the question of whether or not we could have exercised restraint, just as the spectator of an act does not think in terms of the agent's power of self-restraint if the act he has observed is morally innocuous.

Three points may be made regarding Kames's revised account of liberty and necessity. First, it is no less necessitarian than the original account had been. Our freedom is no less a delusion for being the product of our passions than for being a delusion of our God-given nature. The doctrine of universal causality remains the major premiss through the three editions of the *Essays*. As regards human acts, an act of will is a necessary consequence of a desire just as a bodily act is a necessary consequence of the act of will.

Secondly, from a theological perspective the revised version is not quite so obviously provocative as the original version; at least Kames's later doctrine does not proclaim that we were created by a deceiver God. It is, however, doubtful whether the revised version is theologially innocuous; any Calvinist (and most other Christians too) would baulk at his denial of the reality of our freedom, for we are all sinners and a sinful act requires a movement of a free will.

Thirdly, the revised version is in conflict with the philosophy of common sense, which takes seriously the deliverances of consciousness.

We are repeatedly aware of our freedom, especially in moments of moral anguish. In the face of such moments the proper philosophical response is not to see how they should be understood granted the reality of universal causation. Instead we should engage in a process of reflection on our power of self-restraint to see what can be learned about it, and then should see what the implications of the reality of our freedom are for necessitarianism. If the doctrine of the reality of our freedom is incompatible with necessitarianism, then it should not straightaway be assumed that the doctrine of freedom should be transformed into a doctrine of the delusoriness of freedom; we should wonder in what way necessitarianism should be revised in the light of the reality of our freedom. To proceed in that way is to take a Reidian and, more generally, common sense path, which crucially involves privileging consciousness and reflection.

SECTION 8: GEORGE CAMPBELL, COMMON SENSE AND LANGUAGE

George Campbell (1719–96) was born in Aberdeen, attended Aberdeen Grammar School and then went up to Marischal College, Aberdeen. After graduating from there he enrolled as a theology student at Edinburgh University, where he became a close friend of Hugh Blair, who was later to hold two prominent posts: those of minister of the High Kirk of St Giles in Edinburgh and professor of rhetoric and belles lettres at Edinburgh. After his theology studies at Edinburgh Campbell became minister of the kirk at Banchory, a parish close to New Machar, where Reid was then minister. The two men got to know each other well and they remained close friends to the end. Campbell transferred to a post as minister in Aberdeen, and in 1758 he and Reid became members of the Aberdeen Literary Society, a major centre of common sense philosophy. Indeed, in so far as the common sense school can be said to have been more at home in any one part of Scotland rather than any other, its home was surely Aberdeen. Campbell presented to the society a series of papers which were later to form a significant part of his masterpiece *The Philosophy of Rhetoric* (1776). In 1759 he was appointed principal of Marischal College and four years later published his *Treatise on Miracles*. His final appointment, in 1771, was to the chair of divinity at Marischal College. Campbell was a seminal figure in the Scottish school of common sense philosophy, and intellectually was particularly close to Reid. Here I shall discuss a topic on which there appears, at least at first sight, to be a sharp difference between them. The topic concerns universals of language, a field dealt with in Campbell's magisterial *Philosophy of Rhetoric*. For both Reid and Campbell the philosophy of language was central to their intellectual endeavours, so a difference between them on universals of language would not be a negligible matter.

In the *Philosophy of Rhetoric* the concept of common sense is introduced in the course of a discussion of evidence. Evidence is an important topic because the orator seeks to persuade his audience, and the best way to do this is to provide supporting evidence. In some cases the evidence is intuitive, in that we do not come to grasp the truth of the proposition by a process of discursive reasoning; instead our grasp is immediate. Campbell lists three kinds of intuitive evidence, of which the third is 'common sense', and it quickly becomes plain that he understands the term in much the same way that Reid does. For Campbell it is an original source of knowledge common to humankind; by our common sense, we are assured of a number of truths that cannot be evinced by reason, and 'it is equally impossible, without a full conviction of them, to advance a single step in the acquisition of knowledge'.[88] This characterisation of common sense is very similar to Reid's affirmation that 'there are principles common to [philosophers and the vulgar] which need no proof, and which do not admit of direct proof', and these common principles 'are the foundation of all reasoning, and of all science'.[89] James Beattie, colleague and friend of Reid and Campbell, agrees; he uses the term 'common sense' to signify

> that power of the mind which perceives truth, or commands belief, not by progressive argumentation, but by an instantaneous, instinctive, and irrresistible impulse; derived neither from education nor from habit, but from nature; acting independently on our will, whenever its object is presented, according to an established law, and therefore properly called *Sense*; and acting in a similar manner upon all, or at least upon a great majority of mankind, and therefore properly called *Common Sense*.[90]

Of the three kinds of intuitive evidence that Campbell lists, the first concerns our insight into the truth of mathematical axioms; the second concerns the deliverances of consciousness – my being conscious that I am thinking, that I am having auditory sensations, or that I am happy or sad, and so on; and the third concerns common sense. They are all unmediated. Campbell holds that consciousness is a separate principle from common sense, unlike Reid, who says in the formulation of his first principle of common sense: 'The operations of our minds are attended with consciousness; and this consciousness is the evidence, the only evidence which we have or can have of their existence.'[91]

Common sense principles are universal in that, first, *everything* that we know about the world depends upon our antecedent acceptance of those principles, and, secondly, the principles are fundamental to the belief system of *every* human being. But if there are universal features of our experience of the world and if our discourse about the world reflects in some way those universal features, a question arises as to whether the language we use to speak about the world has universal features, in the sense that all languages have those features, perhaps grammatical categories, which are systematically related to the common features of our experience.

Campbell's *Philosophy of Rhetoric* contains a discussion on universals of language in connection with a contrast that Campbell expounds between grammar and logic. Arguments are the province of logic, for logic deals with the rules for determining whether or not a given argument is valid. Any argument is a sequence of well-formed sentences, and it is grammar that contains the rules for determining whether a sentence is well formed. Though intimately related, grammar and logic are logically distinct. Campbell writes:

> The art of the logician is accordingly, in some sense, universal, the art of the grammarian is always particular and local. The rules of argumentation laid down by Aristotle, in his Analytics, are of as much use for the discovery of truth in Britain or in China, as they were in Greece; but Priscian's rules of inflection and construction, can assist us in learning no language but Latin.[92]

There cannot, then, be a universal grammar, for a grammar is the grammar of a given language, and a universal grammar would be a grammar of a universal language. There is no such language, according to Campbell, only English, Latin, Chinese and other particular languages. It should be said, however, that by the mid-eighteenth century there had accrued a rich literature supporting the idea of a universal grammar. The idea had been widely discussed during the Middle Ages and defended on the basis of the authority of St Augustine, Boethius and, ultimately, Aristotle, and post-Middle Ages other great thinkers, such as John Locke, had also defended the idea. Clearly something philosophically significant was perceived to be at issue and Campbell is setting his face against a major current of thought. Among important eighteenth-century texts on universals of language there was James Harris's widely studied *Hermes: or a Philosophical Inquiry Concerning Universal Grammar*, first published in 1751, in which he argues at length for the reality of a universal grammar.

As against Campbell, Reid believes that all languages are grammatically alike, not in every detail of course, but at any rate in philosophically significant measure, where the philosophical significance arises from the extent to which shared features of language reflect shared features of experience. Reid provides scores of examples of grammatical forms that he believes to be universal in human languages, and in an obvious sense he is engaged in the task of framing a universal grammar. As we have seen, Campbell would say that there is no universal language. Reid's reply is that a universal language is not another language alongside English and Latin; instead it informs, or is formally contained in, all such languages at the level of grammar. In that sense we speak a universal language when we speak any language.[93]

Campbell writes:

> The term [universal grammar] hath sometimes, indeed, been applied to a collection of observations on the similar analogies that have been discovered in all tongues, ancient and modern, known to the authors of such collections. I do not mention this liberty in the use of the term with a view to censure it . . . But it is to my purpose to observe, that as such collections convey the knowledge of no tongue whatever, the name *grammar*, when applied to them, is used in a sense quite different from that which it has in the common acceptation.[94]

Reid, on the other hand, would argue that his collection is one of identities that have been discovered in all tongues and that, far from his collection conveying the knowledge of no tongue, it conveys the knowledge of every tongue, and that that is exactly what is to be expected of a universal grammar.

Reid does not invoke Campbell explicitly in any of his discussions on this matter, but he does mention the French Jesuit Claude Buffier (1661–1737) in a manuscript entitled 'Opinions of Buffier concerning language', the first opinion being: 'That there is no such thing as general Grammar, but every Grammar must be the Grammar of some Language.'[95] Reid thinks Buffier totally wrong on this matter, but the opinion he ascribes to Buffier is the same as Campbell's. In the same manuscript of Reid's we find the judgment: 'As there is an Art of Logick and Rhetorick common to all Languages, so there is an Art of

Grammar common to all Languages. This we call Natural or Universal Grammar.' On many philosophical issues Reid and Campbell were very close, but on the important matter of the reality of a universal grammar they present widely divergent doctrines.

SECTION 9: DUGALD STEWART, COMMON SENSE AND MIND

In the Scottish universities during the Age of Enlightenment there were many family ties. We noted the various members of the Gregory family who occupied university chairs in Scotland, in addition to which there was Alexander Gerard, professor of moral philosophy at Marischal College, Aberdeen, who was succeeded in the chair by his son Gilbert, and at Glasgow Robert Davidson, the regius professor of civil law, was by happy coincidence the son of the principal of the university. In Edinburgh, not to be outdone, Alexander Munro *primus*, professor of anatomy, was succeeded in the chair by his son Alexander Munro *secundus*, who was succeeded in the chair by *his* son, Alexander Munro *tertius*.

The Stewarts are a further example. It was Dugald Stewart's good fortune to be the son of his father Matthew, who in 1747 succeeded Colin Maclaurin as professor of mathematics at Edinburgh University. Dugald Stewart (1753–1828) enrolled at the High School of Edinburgh when aged seven and then attended Edinburgh University, where his teachers included Adam Ferguson, professor of moral philosophy, John Stevenson, professor of logic, and Hugh Blair, professor of rhetoric and belles lettres. In 1771 he moved to Glasgow for a session to study under Thomas Reid, who was, after Matthew Stewart, the single most significant influence on his thinking. In Glasgow he shared accommodation with Archibald Alison (1757–1839), who was later to make an immense contribution to the Scottish aesthetic tradition with his *Essays on the Nature and Principles of Taste* (1790). Stewart also wrote a significant work on taste,[96] and he and Alison formed a lifelong friendship.

In the autumn of 1772 Matthew Stewart, then in poor health and unable to lecture, asked his son to return to Edinburgh to take over the mathematics class. After three years of delivering the mathematics lectures Dugald Stewart was appointed mathematics professor conjointly with his father. In 1778 his former moral philosophy teacher, Adam Ferguson, was appointed secretary to the Carlisle Commission, a committee of peace commissioners on a mission to the former American colonies,[97] and Ferguson invited Dugald Stewart to deliver the moral philosophy lectures for the session 1778–9, which he accomplished while also delivering the mathematics lectures. In 1785 he transferred to the moral philosophy chair. He did not, however, forget his mathematics, as witness the fact that from time to time he delivered mathematics lectures when the mathematics professor, John Playfair, was unwell. Indeed Stewart also acted as locum for John Robison,[98] professor of natural philosophy, and as a locum for the professor of logic and for the professor of rhetoric and belles lettres.

It is appropriate to note that Stewart's extraordinary intellectual reach matches his views on education. He noticed that scientists are not content to master just one small area of science, but tend to be curious about and proficient in a number of areas, their curiosity fed by the recognition that knowledge of one discipline can have a helpful effect on one's thinking in other, seemingly disparate disciplines. This point has implications for education, for it suggests that a generalist education has significant advantages over a specialist one. A century and a half before George Davie argued the case for a generalist education,[99] Dugald Stewart had already provided a firm philosophical foundation for the generalist approach.[100]

Stewart occupied the chair of moral philosophy for twenty-five years, during which his students included Lord Brougham, Lord Palmerston, the Marquis of Lansdowne, Henry Cockburn, Sir Walter Scott, Thomas Brown (his successor in the chair), Sydney Smith, Francis Jeffrey, Sir Archibald Alison (son of the Archibald Alison, author of *Essays on the Nature and Principles of Taste*) and James Mill (later a strong critic of Stewart, as also in due course was Mill's son John Stuart Mill). Stewart finally retired from his chair in 1820, though he continued his writings. The first volume of his *Elements of the Philosophy of the Human Mind* appeared in 1792, the second in 1814 and the third in 1827. In 1793 he published his *Outlines of Moral Philosophy* and also in that year read a version of his *Life and Writings of Adam Smith* at a meeting of the Royal Society of Edinburgh. This important document was followed by major biographical essays on William Robertson and Thomas Reid. In 1810 there appeared his *Philosophical Essays*, and in the following two years he produced parts one and two of 'A general view of the progress of the metaphysical, ethical and political philosophy since the revival of letters', for publication in the Supplement to the *Encyclopaedia Britannica*. Finally, not many days before his death in 1828, he published *The Philosophy of the Active and Moral Powers*.

Among his many other smaller works there should be mentioned two polemical pieces that have strong philosophical overtones, though they are no doubt primarily of historical interest. These concern John Leslie, whose application for the chair of mathematics at Edinburgh University was opposed by members of the Edinburgh presbytery who accused him of religious heterodoxy in view of his espousal of Hume's account of causality. Stewart, who was himself not kindly disposed to Hume's account, none the less saw an important principle of academic freedom at stake, and entered the lists on behalf of Leslie with a long 'Statement'[101] in 1805 on Leslie's application and with a 'Supplement' to the 'Statement' in 1806 in response to the presbytery's public attack on the 'Statement'. It should be added that the fight on behalf of Leslie was conducted by others as well as Stewart, and in particular by Stewart's former student Thomas Brown (1778–1820), who wrote a lengthy work, *Observations on the Nature and Tendency of the Doctrine of Mr Hume* (1805), which reassured some of Leslie's accusers. Eventually the defence of Leslie proved successful and he took up the mathematics professorship in succession to Playfair.

Stewart demonstrates a profound knowledge of the philosophy of both Scotland and England during the preceding hundred years, was widely read in French philosophy, and to an extent was influenced by French philosophers such as Cabanis and Destutt de Tracy. Stewart also read Immanuel Kant. Lacking German he read the *Critique of Pure Reason* in Latin translation, and thought ill of the work, perhaps because the Latin text was not the best route to Kant's thought. The fact that Stewart read Kant places him almost at the beginning of a long line of distinguished Scottish philosophers who engaged with Kant's doctrines; as the nineteenth century wore on Kant's voice becomes increasingly influential in Scotland.

The early philosophical influences on Stewart were overwhelmingly those of the common sense school. I have already mentioned that he studied under Ferguson and Reid, and should like to make a brief observation about Ferguson before considering an aspect of Stewart's complex relation with Reid. In 1767 Ferguson published *An Essay on the History of Civil Society* and two years later *Institutes of Moral Philosophy*, which jointly established Ferguson as a thinker of international stature. In both works Ferguson's approach is that of an empirical scientist deploying the Baconian methodology insisted upon by Reid.

One example will suffice to illustrate the method. Ferguson declares that all evidence may be referred to four titles, namely consciousness, perception, testimony and inference, and adds: 'It is the first maxim of reason, that nothing is to be admitted without that degree of evidence with which it should be attended, if true, and that, with this degree of evidence, nothing is to be rejected.'[102] At the start of his *Essay on the History of Civil Society* Ferguson wonders about the claim that before the state of society there was a state of nature; he refers to the 'supposed departure of mankind from the state of their nature' and notes that there have been 'conjectures' about that pre-social state. Two suppositions in particular dominated discussion of the period, one by Hobbes and the other by Rousseau. Without naming the two thinkers Ferguson presents the account that each offers:

> [S]ome [that is, Rousseau] have represented mankind in their first condition, as possessed of mere animal sensibility, without any exercise of the faculties that render them superior to the brutes, without any political union, without any means of explaining their sentiments . . . Others [that is, Hobbes] have made the state of nature to consist in perpetual wars, kindled by competition for dominion and interest, when every individual had a separate quarrel with his kind, and where the presence of a fellow-creature was the signal of battle.[103]

But Ferguson enquires into the evidence for these accounts and in particular enquires into what we actually know from observation and historical record. He finds that the earliest and the latest accounts collected from every quarter of the earth represent people as assembled in troops and companies, as joined by affection with some and as opposed to others, and inclined to communicate their sentiments. From this it follows that it is natural for us to be social, and hence the social state is the state of nature for humankind. Hobbes and Rousseau are telling stories that have no scientific basis; unlike Ferguson they are not practising science.

There appears to be nothing here with which Reid would have disagreed; nor Dugald Stewart, who saw himself as engaged in a systematic scientific study of human beings, where the methodology was exactly according to the prescription of Reid and Ferguson. Pursuing his enquiry into human beings Stewart demonstrates deep knowledge of the writings of his two great teachers and, in particular, he was regarded as the great standard-bearer, after Reid, of the Scottish common sense philosophy. Of course he did not agree with Reid about everything, but he did agree with him about most things. Stewart was, along with James Gregory, a dedicatee of Reid's *Essays on the Intellectual Powers of Man*, and Stewart dedicated to Reid his *Elements of the Philosophy of the Human Mind* (1792).

In terms that Reid could have used Stewart affirms:

> As all our knowledge of the material world rests ultimately on facts ascertained by observation, so all our knowledge of the human mind rests ultimately on facts for which we have the evidence of our own consciousness. An attentive examination of such facts will lead in time to the general principles of the human constitution, and will gradually form a science of mind not inferior in certainty to the science of body.[104]

In this passage 'consciousness' means exactly what Reid said it meant: 'This word denotes the immediate knowledge which the mind has of its sensations and thoughts, and, in general, of all its present operations.' To which Stewart adds:

> The belief with which it [namely, consciousness] is attended has been considered as the most irresistible of any; insomuch that this species of evidence has never been questioned: and yet it rests on the same foundation with every kind of belief to which we are determined by the constitution of our nature.[105]

For example, in discussing the evidence for our freedom of will, Stewart affirms that to settle the question of whether or not we have a free will we should make a direct appeal to the deliverances of consciousness at the moment of the performance of a wicked deed, and adds:

> Will any person of candour deny, that, in the very act of transgressing an acknowledged duty, he is impressed with a conviction, as complete as that of his own existence, that his will is free; and that he is abusing, contrary to the suggestions of reason and conscience, his Moral Liberty.[106]

Reid, who had already said all of this, was, however, strongly hostile to at least one doctrine of Stewart's that relates closely to the evidence of consciousness, and it will be instructive to uncover the grounds of the dispute. Stewart sent Reid a draft of parts of his *Elements of the Philosophy of the Human Mind*, and Reid drafted a hostile response to it.[107] Stewart argues that in important areas of our life our attention is more limited than we believe and that we are misled on this matter because our memory is doing work that we ascribe to attention. Stewart accepts, if somewhat tentatively, the principle 'that the mind can only attend to one thing at once', and argues that though we seem able to attend to several things simultaneously this is due not to the span of our attention but to the speed at which our mind operates. He provides an example:

> It is commonly understood, I believe, that, in a concert of music, a good ear can attend to the different parts of the music separately, or can attend to them all at once, and feel the full effect of the harmony. If the doctrine, however, which I have endeavoured to establish, be admitted, it will follow, that in the latter case the mind is constantly varying its attention from the one part of the music to the other, and that its operations are so rapid, as to give us no perception of an interval of time.[108]

Stewart gives a further example: though the mind seems able to perceive the complete figure of an object at once, it actually attends in succession to different points in the figure but switches its attention from one to another very fast: 'These acts of attention, however, are performed with such rapidity, that the effect, with respect to us, is the same as if the perception were instantaneous.'

In Reid's view, however, Stewart is here being un-Baconian by presenting as facts what are in truth unsupported hypotheses. Reid focuses especially upon Stewart's discussion of a person who is in a room when a clock strikes, though moments later he does not know whether or not he heard it strike. Stewart claims that the person has both an auditory sensation and also a perception of the clock's sound and that in consequence of his lack of attention to these he could not, immediately afterwards, recall either of these mental acts. Reid enquires into Stewart's evidence for this claim. Reid's own view is that the sound probably made an impression on the ear, but that for the occurrence of an auditory perception two additional things were required: an auditory sensation, and a belief that there was a physical sound. In the absence of a recollection of the sound, we are simply not in a position to decide whether or not we heard it.

Reid concludes:

> If therefore one Man says, that in this Case we had both the Sensation & Perception but were not conscious of them; another that we had both with Consciousness, but without any degree of Memory; a third that we had the sensation without the perception; & a fourth that we had neither; I think they all grope in the dark, and I would not trust much to conclusions built upon any of these Hypotheses.[109]

He sums up against his former student:

> Every thing in this Discourse that I dissent from is grounded upon the Hypothesis of hidden trains of thinking of which we have no

Remembrance next Moment, upon the most attentive Reflection. This after considering all you have said seems to me a Hypothesis which admits neither of proof nor of refutation. And I wish you to be much upon your guard against Hypotheses.[110]

We should recall that Reid himself postulates mental acts of which we are unconscious. According to his analysis of a perceptual act, there are three elements: a sensation, a conception of some quality in a thing that causes the sensation, and finally a belief that both the thing and the quality exist. The function of the sensation is to be a natural sign of the quality. Except when our sensations are particularly agreeable or disagreeable we do not normally attend to them; nevertheless by undertaking the task many times over a lengthy period of time, perhaps many years (as Reid did), we can come to be conscious of the sensations that are the natural signs of the objects perceived. That is the difference between our sensations posited by Reid and the rapid mental acts hypothesised by Stewart; we can bring the former to consciousness but not the latter. In short, Reid speaks of objects for which there is empirical evidence, and Stewart speaks of objects for which there is none. Reid was being a practising Baconian and Stewart was not.

It is an open question whether or not Reid sent Stewart his criticisms of the draft of the *Elements*, but if he did there is little if any indication of this in the *Elements*. What Stewart eventually published is open to precisely the criticisms that Reid develops in the draft letter. It is plain that though Stewart was the standard-bearer of the Reidian philosophy of common sense, there was substantial disagreement between the two thinkers on major issues of philosophical concern.

SECTION 10: SIR WILLIAM HAMILTON – A MOMENT OF TRANSITION

Sir William Hamilton (1788–1856), son of the professor of anatomy at Glasgow University, attended school both in Glasgow and in England. Aged twelve he was enrolled in Glasgow University and in 1807 went to Balliol College, Oxford, as a Snell Exhibitioner. Thereafter for some years he practised as a lawyer in Edinburgh without conspicuous success. Despite Dugald Stewart's backing he failed in a bid to become professor of moral philosophy at Edinburgh in succession to the recently deceased Thomas Brown, though a year later he was appointed professor of civil history. He continued to focus on philosophy and in 1829 published in the *Edinburgh Review* his first significant work, an article entitled 'On the philosophy of the unconditioned: in reference to Cousin's Infinito-absolute'.

The article, a lengthy critique of the recently published *Introduction à l'histoire de la philosophie* by Victor Cousin, professor of philosophy at the University of Paris, did not meet with critical acclaim in Scotland or more generally in Britain, though Victor Cousin himself, whose book was attacked with some ferocity by Hamilton, declared himself delighted with the article. In brief, let the term 'unconditioned' stand for the absolute cause or the infinite or pure thought, these last three characterisations being understood as characterisations of one and the same thing. Hamilton argues that if this is what the unconditioned is then it cannot be known or even conceived by us except negatively, that is, as that which is not conditioned, not finite and not determinate thought, from which it follows that Cousin is wrong in holding that the unconditioned is both cognisable and conceivable by a suitably reflective thinker.

What is special about the article is its scholarly sources. Hamilton, who had excellent German, demonstrates extensive first-hand knowledge of the writings of Immanuel Kant, and of Fichte and Schelling, who both made a massive contribution to the development of the Kantian philosophy. Hamilton was the first British philosopher of any significance to immerse himself in the new German philosophy, a form of idealism taking its starting point from Kant's critical analysis of the powers of human cognition. Thereafter in Scotland philosophers could not write as if there had been no Kant, no Fichte, Schelling or Hegel; the Scottish philosophical tradition took on a faint German accent.

In 1836, David Ritchie resigned as professor of logic and metaphysics at Edinburgh, and Hamilton applied for the post, with the support of Francis Jeffrey and Victor Cousin. The application was successful and Hamilton occupied the chair until his death. Hamilton saw himself as a descendent of Reid and Kant, whom he perceived to be descendents of Hume. Kant acknowledged that he was 'roused from his dogmatic slumber' by reading Hume's account of causality and, as we saw in the last chapter, it was as a direct result of reading Hume's *Treatise* and noting Hume's sceptical conclusions that Reid started to investigate the fundamental principles of the mind. Hamilton saw himself as a Reidian and as a Kantian, accepting positions fundamental to both philosophers while rejecting some things that each wrote. He identifies what he characterises as a 'strong analogy' between the philosophies of Reid and Kant: 'Both originate in a recoil against the Scepticism of Hume; both are equally opposed to the Sensualism of Locke; both vindicate with equal zeal the moral dignity of man; and both attempt to mete out and to define the legitimate sphere of our intellectual activity.'[111]

However, where Reid and Kant differed on a central matter, that of sensory perception, Hamilton sides with Reid. Reid thought that 'the principles commonly received with regard to the human understanding', that is, the principles that define the theory of ideas, were the premises from which Hume's sceptical conclusions about the external world were drawn, and Reid therefore sought to demonstrate the error of the theory of ideas. His doctrine was that, contrary to Hume's view, the human mind has direct or unmediated knowledge of the existence of things external to itself, whereas Kant, who was reacting in the first place to Hume's account of causality rather than to his scepticism with regard to the senses, went a good way towards appropriating the theory of ideas. For Kant held

> that the mind has no immediate knowledge of any existence external to itself . . . that the mind is cognisant of nothing beyond its own modifications, and that what our natural consciousness mistakes for an external world, is only an internal phaenomenon, only a mental representation of the unknown and inconceivable.[112]

On this interpretation, Kant conceived his task to be somewhat that of Hume's, namely to explain why, despite the fact that our perceptual knowledge is 'really' a mental representation of something unknown, we believe that we have unmediated knowledge of a reality that is external to us. Plainly, Hamilton judged that Kant would have done well to read Reid.

Kant rejected the Humean account of causality because he thought that the principle that every event has a cause is not an empirical principle but is instead a condition of the possibility of having objectively valid experience. Kant sought to demonstrate that there were twelve such principles, the so-called 'a priori principles of the understanding', without which objectively valid experience is not possible. Hamilton, familiar with these Kantian principles, was no less familiar with Reid's principles of common sense. There are similarities between Kant's a priori principles and Reid's principles of common sense, but the differences are striking.

One such is that Kant's a priori principles are twelve in number. There cannot be more or fewer. He believes that there can only be twelve forms of judgment (for example, the form of the hypothetical judgment 'If p then q') and argues that there must be one a priori principle of the understanding corresponding to each form of judgment. Reid, on the other hand, approaches the question of the number of principles of common sense in an empirical way. We know when we have found one – Reid, as we saw, has a good deal to say about how they are to be recognised – but we cannot possibly know how many there are in advance of finding them, and when we have found some, however many, we cannot be sure that others will not at some stage come to light.

But a striking similarity between the two men is that they both hold that there are certain principles whose operation is necessary if we are to have recognisably human experiences, and the fact that there are such principles is a key feature in their philosophy. In the *Inquiry* Reid writes of certain principles 'which the constitution of our nature leads us to believe, and which we are under a necessity to take for granted in the common concerns of life, without being able to give a reason for them; these are what we call the principles of common sense'.[113] Some of the principles are formulated and discussed in the *Essays on the Intellectual Powers*, essay I, ch. II, and until the middle of the nineteenth century a good deal of the philosophising done in Scotland was an exposition and development of Reid's account of those principles. Then in the 1830s and 1840s Kant's philosophy becomes increasingly influential in Scotland among philosophers who, unlike Dugald Stewart, could read it in German, and one explanation for the fact that Scottish philosophers could feel so much at home with Kant's philosophy is that at least in the earlier stages of the process it bore a significant resemblance to the dominant home-grown philosophy, that of Thomas Reid. Dugald Stewart himself thought that, for those with eyes to see, Kant's teaching on the a priori features of our experience was already there in Reid, and many Scots were later to agree with him, to the extent that Reid came to be termed 'the Scottish Kant'. Though they delved deep into Kant, and into his great successors, Fichte, Schelling and Hegel, they nevertheless thought that they were taking further the great project, the Scottish philosophy, of which Reid was perceived to be the most magisterial representative.

Hamilton, considered as standing in a particular relation to Reid on the one side and German philosophy on the other, may to an extent be considered to have a parallel relation to Reid and French philosophy, for Sir William Hamilton's *The Works of Thomas Reid*, whose first edition appeared in 1846, was dedicated to Victor Cousin, former French minister of public instruction, whom Hamilton greatly admired despite his attack on Cousin in 1829. For all the weaknesses that Hamilton believed himself to have found in Cousin's philosophy, he knew that Cousin had lectured enthusiastically on Reid at the University of Paris and had proved to be a real disciple of Reid's philosophy.

A French version of Reid's *Enquiry into the Human Mind on the Principles of Common Sense* (1764), *Recherches sur l'entendement humain d'après les principes du sens commun*, had been published in 1768, considerably before Cousin's lectures on Reid, and that translation, according to a story whose charm may exceed its trustworthiness, was the basis of a new school of French philosophy. Hippolyte Taine reports that in 1811 Pierre-Paul Royer-Collard, professor of philosophy at the Sorbonne, came upon the 1768 translation, began to read it, and was captivated: 'He had just bought and founded the new French philosophy', claimed Taine.[114] Royer-Collard, already doubtful of the merits of the Lockean philosophy of Condillac and of his heirs the Idéologues, began lecturing on Reid and Scottish common sense philosophy in 1811–12. In his first cohort of students was Victor Cousin, who succeeded Royer-Collard in 1815 and who furthered Royer-Collard's work on behalf of Scottish philosophy, as did other distinguished French thinkers. Among them were Pierre Prévost (translator of Adam Smith's *Essays on Philosophical Subjects*), François Thurot (translator of Reid's *Inquiry into the Human Mind* and of works by Dugald Stewart), Maine de Biran (author of *Comparaison des trois points de vue de Reid, Condillac et Tracy sur l'idée d'existence et le jugement d'extériorité*, published in 1815), Théodore Jouffroy (translator of the *Œuvres complètes* of Reid, who dedicated himself, as did his former professor, Victor Cousin, to the exposition of the Scottish, particularly the Reidian, philosophy) and Baron Joseph Marie Degérando.

Degérando rejected the anti-intellectualist view of Condillac that all mental operations, whether of imagination, memory or reason and so on, are either sensations on a straightforward understanding of the term or are reducible to sensations – this being Condillac's doctrine of 'transformed sensation' (*sensation transformée*) – and argued instead in a Reidian way for the irreducibility of operations such as memory and judgment. In his *Histoire comparée des systèmes de philosophie* (1830) Degérando expounds Reid in detail, providing a strongly supportive account of Reid's attack on the theory of ideas in general and on Hume's version in particular. This is important because the special focus of Degérando's attention was the pair of questions, central also to Reid's philosophy of perception, of whether our knowledge of the external world is mediated by mental representatives of the external objects and whether perception is reducible to sensation. These questions were central to French philosophers well into the nineteenth century, and Reid's answers to them fed directly into French discussions on this topic. It was well-nigh impossible for a French philosopher of the period not to take up a position in relation to Reid's account.

While discussing Hamilton, considered as an intermediary between Reid and both France and Germany, it is appropriate to note that Hamilton's edition of Reid, including Hamilton's extensive commentary, was a major conduit of Reid's ideas to America, where for the greater part of the nineteenth century Reid's work played a conspicuous role in the universities. However, the impact of Scottish philosophy in America long preceded Hamilton, and indeed became significant about half a century before the founding, that is, from the time of Francis Hutcheson. Thus, for example, there was a Scottish influence on the young Jefferson, given his exposure to it at William and Mary College, where he was taught moral philosophy and logic by the Aberdeen-educated William Small, who had arrived in 1758, and of whom Jefferson was later to say that he 'probably fixed the destinies of my life'. Jefferson appears to have had a wide familiarity with the philosophy of the Scottish Enlightenment, including Reid.[115] Reid became a key figure within the American academy after the founding. In particular we must note the significance of John Witherspoon, from Yester near Haddington, who left his post as minister of the kirk in Paisley in 1768 to become president of the College of New Jersey and then, in 1776, the only clergyman to sign the Declaration of Independence. He lectured and wrote extensively and effectively on Reid and Scottish common sense philosophy,[116] a mission that was continued by his great successor at Princeton, Samuel Stanhope Smith, whose enthusiastic championing of Thomas Reid's philosophy had a major outcome for the direction that philosophy took in America. Reid received a very sympathetic reading by Charles Sanders Peirce, who had studied under the Reidian Francis Bowen at Harvard, and there is common agreement that American pragmatism owes a good deal to Scottish common sense philosophy.[117] Hamilton is demonstrably, therefore, a small part of a large story to be told about the presence of Scottish philosophy in general, and the common sense school in particular, in the American academy.

Notes

1. Hume, *My Own Life*, in *Essays*, p. xxxiv.
2. Reid, *An Inquiry into the Human Mind on the Principles of Common Sense*, ed. Brookes, pp. 3–4 (hereinafter *Inquiry*).
3. Datelined King's College, 18 March 1763. Reid, *Correspondence*, ed. Wood, p. 31.
4. Reid, *Essays on the Intellectual Powers*, eds Brookes and Haakonssen, p. 41 (hereinafter *EIP*).
5. *EIP*, p. 421.
6. See for example Nicholas Wolterstorff, *Thomas Reid and the Story of Epistemology* (Cambridge: Cambridge University Press, 2001); and Alvin Plantinga, *Warranted Christian Belief* (Oxford: Oxford University Press, 2001).
7. See Wood, *The Aberdeen Enlightenment*, for detailed information on the Aberdeen teachers and their courses.
8. 'An essay on quantity; occasioned by reading a treatise in which simple and compound ratios are applied to virtue and merit', *Philosophical Transactions of the Royal Society of London*, 45 (1748); reprinted in Reid, *Works*, ed. Hamilton, pp. 715a–719b.
9. See Suderman, *Orthodoxy and Enlightenment*; also H. Lewis Ulman (ed.), *The Minutes of the Aberdeen Philosophical Society, 1758–1773* (Aberdeen: Aberdeen University Press, 1990).
10. Reid had travelled a considerable philosophical distance: 'I once believed this doctrine of ideas so firmly, as to embrace the whole of BERKELEY's system' (*EIP*, p. 142).
11. In 1752, when Adam Smith transferred from the chair of logic and rhetoric to the chair of moral philosophy, the university, through a mis-judgment of cosmic proportions, appointed Clow to the logic and rhetoric chair in preference to Hume. Clow appears to have been a wholly derivative thinker in logic and rhetoric.
12. Jardine, favourite pupil of Adam Smith, friend of Reid and John Millar, and teacher of William Hamilton, made no contribution to logic but was famously innovative in his teaching methods. See his *Outlines of Philosophical Education*.
13. Reid, *Correspondence*, p. 62. Barbara and Celarent are the names of two forms of Aristotelian syllogism. A syllogism in Barbara has the form: 'Every B is C and every A is B, therefore every A is C.' A syllogism in Celarent has the form: 'No B is C and every A is B, therefore no A is C.'
14. *Correspondence*, p. 149.
15. Ibid. pp. 162, 163; and *EIP*, p. 3.
16. *Thomas Reid on the Animate Creation*, ed. Wood, pp. 127–241. Amongst other targets are the following by Joseph Priestley: *An examination of Dr. Reid's inquiry into the human mind on the principles of*

common sense, *Dr Beattie's essay on the nature and immutability of truth, and Dr. Oswald's appeal to common sense in behalf of religion* (London, 1774); *Disquisitions relating to matter and spirit* (London, 1777); *A free discussion of the doctrines of materialism, and philosophical necessity, in a correspondence between Dr. Price, and Dr. Priestley* (London, 1778).

17. *Correspondence*, p. 230.
18. Ibid. p. 197.
19. Ibid. pp. 186–7.
20. Ibid. p. 224.
21. *Inquiry*, p. 12.
22. *Correspondence*, pp. 211–12.
23. *Thomas Reid on Logic, Rhetoric and the Fine Arts*, ed. Broadie, p. 146 (hereinafter *Reid on Logic*).
24. *Inquiry*, p. 13.
25. *EIP*, p. 21.
26. *Inquiry*, p. 14.
27. *EIP*, pp. 60–1.
28. *EIP*, p. 20.
29. Locke, *Essay*, p. 47.
30. *EIP*, p. 53.
31. *EIP*, pp. 52–5.
32. *EIP*, p. 42.
33. *EIP*, p. 43.
34. *EIP*, pp. 45–6.
35. *EIP*, p. 21.
36. *EIP*, p. 26.
37. *EIP*, p. 57.
38. Reid attended classes on Greek but there seems no evidence that he gained a reading knowledge of the language.
39. *EIP*, p. 97.
40. *Inquiry*, p. 60.
41. Ibid. p. 60.
42. *EIP*, pp. 180–1. See also *Inquiry*, pp. 95–8.
43. A. Broadie, 'Thomas Reid, Jules Laforgue et l'art de peindre des impressions', in Arosio and Malherbe (eds), *Philosophie française et philosophie écossaise*, pp. 179–93.
44. *Inquiry*, p. 83.
45. Robert Smith, *A Compleat System of Opticks in Four Books*, 2 vols (Cambridge, 1738), vol. 2, p. 40. Reid seems to have had a real interest in Smith's writings. Elsewhere he refers to Smith's discoveries with regard to tempering of discords in music and tuning of organs. See *Reid on Logic*, pp. 65–6, 305. Smith (1689–1768) was professor of astronomy at Cambridge. It is possible that Reid met him when he visited

Cambridge in 1736, the visit during which he met Nicholas Saunderson.

46. *Inquiry*, p. 183.
47. Ibid. p. 87.
48. Ibid. p. 82.
49. Paul Wood, 'Reid, parallel lines, and the geometry of visibles', *Reid Studies*, 2, 1 (1998): 27–41.
50. Hume, *An Enquiry Concerning Human Understanding*, XII.I, p. 201.
51. Ibid. XII.I, p. 201.
52. Reid, *Essays on the Active Powers*, ed. Hamilton, IV, II, p. 603B (hereinafter *EAP*).
53. *EAP*, IV.I, p. 599A.
54. *EIP*, p. 463.
55. *EIP*, pp. 463–7.
56. *EAP*, IV.VIII, p. 622B.
57. *EAP*, IV.IV, p. 608B.
58. *EAP*, IV.IV, p. 609A.
59. *EAP*, IV.IV, p. 611A.
60. Hume, *Treatise*, p. 302.
61. *EAP*, V.VII, p. 671B.
62. *EAP*, V.VII, p. 676B.
63. *EAP*, III.III.VI, p. 590A–B.
64. *EIP*, p. 414.
65. *EAP*, III.III.VII, p. 592A.
66. *EAP*, V.VII, p. 672B.
67. *EAP*, III.III.VII, p. 592A.
68. *EAP*, V.VII, p. 673A.
69. *EAP*, III.III.VII, p. 592B.
70. *EIP*, p. 573.
71. *EIP*, p. 577.
72. *EIP*, p. 578.
73. *Inquiry*, p. 60.
74. *Reid on Logic*, pp. 287–8.
75. *EIP*, VIII.III, pp. 587–8.
76. For discussion of Reid's philosophy of art see Peter Kivy, 'Reid's philosophy of art', in Cuneo and Woudenberg (eds), *The Cambridge Companion to Thomas Reid*, pp. 267–88.
77. A smuggler, Andrew Wilson, who had robbed a customs officer was sentenced to death in Edinburgh. Many of those who came to witness the execution sympathised with the smuggler, and after the sentence was carried out there was an angry commotion in the crowd, as a result of which Captain John Porteous of the Town Guard ordered his soldiers to fire into the crowd. Perhaps as many as thirty were killed or injured. For this act Porteous himself was put on trial. He was sen-

tenced to death and a crowd came to witness the execution, but they were told that there had been a six-week stay of execution while an appeal for clemency was considered. The crowd then stormed the jail, kidnapped Porteous and hanged him.

78. *EIP*, p. 4.
79. Kames, *Essays*, 1st edn, p. 152 (hereinafter *Essays*).
80. Ibid. p. 155.
81. Ibid. p. 167.
82. Ibid. p. 175.
83. Ibid. p. 179.
84. Hume, *Letters*, ed. Greig, vol. 1, p. 162.
85. George Anderson, *An Estimate of the Profit and Loss of Religion* (Edinburgh, 1753), pp. 122–3. See Harris, *Of Liberty and Necessity*, pp. 97–103.
86. *Essays*, p. 187.
87. *Essays*, 3rd edn, pp. 176–9.
88. Campbell, *The Philosophy of Rhetoric*, vol. 1, p. 114 (I.v). References in parentheses are to book and chapter numbers.
89. *EIP*, p. 39.
90. Beattie, *An Essay on the Nature and Immutability of Truth*, p. 25.
91. *EIP*, p. 41.
92. Campbell, *The Philosophy of Rhetoric*, vol. 1, p. 100 (I.iv).
93. *EIP*, p. 36.
94. Campbell, *The Philosophy of Rhetoric*, vol. 1, pp. 100–1 (I.iv).
95. Claude Buffier, *Cours de sciences sur des principes nouveaux et simples* (Paris, 1723), p. 3. The manuscript is reproduced in *Reid on Logic*, p. 152.
96. Published in his *Philosophical Essays*.
97. See Ferguson's memorandum in Ferguson, *Correspondence*, vol. 2, pp. 556–9.
98. Discoverer in 1769 of the inverse square law of electric force.
99. *The Democratic Intellect* and *The Crisis of the Democratic Intellect*.
100. Stewart, *Elements of the Philosophy of the Human Mind*, introduction, pt. II. VIII (hereinafter *Elements*).
101. Full title: 'A short statement of some important facts, relative to the late election of a Mathematical Professor in the University of Edinburgh' (Edinburgh, 1805).
102. Ferguson, *Institutes*, introduction, sect. VI, pp. 11–12.
103. Ferguson, *An Essay on the History of Civil Society*, ed. Oz-Salzberger, p. 8.
104. Stewart, *Outlines of Moral Philosophy*, introduction, sect. 2.
105. Ibid. pt I, sect. 1.
106. Stewart, *The Philosophy of the Active and Moral Powers of Man*, vol. 2, app. I, sect. 6.

107. *Correspondence*, pp. 211–23. The probable year of the draft is 1791. For discussion of the draft see Daniel N. Robinson, 'Thomas Reid's critique of Dugald Stewart', *Journal of the History of Philosophy*, 27 (1989): 405–22; Broadie, 'The human mind and its powers', in Broadie (ed.), *The Cambridge Companion to the Scottish Enlightenment*, esp. pp. 71–4.
108. *Elements*, pt. I, ch. 2, p. 141.
109. *Correspondence*, p. 214.
110. Ibid. p. 217.
111. Hamilton, *Fragments of the Scottish Philosophy*, in Hamilton, *Lectures on Metaphysics and Logic*, eds Mansel and Veitch, vol. 1, p. 396.
112. Ibid. vol. 1, p. 397.
113. *Inquiry*, p. 33.
114. Hippolyte Taine, *Les philosophies classiques*, 3rd edn (Paris, 1868), pp. 21–2. For my exposition of the French relations to Reid I am indebted to Michel Malherbe's chapter in Broadie (ed.), *The Cambridge Companion to the Scottish Enlightenment* (pp. 298–315), and also to a number of contributions to Arosio and Malherbe (eds), *Philosophie française et philosophie écossaise*.
115. See Gary Wills, *Inventing America: Jefferson's Declaration of Independence* (New York: Vintage, 1978).
116. Douglas Sloan, *The Scottish Enlightenment and the American College Ideal* (New York: Teachers College Press, Columbia University, 1971), ch. 4.
117. For brief surveys with sources, see Benjamin W. Redekop, 'Reid's influence in Britain, Germany, France and America', in Cuneo and Woudenberg (eds), *The Cambridge Companion to Thomas Reid*, pp. 313–39; Michel Malherbe, 'The impact on Europe', in Broadie (ed.), *The Cambridge Companion to the Scottish Enlightenment*, pp. 298–315; and S. Fleischacker, 'The impact on America: Scottish philosophy and the American founding', in Broadie (ed.), *The Cambridge Companion to the Scottish Enlightenment*, pp. 316–37.

CHAPTER 10

The Nineteenth Century: Ferrier to Seth

SECTION 1: WHAT BECAME OF THE SCOTTISH ENLIGHTENMENT?

Scottish philosophy of the eighteenth century and the earlier part of the nineteenth, the period covered by the Scottish Enlightenment, is an extraordinary success story, as is demonstrated by the international impact of its chief participants. The philosophy of Thomas Reid is one of the most significant of Scotland's invisible exports, and no less can be said of David Hume's philosophy. Political economy, represented especially by Adam Smith and Sir James Steuart, and historiography, represented especially by Hume and William Robertson, were also major fields. There is too the work of Scotland's scientists, among them Joseph Black, who discovered carbon dioxide (what he termed 'fixed air') and the phenomena of latent heat and specific heat; James Hutton, whose *Theory of the Earth* (1795) transformed geology, providing the science with the firm foundation on which it has since rested; John Robison, the discoverer of the inverse square law of electric force; and William Cullen, who made significant advances in the field of medical science, as did Alexander Munro II, who engaged in significant research into the nervous system. In engineering, James Watt, a close colleague of Joseph Black's at Glasgow, invented the improved version of the Newcomen steam engine that in due course was to be a major driving force of the industrial revolution. And in mathematics there are Colin Maclaurin, John Stewart and Robert Simson. The point is clear: across a wide range of disciplines the Scottish Enlightenment was a stunning intellectual performance that set the intellectual agenda for many people inside and outside Scotland for many decades thereafter.

Then came the nineteenth century. In *Ferrier and the Blackout of the Scottish Enlightenment* (2003) George Davie argues that Sir William Hamilton's pupil and friend James Frederick Ferrier (1808–64) was in substantial measure responsible for the blackout of the Scottish Enlightenment in the 1850s, when his philosophy ceases to be 'German philosophy refracted through a Scottish medium'[1] and becomes, argues Davie, a form of Platonism in so far as Ferrier holds that in being conscious of our self, and antecedent to our encounter with anyone else, we are already conscious of the existence of other minds. Such a philosophy, Davie believes, has none of the Scottish character of the Scottish Enlightenment, by which he means principally the common sense school. The details are not important here, but the form of the argument is. Davie assumes that philosophy is the only discipline in the Scottish Enlightenment, and he also assumes that a false account of the a priori element in self-consciousness must somehow be fatal to the philosophical project of the Scottish Enlightenment; yet both of these assumptions are deeply implausible.

Whether there was a blackout of the Scottish Enlightenment is an empirical question, one not to be answered by noting a shift in the philosophical thinking of Ferrier to a form of Platonism. Instead we should ask what actually happens as the century wears on, and what we find is that philosophy continues to flourish and indeed to remain in rather close proximity to the philosophy of the Scottish Enlightenment. Different strands are detectable. On the one side we find a flourishing empiricist philosophy being developed most especially by James Mill and Alexander Bain, who are particularly attracted to the associationist theories of Thomas Brown, James Mill's teacher, and Archibald Alison. Everyone on this side of the discussion is indebted to Hume's account of the association of ideas. On the other side many are indebted to Kant, Fichte, Schelling and Hegel, but in this latter group Enlightenment Scotland is not abandoned, for the nineteenth-century Scottish idealist philosophers continue to look over their shoulder at both Hume and Reid while yet edging forward. Representative of the idealist approach is *Scottish Philosophy: A Comparison of the Scottish and German Answers to Hume* (1885) by Andrew Seth (later known as A. S. Pringle-Pattison). This book is rich in deployment of Scottish sources (particularly Reid and Hamilton) and German ones (particularly Kant and Hegel) in the quest for an effective counter to Humean scepticism. In works by others steeped in the German idealist philosophy, such as A. Campbell Fraser, William Wallace, Edward Caird, John Caird, D. G. Ritchie, James Seth, John Watson, W. P. Ker, W. R. Sorley, John H. Muirhead, John Stuart Mackenzie and R. B. Haldane, we again find regard for the Scottish Enlightenment thinkers who posed the questions which the nineteenth-century Scots sought to answer.

Again as with the eighteenth century we find that science is a major feature of the Scottish intellectual scene. The greatest figures are James Clerk Maxwell, who was a student of Sir William Hamilton, and William Thomson, Lord Kelvin. Kelvin of Glasgow and P. G. Tait of Edinburgh collaborated to produce their ground-breaking work on the conservation of energy, *A Treatise of Natural Philosophy* (1867), and in 1873 there appeared Clerk Maxwell's revolutionary *Treatise on Electricity and Magnetism*, whose importance for the development of relativity theory was recognised by Einstein.

Ground-breaking work was also being accomplished in the field of religious and social anthropology. Perhaps the greatest work in this field was James George Frazer's *Golden Bough* (twelve volumes, 1890–1915), but William Robertson Smith's scientifically sophisticated investigations of the Bible were also immensely influential in Britain and far beyond.

All this bespeaks an intellectual scene flourishing at the highest level and prompts doubt over the claim that with Ferrier's later work we reach the 'blackout of the Scottish Enlightenment'. Indeed Cairns Craig has argued that this nineteenth-century phase of Scottish culture might best be described as a 'second Scottish Enlightenment'.[2] I am doubtful about this description in view of the continuity of the cultural movement; there is a single sweep of high-grade intellectual activity through the eighteenth and nineteenth centuries. The two periods are each characteristic of Enlightenment, understanding by that a period of intellectual progress made through the exercise of autonomous reason in circumstances in which people may put their ideas into the public domain without risk of persecution by the authorities, whether political or religious. The term 'Scottish Enlightenment' is now used to refer to a particular time span in the history of Scottish culture, usually taken to start and finish sometime in the eighteenth century but the lack of agreement concerning the length of the span is instructive and it is a consequence of the fact of the sheer continuity to which I have already alluded. The 'second' Enlightenment is part of a larger first.

Regarding the Scottishness of the nineteenth-century performance we should note the self-perception of the thinkers themselves. The philosophers of the age were self-consciously engaged in doing something they described as Scottish. They saw their eighteenth-century predecessors in national terms, as is signalled by James McCosh, a student of Thomas Chalmers at Edinburgh, who in 1868 left Scotland to become the eleventh president of Princeton College. His *The*

Scottish Philosophy (1875) spells out plainly that the title refers to the common sense school even though he includes a chapter on Hume, not as a member of the school but as the person the school most seeks to counter. This concept of Scottish philosophy is in play when Ferrier writes his *Scottish Philosophy: The Old and the New* (1856), when Seth writes his *Scottish Philosophy*, and when an anonymous author pens his *Scottish Metaphysics Reconstructed in Accordance with the Principles of Physical Science* (1887). Thus this last begins with the words: 'Scottish philosophy, founded by Reid and illustrated and adorned by Stewart and others, is here set forth from Hamilton's expository lectures and other sources.'[3] With these works in mind, and others such as them, it should be said that if it is claimed that in the second half of the nineteenth century there was indeed an Enlightenment in Scotland but that there was nothing Scottish about it, those making the claim must at least deal with the fact that it runs strongly counter to the self-perception of those who were participating in that philosophical endeavour. In answer to the question I asked at the start of this section: 'What became of the Scottish Enlightenment?', the evidence suggests that it just kept on running.

SECTION 2: J. F. FERRIER AND THE PHILOSOPHY OF CONSCIOUSNESS

James Frederick Ferrier (1808–64), a native of Edinburgh, was educated at the High School of Edinburgh, then at Edinburgh University and finally at Oxford, from where he graduated in 1831, the year in which he met Hamilton, his future friend and mentor. He was appointed to the chair of civil history at Edinburgh in 1842 and in 1845 was appointed to the chair of moral philosophy at St Andrews, the position he occupied until his death in 1864.

Ferrier was steeped in the Scottish philosophy of the eighteenth century and also in the philosophy of Kant and his heirs Fichte, Schelling and Hegel. These facts played a major role at that crucial moment in his career when he applied for the chair of logic and metaphysics at Edinburgh University in 1856 when it became vacant on the death of Sir William Hamilton. The chair was in the gift of the Edinburgh town council; they wished to appoint someone who would carry on the Reidian tradition, and a question arose as to whether Ferrier's philosophy was Scottish or German. When his application was rejected he wrote a pamphlet, *Scottish Philosophy: The Old and the New*, in which he denounced the corruption of the selection process and declared his philosophical affiliations. 'It has been asserted, that my philosophy is of Germanic origin and complexion . . . My philosophy is Scottish to the very core; it is national in every fibre and articulation of its frame.'[4] As to the accusation that his philosophy was Germanic, his reply was: 'I have read most of Hegel's works again and again, but I cannot say that I am acquainted with his philosophy. I am able to understand only a few short passages here and there in his writings.' This last claim is not persuasive; Ferrier had spent time in Germany, had attended lectures on philosophy at the University of Heidelberg and had made a close study of German philosophy, and there are many traces in Ferrier's writings of the ideas of Kant and his great successors.

It should be said that there was a religious dimension to the war of words that preceded the rejection of Ferrier's application for the chair; for the Disruption, that immense fracture in the Church of Scotland which had taken place in 1843 over the issue of the exercise of patronage, was still resonating strongly in 1856. John Cairns, a minister of the breakaway Free Church, published two pamphlets attacking Ferrier's theory of knowing and being, and argued that Ferrier was not philosophically fit for the chair. There was a subtext to these attacks, for John Cairns was supporting the rival application of Patrick Campbell MacDougall, a philosophy professor in the Free Church stronghold of New College, Edinburgh.[5] Nevertheless hostility to Ferrier was principally focused on his perceived location in relation to the Scottish school of common sense philosophy. The council wanted someone who represented the Scottish philosophical tradition, and many on the council must have felt vindicated in their opposition to Ferrier when they saw what he had to say about recent major figures in Scottish philosophy:

> It is well to know that a candidate for a philosophical chair in the University of Edinburgh need not now be a believer in Christ or a member of the Established Church; but he must be a believer in Dr Reid, and a pledged disciple of the Hamiltonian system of philosophy . . . They [Edinburgh Town Council] are of opinion that no man except the thorough-going disciples of Reid, and Stewart, and Hamilton, ought to get a hearing from our Chairs, and that philosophy has reached its final close, its ultimate development in them.[6]

Ferrier believes himself to be writing Scottish philosophy but not to be writing what Reid, Stewart and Hamilton wrote; philosophy is an ongoing project and Ferrier saw himself as taking the project further. How much further is an interesting question, but there is no doubt that he was in conflict with Reid on essential matters regarding both philosophical method and philosophical doctrine. Aspects of the conflict will surface shortly but it is evident that the conflict runs deep, given Ferrier's disparagement of the principles of common sense. He writes:

> The fundamental principles of the old Scottish philosophy have either no proper place in metaphysics, or else it is just such a place as the facts, that people usually take sugar with their tea, and generally take off their clothes before getting into bed, occupy in the sciences of chemistry, botany, and physiology . . . the first principles of philosophy are *not* the elementary truths which have been enunciated as such by our old Scottish philosophy.[7]

For Ferrier the fundamental difference between the old, Reidian Scottish philosophy and the new, Ferrier's, is that the old holds that philosophy's role is to ratify and systematise what Ferrier terms the 'natural inadvertencies of loose, ordinary thinking', while for the new school, philosophy's role is to correct those natural inadvertencies.

Ferrier's greatest work is perhaps *An Introduction to the Philosophy of Consciousness*, which originally appeared as a series of seven papers in *Blackwood's Magazine* (1838–9). Subsequently he published a number of papers, of which the most important are perhaps 'The crisis of modern speculation' (1841), 'Berkeley and idealism' (1842), 'A speculation on the senses' (1843) and 'Reid and the philosophy of common sense' (1847).[8] In 1854 there appeared his most extensive work, *The Institutes of Metaphysics*, and after his death his lectures on Greek philosophy were published as a unitary work. For the remainder of this section I shall expound his chief ideas, paying particular attention to his *Introduction to the Philosophy of Consciousness*.

Ferrier signals early his dissatisfaction with a major strand of the Scottish philosophical tradition, for though at the start it seems that his target is Hume it quickly transpires that Reid and his followers are also in the firing line. That we should apply to our inner aspect the method, the Baconian experimental method of reasoning, used to investigate the outer world is understandable. From the earliest days our senses are naturally turned outwards, and since it is the outer world that usually holds our attention it is on that that we reflect. A method for enquiring into the outer world is well established, and when people eventually come to enquire into their inner aspect that same method is therefore appropriated for the task. To an extent it is successful, for we can note our sensations and our passions, the changes they undergo and the circumstances in which they undergo them, and we can classify all these things and consider the causal relations between these various states of mind. The states of mind are themselves known to us because of our consciousness of them, evidence that is as strong as any could be. This last point is Reidian and is articulated in the first of his principles of common sense, but Ferrier wishes to add another dimension to this point about the primacy of consciousness. It is that what is conscious is a self, an *I*. It is not my mind, nor any state of my mind that is conscious; it is *I*. As a conscious being, I am the subject in relation to all these things both internal and external which are objects of my consciousness. To which Ferrier adds that the self – as subject – cannot carry out a scientific investigation of itself, but it can carry out a scientific investigation of the acts in which it is engaged and the objects of those acts.

Of course we can carry out a scientific investigation into our mind, we can introspect our sensations, imaginings, rememberings and so on, and reflect upon them; but such investigation is not into the subject, the agent of the mental acts. The conscious subject cannot be objectified into an object of scientific enquiry without being falsified; in so far as the conscious subject is made the object of consciousness it is not the conscious subject. The conscious subject, on this account, is forever concealed from the scientific enquirer because it *is* the scientific enquirer.

The implication of Ferrier's doctrine is that the Humean project of a 'science of man' must fail. A Humean science of man will include an application of the 'experimental method of reasoning' to mental acts and to principles of change in the mind such as the principles of association of ideas, but Ferrier would reply that the science is not properly a science of man if it excludes enquiry into the subject of consciousness, the *I*, the self, that is conscious of the mental existents. Hume might reply that there is nothing more to the self than its various perceptions, but Ferrier's response is that this is an incoherent position. Our perceptions are what we *have*, not what we *are*. Perhaps one way to make this point is to note Hume's famous account of mind as a bundle of perceptions, and to note also the fact that Hume does not account for the fact that the perceptions form a unitary bundle. What is it that makes a given collection of perceptions a single bundle? The obvious answer, Ferrier's, is that all the perceptions are *mine*, or are *yours* or are *hers* and so on Far from the self being identical with its perceptions, it has to be other than them if it is to unify them.

The experimental method of reasoning, which is an essential part of the Scottish philosophical enterprise of the eighteenth century, is held by Ferrier to be inappropriate as a means to attain the truth about the self, and he thereby demonstrates both his distance from the Reidian common sense philosophy and also his closeness to the recent German idealists whose work he knew so well.

It should now be clear that the subject-object relation is at the heart of Ferrier's philosophy of consciousness, and I should like to note the way in which he uses it to reach a major thesis of his philosophical anthropology. My starting point will be a rather common teaching on perception that we find in Hume and in later Scottish philosophers. Thomas Brown, Dugald Stewart's successor in the chair of moral philosophy at Edinburgh, is quoted by Ferrier:

> Perception is a state of mind which is induced directly or indirectly by its external cause, as any other feeling is induced by its particular antecedent. If the external cause or object be absent, the consequent feeling, direct or indirect, which we term perception, will not be induced, precisely as any other feeling will not arise without its peculiar antecedent. The relation of cause and effect, in short, is exactly the same in perception as in all the other mental phenomena, a relation of invariable sequence of one change after another change.[9]

In Chapter 9 we noted that Reid distinguishes between sensation and perception, arguing that sensation is one component, along with conception and judgment, in the complex act he terms 'perception'. Ferrier likewise wishes to make a distinction between the two, though his is grounded instead in the subject/object distinction. Sensation is no doubt to be accounted for entirely in terms of the physical world, and if in the above quotation perception is understood to mean sensation then Ferrier would accept Brown's claim. But Ferrier holds that an act of perception is a sensation accompanied by consciousness of the sensation. Consciousness is an act by an *I* that is conscious of some object, in this case a sensation, and while a causal explanation can be provided of the sensation none can be provided of the act of consciousness.

If something is, through and through, part of the material world, its behaviour must be wholly determined by the causes operating on it, but we, who call ourselves *I*, are not wholly within the scope of empirical causes or, in Ferrier's flamboyant phrase, are not 'engulfed and borne along in their vortices'.[10] There is therefore a distance, which is infinite in the sense of being in principle unbridgeable, between the self and all its objects, which as a collective constitute the not-self, the world out there which is appropriate for investigation by the experimental method of reasoning. The self looks out upon all these things which can make no causal impact upon it, and looking out it knows itself to be free. Consciousness surrounds the self, and keeps the outer world at a distance from it. On this analysis consciousness is the condition of freedom. A being lacking consciousness is overwhelmed by nature whereas a being who has consciousness is so far from being overwhelmed that it is able to use nature to gain ends which nature is in no position to dictate to it.

Consciousness therefore implies an act of negation, for the self must distinguish itself from nature as a self in relation to not-self. Nature can of course have an impact on us in respect of much of what we are, for we have a natural existence in that we are subject to natural causal law in respect both of our material nature and of our sensations, emotions and so on. As something in nature, the human being is wholly under the dominion of causality: 'He dons the sensations and passions that come to him, and bends before them like a sapling in the wind.'[11] But a being who is an *I* is other than nature and therefore able to refrain from bending; he can reject his passions by refusing to act on their dictates even if he may have to put up with their presence. This power of dissent, of being able to say no to nature, is what we call 'will'.

These considerations underpin an important distinction between physical science and philosophy. In the case of physical science, contemplation of the object of study adds nothing to the properties that already belong to the phenomena being studied. The investigative instruments used by a scientist might affect the behaviour of the phenomena being studied, but the scientist's contemplation of the readings on his instruments and of the objects which he investigates with the aid of his instruments can make no difference to the phenomena. But when we think about what kind of beings we ourselves are, this philosophical contemplation adds a new phenomenon, namely the fact of our being contemplative, a fact which cannot be found in nature. Without this additional fact what sort of picture can we construct of ourselves? Ferrier replies:

> Not the picture of a man; but the representation of an automaton, that is what it cannot help being; a phantom dreaming what it cannot but dream; an engine performing what it *must* perform; an incarnate reverie; a weathercock shifting helplessly in the winds of sensibility;

a wretched association machine, through which ideas pass linked together by laws over which the machine has no control; anything, in short, except that free and self-sustained centre of underived, and therefore responsible activity, which we call *Man*.[12]

Though in our earliest years we are such weathercocks, we come to be aware of ourselves as selves over against our sensations and passions, and thereby become aware of them as what we *have*, not what we *are*. Since these things that we have do not determine us as they determine the behaviour of an infant or an animal, the 'enslaving power of nature' (Ferrier's phrase) does not enslave us, but instead provides us with an agenda for our thought. Consciousness of our sensations yields perception of the world over against us, the world that caused the sensations; and consciousness of our passions yields moral judgments concerning how best to respond to those passions, whether to act in the direction dictated by them or to act contrary to their dictates. It is through consciousness of our passions therefore that we become moral beings – something impossible otherwise. For without consciousness we cannot ask ourselves whether it would or would not be right to perform the acts that our passions have demanded of us.

In illustration of the use to which we can put the distance between ourselves and the world of nature Ferrier offers the distinction between love of our friends and of our enemies. The former is according to the dictates of nature; it has, or at least may have, no more moral worth than the girations of the weathercock. Such love is a 'passion' in the proper sense of the term, a passive response to circumstances. It is a 'mere affair of temperament, and in entertaining it, we are just as passive as our bodies are when exposed to the warmth of a cheerful fire. It lies completely under the causal law.'[13] But love of one's enemy is different because it cuts across the grain of nature. Nevertheless our feelings are in some measure under our control; we can act against the hatred to which we naturally succumb. The reason we should so act is that nature presents a permanent threat to our freedom. If nature says: 'Hate your enemy' we best protect our freedom by reflecting on the fact that nature is attempting to colonise us, to absorb us entirely into itself and thereby annihilate our freedom. So we contemplate our natural hatred and ask whether it is right, and then see that there are reasons not to hate; we see that our enemy is another human being, no less worthy of respect than we judge ourselves to be. Our hatred was a capitulation to the forces of nature and thereby implicitly a rejection of our freedom; to love our friends is a natural act, to love our enemies is a moral act.

In Ferrier's eyes, the philosophers of the Scottish common sense school, including Reid and Stewart, were no less in thrall than was Hume to the belief that the experimental method of reasoning was the appropriate method to use in their enquiry into the nature of human beings, and their accounts of the self and morality must also fail. Ferrier sums up his criticism: 'The physical method observes, but the psychological method swings itself higher than this, and observes observation. Thus psychology, or philosophy properly so called, commences precisely at the point where physical science ends.'[14] The experimental method must therefore be supplemented by a different kind of exercise, which Ferrier terms 'reflective consciousness', an exercise by which the self and morality can properly be brought into the enquirer's scope.

Ferrier holds that the self as such is an abstraction and cannot exist in reality. It can exist only in relation to a not-self. He also holds that the world of nature, the not-self, is likewise an abstraction and can exist only in relation to a self of which it is the negation; self and nature therefore exist only as relative and co-relative. On this account what is absolute and not merely relative is the conjunction of the self and not-self, the *I* and the world.[15] This is a version of the doctrine of 'absolute idealism', 'absolute' because it concerns the character that something must have if it is to exist absolutely and is not to exist merely relatively to something else, and 'idealism' because the doctrine affirms that there is no world except as an object in relation to a subject of consciousness. The annihilation of all consciousness would imply the annihilation of the world. This doctrine is closely associated with the post-Kantian German idealists, and though, as we noted earlier, Ferrier said of Hegel: 'I am able to understand only a few short passages here and there in his writings', there is no doubt that he progressed deeply into the philosophy of all three thinkers.

In addition the doctrine is to be found in a rather particular form in George Berkeley, of whom Ferrier wrote: 'His genius was the first to swell the current of that mighty stream of tendency towards which all modern meditation flows, the great gulf-stream of Absolute Idealism.'[16] Berkeley's famous affirmation: 'To be is to be perceived' certainly has absolute idealist overtones in that it implies that there is nothing in the world nor even a system of nature as a whole except it be the object of a perceptual act. Berkeley's doctrine does appear to be in roughly the same territory as Ferrier's doctrine that there is no object except in relation to a subject, and that in particular nothing exists in nature unless there be a knowing subject in relation to which nature and its contents are objects. That said, Ferrier criticises Berkeley's position on the ground that for Berkeley the 'subject' includes our senses, whereas for Ferrier our senses are themselves part of the natural world and must therefore count as on the side of the object in relation to the self which is subject. Nevertheless Ferrier has a good deal in common with Berkeley, as indeed he also has with Kant and the post-Kantian German idealists, perhaps especially Fichte, and these points prompt a question regarding Ferrier's place in the Scottish philosophical tradition and in particular regarding his description of his work as 'Scottish to the very core'. Two points are in order here.

First, the philosopher to whom Ferrier responds most often is Reid, disagreeing with him regarding, first, the propriety of using the experimental method to reach philosophical conclusions in 'the science of man' and, secondly, the status of the principles of common sense. We have just dealt with the first. As regards the second, Ferrier writes:

> Another point of difference – indeed the fundamental difference – between the two Scottish philosophies, the Old and the New, is this, that while I hold that philosophy exists for the sole purpose of correcting the natural inadvertencies of loose, ordinary thinking – that this is her true and proper vocation; the old school, on the contrary, are of opinion that philosophy exists for the very purpose of ratifying, and, if possible, systematising these inadvertencies. This is held by Reid and his followers to be the proper business of metaphysical science.[17]

Among the natural, loose inadvertencies of thinking is the belief in the independence of the outer world from the perceiving subject. Reid seeks to enshrine this belief in his philosophy but, as noted above, Ferrier's philosophical analysis reveals an inseparability of percipient subject and perceived object. Herein lies his absolute idealism. Ferrier might disagree with Berkeley as to what is to count as the 'subject' in relation to the object but there is no doubt that Ferrier sees himself as correcting the Reidian position, advancing beyond it while at the same time remaining within the Scottish philosophical enterprise. With this in mind Ferrier declares:

> Are we to judge of the productions of Scotland by looking merely to what Scotland has *hitherto* produced? May a philosopher not be, heart and soul, a Scotsman – may he not be a Scotsman in all his intellectual movements, even although he should have the misfortune to differ, in certain respects, from Dr Reid and Sir William Hamilton?

> . . . what I assert is, that my system of philosophy – whatever its merit or demerit may be – was born and bred in this country, and is essentially native to the soil.[18]

Secondly, the concept of consciousness is central to the whole philosophical enterprise of Reid. As we have seen, Reid's first principle of common sense concerns the scope of consciousness and the degree of its reliability as evidence of the truth of given propositions. Consciousness could hardly have been given a more conspicuous position in Reid's philosophy. Likewise consciousness could hardly have been given a more conspicuous position in Ferrier's. Ferrier does not reject what Reid says about consciousness but, believing Reid to have said less on the topic than he might have done, he presents an account that is more detailed and more far reaching than Reid accomplished.

SECTION 3: ALEXANDER BAIN AND THE EMPIRICAL STUDY OF THE MIND

Alexander Bain (1818–1903), a native of Aberdeen, went up to Marischal College, Aberdeen, in 1836, graduating in 1840. After some years teaching moral philosophy and natural philosophy there he applied in turn for the chairs of natural philosophy and moral philosophy, the application rejected each time in view of his scepticism on matters religious. In 1845 he was appointed professor of natural philosophy and mathematics at the Anderson College, Glasgow, but after brief occupancy of the chair, he went to London, where his circle of friends and acquaintances included J. S. Mill, Herbert Spencer, Thomas Carlyle and George Grote. He joined the teaching staff of Bedford College, London, in 1851, by which time he had already published on a wide range of subjects philosophical and otherwise. Perhaps his two most important works appeared while he was still in London, *The Senses and the Intellect* (1855) and *The Emotions and the Will* (1859), titles suggestive of Thomas Reid's two late works *Essays on the Intellectual Powers* and *Essays on the Active Powers*. Since Bain read Reid's works repeatedly during the 1850s the resemblance of the titles is unlikely to be coincidental. In 1860 Bain returned to Aberdeen, to the new University of Aberdeen which had just been created by amalgamating King's College and Marischal College. His appointment to the chair of logic was secured despite the formidable rival candidature of James McCosh.

In 1876 Bain founded the journal *Mind*, which is now a philosophy journal, but whose original remit included psychology, including experimental psychology, as well as philosophy. Bain appointed as first editor George Croom Robertson (1842–92), an Aberdonian who graduated from Marischal College and then studied philosophy and psychology in Germany before returning to Aberdeen to work for a year under Bain. Bain's clear intention was to create publishing space for writings on what Hume termed the 'science of man' where that phrase was to be understood much as Hume understood it, though Bain's research within the science of man took him a significant distance into matters on which Hume and his more immediate successors have rather little to say; for example, concerning the relations between psychology and physiology.

The first of Bain's major works, *The Senses and the Intellect*, opens with an extensive exposition of physiology and neurology which is not prefatory to, but is the first part within, his psychological investigation. That first part enables him to give an account of, for example, the establishment of habits. The account takes due note of a physiological aspect of habits, namely the concomitant establishment of neural paths in the brain, and the gradual confirmation of the pathways as the habits themselves become more firm. In *The Senses and the Intellect* Bain also provides a 300-page account of the intellect, an account which consists of an exposition of the laws of association, principally the law of contiguity and the law of similarity, and it is plain that he regards the physiological underpinning of association as an integral part of the science he is investigating. His version of the 'science of man' is thus empirical psychology with a strong experimental basis.

Another philosopher with a similar vision of philosophy was G. F. Stout (1860–1944), a younger friend of Bain's, who occupied the chair of logic at St Andrews and, like Croom Robertson, was also for some years editor of *Mind*. Thus in the second half of the nineteenth century experimental psychology was taught as an integral part of philosophy courses in Scottish universities. This implies the deployment of a concept of philosophy far removed from Ferrier's, but for some decades the different concepts lived more or less amicably side by side in the philosophy courses.

Section 4: Andrew Seth Pringle-Pattison and personal idealism

Andrew Seth Pringle-Pattison (1856–1931) was born plain Andrew Seth and remained so until 1898, when as a result of a bequest he added 'Pringle-Pattison'. He attended the Royal High School in

Edinburgh and then went up to Edinburgh University, where he read classics and philosophy. In 1878 he spent two years in Germany, attending classes at the universities of Berlin, Jena and Göttingen and reading the German idealist philosophers. On his return in 1880 he was appointed assistant to A. Campbell Fraser, the professor of logic and metaphysics at Edinburgh, and two years later he published *The Development from Kant to Hegel*, a book that in some ways set his philosophical agenda for the rest of his life. In 1883 he took up the chair of logic and philosophy at University College, Cardiff, returning to Edinburgh in 1887 to occupy the chair of logic and metaphysics from which Campbell Fraser had just retired. (In 1898 his brother James Seth, author of *Ethical Principles*, was appointed to Edinburgh's chair of moral philosophy, which he occupied until 1924.)

By the time of Andrew Seth's return to Edinburgh in 1887 he had published two further books, *Scottish Philosophy: A Comparison of the Scottish and German Answers to Hume* (1885) and *Hegelianism and Personality* (1887). Thereafter his principal writings, *The Idea of God* (1917), *The Idea of Immortality* (1922) and *Studies in the Philosophy of Religion* (1930), were based on two sets of Gifford Lectures. Here I shall give a sense of the range of ideas in Andrew Seth Pringle-Pattison's writings, attending chiefly to the first three of his books. My intention is to note certain ideas of the German idealists that were particularly influential on him, to indicate some of the grounds of his dissatisfaction with German idealist thinking, and to indicate also where he stands in relation to the tradition of Scottish philosophy.

That this last question was of interest to him is suggested by a revealing comment at the start of *Scottish Philosophy: A Comparison of the Scottish and German Answers to Hume*:

> The thread of national tradition, it is tolerably well known, has been but loosely held of late by many of our best Scottish students of philosophy. It will hardly be denied that the philosophical productions of the younger generation of our University men are more strongly impressed with a German than with a native stamp.[19]

His interest in the question is shown also by the following observation:

> The *Fachmann*, or specialist, has hitherto not flourished among us, and the disadvantages of his absence are obvious. But it is possible that what Scottish philosophy has lost in scientific precision may have been compensated for, in part, by the greater influence which it has

exerted upon the body of the people – an influence which has made it a factor, so to speak, in the national life. It is a matter of history, on the other hand, that the great idealistic movement in Germany in the beginning of this century passed to a great extent over the heads of the German people . . . Hegel's philosophy has had a wide, and frequently unobserved, influence in moulding many departments of thought; but, as *philosophy*, it never lived in German beyond the confines of the schools. It spoke in an unknown tongue, and the people were not edified; it may be said to have died of its technical dialect.[20]

This is a heartfelt cry from Seth, as is his understated summing up: 'things cannot be altogether healthy, when there is no manner of touch whatever between the many and the few.' Seth sees philosophers as having a role in society, as educating the people and also as providing a principle of unity of the culture. Philosophers who do not contribute to these cultural goals have failed in an important dimension of their lives. Scottish philosophy has been singularly successful in this respect; the best has been metaphysically and morally strong and been comprehensible to the non-specialist, this in contrast to the German philosophy on which Seth focused. Seth plainly preferred the Scottish way of doing philosophy. Few nineteenth-century Scottish philosophers dedicated themselves more steadfastly than did Seth to exploring German philosophy, but in the end so far as he found weaknesses there he found space within which a modified form of Reidian philosophy would grow.

The Development from Kant to Hegel was the immediate product of Seth's two-year sojourn in Germany. The development he traces is via Fichte and Schelling, concluding with Hegel because: 'Hegel is the summing up and most perfect expression of the general movement of thought known as German Idealism.' Nevertheless he judges Hegel's philosophy to have fatal weaknesses, and I shall consider that judgment shortly, but first something should be said about Seth's satisfaction and dissatisfaction with Kant. Seth's baseline is the philosophy of Hume.

As regards the dissatisfaction, Hume had inherited a dualist conception according to which on the one side there are thinkers or minds and on the other there is a real world out there, two things connected if by nothing else then by the thinker's knowledge of the real world. But a question arises as to how this knowledge is possible. Hume understood his great predecessors Descartes and Locke to have answered this question by showing that if we start, as we must, with what is in the mind, namely our ideas, then we are able to know the real world through the ideas because we can trust to their veracity.

Seth interprets Hume as responding sceptically to this line of thought on the grounds that if we have to start with elements in our mind then we cannot progress cognitively to a reality outside our mind. But Hume, like the rest of us, believes there to be such a reality, and he argues that we construct it by the exercise of our imagination working on our perceptions. In a word, and it is the word Hume uses in this context, external reality is a 'fiction'. Kant, on Seth's interpretation, believes that he can refute Humean scepticism regarding the outer world, but Seth holds that the refutation fails because on the Kantian account we in fact remain trapped, as Hume believes us to be, within the world of appearances or 'phenomena'. We bring the sensory data under given concepts or categories, and what we believe to be the outer world is unknowable by us except as grasped under these categories. We can therefore never be face to face with outer reality because the categories we must deploy in order to have objectively valid knowledge prevent us seeing things in themselves or as they really are. Seth argues that this is true not only of the human race, since objectively valid knowledge for a being of any kind must involve the deployment of concepts under which reality is presented.

The implication of this position, from a Sethian perspective, is bizarre, for though we fondly imagine that our cognitive apparatus yields up knowledge of reality, on Seth's interpretation of Kant our cognitive apparatus in fact does the precise opposite, for it constitutes an obstacle to our apprehension of reality. On Kant's account, on the one hand there are 'noumena' or real things, things as they are in themselves (assuming it to be appropriate to use the plural, or even to use the singular as an alternative), and on the other hand there are 'phenomena' or appearances of these real things. Phenomena are substances standing in causal relation to each other but, since such categories as substance and causal necessity are provided by the mind, real things are in themselves neither substantial nor related by causality to anything. Hence in so far as the world we know is populated with substances related to each other in relations of causal necessity, the world we know is not real. This Kantian picture is rejected by Seth:

> We have vindicated rationality and necessity of connection for our universe; and we have now a cosmos, or nature, in which science can work. But this has been achieved at a terrible cost. For we have to bear in mind that, without exception, as Kant puts it, the objects we are dealing with are 'not things-in-themselves, but the mere play of our ideas, which in the end are merely determinations of the internal sense'.[21]

Seth concludes that at a certain level of abstraction Kant's position points, no less than does Hume's, to a total scepticism about the existence of reality. If we ask: 'What reality?', how can that be answered if cognitive contact with reality is ruled out? We are left with appearances, but not with something, a reality, of which the appearances are appearances. Hume's doctrine that the outer world, the 'real' world, is a fiction produced by the imagination seems to live on in Kant even if the account is modulated in certain significant ways. We can *say* that what we know is reality, but on the analysis of both Hume and Kant, the reality that we know seems entirely on the side of the subject.

Seth complains: 'It is hardly possible to open a scientific or semi-philosophical work, without meeting the complacent admission that our knowledge is "only of phenomena".'[22] As against this 'complacent admission' Seth argues that we do know noumena. A phenomenon is what reality or the noumenon becomes by being known by us. As Seth puts the point: 'to say that the noumenon becomes a phenomenon is only to say that the noumenon is known.'[23] On this account we do have cognitive access to reality, and in distinguishing between noumenon and phenomenon we do not thereby distinguish between a reality to which we can have no cognitive access and something else, a phenomenon, to which we do; it is instead to distinguish between reality and that same reality in so far as it is actually accessed by us. The difference between the two is that we do not always, or perhaps ever, know everything that there is to be known about something real. If we had exhaustive knowledge of a given individual reality then we would know that individual reality all the way through, and then, in Seth's words, 'the knowledge of the phenomenon would be, in that case, in the strictest sense the knowledge of the noumenon'. On this account phenomenon and noumenon are the same thing. Far from the two terms marking the difference between the known and the unknown, they mark the difference between the one thing so far as it is known and that same thing which is perhaps partly known and partly not yet known. But the fact that reality is inexhaustible as to what there is to know about it does not mean that reality is simply unknowable; it means only that it is not wholly knowable. This doctrine of Seth's is deeply anti-Kantian on what for Kant is a central issue.

Seth is here making the point that though Kant sought to 'answer' Humean scepticism he in fact produced a more sophisticated version of it. Kant, no less than Hume, operated within the framework of the theory of ideas, the theory of 'mental representations', and since scepticism is, on a Reidian interpretation, an inevitable consequence of the theory of ideas, Kant could no more escape scepticism than could Hume. Seth, who was entirely on Reid's side in Reid's critique of the theory of ideas, declares:

> Instead of, like Reid, abandoning 'the ideal system', he [Kant] elaborately reconstructed it, endeavouring to give it a more rational and tenable form. Kant is, indeed, the very prince of Representationalists, and the Representationalism of the present day has its roots almost entirely in the Kantian theory.[24]

Seth's analysis has an implication for the common claim that Reid is 'the Scottish Kant'. The negative dimension of Reid's philosophy is an attack on the theory of ideas, and it is on the ruins of that theory that Reid constructs his own positive philosophy of perception and liberty. If, then, Kant embraces a version of the theory of ideas, he stands for something which, in Reid's view, was blocking progress towards a proper account of the relation between the knower and the known, between a cognitively active subject and an object located in the real world. To call Reid the 'Scottish Kant' is to fail to note that, though Reid had not read Kant, Kant was, virtually, no less a target of Reid's attack than was Hume.

Seth's conception of the relation between Hume and Kant focuses on a significant respect in which Kant's philosophy is an advance on Hume's, namely Kant's definitive reshaping of the way in which philosophers understand the difference between subject and object. On Kant's account the object cannot be at a distance from the subject if the object exists purely as the product of a unifying or 'synthesising' act performed by the subject on its own impressions. Without the subject's synthesising acts there is no object nor, as Seth indicates, a subject either. Subject and object are in themselves empty abstractions. What is not an abstraction is the subject and the object united in an act of knowledge. In that act subject and object are one, but the one is a duality, that is, two things united. Hence knowledge that excludes division is not knowledge. We shall need to revisit shortly the relation of subject to object. The history of nineteenth-century Scottish philosophy can almost be described as an exploration of the subject–object relation.

In his *Scottish Philosophy: A Comparison of the Scottish and German Answers to Hume* Seth criticises Hegel, and in *Hegelianism and Personality*, published two years later, he takes the criticisms much further, sufficiently far to call in question the description of Seth as a neo-Hegelian. Seth's Hegel is an absolute idealist in the sense that he holds that 'the real is rational'. We are to understand by this phrase that reality is a system and that both the system and its parts are intelligible, though the parts are not intelligible except as within the system.[25] Since the real is rational it must be cognitively accessible to rational beings. Nature is real; it must also be rational, for we know its laws and we know how to manipulate it in the light of these laws. Since we are rational, that is, can think logically, and nature is rational, nature is therefore *formally* like us. Hegel concludes that when we look out upon nature we find ourselves reflected in it – the logical reflected in the logical. This is a tight unity since a spirit, a self, is not separable in reality from the other in which it finds itself reflected, nor is nature separable in reality from the spirit whose reflection is in nature. Hence both nature and spirit are, by themelves, abstractions, and logic also is an abstraction except so far as it is actualised both in the thinking subject and also in nature considered as an object of thought.

There is here reference to spirit, nature and logic. Hegel holds that while these things are three *in abstracto* they are in reality not three but one, for nature and logic do not really exist except in relation to the life of the spirit.[26] But Seth asks whether there is in reality only one spirit, and argues that Hegel's answer is that there is only one and that it may be called the Absolute. This is not to deny that we also may be called spirits, but we finite spirits are no more than qualifications or perhaps modifications of the one spirit. In so far as we are real, we are identical with the one spirit which is the Absolute, and hence, as Seth formulates Hegel's doctrine, there is a unification of the human and the divine self-consciousness in a single Self.

Seth, on the other hand, rejects the doctrine that there is just one spirit and that that spirit is what reality is. He holds that we are unique real spirits, separate from each other and 'impervious' to each other, 'impervious', as he puts the point, 'in a fashion of which the impenetrability of matter is a faint analogue'.[27] The impenetrability does not imply that there is no interaction between selves, separate spirits, nor that no spirit can know another; what it implies is that each self is a unique centre of consciousness and of will, necessarily exclusive of every other. As to the evidence for this exclusiveness, it is evidence of the kind to which Thomas Reid ascribed priority in his ordering of the principles of common sense:

There is no deliverance of consciousness which is more unequivocal than that which testifies to this independence and exclusiveness. I have a centre of my own – a will of my own – which no one shares with me or can share – a centre which I maintain even in my dealings with God Himself. For it is eminently false to say that I put off, or can put off, my personality here. The religious consciousness lends no countenance whatever to the representation of the human soul as a mere mode or efflux of the divine.[28]

Instead our religious consciousness testifies to our own subjectivity, something that we have no less than God does, even if God's subjectivity transcends ours infinitely and in innumerable ways. Seth's claim therefore is that a self must be a self for itself, not just an object to another who is subject in relation to our self-as-object; a self must be conscious of itself as a subject in relation to something other. It is this, our subjectivity, that is the source of dignity and worth in ourselves; and since subjectivity is the highest category in our reach it is hardly for us to hold back from ascribing subjectivity to God also.

This implies not that we are divine but that we finite spirits are no less truly selves than God is a self, that we are neither an adjectival qualification nor an adverbial modification of him, and we are therefore, as Seth affirms, exclusively ourselves, where the exclusiveness is so exclusive that it excludes even God. Our exclusiveness cannot be overcome except by means of our annihilation – we would cease to be selves in ceasing to stand over against other selves. This is a deeply un-Hegelian picture driven partly by a deliverance of consciousness as endorsing an uncompromising, unsurmountable real plurality as contrasted with the Hegelian idea that the real is one. The outcome is a version of personal idealism or personalism. Seth was the first of the Scottish, indeed the British, idealists to provide a detailed statement of personalism, and many followed him.

I have sought here to indicate the character of the philosophy of the nineteenth-century Scottish idealists, but it should be added that many of them wrote extensively on the practical implications, whether social or political, of their philosophy. Here I have in mind such writings as *The Ethics of Citizenship* (1894) by John MacCunn (uncle of the composer Hamish MacCunn); *The Principles of State Interference* (1891), which had a wide readership, *Natural Rights* (1894) and *Studies in Political and Social Philosophy* (1902), all of these by David George Ritchie, an early member of the Fabian Society; *An Introduction to Social Philosophy* (1890) by John Stuart Mackenzie (who stood as a Labour candidate in the 1918 General

Election); *The Service of the State* (1908), *By What Authority?* (1909) and *German Philosophy in Relation to the War* (1915), all these by John H. Muirhead; *The State in Peace and War* (1919) by John Watson; *The Working Faith of the Social Reformer* (1910) and *The Principles of Citizenship* (1919) by Henry Jones;[29] and *The Philosophy of Humanism* (1922) and *Human Experience* (1926) by Richard Burden Haldane, Liberal MP, and lord chancellor 1912–15. Most of these philosophers, though not all – Jones stayed close to Hegel's absolute idealism – were personal idealists, and since therefore the concept of the person lay at the heart of their philosophy, the question of the proper way for a person to live was bound to press hard on them. What is impressive is the range of first-order moral, social and political concerns to which they gave their attention, concerns such as factory working conditions, provision of education, and the need to remove barriers to the advancement of women.

Notes

1. Davie, *Ferrier and the Blackout of the Scottish Enlightenment*, p. 1.
2. Craig, 'Nineteenth-century Scottish thought'.
3. *Scottish Metaphysics*, p. 1.
4. Ferrier, *Scottish Philosophy*, p. 12.
5. For details see Davie, *Ferrier and the Blackout of the Scottish Enlightenment*. See also Graham, 'The Scottish tradition in philosophy'.
6. Ferrier, *Scottish Philosophy*, pp. 7–8.
7. Ibid. p. 11.
8. The *Introduction to the Philosophy of Consciousness* and the four papers are in Ferrier's *Lectures on Greek Philosophy and Other Philosophical Remains*, vol. 2 (herinafter *Lectures*).
9. Ferrier, *Lectures*, vol. 2, pp. 115–16, quoting Brown, *Sketch of a System of the Philosophy of the Human Mind*, pp. 125–6. The quotation is accurate aside from some details that do not affect the sense.
10. *Lectures*, vol. 2, p. 133.
11. Ibid. vol. 2, p. 188.
12. Ibid. vol. 2, p. 195.
13. Ibid. vol. 2, p. 211.
14. Ibid. vol. 2, p. 250.
15. This doctrine occurs in several of Ferrier's writings and is the single topic of his essay 'The crisis of modern speculation', in *Lectures*, vol. 2, pp. 261–88.
16. Ferrier, 'Berkeley and idealism', in *Lectures*, vol. 2, p. 293.
17. Ferrier, *Scottish Philosophy*, p. 12.
18. Ibid. pp. 12–13.

19. Seth Pringle-Pattison, *Scottish Philosophy*, pp. 1–2.
20. Ibid. pp. 129–30.
21. Ibid. pp. 136–7.
22. Ibid. p. 175.
23. Ibid. p. 176.
24. Ibid. p. 149.
25. Ibid. p. 202.
26. 'Hegel suggestively calls the Logic "the kingdom of shades", as if to hint that it is but the ghost of reality.' See Seth Pringle-Pattison, *The Development from Kant to Hegel*, p. 84.
27. Seth Pringle-Pattison, *Hegelianism and Personality*, p. 227.
28. Ibid. pp. 228–9.
29. Jones was a Scot by adoption. He was born in Wales, was a student at Glasgow University and then Edward Caird's assistant there, was professor of logic, rhetoric and metaphysics at St Andrews, 1891–4, in succession to Andrew Seth, and finally professor of moral philosophy at Glasgow, 1892–1922, in succession to Caird.

CHAPTER 11

Realism and Idealism: Some Twentieth-century Narratives

SECTION 1: INTRODUCTION

Writing in the 1950s John Passmore affirms: '[A]t the Scottish universities, particularly, Idealism is still the predominant tendency in philosophy.'[1] He thereupon mentions representative works by three leading figures: *Scepticism and Construction* (1931) by Charles A. Campbell, professor of logic and rhetoric at Glasgow; *The Natural History of Mind* (1936) by Arthur D. Ritchie, professor of logic and metaphysics at Edinburgh (and son of D. G. Ritchie, professor of logic and metaphysics at St Andrews from 1894 to 1903, and a relative also of David Ritchie, who had been Sir William Hamilton's predecessor in the chair of logic and metaphysics at Edinburgh); and *The Boundaries of Science* (1931) by John Macmurray. Passmore also refers in this context to Donald M. MacKinnon, a native of Oban, who was regius professor of moral philosophy at Aberdeen (1947–60) before occupying the Norris Hulse chair of divinity at Cambridge (1960–76); in the 1940s and 1950s MacKinnon published several articles of an idealist hue.[2] Passmore had previously spoken also of Norman Kemp Smith as an idealist of sorts, pointing as evidence to Kemp Smith's *Prolegomena to an Idealist Theory of Knowledge* (1924). Mention might also have been made of William D. Lamont, reader in philosophy at Glasgow, whose writings, including *Introduction to Green's Moral Philosophy* (1934) and *The Principles of Moral Judgement* (1946), are of a strongly idealist bent.

These thinkers were all major representatives of Scottish philosophy up to the end of the 1950s and were alive at the time Passmore was passing judgment on the predominant tendency then discernible in Scotland's universities. A case can be made out that all were idealists of sorts, though, of course, it would be necessary to say what is meant by 'idealist', for they were not all idealists in an equally tough sense – far from it. It may also be the case that idealism, in whatever sense or senses, predominated in the Scottish universities during the period to which Passmore refers. In which context mention might fairly be made also of A. A. Bowman (1883–1936), professor of logic and rhetoric and then of moral philosophy at Glasgow, whose two books *Studies in the Philosophy of Religion* and *A Sacramental Universe*, both published posthumously in 1938, are quite firmly on the side of idealism, and A. E. Taylor (1869–1945), professor at Edinburgh, author of *The Faith of a Moralist* (1930) and *Philosophical Studies* (1934). William Maclagan (1903–72), a successor of Bowman's in the chair of moral philosophy at Glasgow, should also be mentioned here on account of the Kantian idealism manifest in his early papers on moral philosophy as well as in his *The Theological Frontier of Ethics* (published in 1961, long after first drafted). Maclagan had been a doctoral student under Kemp Smith at Edinburgh while the latter had been working on his translation of Kant's *Critique of Pure Reason*.

Nevertheless some of the major figures of the time produced works that were not idealist in any obvious sense, and here I have in mind, among others, John Laird, author of *A Study in Realism* (1920), and John Anderson, whose *Studies in Empirical Philosophy*, a collection of papers that he had published during a forty-year period, appeared in 1962 shortly after his death. Despite Passmore's judgment I also wish to add as on the side of the realists Norman Kemp Smith, whose *Prolegomena to an Idealist Theory of Knowledge* is, as I hope will become clear, a major presentation of a realist position on the theory of knowledge. In fact the various works mentioned in this paragraph and the preceding ones are spread rather widely on the idealism-realism spectrum and, in view of the importance of their authors, the works ought to give one pause before reaching a decision on what was or was not the predominant position during the period that Passmore had in view. Perhaps Passmore's judgment is correct, but I suspect that his term 'predominant' is too heavy, for reasons that I hope will become clear as this chapter proceeds.

SECTION 2: ASPECTS OF REALISM: NORMAN KEMP SMITH, JOHN ANDERSON AND JOHN LAIRD

Norman Kemp Smith (1872–1958) was born in Dundee and educated first at the High School and then at Harris Academy in Dundee. He proceeded to St Andrews University in 1888, as a student of Andrew Seth, John Burnet and Henry Jones, and graduated in philosophy in 1893. It was under what he termed 'the genial and inspiring guidance' of Jones at St Andrews that Kemp Smith began his study of Kant's *Critique of Pure Reason*. After a year spent at Jena he passed most of the following dozen years (1894–1906) at Glasgow, first as assistant to his old teacher Henry Jones, by then professor of moral philosophy there, and then as assistant to Robert Adamson, professor of logic and rhetoric, a distinguished scholar whom John Laird was later to describe as 'the best Kantian scholar in the country',[3] a judgment that could not have been far wrong given that Adamson was the dedicatee of Kemp Smith's *Commentary to Kant's 'Critique of Pure Reason'* (1918). Between these two assistantships Kemp Smith attended the universities of Zurich, Berlin and Paris. It was during the second assistantship that he published his *Studies in the Cartesian Philosophy* (1902), for which he was awarded his St Andrews doctorate.

In 1906, following an interview by Woodrow Wilson, president of Princeton University, Kemp Smith took up a professorship of psychology there, shifting in 1914 to become the McCosh professor of philosophy at Princeton. Kemp Smith had been christened Norman Duncan. It was only after his marriage in 1910 to Amy Kemp that he adopted 'Kemp' instead of 'Duncan' as his middle name. He returned to Britain in 1916, published his *Commentary to Kant's 'Critique of Pure Reason'* in 1918, and in 1919 succeeded his old teacher Andrew Seth Pringle-Pattison as professor of logic and metaphysics at Edinburgh. In 1924 he published *Prolegomena to an Idealist Theory of Knowledge* and in 1929 there appeared the work for which he is now best known, his translation of Kant's *Critique of Pure Reason*, still the standard translation of the *Critique*. He published his *Philosophy of David Hume* in 1941, developing work that he had published four decades earlier in which he had expounded his immensely influential 'naturalistic' interpretation of Hume. Kemp Smith was a Calvinist Presbyterian, though he was not active in the life of the church; it has been argued that his philosophy was affected in significant ways by his Calvinism,[4] and it is perhaps also significant that when Kemp Smith took over one of A. E. Taylor's classes, during the term-long absence of Edinburgh's professor of moral philosophy, he decided that the class should study *An Interpretation of Christian Ethics* by Reinhold Niebur.

The greater part of Kemp Smith's writings are commentaries, chiefly on Descartes, Hume and Kant. From these a good deal is of course to be learned on Kemp Smith's views on many issues. In just one book, his *Prolegomena*, he tells us where he stands and does so in systematic fashion rather than according to an order dictated by the text being commented on. It is therefore on the *Prolegomena* that I shall focus in my discussion of his philosophy.

Kemp Smith is a distinguished member of a distinguished line of Scottish philosophers who helped to bring German idealist philosophy into the anglophone philosophical culture, but though his translation of Kant's *Critique of Pure Reason* and his *Commentary* on the *Critique* remain major research resources, Kemp Smith was in important respects un-Kantian, even anti-Kantian; Kant would assuredly have rejected much of Kemp Smith's *Prolegomena*, a work that Kemp Smith describes as 'the formulation of an idealist theory of knowledge on realist lines',[5] where 'idealist' describes a philosophy which maintains that 'spiritual values have a determining voice in the ordering of the Universe' or that 'spiritual values can be credited as operating on more than a planetary, that is, on a *cosmic* scale'. We are the outcome of the unfathomably rich processes of nature itself; and nature, whatever the arguments of some idealists, is not a product of our own activity. He invites us to recognise as supremely significant the seemingly accidental by-products of nature's animal devices: 'Nature – such, at least, has been her actual behaviour – seeks man out; she creates him, endows him with theoretical as well as with other needs, and then progressively responds to these needs, the more he seeks her aid.'[6] The entire argument of the book suggests that this remarkable statement should not be understood as merely an extended metaphor, a personification of nature for purely rhetorical or dramatic purposes, and Kemp Smith's reference to Baron von Hügel's *The Mystical Element of Religion* (1908) at this point in his argument tends to reinforce this view.[7]

The idealism that Kemp Smith espouses plainly implies a realist view of nature. The realism in question is a tough sort that bears a notable resemblance to Thomas Reid's and that is utterly at odds with Kant. To get the measure of Kemp Smith's distance from Kant it will be sufficient to make a point regarding space, time and the categories of the understanding. Kant affirms that the things we experience as out there in the 'real' world are spatial and temporal, and he holds that in that same 'real' world there are substances, which are wholes composed of parts and which stand in causal relations to each other. These categories, of causality, of substance and of whole and part, are three of the twelve that Kant lists and I shall take them, as Kemp Smith does, as representative of the categories as a whole. The categories are objective features of the world, so constituting it that it is experienced as objectively valid, and not a mere stream of consciousness, in relation to us rational spectators.

To this claim regarding the objectivity of space, time and the categories, Kant adds a transformative insight. It is that these objectively valid features of the world are there in the world because we put them there. They are products of our reason which are read into the sensory data that we receive and are the means by which we render our perceptual experience intelligible to ourselves. Kant speaks of all these features as 'a priori' because they are 'antecedent' to experience, and they are antecedent because they are necessary conditions of our having objectively valid perceptual experience. On this account space, time and the categories are not only objective but also subjective in so far as they are products of mental acts. They are thus not less on the side of the subject than of the object.

The negative aspect of Kemp Smith's position in relation to Kant can be stated simply – he rejects Kant's claim that space, time and the categories are subjective features of our experience; they are instead solely on the side of the object. Kemp Smith sets out his programme as follows:

> Since time and space are as real as the revolutions of the planets and the growth of trees, to regard them as being subjective is to reduce external Nature to the level of an illusory appearance. In order, therefore, to uphold a realist view of Nature, I shall contend that time and space are independently real, that as such they disclose themselves directly to the mind, that in so doing they prescribe certain categories which are involved in their apprehension, and that these categories equip the mind for discerning those ideals which constrain it to the pursuit of science and philosophy.[8]

Space, time and the categorial features of perceptual experience are, however, not apprehensible separately from other features or elements in experience, and in particular our grasp of them depends on a grasp of the colours, tastes, smells, sounds and tactile qualities (hardness, smoothness, warmth) of things. These sensory qualities, termed 'sensa', are treated in the *Prolegomena* as public in the sense that a given sensum is available for apprehension by several percipient beings. Several people looking at the same leaf all see the same patch of green, and listening to the same trumpet all hear the same sound. This does not imply that all percipients looking at the same leaf or listening to the same sound have exactly the same kind of sensory experience, for, as Kemp Smith emphasises, the particular experience each has depends on his position in relation to what he is seeing or listening to – where he stands in relation to, for example, the leaf or the trumpet – and also on particular features of the physiology of the percipient's reception apparatus.

It follows that sensa, though objective, are private, in the sense that they are open to the observation of only one percipient;[9] for no two individuals can touch the same object at the same time in the same place, or can taste the same morsel, or can see that patch of colour from that place at that moment.

Kemp Smith holds that it is only in terms of sensa that we come to have an articulated view of space and time, though he also argues that sensa are not in themselves either spatial or temporal. There are two acts of mind involved here: sensation and intuition. By sensing we come to an apprehension of sensa and by intuiting we come to an apprehension of space and time, two of the non-sensory elements in sense experience. It is because intuition of space and sensation of colour always go together that it is naturally supposed that colours are by their very nature spatially extended.

Space and time are not the only non-sensory elements in sense experience. There are in addition the categories, such as causality, substance, and whole and part, mentioned some paragraphs earlier in the course of our reference to Kant's subjectivisation of what we naturally suppose to be objective. On Kemp Smith's account, the categories are no less objective than are space and time nor, *pace* Kant, are they in the least subjective in origin.[10] They are further connected in that two of the categories, those of totality (or whole and part) and necessity, are indispensable for our apprehension of space and time. It is impossible to conceive of a given time or space that is not part of a wider time or space, and in so far as the given time or space is a part the concept of the whole or the totality is at work, for part and whole are correlatives.

For example, though it is the now that is immediately apprehended, it would not be apprehended were it not for our act of transcending the now and contextualising it in a wider time that includes the no longer and the not yet. In the same way, our apprehension of a triangle requires our transcending the triangle by contextualising it in a wider space that bounds the triangle. Likewise any span of space and time is continuous in the sense that between any two spatial points there are others and between any two moments there are others – there cannot be contiguous points or contiguous moments. The space and time that are immediately apprehended are themselves apprehended as the context within which other, lesser spaces and times are situated. Consequently the category of whole and part is deeply implicated in our apprehension of space and time.

Closely related to this observation is the doctrine that the category of necessity is no less deeply implicated than is that of totality in our apprehension of space and time. There can be no now that is not conditioned and made possible by a no longer and a not yet which frame the now. The temporal frame is therefore necessary for the now; it determines, or is the necessary condition of, the now, just as there cannot be a triangle that is not conditioned and made possible by the space that bounds it. The spatial frame determines, or is the necessary condition of, the triangle.[11]

It has to be concluded therefore that intuition and categorial thought play as great a part in our apprehension of the green of a leaf as does our sensation of the green. Since, on Kemp Smith's account, all these things – the sensa, space and time and the categories – have their origin outside our minds, it has to be concluded also that Kemp Smith, one of the greatest of Kant's commentators, is also one of his fiercest critics.

Kemp Smith pays particular attention to the immense richness of nature's resources as these are manifested in our ability to cope with our natural environment. Science probes nature and opens up the unfathomable complexities of the natural world, but much of what nature reveals of itself to scientists is of no use to us as we go about our daily business, and if we were suddenly able to perceive directly the things that scientists have discovered or deduced we would almost certainly cease to be viable. As Kemp Smith puts the point: 'such exhaustive experience, even if possible, would so bewilder and distract the mind that its primary function, viz. the initiating and directing of bodily movements, could not be efficiently exercised. Such consciousness would be self-defeating.'[12] For us to be able to cope three things are required: first, a grand simplification that involves the concealment of almost all of the endless complexity of nature; secondly, the visibility of all the things that we need if our practical needs are to be satisfied; and thirdly, an appropriate level of definition and precision of the things that we need if we are to be able to manipulate nature and to defend ourselves. The sensa are nature's solution to this practical problem. To be viable we need water. A drop of water, as scientists teach us, contains countless millions of atomic and subatomic particles moving at barely imaginable speeds, but we do not require to apprehend these bewilderingly fast countless millions; to do so would make us incompetent at the ordinary business of keeping ourselves alive. Fortunately a drop of water is apprehended as a uniform whitish globule and, as thus apprehended, presents us with no practical problems. As Kemp Smith says, there is omission in our apprehension – in fact almost everything is omitted – but there is also in our apprehension no lack of definiteness and precision as regards what needs to be definite and precise, and it is for this reason that sensa have to be regarded as nature's brilliant solution to a practical problem. They vindicate their reality by 'the indispensible part which they play in Nature's ordered and complex economy'.[13]

A point needs to be emphasised here regarding the knowability of reality. We have a variety of theoretical needs, the need to grasp scientific truth and to grasp philosophical truth also, for we are drawn into philosophy to investigate the implications of such facts as that apprehension of the present involves apprehension of the present-transcending-itself-into the no longer and the not yet, an apprehension that implies that any span of time is situated within a wider span, with no apparent reason why time should not be unboundedly past and future. Scientists and philosophers are engaged in the progressive penetration of a mind-independent reality, and their 'mind-independent reality' is the same as everyman's. Kemp Smith does not accept the distinction between appearance and reality, in Kantian or Hamiltonian fashion, as a metaphysical distinction, one between phenomena, which are knowable appearances, and noumena, which are unknowable reality; his appearances are appearances-of-reality. We may not be able to plumb the deepest depths of reality but it can, and does, become increasingly well known to to us. This aspect of Kemp Smith's teaching is strongly reminiscent of his teacher Andrew Seth Pringle-Pattison and also of Thomas Reid.

The fact that practical apprehension precedes theoretical is an element in a quasi-religious doctrine of Kemp-Smith's that requires to be noted. He writes:

> All along Nature has, seemingly, been intent upon providing her creatures, in their conscious experience, with an adequate instrument of practical adaptation. And now we find that while successfully doing this, she has at the same time, as it were inadvertently, provided the last-born of her children with the means of setting aside all immediate practical purposes, and indeed of establishing himself in her ancient rights, taking the future into his own hands, and deliberately thwarting her when her ways do not conform to his own preferred plans. Discerning truth, beauty, and goodness, he adopts the attitude of contemplation, and in view of these absolute values organises even his practical life on a different plane.[14]

In this passage Kemp Smith prompts the suspicion that he attributes personhood or near-personhood or quasi-personhood to nature, and this suspicion is quickly reinforced by his clarification of the phrase 'as it were inadvertently' in the passage just quoted:

> Can Nature's proceedings be so purely accidental as this account of them would imply? Is it not truer – keeping merely to the bare facts – to reverse the point of view, and to recognise as supremely significant the seemingly accidental bye-products of Nature's animal devices? Nature – such, at least, has been her actual behaviour – seeks man out; she creates him, endows him with theoretical as well as with other needs, and then progressively responds to these needs, the more he seeks her aid. Is not Nature here revealing herself – I raise the question, but shall not attempt to discuss it – as Super-Nature; and can she be synoptically envisaged save when so conceived?[15]

There are many theologians who have spoken of God in terms not dissimilar to these, and indeed those same theologians would also be likely to say of God what Kemp Smith says further of Nature:

> in endowing man with those instinctive, emotional needs which finally develop into intellectual curiosity and the passionate ambition to discover truth, she has also contrived to provide him with the necessary driving power that enables her, working from her own side, to make her revelation of herself to him more and more complete.[16]

In the light of these passages it is helpful to recall Kemp Smith's description of his project as 'the formulation of an idealist theory of knowledge on realist lines', where the term 'idealist' indicates the doctrines that 'spiritual values have a determining voice in the ordering of the Universe' and that 'spiritual values can be credited as operating on more than a planetary, that is, on a *cosmic* scale'. Kemp Smith aims to replace a subjectivist philosophy that emphasises the role of the human mind in the formation, or even 'creation', of the world. The subjectivist characteristically says that many things (such as space, time and causal necessity) that we take to be objectively valid features of what we fondly suppose to be reality are in fact provided by ourselves. The subjectivist, from a Kemp Smithian realist perspective, despoils reality, leaving it severely diminished, and donates the booty to mind. On behalf of realism Kemp Smith undertakes to return the booty to the real world, and is therefore committed to a philosophical programme, performed in his *Prolegomena to an Idealist Theory of Knowledge*, of rehabilitating reality by drawing our attention to the many-layered richness which is integral to nature and which is not at all dependent upon the activity of our minds.

The realism that Kemp Smith espouses is of a very different sort from that associated with John Anderson (1893–1962), a philosopher now little read in Scotland though a major figure in Australia, where he was a professor in philosophy at Sydney after emigrating in his mid-thirties. Indeed he is the founder and presiding genius of the school of philosophy known as 'Australian realism', a school that includes J. L. Mackie, Eugene Kamenka, David Armstrong, David Stove and John Passmore. Anderson, born in Stonehouse, Lanarkshire, attended Hamilton Academy and then in 1911 went up to Glasgow University, where he studied mathematics, natural philosophy and philosophy, graduating in 1917. His philosophy professors were the absolute idealist Henry Jones (in the chair of moral philosophy) and Robert Latta (in the chair of logic and rhetoric), a distinguished Leibniz scholar who was an idealist of sorts, though not embracing idealism in its most heroic form as Jones did. Anderson also heard some at least of the Gifford Lectures in natural theology delivered in Glasgow (1916–18) by Samuel Alexander under the title 'Space, Time and Deity'.[17] These lectures were an important part of Anderson's education; they presented a realist doctrine with which in the main he was in sympathy. Anderson lectured for two years at the University College of South Wales (1917–19), before returning to Scotland to lecture first for a year at Glasgow University (1919–20) and then for six years at the University of Edinburgh, where the professor of logic and metaphysics was Norman Kemp Smith, who had just taken up the post in succession to Andrew Seth Pringle-Pattison. Anderson then went to Sydney University in 1927 to become the Challis professor of philosophy, retiring from that post in 1958. Before his departure from Scotland Anderson had published three papers in defence of realism in metaphysics and epistemology;[18] he was later to make substantial contributions to ethics and aesthetics, and here again realism was in the driving seat. I shall indicate some of the leading ideas in his account of realism.

Empiricism is commonly presented as a theory of knowledge, but in Anderson's view it is primarily a metaphysical theory, about ways of being, not ways of knowing being, although of course empiricists have a good deal to say about the role of sensory perception in the acquisition of knowledge. The opposing theory of rationalism is likewise a theory about being, not about knowing being, although rationalism has a good deal to say about the role of reason in the acquisition of knowledge. Rationalists characteristically invoke orders of being, with one order the highest, absolute being. This is 'true reality' and it is commonly thought to transcend experience, though some rationalists allow that a mystical, but certainly non-natural experience might enable us to overcome the natural obstacles to knowledge of transcendental reality. Kantianism rejects the idea of us managing by any means to gain intellectual access to real things, things as they are in themselves, not as formed by space and time and processed by the a priori categories. Anderson is wholly opposed to this rejection. Philosophy must make sense to us, including to philosophers, and it cannot do so unless it respects the constraints of our discourse, which is based on or shaped by our observations of a shared world. Talk about an 'ideal' world which is beyond our experience is empty. There is, for Anderson, only one realm of being and it is one to which we all have access; it is the natural world, the 'real' world, that provides the subject matter of our shared discourse.

Anderson takes the example of geometry. It is said to be a rational science, a science about a wholly rational world, one therefore that can be accessed only by the faculty of reason and is not an object of sensory perception. Nothing could better capture the idea that geometry is about a supra-sensible world than Leibniz's claim that the truths about the world of geometry are derivable from the principle of non-contradiction – 'It is not possible for both a proposition and its negation to be true.' But how, from that highly abstract principle, are we to construct the much more concrete concepts on the basis of which we engage in geometrical reasoning? If we are to understand that the internal angles of a triangle are equal to two right angles we need to know what angles and triangles are. How do we come by such knowledge? It is Anderson's contention that such concepts are learned by looking at the natural world, which is full of straight lines, curves, circles, angles and other geometric forms. Why then say that these figures are to be found only in a supra-sensible world and that therefore the natural world, what we like to think of as the 'real' world, is not the only world nor even the most real one?

Geometers draw geometrical figures at the head of their proofs. Euclid proved precise things about triangles, for example the theorem just mentioned concerning the internal angles, and it might be said that the triangles drawn on paper or scratched in the sand are not real triangles, because if we measure them we will discover that their internal angles do not precisely equal two right angles. Suppose, however, that empirical measurement reveals that the internal angles of a given drawn triangle do indeed equal two right angles; it might be said that that proves nothing beyond the fact that the instruments used are themselves as imperfect as the drawing of the triangle. But we might take the opposite line, the one that Anderson in fact takes, namely that people knew what triangles were long before Euclid proved his theorems and demonstrated what necessarily is, or alternatively what necessarily is not, true of them.

This point leads us to something philosophically important about geometers' use of supposedly imperfect figures in their proofs. The geometer can draw his 'imperfect' figure of a triangle and say that the imperfection does not matter because he is not talking about precisely *that* figure; he is simply drawing a figure and saying: 'Let us suppose that that is a triangle.' If he has drawn what looks like a triangle we will say 'yes' without a qualm, beyond perhaps wondering what the figure could possibly be if not a triangle. But suppose he had said of the taste of coffee or the smell of coffee: 'Suppose that that is a triangle', we would simply be baffled because we know very well that tastes and smells are not the kinds of thing that could conceivably be triangular. The point here, Anderson's, is that we arrive at the science of geometry already in possession of a battery of geometric concepts got by living in the spatio-temporal world, the world of nature and of human artefacts.

It is in the light of these considerations that Anderson argues[19] that the question whether our space is Euclidean or not is an empirical question. It is to be answered by observation and experiment, and that this is so demonstrates that the geometers' discourse is part of everybody's discourse. The concepts they use are of things in our world or are reducible to such concepts. There is nothing that the geometer does that gives us grounds to argue that there is another world, an ideal world populated by supra-sensible geometrical objects that are truly real or are at least more real than are the things with which we are acquainted in our world. It is Anderson's broad contention that there are no degrees of reality; whatever is has just as much reality as anything else that is. And he is not saying that they are different kinds of reality but somehow equal in their being; he is saying, on the contrary, that there is just one realm of being investigated by mathematicians, physicists and ordinary people. As Anderson puts the point at the end of his article 'Empiricism': 'There are only facts, i.e., occurrences in space and time.'[20]

As said earlier, although empiricism is primarily a metaphysical theory, a theory about being, there is an epistemological companion to empiricist metaphysics since we are not well placed to say what *is* if we have no cognitive access to it. A question therefore arises as to the nature of that access. Anderson emphasises the role of sensory perception and does so in the course of making a point that he believes takes us to the heart of empiricism and realism. It is a point stressed by Kemp Smith and by his predecessor Andrew Seth Pringle-Pattison: that what we are acquainted with *is*. It may not be all that there is and no doubt there will always be more to investigate and to discover, but what we are acquainted with is not appearance as contrasted with reality. It is instead reality itself as it appears, so that we can say of what appears to us: 'This is real.'

Anderson's realism left no room for God; he believed there to be only occurrences in space and time. But others of Anderson's generation, who were no less realist than he, were persuaded of God's existence and thought that realist philosophical arguments supported their position. Among the theistic realists was John Laird (1887–1946), from the Kincardineshire village of Durris, in a parish next to that in which Thomas Reid was born. Laird, like Reid, was the son, grandson and great-grandson of ministers of the kirk, and, like Reid, attended school in Aberdeen. His realist philosophy was also, in important respects, very close to the common sense philosophy of Reid. Laird studied philosophy in Edinburgh under Andrew Seth Pringle-Pattison, graduating in 1908, before going to Cambridge to continue his philosophical education. Thereafter he held a series of teaching posts at St Andrews University, Dalhousie University in Nova Scotia and Queen's University, Belfast, before his appointment in 1924 as regius professor of moral philosophy at Aberdeen, the post he held till his death. He was appointed Gifford Lecturer in natural theology by Glasgow University and subsequently published the lectures as two books, *Theism and Cosmology* (1940) and *Mind and Deity* (1941). The score of books that he published ranged widely across philosophy while also displaying a formidable breadth of knowledge about the natural sciences, a breadth hinted at in his brief but packed *Recent Philosophy* (1936), which displays familiarity with Lorentz, Einstein, Planck, Heisenberg and many other physicists; Edmund Husserl (with whom Laird corresponded), Henri Bergson (another of his correspondents), Meinong and Heidegger, among continental philosophers; and Russell, Schlick, Carnap, Popper and Reichenbach, among others of the analytic school.

Laird presents as the main assumption of realism the proposition that 'things can be known as they really are'.[21] He also tells us: 'The general thesis of realism is that knowledge is a kind of discovery in which things are directly revealed to or given to the mind.'[22] However, the directness of knowledge is one of the great battlefields of philosophy. Laird, who spent a year as philosophy assistant at St Andrews, takes the example of our perception of a golf ball. But what exactly do I perceive? Surely not all of the golf ball, since we can see neither the back of it nor the interior, and while I can at least touch the back even when I cannot see it, I can touch only the surface, not the interior. Do we perceive the ball if we are in perceptual contact with so little of it – just some patches of colour and the tactile equivalents – properties that were then termed 'sense data', the sensorily given? If we do, then in what sense do we have direct knowledge of the object? Sense data, after all, are 'fleeting existences' (I borrow Hume's description of perceptions) as contrasted with physical things, such as golf balls, which preserve the same recognisable spatial contours for a long period of time. In addition physical objects seem to be unlike sense data in that physical objects stand to each other in a variety of causal relations. Soap, Laird adds, dissolves in water and can stop a leak in a gas pipe. Sense data do not dissolve in water nor stop gas leaks.

However, it is Laird's contention that these statements do not do justice to sense data, for they omit the fact that they are 'suffused with meaning'. They are not just sense data, they are sign-facts and we know how to 'read' them. We read some of them as physical objects, objects that are simply given or found and that are not in any way affected by our knowing them. This way of putting the matter points to a possible problem. If sense data are signs and signs have a meaning then, it may be argued, they cannot be independent of the knower; to say that something has a given meaning is to say that it is understood in a given way. Meanings are therefore inseparable from acts of understanding and are therefore mind-dependent.

To this line of argument Laird responds that a meaning need not be either a mental entity or something imposed by a mind. The apprehension of meaning is of course a mental act, but the meaning apprehended may belong to the meaningful thing no less than does the thing's sensory qualities. The meaning of the approaching rain clouds belongs to the clouds no less than do their shape and colour. Not always, but often enough, the sign-facts, meaningful sense data, are read by us as physical objects in causal relations, and as such they are fragments of the world that we ourselves inhabit. Laird concludes that though it is only through the senses that we have evidence of the existence of the physical world, it does not follow that there is room for scepticism about whether the physical world 'really' exists. In a passage that could have been penned by Reid (and in a sense was), Laird affirms:

> the *onus probandi* [burden of proof] certainly rests with the doubter of sensory testimony. Credulity is more ancient than doubt, and although credulity is the philosopher's bane, disbelief or suspension of judgment is a logical attitude when, and only when, there are positive reasons for denying that something is as it appears to be.[23]

Laird has looked at the reasons brought forward by some philosophers, believes himself to have undermined them, and concludes that physical things may be revealed to us as they really are.

In a way that is precisely matched by Norman Kemp Smith and by John Anderson, Laird rejects the view that there is a something which appears to us but which is in itself unknowable by us, and that the appearance alone is an object of knowledge. It might be added that in an interesting comment on Robert Adamson (1852–1902), professor of logic and metaphysics at Glasgow, Laird affirms that Adamson 'was developing a Kantian form of "realism" when he died'.[24] The kind of realism for which Laird argues in *A Study in Realism* is far removed from, indeed is incompatible with, the kind of realism he took Adamson to be developing in *The Development of Modern Philosophy*, published in 1903, a year after Adamson's untimely death.[25]

There is no hint in this that we can know things all the way through as they really are, but such partial knowledge as we have is of what is real. Our knowledge is not of appearance as opposed to reality; it is of reality, and we have that knowledge because it is reality that appears to us, a reality that, in a common sense way, we identify with the world we inhabit and therefore with the world that is investigated by scientists.

This last point prompts a question that Laird meets head-on. Science aims to deliver up a description of reality, and yet an exercise of scientific imagination is required if scientific progress is to be made. If what the scientist produces is a product of an exercise of imagination, then the world, as seen by him and by the rest of us who accept the scientific narrative, is surely an imaginative artefact. But this argument, in Laird's view, is based on a misunderstanding of the role of the scientific imagination. To have a scientific imagination is one way, perhaps the most important way, of being scientifically insightful; what it delivers up, as Laird describes its role, is 'either a profounder analysis than is common, or a greater genius for detecting analogies, or both combined'.[26] Of course some analogies may prove unfruitful, but not all do, and those that succeed give us a new insight into reality. That the scientist needed to exercise his imagination to reach the truth does not imply that the object that he was investigating was after all merely the product of his imagination, and is somehow only held in existence by his imaginative act. Throughout his *Study in Realism* Laird treats realism as the doctrine that things can be known as they really are. Sometimes, as he allows, they can be so known only after a good deal of hard mental labour, involving sensory perception, intellect, imagination and will. This scientific labour does not constitute an obstacle to our cognitive access to the real world; it is one of the chief means by which access is gained and extended.

SECTION 3: ASPECTS OF IDEALISM: H. J. PATON, C. A. CAMPBELL AND JOHN MACMURRAY

The question discussed in the preceding section concerning the possibility of cognitive access to reality is uppermost in the mind of several other Scottish philosophers of the same period, whom I shall now discuss and who have a strong sense of the obstacles in the way of such access. I shall briefly discuss aspects of the work of H. J. Paton and then focus on Charles Arthur Campbell and John Macmurray, though, as noted in Section 1, a number of philosophers in addition to these three could fairly be invoked in support of John Passmore's claim that idealism was the predominant tendency in philosophy in the Scottish universities.

Herbert James Paton (1887–1969), from Abernethy in Perthshire, attended the High School of Glasgow and thereafter went up to Glasgow University to study classics, though he also attended Henry Jones's classes in idealist philosophy. He then went up to Oxford, where he spent six years, first as a student at Balliol and then as a fellow at Queen's. Following his war service he worked on a book of idealist ethics which was eventually published in 1927 under the title *The Good Will: A Study in the Coherence Theory of Goodness*. In that same year he was appointed to the chair of logic and rhetoric at Glasgow in succession to A. A. Bowman, who had transferred to the chair of moral philosophy. The next ten years were a period of intense work on the philosophy of Kant culminating in the publication of

Paton's *Kant's Metaphysic of Experience* (1936), a magisterial commentary on the first half of Kant's *Critique of Pure Reason*. The following year he became White's professor of moral philosophy at Oxford, publishing first *The Categorical Imperative* (1947), an insightful commentary on, and defence of, Kant's *Groundwork of the Metaphysic of Morals*,[27] and then *The Defence of Reason* (1951), a collection of essays devoted almost entirely to a critical analysis and defence of Kant. On retirement from his Oxford chair in 1952 he returned to Scotland, in due course taking up the post of crown assessor for St Andrews University. Paton had previously been Gifford Lecturer at St Andrews (1950–1), delivering two series of lectures under the joint title *The Modern Predicament*. His last substantial publication was a powerfully argued case for Scottish devolution; his *The Claim of Scotland* (1968) argues that 'under the Crown and within the framework of the United Kingdom, Scotland should have her own Parliament with genuine legislative authority in Scottish affairs'.[28]

Paton was one of the two or three foremost Kant scholars of the century. Space could be devoted here both to an exploration of his scholarly writings in the field of Kant studies and perhaps also, and relatedly, to a comparison between those writings and the corresponding writings of Norman Kemp Smith. Such an approach may have particular merit in view of the fact that on a number of issues regarding Kant these two great scholars are in deep disagreement, with, to generalise, Paton defending Kant and Kemp Smith opposing.[29] I should, however, prefer instead to make brief comment on another project of Paton's, his Gifford Lecture series *The Modern Predicament*, though in this as in most of his books Paton writes as a Kantian, seeing both the problem and the solution in a manner of which Kant would have been likely to approve.

Paton's purpose is to probe the relation between science and religion and to see what might be said about the predicament of religion in the face of the success of science. What space is there for religious belief if science can say so much, and so persuasively, about our world? If science can find no God why should we not draw the conclusion that religion does not indicate to us a valid way forward? The predicament that emerges from this approach is one for the religious consciousness, not for the scientific; science has no trouble defending itself. Religion, which is not bereft of questions, has struggled to say anything persuasive in answer to even the most pressing of them, such as why we should believe that there is a God.

Paton's Kantian response is to develop the fact that the brilliant success of science is due at least in part to the fact that scientists have asked questions amenable to investigation in accordance with scientific methodology; questions for which scientifically testable answers have been provided. There are, however, other questions that are important and that seem not to be amenable to scientific investigation, such as are asked in respect of the moral worth of an act or of the beauty of an object or event. If there are aspects of human experience that are real but are not the proper domain of science, then perhaps the religious aspect is another such to be set alongside those of the moral and the aesthetic. It is then on the limits of science, and on what might lie beyond those limits, that Paton focuses. He is committed to Kant's doctrine that science does not deal with reality except in so far as it appears to us under the forms of space and time and under the categories of the understanding, and holds that the question whether there is more than the world as investigated by science is not itself a question that science can answer; it is a question in philosophy. Scientists can of course seek to answer it but not as scientists.

These considerations are deployed by Paton as a way of introducing the idea that since science does not deal with the world as it really is but only as it appears to us, room is left for the reality to which religion refers. But by what means can we say anything about this special area? Paton is doubtful that natural theology can help here, except perhaps in a negative way by enabling us to avoid contradiction, and instead he focuses on religious experience, and notes particularly the idea of the *mysterium tremendens et fascinans* developed by Rudolf Otto, in his *The Idea of the Holy*,[30] and of the distinction between the 'I-thou' and the 'I-it' developed by Martin Buber in his *I and Thou*.[31] However, in respect of both these great writers on the psychology of religious experience Paton is doubtful whether they made much progress regarding our understanding of God and of our relation to him. Nowhere more than in dealing with the question of our experience of God does Paton display his Kantian predilections. Kant, most rational of people, argues that there is no possibility of our having a theoretical cognition of God; it is legitimate to use the idea of God as a regulative principle, guiding our investigations, but he is not a possible object of experience. Otto speaks of a particular feeling of awe and Buber speaks of a certain kind of encounter; but in each case, when we try to probe the object, whether of the awe or of the encounter, we find ourselves, if Kantians, up against an unsurmountable barrier. We have to recognise our intellectual pretensions for what they are, a motive to overreach ourselves, to use reason in a role for which reason is wholly unfitted. Paton, fully committed to Kant's critical philosophy, does not come an inch closer than did Kant to rendering God intelligible to us. The faithful, reading Paton in hope of finding a sound intellectual underpinning to their faith, could gain no solace from his words. As we shall now see, the faithful would derive little more joy from C. A. Campbell, Paton's successor in the chair of logic and rhetoric at Glasgow.

Charles Arthur Campbell (1897–1974) went almost without a break from Glasgow Academy to service in the First World War. Thereafter he was a student first at Glasgow University (where, as with John Anderson, he studied under the Hegelian Henry Jones and the Leibniz scholar Robert Latta) and then at Balliol College, Oxford. He returned to Glasgow to be first an assistant and then a lecturer in moral philosophy, during years when A. A. Bowman and H. J. Paton occupied the philosophy chairs. From 1932 to 1938 Campbell was professor of philosophy at the University of North Wales at Bangor, returning thereafter to the chair of logic and rhetoric at Glasgow in succession to Paton. He occupied the chair for twenty-three years. During the years 1953–5 he was Gifford Lecturer in natural theology at St Andrews. His first book, *Scepticism and Construction: Bradley's Sceptical Principle as the Basis of Constructive Philosophy* (1931), was followed by *Moral Intuition and the Principle of Self-Realisation* (1952) and a version of his Gifford Lectures *On Selfhood and Godhood* (1957). His final book, *In Defence of Free Will, with Other Philosophical Essays*, appeared in 1967. The essay mentioned in the last title, 'In defence of free will', is Campbell's inaugural lecture at Glasgow delivered in 1938. The basic philosophical position that he first took up in *Scepticism and Construction* changed little, if at all, through his career, though he continued to add to his system, perhaps most importantly in his Gifford Lectures. Tightly packed, his claim is that though scepticism is appropriate in respect of the possibility of gaining cognitive access to reality, it is possible to construct a positive philosophy, particularly regarding morality and, to a lesser extent, religion, on the basis of that same scepticism. I shall now try to unpack this version of the Scottish metaphysical preoccupation with the question of the knowability (or unknowability) of reality.

The English idealist philosopher F. H. Bradley (1846–1924)[32] argued that we could not secure an intellectual grasp of what really is, and his reason is that reality has a oneness that necessarily eludes us. This Bradleian position is Campbell's starting point, but he moves from it to doctrines that are not Bradley's. Reason seeks oneness, as is evidenced by the way reason responds to scientific judgments. Suppose we notice that whenever a carburetter-jet is partially choked the engine misfires, and wonder what the mediator is that links the two apparently disparate events and explains the connection. We decide that the explanatory mediator is the thinning of the petrol supply, for whenever the carburetter-jet is partially choked the petrol supply is thinned and whenever the petrol supply is thinned the engine misfires. So the thinning process is the principle of unity. However, it is inadequate as a principle of unity since it leads directly to two questions: why should the partial choking of the carburetter-jet lead to a thinning of the petrol supply, and why should a thinning of the petrol supply lead to the engine misfiring? And so on. If anything, the supposed principle of unity, is a principle of disunity since it prompts two questions when previously there had been only one. But this process, which exemplifies the way reason works, cannot produce a final principle of unity, since reason's way forward is to seek a mediator between disparate things and hence it proceeds by opening up a question concerning what it is that mediates between the mediator and each of the mediated terms. Hence, though reason is compelled by its nature to seek unity, its method ensures that it will fail.

Campbell identifies reality with the unitary totality and, in the light of considerations such as those just rehearsed, he shows that reality is forever beyond the grasp of reason. It is not that we can get forever closer to reality without reaching it; inventing more and more thought-products, such as the mediators we think up in order to unify disparate terms, does not help us in our metaphysical question because, as Campbell affirms: 'Reality in its true character must be pronounced to be disparate from each and every thought-product . . . I mean that there is a fundamental difference in kind, such as renders thought-products and Reality strictly incommensurable.'[33] As against a large swathe of nineteenth-century idealism which holds that the real is rational, Campbell holds that it is not rational but, to use his own term, 'supra-rational'. Not 'irrational', for it is not being said (yet) that the search harbours a contradiction, but neither is it rational, for the task which we undertake and in which we are bound to fail has to be undertaken by reason or not at all; the task is to seek an explanation for things by identifying a mediator which will unite apparently disparate things, and that is the task of reason *par excellence*; no other of our faculties could aspire to it. So it is beyond what reason can accomplish – it is supra-rational. The term seems apt.

One aspect of the supra-rationality of reality has a direct bearing on the question of whether our supposedly free acts are indeed free, and an important part of the 'construction' indicated in the title *Scepticism and Construction* is the positive metaphysic of freedom that Campbell constructs on the basis of his scepticism about the power of reason to gain access to reality. Granted that two things are 'continuous' with each other if there is no gap between them, one task of reason is to demonstrate continuities where there appear to be discontinuities. However, as already noted, each time we identify a mediator that would overcome the apparent discontinuity, the mediator points us towards further apparent discontinuities. Since this is a process which in principle is without end, Campbell affirms that the world is rationally discontinuous, which implies that universal determinism cannot be demonstrated. The doctrine of universal determinism can perhaps be accepted as a matter of faith, but reason cannot provide a demonstration. Its failure to do so is not itself proof that we can perform free acts, but does open up the possibility of freedom. Campbell moves in on the space created by the demonstrated lack of a rational basis to the claims on behalf of universal determinism and seeks to make out a case for freedom.

There is a 'vulgar' concept of freedom, the concept used by the philosophically unsophisticted all the time and even by all determinist philosophers when they are going about their ordinary lives and are not writing about freedom. It is this: whatever free agents do, they could in those very same circumstances have done something different; in Campbell's phrase, 'there are genuinely open possibilities'. Such freedom, which Campbell also terms 'moral freedom', is so called in virtue of its relation to moral responsibility. To be morally responsible for a given act implies being worthy of moral praise or moral blame for the act, but the worthiness of such a judgment implies that the act has been performed freely. If freedom is a sham or illusion then so also must be moral responsibility.

Campbell sets out two conditions for an agent's moral responsibility. The first is that the self is the sole cause of the act; if there are causal influences other than the self then the agent is not in an unqualified sense morally responsible for the act. But this condition might be satisfied by an act for which the agent is not morally responsible; if the agent is the sole cause but his act is necessitated by some property essential to him – as some have said about God in respect of his creation of the world – then the agent lacks moral responsibility for the act. A further condition must therefore be posited, namely that there were real alternative possibilities open to an agent in the moment when he performed the act. The doctrine that an act's being free is its satisfying both of these two condition is libertarianism. In Campbell's view non-libertarian free will is a sham.

Can there be acts which satisfy both conditions? The answer, obvious to determinists, is 'no', for it is surely past belief that agents are not every inch of the way influenced in their behaviour by the hereditary and environmental factors that agents bring with them into the decision-demanding situations. Is this not to say that there is a battery of external causal factors influencing the choices and decisions we take, and does it not follow that the self is never the sole cause of its acts and therefore never acts freely? In fact some would reject this line of thought on the grounds that what happens in these cases is that such of our propensities as come to us via heredity or environment do not *as such* influence our choices and decisions, but influence them only in so far as certain of the suggestions of the propensities are taken up by the self into its concept of what is good for the self. If that is indeed what happens, then it might seem that what is actually influencing our choices and decisions are not things external to the self but suggestions which, though originally made by something external, have been taken up into the self.

This line of thought is identified by Campbell as a move made by the great Oxford idealist T. H. Green.[34] It is, however, a move that Campbell rejects on the grounds that even if, as Green holds, our choices and decisions are made on the basis of our conception of what is for the good of the self, that conception is itself influenced by such factors as heredity and environment, and in that case those factors, which in themselves are indeed external to the self, must have an influence on our choices and decisions. Campbell finds support for his line of attack on Green in biographical practice. In serious biographical studies the author's moral assessment of his subject is based in part on precisely such considerations as heredity and environment. These factors are seen as having an influence on the subject's choices and decisions, and our assessment of the agent's moral responsibility for his actions must take into account the possibilities realistically open to him given the various sorts of factors we have been considering. The factors in question are seen as external to the subject and as limiting his freedom. Green's account is at odds with this practice of biographers, though it is a practice we all engage in, not just biographers.

Granted therefore that acts influenced by these factors are not free, a question arises as to whether there are or at least might be acts we perform on which these factors have no influence. The determinist philosopher might insist that the world is characterised by universal rational continuity, and perhaps the idea that there is such continuity is an essential principle for science, a regulative principle without which science could make no progress. If the world is constituted by a rational continuity then there can be no break in the continuity; every event is an effect of an antecedent event and explicable at least partly in terms of the antecedent event, and there is therefore no possibility of a true initiation of a causal series. But Campbell has already argued against the demonstrability of universal rational continuity, and in the absence of a demonstration we have to be open to the suggestion that a brand-new causal series can be initiated. If there is evidence of a free action anywhere it must be where we believe there to be just such an initiation, and Campbell is clear where we should look, namely at ourselves when we engage in an effortful act of will.[35]

Suppose I judge it morally right for me to do X, and suppose also that in virtue of the system of conative dispositions that constitute my formed character I desire to do Y, even though Y is incompatible with X and I believe Y to be wrong. One possible outcome is the following: though Y continues to be the line of least resistance, in that, in relation to what I want to do, Y is the easy option, I nevertheless engage in an effortful act of willing to do X. The willing has to be effortful because the desire to do Y is strongly resistant to anything that works to thwart the performance of Y. This situation satisfies the two conditions for free action that were laid down earlier. For first, the agent facing the moral temptation as just described must believe himself open to genuine alternatives, X and Y, both possible acts. He thinks that Y is possible for him, indeed is the line of least resistance, and that X is also possible for him, and would be what he would do if, which is again possible for him, he makes an effort of will.

The second condition, namely that the self determines the act without any external factor exercising causal influence, is also satisfied. In our moral temptation scenario the agent's formed character is clearly influential in some way, and hence hereditary and environmental factors are at work in respect of the agent's act of will, but they are not present as causal determinants; they produce the desire Y which is the path of least resistance. If, however, the agent makes an effort of will on behalf of what he believes to be the morally right thing to do then the desire to do Y will not have been efficacious. What the agent's formed character has done is to set the agent's agenda; the agent wants to do Y, but wanting to do Y is not the same as willing to do it. The question arises therefore as to whether it would be morally right to do Y, and he judges that it is X, not Y, that would be the morally right thing to do. He thereupon wills to do X. So the agent's wanting to do Y has not causally influenced him to do Y, since it was not Y that he decided to do but X. Campbell concludes:

> the agent believes that through his act of decision he can oppose and transcend his own formed character in the interest of duty. We are therefore obliged to say, I think, that the agent *cannot* regard his formed character as in any sense a determinant of the act of decision as such.[36]

That the agent believes that he can transcend his own formed character is not by itself proof that he succeeds in this. A question must therefore be faced as to whether the agent's belief is to be trusted, and on this matter Campbell makes a move identical to one made by Reid in his *Essays on the Active Powers* when faced with the identical question. Campbell writes:

> we should begin by noting that the onus of proof rests upon the critic who rejects this belief. Until cogent evidence to the contrary is adduced, we are entitled to put our trust in a belief which is so deeply embedded in our experience as practical beings as to be, I venture to say, ineradicable from it.[37]

There are counter-claims that have to be resisted, however, of which perhaps the commonest is that we are, after all, predictable and predictability is a phenomenon on the side of determinism. In response Campbell agrees that we are predictable 'within limits' that are due to our character to the extent that it sets limits to what we will desire. However, no one makes predictions infallibly about how others will behave, and no doubt the reason is the one Campbell gives, namely that character sets the agenda rather than decides the issue. There are also limits due to the sheer strength of the desires that we sometimes have to overcome if we are to do what we think morally right; we may therefore have to make a great effort – which no doubt makes it more likely that we will follow the line of least resistance. Campbell reminds us, however, that we might not follow it, even if the desire that runs contrary to our moral judgment is immense. Prediction therefore in the case of moral temptation is an uncertain business.

Suppose finally that the determinist asks the libertarian to explain why an agent sometimes makes an effort of will and sometimes does not. The libertarian cannot ever give an explanation, unlike the determinist, who can at least sometimes provide a causal story. Nevertheless this does not indicate a weakness in the libertarian's position for he does not believe that there is a scientific causal explanation. Sometimes we rise to the challenge and make an effort in line with our moral insights and sometimes we do not, and when we fail we are always conscious of the fact that the failure is something for which we are accountable. Though we gave into temptation, there was no necessity for that; we could have done otherwise. On Campbell's analysis the determinist has not provided a plausible refutation of the libertarian position.

If Campbell is right about this, then the freedom of our will is a fact in accord with his claim that reality is supra-rational. The free agent performs an act that he believes to be the right one to perform and yet the act is not rationally continuous with other antecedent events or states of affairs. A rationally continuous world is deterministic all the way through but in our world there are genuine alternatives open to us; where the alternative that is realised is determined by an act of an agent, and not by anything external to the agent. We have power over the determinations of our will. If this power is to be classed as a form of causation then the form is that of the agent-causation of the libertarians and not the event-causation of the natural scientists. By virtue of our having this kind of power our world has an open future.

This doctrine gives a clue to the kind of idealism that Campbell espouses. His concept of free will points to the existence of a self, a finite self (for it is a human, not a divine self) that is an individual agent. The self is not rationally continuous with the world for it can stand back from the world and decide how to act in and on the world. The world is, as we have seen, not a causal determinant of free acts, but instead the agent's environment sets the agenda for practical reflection on what to do. Freedom, as so understood, is a problem for absolute idealism, for that philosophy holds that the real is rational and therefore forms a whole that is rationally continuous. There is no room in such a philosophy for finite individuals, but only for one individual, namely the absolute, the rationally continuous whole itself; selves have degrees of individuality only in the sense that, to a greater or lesser extent, they are manifestations of the character of the absolute, the sole true individual. But even if this is individuality in some sense or other, it is not of the kind that is at issue when we speak about us finite agents as able to stand back from the world and think of it as providing us with an agenda for practical reflection.

Campbell's position here is very close indeed to that of Andrew Seth Pringle-Pattison in the latter's development of his personal absolutism or 'personalism'. In our discussion of Seth we noted his doctrine that each self is a centre of consciousness and will that is unique, not merely different from every other self but necessarily exclusive of every other. As to the evidence that Seth invokes regarding the exclusiveness of self, it is this:

> There is no deliverance of consciousness which is more unequivocal than that which testifies to this independence and exclusiveness. I have a centre of my own – a will of my own – which no one shares with me or can share – a centre which I maintain even in my dealings with God Himself.[38]

This passage by Seth would have been at home in Campbell's *Scepticism and Construction*. It also prompts a question concerning Campbell's perspective on the relation between religion and suprarationalism. This question is dealt with rather briefly in *Scepticism and Construction*, amounting to a tenth of the book, and I shall deal with it rather briefly here, though also noting that the question is considered in Campbell's Gifford Lectures *On Selfhood and Godhood*, where the material on religion in *Scepticism and Construction* is greatly expanded.[39]

It is with considerable diffidence that Campbell probes the relation between religion and supra-rationalism. His reason for this is that the content of religious consciousness is fundamentally different from the contents of perceptual consciousness and of practical consciousness, for whereas the latter two contents include beliefs, in the external world and in our freedom of will, that are foundational and irremovable aspects of everyone's experience, the content of the religious consciousness includes a belief, in the existence of God, that is far from being either foundational or irremovable. Campbell affirms therefore that in respect of religion he is writing in hypothetical mode, for his chief claim is that if the content of religious consciousness is valid then reality is supra-rational. He has no reason to say 'if' in relation to the existence of the external world or of our our freedom of will.

His starting point is the fact that two central features of religious experience appear to be mutually incompatible: (1) the serene confidence that comes with the belief that the universe is permeated by the divine presence, and (2) the demand that we cleanse the world and our souls of impurity and imperfection. They appear mutually incompatible since (1) implies that what ought to be is (since perfection is everywhere if the perfect God is everywhere) while (2) implies that what ought to be is not (since the purity and perfection that ought to be everywhere have to be fought for by the faithful). In short, reality is both perfect and also shot through with imperfection. How to avoid this conclusion?

Campbell's solution is to postulate a God who is unknowable in the sense of being supra-rational.[40] We know what wisdom is because we know wise people, but God's wisdom is perfect and therefore transcends ours; the same should be said of the other moral and intellectual perfections to which we aspire. In each case God has these perfections while transcending the finite mode of functioning that they display in our lives. We can assign the names of these perfections a definite meaning in respect of the way they function in us, and cannot do so as regards their functioning in God, and in that sense we cannot know the God in whom these perfections function with their full vigour. The concept just expounded is of a supra-rational God.

On the basis of this concept Campbell seeks to resolve the apparent contradiction committed by the believer who holds both that the world is permeated by divine perfection and that we have a duty to tackle the imperfections of the world. Campbell's resolution is that God's perfection is not of the same type as human perfections and that God's perfection cannot be measured by human standards, hence the imperfections we find in the world and in ourselves are not existentially incompatible with the perfections that are God's. This approach does of course prompt a question about the concepts we deploy in our attempt to understand God, and it becomes clear, particularly from Campbell's Gifford Lectures, that he believes that the terms we predicate of God are to be understood 'symbolically', not literally.

The 'supra-rational theism' or, as Campbell also terms it, 'symbolic theism' that emerges from these thoughts about divine perfection takes its starting point from Rudolf Otto's concept of religious experience as experience of the numinous, the awesome majesty of the divine and our corresponding sense of our own nothingness in the presence of a supreme being.[41] Otto's concept of the *numen*, understood as *mysterium tremendum et fascinans*, is of our sense of contact with an *other* whose being is incommensurable with ours and who eludes the very possibility of rational enquiry, whose awe-inspiring nature is such as to produce an 'inward shudder of the soul' but also an entrancement and blissful rapture. Campbell introduces the idea of 'symbolic knowledge' in an attempt to capture a concept of God that we reach by way of a consideration of a psychological fact about us, namely the battery of affective responses we have to something whose being we find ourselves obliged to accept even though the nature of the being eludes the very possibility of rational enquiry. As surpassing our understanding, the reality here at issue is supra-rational, as is the reality of the world of theoretical experience and of practical, specifically moral, experience, with this difference, that the experience associated with the numinous, the experience of a *mysterium tremendum et fascinans*, is not given to all of us, perhaps not even to many, and those lacking such an experience will remain unconvinced by Campbell's argument. The experience of the numinous is, as he says, to be understood as a hypothesis, not as an assured datum – this in contrast with our experience of the perceptual world and of our moral freedom, which we all know from the inside. Campbell leaves us in no doubt that he himself writes of the numinous from his own experience, but he believes that even if the theistic aspect of his philosophy is set aside he has said sufficient concerning our theoretical and practical experience to have made out a strong case for the claim that reality is supra-rational.

At the start of this chapter I mentioned John Passmore's list of thinkers who typified the predominant philosophical tendency in the Scottish universities in the earlier part of the twentieth century, namely idealism. The last person on the list was John Macmurray, to whom I now turn. John Macmurray (1891–1976), from Maxwellton in Kirkcudbrightshire, was born into a family of committed Calvinists and was educated into Calvinist tenets and values. The family moved north and John Macmurray attended first Aberdeen Grammar School and then Robert Gordon College, Aberdeen, before going up to Glasgow University in 1909 to study classics. In 1913 he enrolled at Balliol College, Oxford, as a Snell Exhibitioner to read Greats. At the start of the Great War Macmurray, already a committed pacifist, enlisted as a nursing orderly in the Medical Corps, but then decided that since he was part of the war machine he should participate in the fighting. He fought at the battle of the Somme, was badly injured during fighting in defence of Arras, an action in which he was the only survivor of his Cameron Highlander company, and was awarded the Military Cross. He returned to Balliol to complete his studies and then held a series of academic appointments, including a fellowship at Balliol (1922–8) and the Grote chair of the philosophy of mind and logic at University College London

(1928–44).[42] In London he came into contact with philosophers, including Theodor Adorno, Karl Popper, Gabriel Marcel and Martin Buber, seeking refuge from Nazi-occupied Europe. Finally Macmurray was appointed to the chair of moral philosophy at Edinburgh (1944–58) in succession to A. E. Taylor. Macmurray's opposite number in the chair of logic and metaphysics at Edinburgh was Norman Kemp Smith.

By the time of his Edinburgh appointment Macmurray had already published many works, including *Freedom in the Modern World* (1932), *Interpreting the Universe* (1933), *The Philosophy of Communism* (1933), *Reason and Emotion* (1935), *The Structure of Religious Experience* (1936) and *The Boundaries of Science* (1939). During the 1930s Macmurray reached out beyond the groves of academe, particularly via many talks on the BBC through which he acquired an immense reputation as a sage on matters moral, political and religious. He had no sympathy for the Marxist rejection of religion nor much, if any, for the other-worldly doctrines of Christianity, but he was developing a philosophy grounded in the centrality of personal relations and community in our lives, and he believed the doctrine to be close to aspects of Christianity and Marxism. In 1953 and 1954 Macmurray delivered two series of Gifford Lectures at the University of Glasgow. These, published as *The Self as Agent* (1956) and *Persons in Relation* (1961), are his principal works. Following his retirement in 1958, he moved with his wife to the Quaker village of Jordans in Buckinghamshire in which he had lived during the early years of the Second World War. They stayed at Jordans until 1968 and then returned to Edinburgh, where Macmurray died eight years later. His ashes were buried at Jordans.

The book titles *The Self as Agent* and *Persons in Relation* encapsulate Macmurray's philosophy. He argues, first, against those who identify the self as primarily a thinker and knower, and, secondly, against those who identify the self as a solitary being for whom it makes sense to ask whether there are other selves. In contrast, and this is the positive side of his philosophy, Macmurray emphasises, first, the role of agency in our lives; primarily we are agents, and thought, knowledge and science are for the sake of action, not vice versa. Secondly, he emphasises the role of relationships in our lives; he believes that there is no person except in relationship with other persons, hence a person considered as outside all personal relationships is considered only abstractly, not as a concrete historical reality.

For Macmurray, the reality is the person in relation with others, and personhood is most fully realised in relations in which the person opens or reveals himself to another equally revealing self. In relations of enmity (also a kind of personal relation), we find not disclosure but concealment; it is only in relations of love that a person can fully realise himself. Such relations Macmurray describes as a fellowship or communion. 'Communion' is a term associated particularly with religion, and Macmurray intends us to make the association, for he holds religion to be inseparable from communion. This inseparability is a central plank of his philosophy.

There are types of human act in which the agent conceives the person, on whom or for whom he is acting, in terms which are impersonal or abstract rather than personal, and we can learn a good deal about Macmurray's understanding of persons by considering these other types of act. He has in mind two in particular, namely the scientific and the artistic, which he contrasts with the kind of loving act that constitutes the distinctive datum of religion.

Let us look at science first. Scientific papers have a distinctive rhetoric, one element of which is their impersonality; they reveal little if anything about the scientist's personality. They do not reveal what he feels about anything, what his likes and dislikes are, not even whether he loves the science he writes about or enjoyed performing the experiments described in his papers. He is therefore present in his papers as an impersonal person. All that matters is that he has performed the experiments, has done the extrapolations according to due procedures, and has drawn appropriate conclusions. Since he is an impersonal person it is fitting that the rhetoric of his papers should be marked by an 'un-self-consciousness'. The presence of the self in the papers would be an intrusion, a rhetorical impropriety.

It might be thought that sometimes scientists should have an explicit presence in their paper, for they are observers and famously in some scientific contexts the question of the effect of an observer's observation on the behaviour of what he is observing is a serious one.[43] Nevertheless even then the self is not given space. What is reported in the paper is the effect of observational apparatus on the things to be observed, and that says nothing about the scientist. What affects the behaviour of molecules in a gas chamber is not the visual perception of the scientist but the instrumentation he has deployed to measure that behaviour. The rationale for the rhetoric of impersonality in scientific papers is therefore quite plain; it is based on the scientific methodology and scientific values that are in place in the real world of scientific research.

From Macmurray's perspective the work of certain psychothera-pists and psychiatrists is vitiated by the fact that they see themselves as scientists and therefore as bound to look upon their client in a detached, dispassionate way, when in fact they cannot provide help except through the kind of knowledge of their client that comes with, and is part of, the personal encounter between the two. Macmurray's criticism of the encroachment of scientific methods and scientific values into areas where these are wholly inappropriate is also to be found in the writings of several other Scottish thinkers of the period, notably Ian Suttie (1889–1935), R. D. Laing (1927–89), W. R. D. Fairbairn (1889–1964) and John D. Sutherland (1905–91), all of whom owed something to Macmurray's work on the subject of psy-chotherapy as well as in the wider fields of science and of interper-sonal relations.[44]

Another aspect of the rhetorical performance of the scientist should here be noted. Not only is his paper impersonal, so also is the intended readership. He must have a readership in mind, for why publish if not to make his work available to a reader? But to whom in particular? The short answer is that it does not matter; the scien-tist has not written the paper for some person in particular, even if the paper is a response to one written by some other scientist and even if he expects to prompt a responding scientific paper from that other sci-entist. Such exchanges happen often enough in the scientific literature, but they do not make the exchange personal.

The situation, as Macmurray points out, is comparable to an exchange between two mutual strangers who have no personal inter-est in each other and who are seeking information from each other and nothing more.[45] That the interchange is between two persons does not of itself imply that it is personal. For that, they would have to be responding to each other in a personal way, such that for each the significance of the interchange is a product not only of what is being said but also of the personal relations between the persons who are saying it. If the traveller informs the booking clerk of his intended destination and the clerk informs the traveller of the best way to reach that destination, their exchange, though significant for each, is not in the least significant because of the personal relations between the speakers. Scientists engaged in exchanges in the pages of a scientific journal are similarly engaged in communicating impersonally with an impersonal recipient. There is, then, a sense in which scientific rhetoric rejects both the first person and the second, and recognises the reality only of the third person, the 'it' which is the subject matter of the scientific research. Macmurray writes:

> For science is only interested in the object, and therefore writes, speaks and thinks, even of itself, in the third person; like a child that has not yet become self-conscious. There is no 'I' nor 'you' for science, only 'it'; and because of this science is utterly at sea in the personal field.[46]

However, Macmurray also wishes to draw attention to the particular kind of knowledge that the scientist seeks to gain by his work on the things that are the objects of his observation and experiments, for it marks a contrast with the kind of knowledge that Macmurray believes to have priority for all of us in our real-life living. Though the object that the scientist observes is an individual thing, a singularity, it is not the thing in respect of its individuality that interests the scientist, but instead the thing as embodying something general or even universal. It behaves in a law-like way and the scientific question is: 'What is the law that it embodies?' or 'What is the general concept under which it falls?' When that knowledge is secured the scientist knows something about the object, namely that it exemplifies something general – that, say, bodies with these properties behave in this way. Nevertheless, that sort of knowledge is consequent upon another sort, for the scientist does science by reflecting on things that he already knows non-reflectively and non-scientifically, things of which he has direct experience and which he has to learn to manipulate if he is to stay alive. Our knowledge of this real-life world is practical in that we deal with the world as agents.

A pre-scientific knowledge is implicit in our ordinary manipulations of things, for our learning to manipulate them implies a practical understanding of the conditions that determine things to behave in one way rather than another, and such an understanding implies a grasp of generalities of such a kind as scientists focus on. Macmurray contends that our practical knowledge of the world, knowledge of a kind well-nigh universal amongst us, is not inferior in kind to the knowledge of a specifically scientific character that is acquired by a small intellectual elite of reflective persons. It has to be recalled that Macmurray was writing defensively in the light of a common philosophical view that elevated scientific knowledge to a pre-eminent position, and regarded other forms of knowledge as inferior, and perhaps not to be termed knowledge at all.

How does the scientist's performance in respect of the first and second person compare with the artist's? To return to Macmurray's thinking on conversation: I might be talking to a friend about a joyous occasion;[47] I speak lyrically about the event and start to relive the occasion in my imagination, by which point I could be speaking to anyone; the identity of the audience has lost significance because I am entranced by my recollection. I am disclosing my feelings to my friend but by this point he is a cypher – anyone could have been the recipient of my disclosures. In this sense my audience is as impersonal as is the readership of the scientific paper, but I am not as impersonal as the scientist, for my feelings take centre stage in my self-revelatory narration. It is directed to whoever will listen, and is in no way part of an exercise in mutuality by which my self-revelation is matched by that of the person to whom I am speaking.

This kind of discourse is, according to Macmurray, a model for the artistic performance. The artist pours himself into his work, discloses himself in his products. This is not to say that the artist must then and there be having the very feelings in terms of which his work will be interpreted by an audience educated in these matters, for the artist knows how to produce a product which will be read in given emotional terms whether or not he has those very emotions during the creative act. He must at some time, however, have lived through those emotions and learned how to produce a work that, as we say, 'expresses' them. What, however, to say about the second person, the one for whom the work is produced? Macmurray replies:

> [T]he second person is generalized to a listener, negative and receptive, and tends to fade out of the picture and become hypothetical and imaginary. The artist can write his description for anyone to read, or paint his picture for anyone to see. He gives himself, not to anyone in particular, but to the world at large.[48]

Elsewhere Macmurray presents this position again but with details added:

> In aesthetic reflection, we may say, the second person is intentionally excluded. The 'you' cannot, of course, be excluded as a matter of fact, for the 'I' is constituted by his relation to the 'You', but he can be excluded by a limitation of attention. The second person, excluded from attention, is not abolished, but he is not individualized. He is, as it were, treated as a negligible constant. The artist's activity is one of expression; it is not complete until its product is exhibited, or at least externalized in a form which can be exhibited, to other people.

> Expression implies exhibition, and exhibition implies communication. But the communication is not to another person to whom the artist stands in a personal relation. It is to a public; to anyone who has the interest to accept and the ability to understand it.[49]

On this account the scientist is unlike the artist and like him; unlike him in so far as the scientist does not represent his own feelings, and like him in so far as both communicate to an impersonal recipient. Scientist and artist are citizens in the republic of letters, putting their ideas into the public domain to be taken up by whoever has the intellect and will to make something of them. The identity of the persons who take up the ideas is not part of the story about the scientific or artistic performance, and the second person to whom scientist and artist direct their product is therefore in that sense an impersonal person.

From the foregoing there follows a consequence of the greatest importance to Macmurray, namely that artist and scientist, *qua* artist and scientist, lead incomplete lives. As Macmurray affirms: 'the "I" is constituted by his relation to the "You"'. What is required to complete their lives is other selves, persons with whom they are in personal relations, and with whom they are bound in fellowship or communion. To reactivate Macmurray's model of a conversation, communion is expressed in two people for whom the conversation they are having has significance not only on account of its ideational content but also on account of the fact of communion, friends each of whom is enjoying the conversation partly because it is with this friend that he is having it. Of course the content of the conversation is significant for each; they attend to what is being said and respond appropriately. Something else, however, is also in play, namely the friendship of which the conversation is in part an expression. For each participant in the conversation, to deploy Macmurray's terminology, the second person is not 'generalised to a listener, negative and receptive'; he is not, in respect of his individuality, 'excluded by a limitation of attention'. Macmurray's contention is that an artist giving a performance, whether painting a picture, writing a novel or giving a musical performance and so on, is not like someone in conversation with a friend, for the latter case exemplifies communion and in the former, artistic case there is no role for communion.

Macmurray writes:

> The artist wants to give, not to receive; so that mutuality is lost, and his experience, though it remains intensely personal, is one-sided, has

lost part of the fullness of personal experience. Knowledge there is, and the pouring out of knowledge, which is self-expression, but not mutuality.[50]

Yet this may not seem quite right, for performers respond to their audience. In such a case the audience is not to be classed as 'not abolished but not individualised', for the performer is responding not to an abstraction but to that audience, an individual whose appreciation, whose values and expectations the artist senses.

It is open to Macmurray to respond that in the case of a musician's performance to an empty recording studio the performance is not any the less a work of art for the audience being a 'second person' which is 'hypothetical and imaginary'. The performance might have been better if there had been an audience, but in the absence of such the performance is not the less a work of art. In this respect the artist is just like the scientist who directs his papers at a 'hypothetical and imaginary' readership. The scientist has in mind readers who can understand and evaluate his papers – that is all he needs to know about the readership – just as a musician plays for an audience who can understand and evaluate his performance. That is all he needs from his audience. Hence, in describing the scientific and the artistic performance there is no need to invoke the mutuality of fellowship or communion.

I turn now to Macmurray's claim that artist and scientist, *qua* artist and scientist, lead incomplete lives. There is nothing disparaging or dismissive implied in the claim; Macmurray is alive to the awesomeness of the achievements of artists and scientists. His point is that full realisation of a person requires mutual relations with other persons, and scientific and artistic performances do not require the mutuality of persons in relation. He does not, however, imply that any form of personal association is sufficient for full realisation of ourselves as persons, but notes instead a distinction between two forms of human association: one negative and impersonal, for which he uses the term 'society', and the other positive and personal, for which he reserves the term 'community'.[51] The two sorts are represented by the two sorts of conversation noted earlier, that between a ticket clerk and a passenger and that between two friends. Macmurray discusses two sorts of society marked by negativity and impersonality, those described by Hobbes and by Rousseau. Hobbesian society is formed because antecedent to it, that is, in the state of nature, the life of man is, in his famous phrase, 'solitary, poor, nasty, brutish and short'.[52] People come together in society out of fear of an early and violent death, and social living therefore has a purely prudential and pragmatic basis. While Rousseau's account of human beings in a state of nature is less bleak than Hobbes's, Rousseau agrees with Hobbes in describing the motivation for social relations in prudential terms. He speaks of society, as Macmurray points out, as 'a form of association which will protect . . . the person and goods of each associate'.[53] Rousseau therefore, no less than Hobbes, sees social relations as grounded on the need for protection and on our fear of failing to satisfy the need.

In contrast with both these accounts there is the relation between two people who each care for the other out of love for the other. Hence however much they cooperate, and enjoy the benefits of cooperation, the relation is not driven by perceived benefits; they are friends and not just associates. The model Macmurray focuses on is the family in so far as it is a community neither established by force nor maintained by a sense of duty, but both established and maintained by natural affection.[54] The focus of the friend is precisely the second person regarded not as an abstraction or as an 'impersonal person' but instead as an individual who is valued for being precisely *that* individual. Here, then, is a sharp contrast between on the one hand an artist or scientist and on the other a friend. As we shall see, it is on the basis of this contrast that Macmurray constructs his account of religious experience.

As already noted, we all have the kinds of experience on the basis of which scientific reflection is possible, and perhaps we all have some scientific knowledge even though very few of us are specialists in the field. Likewise we all have aesthetic experience, experience of the beauty, sublimity or awesomeness of things. Artists are special in respect of their ability to produce works which embody these qualities, and Macmurray holds that their reflections are unlike those of scientists, for while scientists observe things in respect of their common properties, artists reflect on things in respect of their individuality or uniqueness. We see something and admire it in virtue of something in it that we feel to be unrepeatable. Science, in contrast, looks for the repeatable and seeks to repeat or reproduce it, or at least to demonstrate how it can be reproduced. Relatedly, scientists are concerned with the utility-value of things whereas artists are concerned with their intrinsic value. Hence the artist values things for their own sake and not merely for their effectiveness at producing a given outcome when appropriately deployed.

Macmurray holds that religion arises from our experience within a relation of communion, and this doctrine is suggested to him by the following four considerations.[55] (1) Religion has always been a matrix in which all aspects of culture have crystalised – he has in mind such institutions and activities as science, philosophy, morality, law, politics and art. (2) Religion is universal amongst societies, as also is our experience of communion, fellowship or friendship. (3) There appears to be nothing analogical to religion in the life of other animals, which suggests, as Macmurray puts the point, that religion is rooted in the personal life and not in the merely organic. (4) Religion has a 'universality of intention' in so far as it aims to include all members of society, not just an elite. In this respect it is to be contrasted with science and the fine arts, both of which are directed to an elite.

In so far as religion arises as a response to our experience of ourselves as in personal relationships, it follows that religion will remain with us as long as we live in fellowship with others, and, while it remains, it does so as a principle of activity, for it tends to develop and enhance our experience of fellowship in the sense both of intensifying the experience and of drawing others into the community. Macmurray does not have in mind a credal religion; he thinks instead that religion is something that we do, namely, enter into, maintain and seek to intensify personal relations marked by mutual love and a mutual attitude of caring. These are relations which find their satisfaction in themselves in the sense that love and friendship are for the sake of the love and friendship, not for the sake of something that will be an effect of these. They have no purpose beyond themselves, though, as already hinted, they do have a dynamic, at least in intention, that both leads these relations to draw in other persons, so that the community is widened, and also leads these relations to be intensified. Since the community is such a precious thing its members seek to preserve it, and a main way this is done is by common celebration of the communion, a celebration that enhances consciousness of one's membership. The celebration, no matter what form the ceremony or ritual may take, is a representation or symbol of the fellowship.

But where is God in all this? God is rarely mentioned by Macmurray and when he is it is in highly elusive terms. It is made clear that we are to understand God not as a supernatural being, nor as the object of a mystical experience or of an experience that is in some other way peculiarly religious. Instead he is to be met with and known in our common, frequent, even everyday experience of caring and loving relations that bind persons one to another in fellowship. If he is met with, then of course he exists, but Macmurray does not approve of the form of the question 'Does God exist?', for it is the form of a theoretical question. It is like the question 'Is there a telephone in the room?' as contrasted with the practical question 'What should I do?' Macmurray holds that, properly interpreted, the question 'Does God exist?' is practical – or as he says: 'If it made no difference to action it would be meaningless – a merely speculative metaphysical conundrum.'[56]

If Macmurray, reluctant to answer the question whether God exists, is pressed on the matter of what God is, he replies in terms of a personal universal other which is the common conception of all those who participate in a communion of finite persons.[57] This, however, is to be carried lightly, since it hints at theory whereas Macmurray insists that religion is about practice and in its mature form is not credal. Somehow therefore we are to understand God's existence in terms of the life of communion. Those who live such a life, as members of loving, caring relations, are religious in the way that matters most, whatever the narrative, if any, that they might give regarding the existence of God. Macmurray affirms:

> [B]ecause religious reflection is not primarily expressed in thought but in action, God is not primarily apprehended as an idea, but in life which is centred in the intention of mutuality, as that personal infinite in which our finite human relationships have their ground and their being.[58]

Macmurray believes that religion in his day, and in earlier days, is in an immature state as compared with science, and that part of the weakness of contemporary religion is precisely its emphasis on credal and therefore theoretical matters, matters regarding the existence and nature of given persons and events. In this respect religion is all too like a science, for it is characteristic of science to be concerned with the existence and nature of things. Macmurray's doctrine, on the contrary, is that for religions to move towards maturity they must abandon their emphasis on the theoretical and focus instead on practical matters, and above all on ourselves as agents in the world, not as spectators, and on ourselves not as discrete individuals in merely functional relations with others, but as persons who find fulfilment or full self-realisation, when freely linked to others in relations of caring and of love. Does Macmurray believe that God exists? Well yes, but his believing this is his subscribing to the doctrine that I have just formulated; it is a long way from traditional Christian theology, but Christianity is by no means out of sight, and in particular Macmurray has not lost sight of a concept of Christianity that was dominant among Scottish philosophers in the latter decades of the nineteenth century. Seth affirmed: 'The essential feature of the Christian conception of the world, in contrast to the Hellenic, may be said to be that it regards the person and the relation of persons to one another as the essence of reality', and he notes A. Campbell Fraser's approbatory use of the phrase 'the profound personalism of Christianity'.[59] These passages are a reminder that in important ways Macmurray's work was continuous with earlier elements in the Scottish philosophical tradition.

Notes

1. Passmore, *A Hundred Years of Philosophy*, p. 313.
2. MacKinnon, *Borderlands of Theology*.
3. Laird, *Recent Philosophy*, p. 45.
4. Davie, *Crisis of the Democratic Intellect*, pp. 46–61. See also Barmann (ed.), *The Letters of Baron Friedrich von Hügel and Professor Norman Kemp Smith*, passim.
5. Kemp Smith, *Prolegomena*, p. ix (herinafter *Prolegomena*).
6. Ibid. pp. 231–2.
7. Kemp Smith conducted an eight-year correspondence with von Hügel on matters philosophical and religious and there reveals himself open to Hügel's ways of thinking – even if quite often not agreeing with him. Kemp Smith's *Prolegomena* was published one year before von Hügel's death. See Barmann (ed.), *Letters*.
8. *Prolegomena*, p. 10.
9. Ibid. p. 71.
10. 'The subjectivist tendencies which continue into, and so greatly pervert, Kant's teaching are, it may be noted, one and all bound up with his conviction that the categories are of subjective origin' (*Prolegomena*, p. 124, n. 1).
11. *Prolegomena*, pp. 134–8.
12. Ibid. p. 11.
13. Ibid. p. 37.
14. Ibid. p. 231.
15. Ibid. pp. 231–2.
16. Ibid. p. 232.
17. Alexander, *Space, Time and Deity*, 2 vols (London: Macmillan, 1920).
18. John Anderson, 'Propositions and judgments' and 'The truth of propositions', both in *Mind*, 35 (1926); and 'The knower and the known', *Proceedings of the Aristotelian Society*, 27 (1926–7). All three are reprinted in his *Studies in Empirical Philosophy*.

19. Anderson, *Studies in Empirical Philosophy*, pp. 8–9.
20. Ibid. p. 14.
21. Laird, *A Study in Realism*, p. 8.
22. Ibid. p. 14.
23. Ibid. p. 43.
24. Laird, *Recent Philosophy*, p. 45.
25. Adamson had already started to explore Kantian 'realism' in his *On the Philosophy of Kant* (1879).
26. Laird, *A Study in Realism*, p. 203.
27. In 1948 Paton also published an authoritative translation of Kant's *Groundwork* under the title *The Moral Law*.
28. Paton, *The Claim of Scotland*, p. 254.
29. See, for example, Paton's paper 'Is the Transcendental Deduction a patchwork?' in *The Defence of Reason*, pp. 65–90, in which he defends Kant against the 'patchwork theory' of the first *Critique* propounded by Hans Vaihinger and Norman Kemp Smith.
30. Paton, *The Modern Predicament*, pp. 130–45. Paton is, however, critical of Otto's appropriation or rather misappropriation of Kantian terminology.
31. Paton, *The Modern Predicament*, pp. 162–73.
32. The writings of Bradley to which Campbell is chiefly reacting in *Scepticism and Construction* are *The Principles of Logic* (1883), *Appearance and Reality* (1893) and *Essays on Truth and Reality* (1914).
33. Campbell, *Scepticism and Construction*, pp. 19–20.
34. Campbell, *In Defence of Free Will*, p. 39.
35. Campbell, *Scepticism and Construction*, pp. 130–1. See also *In Defence of Free Will*, p. 41.
36. Campbell, *In Defence of Free Will*, pp. 43–4.
37. Ibid. p. 44.
38. Seth, *Hegelianism and Personality*, p. 228.
39. Campbell's ideas on this matter are developed in *Scepticism and Construction*, ch. 8, and in his Gifford Lectures *On Selfhood and Godhood*, esp. lectures 16–17.
40. Campbell, *Scepticism and Construction*, p. 293; also *On Selfhood and Godhood*, chs. 16, 17.
41. Rudolf Otto, *The Idea of the Holy*, trans. J. W. Harvey (London: Oxford University Press, 1929), passim.
42. His successor in the chair was A. J. Ayer, who in his inaugural lecture conspicuously failed to make any mention of his immediate predecessor. Ayer's philosophy – at that point in his career he was a logical positivist – could hardly have been further removed from Macmurray's.
43. Macmurray invokes the question of the status of the scientific observer in *Reason and Emotion*, p. 151.

44. See R. D. Laing's *The Divided Self*, where there is due acknowledgement of Macmurray, and Gavin Miller, *R. D. Laing*, which contains an extensive discussion of Macmurray in his relation to main themes of Laing. For Macmurray's relation to Fairbairn and Sutherland see Miller, and also *The Legacy of Fairbairn and Sutherland*, eds Jill Savege Scharff and David E. Scharff (London: Routledge, 2005). Suttie's *The Origins of Love and Hate* (London: Kegan Paul, 1935) was probably uninfluenced by Macmurray directly, though there is a striking similarity between the views of the two men on the treatment of psychiatric disorders.

45. Macmurray, *Reason and Emotion*, p. 149.

46. Ibid. p. 150.

47. Ibid. p. 153.

48. Ibid. p. 154.

49. Macmurray, *Persons in Relation*, p. 179.

50. Macmurray, *Reason and Emotion*, p. 154.

51. Macmurray, *Persons in Relation*, ch. 6.

52. Hobbes, *Leviathan*, pt. 1, ch. 13.

53. Macmurray, *Persons in Relation*, pp. 150–1.

54. Ibid. p. 156.

55. Ibid. pp. 156–7.

56. Ibid. p. 215.

57. Ibid. p. 215.

58. Macmurray, *The Structure of Religious Experience*, p. 54.

59. Seth Pringle-Pattison, *The Idea of God*, p. 291; see also Fraser, *The Philosophy of Theism*, vol. 1, p. 77.

CHAPTER 12

Conclusion

As this book demonstrates, there has been a long tradition of philosophising in Scotland. Though the first great Scottish philosopher, John Duns Scotus, educated in the Scottish Borders until the age of about twelve, pursued his philosophical and theological studies furth of Scotland partly because there was no university here, during the fifteenth century three Scottish universities were founded, at St Andrews, Glasgow and Aberdeen, and philosophy figured high on the agenda of all of them. By the end of the sixteenth century, with the foundation of Edinburgh University and Marischal College, Aberdeen, the country had brought its tally of universities to five, an impressive number in a country of one million inhabitants.

All five universities had a strong international dimension. At the start their internationalism was a necessity, for in order to have teaching staff the universities had to recruit Scots who had gone abroad for their education. In those earliest centuries the chief source of Scottish recruits was Paris, Scotus's university, which in due course was attended by Lawrence of Lindores, John Ireland, James Liddell, John Mair, George Lokert, William Manderston, George Buchanan, William Cranston; it is a formidable list. The outcome of the recruitment process was entirely to Scotland's benefit, since the country's high culture came to be served by men who had been educated at as high a level as was available anywhere, who had lively, creative imaginations, deep learning, and an awareness of what was taking place at the cutting edge of the various academic disciplines. Many of them indeed were contributing cutting-edge work and were in consequence setting the agenda for the thinking of others, especially of their students.

After the Reformation Scottish philosophers were no less interested than their predecessors had been in the philosophy being done furth of Scotland. Teaching was up to date. The international nature of the western philosophical enterprise was fully appreciated by its Scottish practitioners and so also was the universality of its disciplinary reach;

there was no academic field on which philosophers could not make philosophical comment. In consequence the whole gamut of arts and sciences practised in Scotland was likely to be affected by the philosophical education of the many students in the country, and so it proved; it can be argued that philosophy was a principle of unity of Scottish culture for centuries. To take some examples: first, poetry. The great fifteenth-century poet Robert Henryson wrote a magnificent poem 'The preaching of the swallow' that is not merely replete with philosophical references but also reveals him as a sophisticated philosophical thinker, well informed about the kind of philosophy then being taught in the Scottish universities. A second example from Scotland's poetical heritage links Robert Burns to Adam Smith. A copy of *The Theory of Moral Sentiments* was owned by Robert Burns's father, and Burns himself is known to have read the book. It is therefore of more than passing interest that Smith wrote: 'If we saw ourselves in the light in which others see us, or in that in which they would see us if they knew all, a reformation would generally be unavoidable. We could not otherwise endure the sight.' Comparison with Burns is irresistible: he sat in church watching a louse walking up a lady's bonnet and from that experience he produced the lines: 'O wad some Pow'r the giftie gie us / To see oursels as others see us! / It wad frae mony a blunder free us / An' foolish notion.' It is probable that Burns wrote this with Smith's sentences in mind, but whether he did or not his poem 'To a louse' entitles us to locate Burns within the philosophy of the Scottish Enlightenment.

Regarding the field of literary fiction, the hugely popular novel *The Man of Feeling*, by Henry Mackenzie (1745–1831), is plainly an outrider of the sentimentalist moral philosophy of which Mackenzie's friend Adam Smith was the leading exponent through his *Theory of Moral Sentiments*.

As with poetry and literary fiction, philosophy is also at or close to the surface of some of the main legal texts produced by Scottish lawyers, for example, *Institutions of the Laws of Scotland* (1681) by Sir James Dalrymple, later Viscount Stair (1619–95), and *An Institute of the Law of Scotland* by John Erskine of Carnock (1695–1768), published posthumously in 1773. Nor can Scottish philosophy be detached from its economic theorising. This is spectacularly the case as regards Adam Smith's *Wealth of Nations*, the greatest work on economics to have been produced in the European Enlightenment. In this work philosophy, particularly moral philosophy, is never far from the surface, as is indicated by the fact that Smith's early thinking on matters relating to political economy was done during his occupancy of the chair of moral philosophy at Glasgow. He held that to impose an economic policy without having taken due account of the moral implications of the policy's implementation is itself a morally unjustifiable act.

Scottish philosophy is also inextricably bound up with mathematics and the natural sciences. As regards philosophy and mathematics, the greatest of the Scottish critics of Hume's sceptical philosophy was Thomas Reid, now known principally as a philosopher, though in fact a high proportion of his manuscripts are on mathematics and he was one of the leading Scottish mathematicians of his day. In the course of one particular attack on Hume Reid develops a geometric system significantly different from any produced before.[1] The system is of a kind that would now be termed 'non-Euclidean' and is a brilliantly innovative piece of work deeply embedded within the kind of philosophy, the 'philosophy of common sense', then prevalent in Scotland.

Finally, as regards philosophy and the natural sciences, in 1714 Colin Maclaurin, then a fifteen-year-old student at Glasgow, displayed in a thesis, *Power of Gravity*, so deep an insight into Newton's *Principia Mathematica* that Newton himself was impressed by the thesis. Thereafter as professor of mathematics first at Marischal College, Aberdeen, and then at Edinburgh (for which latter post Newton was Maclaurin's referee), Maclaurin continued his researches into Newton's theories. At the end of his days Maclaurin wrote a large book, *An Account of Sir Isaac Newton's Philosophical Discoveries*; the 'philosophical discoveries' in question were in natural philosophy, principally in physics. But the long first chapter is a highly sophisticated and well-informed piece of writing on the philosophy of religion, in which Maclaurin follows through the idea that a suitably slanted scientific investigation of nature can yield up both evidence of the existence of God considered as the cause of nature and evidence of the attributes of a being who is able to produce the natural world.

These facts, concerning philosophy's impact on Scotland's poets, novelists, lawyers, economists, mathematicians and physicists, are a few among the thousands that could be produced in support of the claims that Scottish philosophy is inextricably bound up with the wider culture of Scotland. Of course Scottish philosophers have discussed problems of interest to all philosophers; there are perennial problems in philosophy, and the history of Scottish philosophy is focused on these. But the extent to which philosophy has penetrated deeply and widely within Scottish culture means that, in spite of its universality, Scottish philosophy is a citizen of its country.

Its citizenship is not based on a distinctive set of doctrines and, in any case, given the universality of its subject matter it is hard to see how doctrine could be the basis of it. Nevertheless some doctrines have had a high profile over the centuries, perhaps none more so than libertarianism, a strong doctrine of moral freedom according to which we are, in respect of our determinations to act, independent of natural causation and therefore open to alternative possible acts. As we have seen, this doctrine, which had been worked out in detail by Duns Scotus and was also favoured by Mair, was central for both Reid and Ferrier and was also crucial for Andrew Seth Pringle-Pattison and then, in the twentieth century, for C. A. Campbell. In that sense, there has been a seven-centuries-long Scotistic vein in the tradition of Scottish philosophy. Of course many outside that tradition have taught that same doctrine, perhaps no one more conspicuously than Immanuel Kant, and it is perhaps primarily in the light of this fact about Kant that Scottish philosophers were, as we noted, so receptive to his ideas. By the time he arrived there was already a Kant-shaped space within the Scottish philosophical culture that made it possible for his ideas to find a home here.

I have brought my narrative to the 1960s, no further despite the fact that there is still a good deal of philosophical activity in the Scottish universities. I have done this because temporal distance is required if there is to be a reasonable prospect that my judgment about the importance of a philosophical work will not seem bizarre within a few years. Nor do I need to bring the story up to the very recent past. My aim, as indicated in the Introduction, has been to give the reader an idea of what has gone on in Scottish philosophy, and I think that this can be accomplished without coverage of the most recent years. As it is the book covers about seven centuries of philosophising.

I said in the Introduction that during my four years as an undergraduate philosophy student at Edinburgh in the 1960s I was taught almost nothing about the Scottish philosophical tradition. Hume was a major subject of study and that, apart from stray judgments, was all; no word on the philosophy of Scotus, Ireland, Mair, Hutcheson, Smith, Reid, Kames, Stewart, Ferrier, Seth Pringle-Pattison, Kemp Smith or Macmurray, as if by a conspiracy to erase the story. This book has been written to demonstrate the longevity and richness of the Scottish philosophical tradition. Scottish philosophy is not just

Hume nor even just the philosophy of the Scottish Enlightenment; it flourished for half a millennium before the Enlightenment and has outlived that wondrous event by two centuries. Scottish philosophy is unfinished business and this book is perforce an interim report.

Note

1. Thomas Reid, *An Inquiry into the Human Mind on the Principles of Common Sense*, ch. 6, sect. 9.

Bibliography

Addison, Joseph and Sir Richard Steele, *The Spectator*, ed. Donald F. Bond, 5 vols, Oxford: Clarendon Press, 1965.

Alison, Archibald, *Essays on the Nature and Principles of Taste*, Edinburgh: J. J. G. and G. Robinson, 1790.

Allan, David, *Virtue, Learning and the Scottish Enlightenment*, Edinburgh: Edinburgh University Press, 1993.

——. *Philosophy and Politics in Later Stuart Scotland*, East Linton: Tuckwell Press, 2000.

Anderson, John, *Studies in Empirical Philosophy*, Sydney: Angus and Robertson, 1962.

Anonymous (Ebenezer Edmond), *Scottish Metaphysics*, Edinburgh: Blackwood, 1887.

Árdal, Páll, *Passion and Value in Hume's Treatise*, Edinburgh: Edinburgh University Press, 1966.

Arosio, Elisabetta and Michel Malherbe (eds), *Philosophie française et philosophie écossaise, 1750–1850*, Paris: J. Vrin, 2007.

Balfour, Robert, *Commentarius R. Balforei in organum logicum Aristotelis*, Bordeaux, 1616.

——. *Commentarii in Aristotelis Ethica*, Bordeaux, 1620.

Barmann, Lawrence F. (ed.), *The Letters of Baron Friedrich von Hügel and Professor Norman Kemp Smith*, New York: Fordham University Press, 1981.

Beattie, James, *An Essay on the Nature and Immutability of Truth in Opposition to Sophistry and Scepticism*, Edinburgh: A. Kincaid and J. Bell, 1770; reprint, ed. James Fieser, Bristol: Thoemmes Press, 2000.

Blair, Hugh, *Sermons to which is Prefixed A Short Account of the Life and Character of the Author*, 2 vols, Edinburgh: Anderson, 1824–5.

Boucher, David (ed.), *The British Idealists*, Cambridge: Cambridge University Press, 1997.

——. *The Scottish Idealists: Selected Philosophical Writings*, Exeter: Imprint Academic, 2004.

Boutroux, Émile, 'De l'influence de la philosophie écossaise sur la philosophie française', in *Études d'histoire de la philosophie*, Paris: Alcan, 1897.

Bowman, Archibald Allan, *Studies in the Philosophy of Religion*, ed. N. Kemp Smith, London: Macmillan, 1938.

——. *A Sacramental Universe: Being a Study in the Metaphysics of*

Experience, ed. J. W. Scott, Princeton, NJ: Princeton University Press, 1939.

Broadie, Alexander, *George Lokert: Late-Scholastic Logician*, Edinburgh: Edinburgh University Press, 1983.

——. *The Circle of John Mair: Logic and Logicians in Pre-Reformation Scotland*, Oxford: Clarendon Press, 1985.

——. *Notion and Object: Aspects of Late-Medieval Epistemology*, Oxford: Clarendon Press, 1989.

——. *The Tradition of Scottish Philosophy*, Edinburgh: Polygon, 1990.

——. *The Shadow of Scotus: Philosophy and Faith in Pre-Reformation Scotland*, Edinburgh: T & T Clark, 1995.

——. *Why Scottish Philosophy Matters*, Edinburgh: Saltire Society, 2000.

——. *The Scottish Enlightenment: The Historical Age of the Historical Nation*, 2nd edn, Edinburgh: Birlinn, 2007.

Broadie, Alexander (ed.), *The Scottish Enlightenment: An Anthology*, Edinburgh: Canongate, 1997.

——. *The Cambridge Companion to the Scottish Enlightenment*, Cambridge: Cambridge University Press, 2003.

——. *Thomas Reid on Logic, Rhetoric and the Fine Arts*, Edinburgh: Edinburgh University Press, 2005.

Brown, Thomas, *Observations on the Nature and Tendency of the Doctrine of Mr Hume*, Edinburgh: Mundell, 1805; reprinted in *Life and Collected Works of Thomas Brown*, ed. T. Dixon, vol. 3, Bristol: Thoemmes Press, 2003.

——. *Inquiry into the Relation of Cause and Effect*, Edinburgh: Constable, 1818; reprinted in *Life and Collected Works of Thomas Brown*, ed. T. Dixon, vol. 4, Bristol: Thoemmes Press, 2003.

——. *Sketch of a System of the Philosophy of the Human Mind; Part First: The Physiology of the Mind*, Edinburgh: Bell and Bradfute, 1820; reprinted in *Life and Collected Works of Thomas Brown*, ed. T. Dixon, vol. 5, Bristol: Thoemmes Press, 2003.

Buchan, James, *Adam Smith and the Pursuit of Perfect Liberty*, London: Profile Books, 2006.

Burnet, Gilbert and Francis Hutcheson, *Letters Between the Late Mr. Gilbert Burnet, and Mr. Hutcheson, Concerning the True Foundation of Virtue or Moral Goodness. Formerly Published in the London Journal*, London: W. Wilkins, 1735.

Burnett, James, Lord Monboddo, *Antient Metaphysics*, 6 vols, Edinburgh: J. Balfour, 1779–99.

Burns, J. H., 'The Scotland of John Major', *Innes Review*, 2 (1951): 65–76.

——. 'New light on John Major', *Innes Review*, 5 (1954): 83–100.

——. '*Politia regalis et optima*: the political ideas of John Mair', *History of Political Thought*, 2 (1981): 31–61.

Campbell, Charles A., *Scepticism and Construction: Bradley's Sceptical*

Principle as the Basis of Constructive Philosophy, London: Allen & Unwin, 1931.

——. *On Selfhood and Godhood*, London: Allen & Unwin, 1957.

——. *In Defence of Free Will, with other Philosophical Essays*, London: Allen & Unwin, 1967.

Campbell, George, *The Philosophy of Rhetoric*, 2 vols, London: W. Strahan and T. Cadell, 1776.

Carey, Daniel, *Locke, Shaftesbury, and Hutcheson: Contesting Diversity in the Enlightenment and Beyond*, Cambridge: Cambridge University Press, 2006.

Carmichael, Gershom, *Natural Rights on the Threshold of the Scottish Enlightenment: The Writings of Gershom Carmichael*, eds James Moore and Michael Silverthorne, Indianapolis, IN: Liberty Fund, 2002.

Carter, Jennifer J. and Joan M. Pittock (eds), *Aberdeen and the Enlightenment*, Aberdeen: Aberdeen University Press, 1987.

Cooper, Anthony Ashley, Third Earl of Shaftesbury, *Characteristics of Men, Manners, Opinions, Times*, ed. Lawrence E. Klein, Cambridge: Cambridge University Press, 1999.

Craig, Cairns, 'Nineteenth-century Scottish thought', in *The Edinburgh History of Scottish Literature*, vol. 2, *Enlightenment, Britain and Empire (1707–1918)*, ed. Susan Manning, Edinburgh: Edinburgh University Press, 2007, pp. 267–76.

——. *Intending Scotland: Explorations in Scottish Culture since the Enlightenment*, Edinburgh: Edinburgh University Press, 2009.

Cranston, David, *Tractatus noticiarum parvulis et provectis utilissimus*, Paris, 1517.

Cross, Richard, *Duns Scotus*, Oxford: Oxford University Press, 1999.

——. *Duns Scotus on God*, Aldershot: Ashgate, 2005.

Cuneo, Terence and René van Woudenberg (eds), *The Cambridge Companion to Thomas Reid*, Cambridge: Cambridge University Press, 2004.

Davidson, William, *Gulielmi Davidson aberdonani institutiones luculentae iuxta ac breves in totum Aristotelis organum logicum*, Paris, 1560.

Davie, George E., *The Democratic Intellect: Scotland and Her Universities in the Nineteenth Century*, 2nd edn, Edinburgh: Edinburgh University Press, 1964.

——. *The Crisis of the Democratic Intellect: The Problem of Generalism and Specialism in Twentieth-Century Scotland*, Edinburgh: Polygon, 1986.

——. *Ferrier and the Blackout of the Scottish Enlightenment*, Edinburgh: Edinburgh Review, 2003.

Dickinson, W. C. (ed.), *John Knox's History of the Reformation in Scotland*, 2 vols, London: Nelson, 1949.

Dickinson, W. C., Gordon Donaldson and Isabel A. Milne (eds), *A Source Book of Scottish History*, vol. 1, Edinburgh: Nelson, 1952.

Duns Scotus, John, *Opera Omnia*, ed. L. Wadding, 26 vols, Paris: Vivès, 1891–5.

——. *Opera Omnia*, ed. C. Balić, Civitas Vaticana: Typis Polyglottis Vaticanis, 1950–.

——. *Duns Scotus on the Will and Morality*, ed., tr. and intr. Allan B. Wolter, Washington, DC: Catholic University of America Press, 1986.

——. *Philosophical Writings*, ed. and tr. Allan Wolter, Indianapolis, IN: Hackett, 1993.

——. *Duns Scotus Metaphysician*, tr. and intr. William A. Frank and Allan B. Wolter, West Lafayette, IN: Purdue University Press, 1995.

——. *John Duns Scotus' Political and Economic Philosophy*, ed. and tr. Allan B. Wolter, St Bonaventure, NY: Franciscan Institute, 2001.

Durkan, John, 'John Major: after 400 years', *Innes Review*, 1 (1950): 131–9.

——. 'The school of John Major: bibliography', *Innes Review*, 1 (1950): 140–57.

Durkan, John and James Kirk, *The University of Glasgow, 1451–1577*, Glasgow: University of Glasgow Press, 1977.

Fairbairn, W. R. D., *From Instinct to Self: Selected Papers of W. R. D. Fairbairn*, vol. 1, *Clinical and Theoretical Papers*, eds David E. Scharff and Ellinor Fairbairn Birtles, London: Aronson, 1994.

Farge, James K., *Biographical Register of Paris Doctors of Theology, 1500–1536*, Toronto: Pontifical Institute of Mediaeval Studies, 1980.

Ferguson, Adam, *Institutes of Moral Philosophy*, 3rd edn, Edinburgh: J. Bell and W. Creech, 1785.

——. *The Correspondence of Adam Ferguson*, 2 vols, ed. V. Merolle, London: Pickering, 1995.

——. *An Essay on the History of Civil Society*, ed. Fania Oz-Salzberger, Cambridge: Cambridge University Press, 1995.

——. *Selected Philosophical Writings*, ed. E. Heath, Exeter: Imprint Academic, 2007.

Fergusson, David (ed.), *Scottish Philosophical Theology 1700–2000*, Exeter: Imprint Academic, 2007.

Ferrier, James Frederick, *Institutes of Metaphysics: The Theory of Knowing and Being*, 2nd edn, Edinburgh: Blackwood, 1856.

——. *Scottish Philosophy, the Old and the New: A Statement*, Edinburgh: Sutherland and Knox, 1856.

——. *Lectures on Greek Philosophy and Other Philosophical Remains of James Frederick Ferrier*, 2 vols, eds A. Grant and E. L. Lushington, Edinburgh: Blackwood, 1866.

Fordyce, David, *The Elements of Moral Philosophy*, ed. Thomas D. Kennedy, Indianapolis, IN: Liberty Fund, 2003.

Fraser, A. Campbell, *Philosophy of Theism*, 2nd edn, Edinburgh: Blackwood, 1899.

Galbraith, Robert, *Quadrupertitum in oppositiones conversiones hypotheticas et modales*, Paris, 1510.

Gerard, Alexander, *An Essay on Taste*, London: A. Millar, 1759.

Gill, Michael B., *The British Moralists on Human Nature and the Birth of Secular Ethics*, Cambridge: Cambridge University Press, 2006.

Graham, Gordon, 'The Scottish tradition in philosophy', *Aberdeen University Review*, 58 (1999): 1–12.

Graham, Gordon (ed.), *Scottish Philosophy: Selected Writings 1690–1960*, Exeter: Imprint Academic, 2004.

Haakonssen, Knud, *The Science of a Legislator: The Natural Jurisprudence of David Hume and Adam Smith*, Cambridge: Cambridge University Press, 1981.

Haakonssen, Knud (ed.), *The Cambridge Companion to Adam Smith*, Cambridge: Cambridge University Press, 2006.

Haldane, John and Stephen Read (eds), *The Philosophy of Thomas Reid: A Collection of Essays*, Oxford: Blackwell, 2003.

Hamilton, Sir William, 'On the philosophy of the unconditioned: in reference to Cousin's doctrine of the infinito-absolute', *Edinburgh Review*, 50 (1829): 194–221; reprinted in William Hamilton (ed.), *Discussions on Philosophy and Literature, Education and University Reform*, 3rd edn, Edinburgh: Blackwood, 1866, pp. 1–38.

——. *Lectures on Metaphysics and Logic*, eds H. L. Mansel and J. Veitch, 2 vols, Edinburgh: Blackwood, 1859–60.

Harris, James A., *Of Liberty and Necessity: The Free Will Debate in Eighteenth-Century British Philosophy*, Oxford: Clarendon Press, 2005.

Home, Henry, Lord Kames, *Essays on the Principles of Morality and Natural Religion*, Edinburgh, 1751; 3rd edn, Edinburgh, 1779; reprint, intr. John Valdimir Price, London: Routledge/Thoemmes Press, 1993.

——. *Sketches of the History of Man*, 2 vols, Edinburgh: W. Creech, 1774.

Houston, Joseph (ed.), *Thomas Reid: Context, Influence, Significance*, Edinburgh: Dunedin Academic Press, 2004.

Hume, David, *The Letters of David Hume*, 2 vols, ed. J. Y. T. Greig, Oxford: Clarendon Press, 1932.

——. *Essays Moral, Political, and Literary*, ed. Eugene F. Miller, rev. edn, Indianapolis, IN: Liberty Fund, 1985.

——. *Principal Writings on Religion including 'Dialogues concerning Natural Religion' and 'The Natural History of Religion'*, ed. J. C. A. Gaskin, Oxford: Oxford University Press, 1993.

——. *An Enquiry Concerning the Principles of Morals*, ed. Tom L. Beauchamp, Oxford: Oxford University Press, 1998.

——. *An Enquiry Concerning Human Understanding*, ed. Tom L. Beauchamp, Oxford: Oxford University Press, 1999.

——. *A Treatise of Human Nature*, eds David Fate Norton and Mary Norton, Oxford: Oxford University Press, 2000.

Hutcheson, Francis, *An Inquiry into the Original of our Ideas of Beauty and Virtue*, London, 1726; reprint, ed. W. Leidhold, Indianapolis, IN: Liberty Fund, 2004.

——. *An Essay on the Nature and Conduct of the Passions and Affections, with Illustrations on the Moral Sense*, London, 1728; reprint, ed. A. Garrett, Indianapolis, IN: Liberty Fund, 2002.

——. *Logic, Metaphysics, and the Natural Sociability of Mankind*, eds James Moore and Michael Silverthorne, Indianapolis, IN: Liberty Fund, 2006.

——. *Philosophiae Moralis Institutio Compendiaria, with a Short Introduction to Moral Philosophy*, ed. Luigi Turco, Indianapolis, IN: Liberty Fund, 2007.

——. *Letters*, *see* Burnet, Gilbert and Francis Hutcheson

Ireland, John, *The Meroure of Wyssdome*, vol. 1, ed. C. Macpherson, Edinburgh: Blackwood, 1926; vol. 2, ed. J. F. Quinn, Edinburgh: Blackwood, 1965; vol. 3, ed. C. McDonald, Edinburgh: Blackwood, 1990.

Jardine, George, *Outlines of Philosophical Education, Illustrated by the Method of Teaching the Logic Class in the University of Glasgow*, 2nd edn, Glasgow: Oliver and Boyd, 1825.

Kail, Peter J. E., *Projection and Realism in Hume's Philosophy*, Oxford: Oxford University Press, 2007.

Kames, *see* Home, Henry, Lord Kames

Kemp Smith, Norman, *Studies in the Cartesian Philosophy*, London: Macmillan, 1902.

——. *Prolegomena to an Idealist Theory of Knowledge*, London: Macmillan, 1924.

——. *A Commentary to Kant's 'Critique of Pure Reason'*, London: Macmillan, 1918.

——. *The Philosophy of David Hume*, London, 1941; reprint, intr. D. Garrett, Basingstoke: Palgrave Macmillan, 2005.

Kretzmann, Norman, Anthony Kenny and Jan Pinborg (eds), *The Cambridge History of Later Medieval Philosophy*, Cambridge: Cambridge University Press, 1982.

Kuehn, Manfred, *Scottish Common Sense in Germany, 1768–1800: A Contribution to the History of Critical Philosophy*, Kingston: McGill-Queen's University Press, 1987.

Laing, R. D., *The Divided Self: An Existential Study in Sanity and Madness*, London: Penguin, 1960.

Laird, John, *A Study in Realism*, Cambridge: Cambridge University Press, 1920.

——. *Recent Philosophy*, London: Thornton, Butterworth, 1936.

Laurie, Henry, *Scottish Philosophy in its National Development*, Glasgow: Maclehose, 1902.

Ledelh, Jacobus (= James Liddell), *Tractatus conceptuum et signorum*, Paris, 1495.

Lindsay, David, 'Testament of the Papyngo,' in *The Works of Sir David Lindsay of the Mount, 1490–1555*, 4 vols, ed. Douglas Hamer, Edinburgh: Blackwood, 1931–6.

Locke, John, *An Essay Concerning Human Understanding*, ed. P. H. Nidditch, Oxford: Oxford University Press, 1975.

Lokert, George, *Scriptum in materia noticiarum*, Paris, 1514.

McCosh, James, *The Scottish Philosophy, Biographical, Expository, Critical, from Hutcheson to Hamilton*, London, 1875; reprint, Bristol: Thoemmes, 1990.

MacIntyre, Alasdair, *Whose Justice? Which Rationality?*, London: Duckworth, 1988.

MacKinnon, Donald M., *Borderlands of Theology, and Other Essays*, eds G. W. Roberts and D. E. Smucker, London: Lutterworth Press, 1968.

Maclagan, William, *The Theological Frontier of Ethics*, London: Allen & Unwin, 1961.

Maclaurin, Colin, *An Account of Sir Isaac Newton's Philosophical Discoveries*, London, 1748.

Macmurray, John, *Reason and Emotion*, London: Faber & Faber, 1935.

——. *The Structure of Religious Experience*, London: Faber & Faber, 1936.

——. *The Boundaries of Science*, London: Faber & Faber, 1939.

——. *The Self as Agent*, London: Faber & Faber, 1956.

——. *Persons in Relation*, London: Faber & Faber, 1961.

——. *John Macmurray: Selected Philosophical Writings*, ed. Esther McIntosh, Exeter: Imprint Academic, 2004.

Mair, John, *Exponibilia*, Paris, 1499.

——. *Inclitarum artium ac sacra pagine doctoris acutissimi magistri Johannis Majoris, [. . .] Libri quos in artibus in collegio Montis Acuti Parisius regentando compilavit*, ed. Antonio Coronel, Paris, 1506.

——. *Quartus sententiarum Johannis Majoris*, ed. David Cranston, Paris, 1509.

——. *In primum sententiarum*, Paris, 1510.

——. *In secundum sententiarum*, ed. Antonio Coronel, Paris, 1510.

——. *Editio Joannis Majoris [. . .] super tertium sententiarum de novo edita*, Paris, 1517.

——. *Ethica Aristotelis peripateticorum principis. Cum Johannis Majoris Theologi Parisiensis commentariis*, Paris, 1530.

——. *A History of Greater Britain as well England as Scotland Compiled from the Ancient Authorities by John Major, by Name Indeed a Scot, but by Profession a Theologian, 1521*, tr. and ed. Archibald Constable, Edinburgh: Printed by T. and A. Constable for the Scottish History Society, 1892.

Malherbe, Michel, 'Reid et la possibilité d'une philosophie du sens commun', *Revue de métaphysique et de morale*, 96 (1991): 551–71.

Manderston, William, *Bipartitum in morali philosophia*, Paris, 1518.

Mason, Roger A., *Kingship and the Commonweal: Political Thought in Renaissance and Reformation Scotland*, East Linton: Tuckwell Press, 1998.

Millar, John, *The Origin of the Distinction of Ranks*, reprinted in William C. Lehman (ed.), *John Millar of Glasgow*, Cambridge: Cambridge University Press, 1960, pp. 173–332.

Miller, Gavin, *R. D. Laing*, Edinburgh: Edinburgh Review in assoc. with Edinburgh University Press, 2004.

Millican, Peter (ed.), *Reading Hume on Human Understanding: Essays on the First Enquiry*, Oxford: Clarendon Press, 2002.

Monboddo, *see* Burnett, James, Lord Monboddo

Oswald, James, *An Appeal to Common Sense in Behalf of Religion*, Edinburgh: A. Kincaid and J. Bell, 1766.

Passmore, John, *A Hundred Years of Philosophy*, London: Duckworth, 1957.

Paton, Herbert James, *Kant's Metaphysic of Experience*, 2 vols, London: Allen & Unwin, 1936.

——. *The Categorical Imperative: A Study in Kant's Moral Philosophy*, London: Hutchison, 1947.

——. *The Defence of Reason*, London: Hutchinson, 1951.

——. *The Modern Predicament: A Study in the Philosophy of Religion*, London: Allen & Unwin, 1955.

——. *The Claim of Scotland*, London: Allen & Unwin, 1968.

Pringle-Pattison, Andrew, *see* Seth Pringle-Pattison, Andrew

Rae, John, *Life of Adam Smith*, London: Macmillan, 1895.

Reeder, John (ed.), *On Moral Sentiments: Contemporary Responses to Adam Smith*, Bristol: Thoemmes Press, 1997.

Reid, Thomas, *Essays on the Intellectual Powers of Man*, eds Derek R. Brookes and K. Haakonssen, Edinburgh: Edinburgh University Press, 2002.

——. *An Inquiry into the Human Mind on the Principles of Common Sense*, ed. Derek R. Brookes, Edinburgh: Edinburgh University Press, 1997.

——. *Œuvres complètes de Thomas Reid, chef de l'école écossaise*, tr. and intr. Théodore Jouffroy, with fragments by Paul Royer-Collard, 6 vols, Paris: Victor Masson, 1828–36.

——. *The Works of Thomas Reid, DD, FRSE*, ed. Sir William Hamilton, 6th edn, 2 vols, Edinburgh, 1863; reprint, Bristol: Thoemmes, 1994. It includes *Essays on the Active Powers of the Human Mind*, vol. 2, pp. 509–679.

——. *Thomas Reid on the Animate Creation: Papers Relating to the Life Sciences*, ed. Paul B. Wood, Edinburgh: Edinburgh University Press, 1995.

——. *The Correspondence of Thomas Reid*, ed. Paul Wood, Edinburgh: Edinburgh University Press, 2002.

——. *Thomas Reid on Logic, Rhetoric and the Fine Arts*, ed. Alexander Broadie, Edinburgh: Edinburgh University Press, 2005.

——. *Practical Ethics*, ed. K. Haakonssen, Edinburgh: Edinburgh University Press, 2007.

Richard of St Victor (= Ricardus de Sancto Victore Scotus), *De Trinitate*, ed. J. Ribailler, in *Textes philosophiques du moyen âge*, Paris: Éditions du Cerf, 1959.

Ritchie, Arthur D., *The Natural History of Mind*, London: Longmans Green, 1936.

Ross, Ian Simpson, *Lord Kames and the Scotland of his Day*, Oxford: Clarendon Press, 1972.

——. *The Life of Adam Smith*, Oxford: Clarendon Press, 1995.

Rothschild, Emma, *Economic Sentiments: Adam Smith, Condorcet, and the Enlightenment*, Cambridge, MA; London: Harvard University Press, 2001.

Rowe, William L., *Thomas Reid on Freedom and Morality*, Ithaca, NY; London: Cornell University Press, 1991.

Rutherford, John, *Commentariorum de arte disserendi libri quatuor*, Edinburgh, 1557; 2nd edn, Edinburgh, 1577.

Seth Pringle-Pattison, Andrew, *The Development from Kant to Hegel*, London: Williams and Norgate, 1882.

——. *Scottish Philosophy: A Comparison of the Scottish and German Answers to Hume*, Edinburgh: Blackwood, 1885.

——. *Hegelianism and Personality*, Edinburgh: Blackwood, 1887.

——. *The Idea of God in the Light of Recent Philosophy*, 2nd edn, Oxford: Oxford University Press, 1920.

——. *The Idea of Immortality*, Oxford: Clarendon Press, 1922.

Shaftesbury, Earl of, *see* Cooper, Anthony Ashley, Third Earl of Shaftesbury

Skinner, A. S. and T. Wilson (eds), *Essays on Adam Smith*, Oxford: Clarendon Press, 1975.

Skoczylas, Anne, *Mr Simson's Knotty Case: Divinity, Politics, and Due Process in Early Eighteenth-Century Scotland*, Montreal: McGill-Queen's University Press, 2001.

Smith, Adam, *An Inquiry into the Nature and Causes of the Wealth of Nations*, eds R. H. Campbell, A. S. Skinner and W. B. Todd, 2 vols, Oxford: Clarendon Press, 1976; Indianapolis, IN: Liberty Classics, 1981.

——. *The Theory of Moral Sentiments*, eds D. D. Raphael and A. L. Macfie, Oxford: Clarendon Press, 1976; Indianapolis, IN: Liberty Fund, 1982.

——. *Lectures on Jurisprudence*, eds R. L. Meek, D. D. Raphael and P. G. Stein, Oxford: Clarendon Press, 1978; Indianapolis, IN: Liberty Classics, 1982.

——. *Essays on Philosophical Subjects*, eds W. P. D. Wightman, J. C. Bryce and I. S. Ross, Oxford: Clarendon Press, 1980; Indianapolis, IN: Liberty Classics, 1982.

——. *Lectures on Rhetoric and Belles Lettres*, ed. J. C. Bryce, Oxford: Clarendon Press, 1983; Indianapolis, IN: Liberty Classics, 1985.

——. *Correspondence of Adam Smith*, 2nd edn, eds E. C. Mossner and I. S. Ross, Oxford: Clarendon Press, 1987; Indianapolis, IN: Liberty Classics, 1987.

Stewart, Dugald, *The Collected Works of Dugald Stewart*, ed. William Hamilton, Edinburgh: T. Constable, 1854–60; reprint, intr. K. Haakonssen, Bristol: Thoemmes, 1994. It includes *Elements of the Philosophy of the Human Mind* (vols 2–4); *Philosophical Essays* (vol. 5); *The Philosophy of the Active and Moral Powers of Man* (vols 6–7); *Outlines of Moral Philosophy* (vols 2, 6 and 8 for parts 1, 2 and 3 respectively of the *Outlines*).

——. *Selected Philosophical Writings*, ed. E. L. Mortera, Exeter: Imprint Academic, 2007.

Stewart, M. A. (ed.), *Studies in the Philosophy of the Scottish Enlightenment*, Oxford: Clarendon Press, 1990.

Stewart, M. A. and John P. Wright (eds), *Hume and Hume's Connexions*, Edinburgh: Edinburgh University Press, 1994.

Stirling, James Hutchison, *The Secret of Hegel*, London: Longman, Green, 1865.

Suderman, Jeffrey, *Orthodoxy and Enlightenment: George Campbell in the Eighteenth Century*, Montreal: McGill-Queen's University Press, 2001.

Sutherland, John D., *Fairbairn's Journey into the Interior*, London: Free Association, 1989.

Torrance, Thomas F., '1469–1969: La philosophie et la théologie de Jean Mair ou Major, de Haddington (1469–1550)', *Archives de Philosophie*, 32 (1969): 531–47; 33 (1970): 261–93.

——. *The Hermeneutics of John Calvin*, Edinburgh: Scottish Academic Press, 1988.

Turnbull, George, *Theses philosophicae de scientiae naturalis cum philosophia morali conjunctione*, Aberdeen: James Nicol, 1723.

——. *Theses academicae de pulcherrima mundi cum materialis tum rationalis constitutione*, Aberdeen: James Nicol, 1726.

——. *A Treatise on Ancient Painting*, London: A. Millar, 1740.

——. *Observations upon Liberal Education*, London: A. Millar, 1742; reprint, ed. and intr. Terrence O. Moore, Jr, Indianapolis, IN: Liberty Fund, 2003.

——. *The Principles of Moral and Christian Philosophy*, 2 vols (vol. 1, *The Principles of Moral Philosophy*; vol. 2, *Christian Philosophy*), London: A. Millar, 1740; reprint, ed. and intr. Alexander Broadie, Indianapolis, IN: Liberty Fund, 2005.

Veitch, John, *Hamilton*, Edinburgh: Blackwood, 1882.

Vos, Antonie, *The Philosophy of John Duns Scotus*, Edinburgh: Edinburgh University Press, 2006.

Wood, Paul B., *The Aberdeen Enlightenment: The Arts Curriculum in the Eighteenth Century*, Aberdeen: Aberdeen University Press, 1993.

——. 'George Turnbull', in *The Oxford Dictionary of National Biography*, Oxford: Oxford University Press, 2004.

Wright, John P., *The Sceptical Realism of David Hume*, Manchester: Manchester University Press, 1983.

Yaffe, Gideon, *Manifest Activity: Thomas Reid's Theory of Action*, Oxford: Clarendon Press, 2004.

Index